Hiking

Hells Canyon and
Idaho's Seven Devils Mountains

Help Us Keep This Guide Up to Date

Every effort has been made by the author and editors to make this guide as accurate and useful as possible. However, many things can change after a guide is published—trails are rerouted, regulations change, techniques evolve, facilities come under new managment, etc.

We would love to hear from you concerning your experiences with this guide and how you feel it could be improved and kept up to date. While we may not be able to respond to all comments and suggestions, we'll take them to heart and we'll also make certain to share them with the author. Please send your comments and suggestions to the following address:

The Globe Pequot Press
Reader Response/Editorial Department
P.O. Box 480
Guilford, CT 06437

Or you may e-mail us at:

editorial@globe-pequot.com

Thanks for your input, and happy travels!

Hiking

Hells Canyon and Idaho's Seven Devils Mountains

Fred Barstad

FALCON®

GUILFORD, CONNECTICUT
AN IMPRINT OF THE GLOBE PEQUOT PRESS

_A_ FALCON GUIDE ®

Cover photo: RO-MA Stock
All photos by the author unless otherwise indicated.

Library of Congress Cataloging-in-Publication Data
Barstad, Fred.
Hiking Hells Canyon and Idaho's Seven Devils/Fred Barstad.
     p. cm. — (A Falcon guide)
Includes bibliographical references (p.) and index.
ISBN 1-58592-120-3
     1. Hiking—Hells Canyon (Idaho and Or.)—Guidebooks. 2. Mountaineering—Hells Canyon (Idaho and Or.)—Guidebooks. 3. Backpacking—Hells Canyon (Idaho and Or.)—Guidebooks. 4. Hells Canyon (Idaho and Or.)—Guidebooks. I. Title. II. Series.

GV199.42.H45 B37 2001
917.95'73—dc21   2001033078

♻ Text pages printed on recycled paper.
Manufactured in the United States of America
First Edition/First Printing

Contents

Acknowledgments

Thanks to Gretchen Weeks and Bob Barstad for hiking with me, and to Kati Smith, Dave Kaufman, Brian Barstad, Jen Barstad, Gina Barstad, Diana Strickland, Jason Sharp, Tiffany Noel, Jeremy Younggren, Dane Johnson, Dylan Botham, Darin Larvik, and Bruce Johnson for hiking and camping with me. Thanks to Dr. Lowell Euhus for hiking with me and providing information about snake bite treatment, and to Ettore Negri, Jerry Lavender, Oliver Boeve, and Gary Fletcher for hiking, camping, and furnishing photos. Thanks also to Bret Armocost, Butch Brown, and Linda Mink of Hells Canyon Adventures for providing jet boat service and valuable information. Thanks to Beamer's Hells Canyon Tours for meals, lodging, and jet boat transportation, and to Joe Spence of Spence Air Service for providing flights to backcountry airstrips and valuable information. Thanks to all of the employees at the Riggins and Enterprise offices of the USDA Forest Service and especially to Cathy Conover and Leigh Dawson for supplying trail information and reviewing the text. Most of all, thanks to my wife, Suzi Barstad, for hiking and camping with me and editing my raw text.

Map Legend

U.S. Highway	(95)	Town	○ **Riggins**
State Highway	(350) (86)	Picnic Area	🛆
County Road	(727)	Campground	⏶
Forest Road	4201	Parking Area	Ⓟ
Paved Road	——⇒	Bridge	⌣⌣
Gravel Road	——⇒	Building	■
Dirt Road	======⇒	Ruin	⌐
Trailhead	○	Peak/Elevation	⛰ 9,782 ft. X
Featured Trail	▬ ▬ ▬ ▬ ▬	Overlook/Point of Interest	•
Secondary Trail	– – – – –	Corral	↺
X/C Route	• • • • • • •	Power Transmission Line	•——•——•
Pass or Saddle	⌣⌢	Fence	×—×—×—×—×
Mine Site	⚔	Wilderness Boundary	▬ ▬ ▬
Cave	⟩—	State Boundary	O R E G O N
River/Creek	∿		I D A H O
Lake	⬭	Map Orientation	N ↑
Waterfall/Rapids	∿//		
Spring	○~	Scale	0 0.5 1 Miles

ix

Overview Map

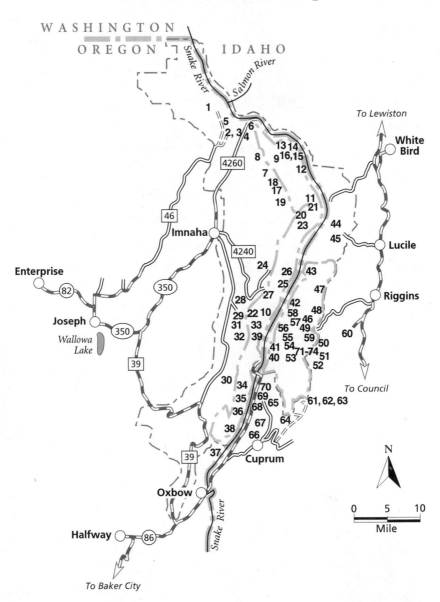

WASHINGTON
OREGON   IDAHO

Snake River
Salmon River

To Lewiston

White Bird

1
5
2, 3 4
6
13 14
8 9 16,15
4260 7 12
18
17
19
11
21
20
23
44
45
Lucile

46
Imnaha
4240
24
26 43
25
47
Enterprise
82
350
28
27
42
48
29 22 10 58 57 46
31 33 56 49
32 39 55 59 50
41 54 71-74 51
40 53 52
60
Riggins
Joseph
350
Wallowa
Lake
39
30 34
35
36
70
69
68 65
61, 62, 63
38 67
37 66 64
Cuprum

To Council

N
0 5 10
Mile

39
Oxbow

Snake River

Halfway
86

To Baker City

Topographical Map

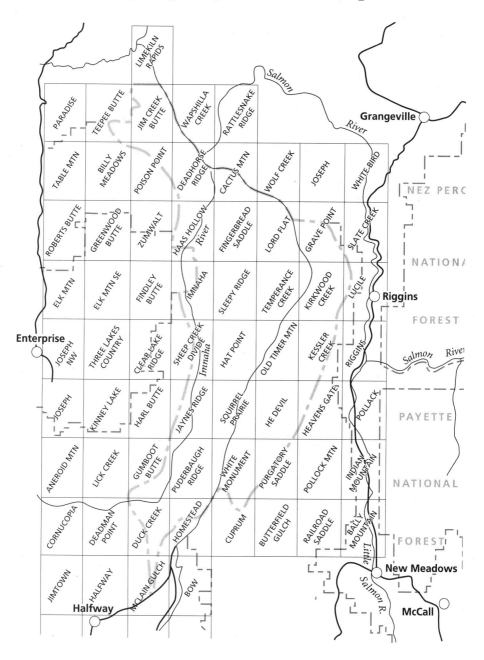

Introduction

The 1,020-square-mile Hells Canyon National Recreation Area straddles the Oregon–Idaho border for 70 miles. Within the NRA, 334 square miles of designated wilderness protect the most spectacular part of the canyons and mountains. Hundreds of miles of trails allow the hiker access to the rugged scenery, historical sites, and wildlife viewing opportunities of the cavernous gorge and the mountains that adjoin it.

GEOGRAPHY OF HELLS CANYON

Hells Canyon is a huge river-cut canyon or, to be more exact, system of canyons. The Snake River rushes at a steep gradient through the gorge, descending from 1,520 feet above sea level at the base of Hells Canyon Dam to 920 feet elevation at Salmon Bar. Along the river, the country is semiarid, almost a desert.

The western rim of the canyon is a long narrow plateau ranging in elevation from 5,500 to nearly 7,000 feet, along its north–south axis. Known as Summit Ridge, this plateau is mostly timbered, but scattered ridgetop meadows and other openings in the trees make for eye-popping views both to the east and to the west.

On the eastern side of Hells Canyon rise the Seven Devils Mountains. The Seven Devils top out at the 9,393-foot summit of He Devil Mountain, 7,900 vertical feet above the frothing Snake River. The mountains contain many beautiful lakes and some of the best alpine scenery anyone could hope for.

HUMAN HISTORY

People have inhabited Hells Canyon for much of the last eight thousand years, leaving their mark in the form of pictographs and petroglyphs on the dark rock of the canyon. Not much is known about these early inhabitants. In the early part of the nineteenth century, interest in this rugged land, which was then the domain of the Nez Perce and Shoshone tribes, began to build.

By the late nineteenth century, copper and other minerals had been discovered in the canyon as well as in the Seven Devils Mountains, and settlers were beginning to stake their claims to the small spots of workable land. During the depression years of the 1930s, approximately one hundred families were living in Hells Canyon. This influx of people was to be short lived, however, as most of the settlers left for greener pastures and sold their land to a few larger ranchers. These larger ranch operations raised sheep and cattle in the canyon for several decades, but their time was also limited. In 1976, the U.S. Congress declared Hells Canyon a national recreation area and designated much of the canyon and the Seven Devils Mountains as wilderness. The government bought out most of the landowners, and the canyon reverted to public domain.

Hells Canyon has come full circle, from people being visitors to being settlers and then back to being just visitors again. Hells Canyon is one of the few areas that is getting wilder with time rather than becoming more subdued.

CLIMATE

The climate of Hells Canyon and the mountains that adjoin it is widely diverse. May and June have the heaviest precipitation, but a fair amount of snow falls from November through April.

Winter temperatures even in the bottom of the canyon can drop to well below zero. Extremely cold temperatures are the exception rather than the rule along the Snake River, however. Much of the winter in the bottom of the canyon is mild, and by March the grass starts to grow and the first flowers begin to bloom. As you climb above the river the climate cools and the rainfall increases.

Above 4,000 feet elevation, snow generally covers the ground from December through March. At 6,000 to 7,000 feet elevation, the canyon rim on the Oregon side is usually snowed in until mid-June. The higher parts of the Seven Devils Mountains, above the 7,000-foot level, generally have snow cover from late October until mid-July.

Summer temperatures in the depths of Hells Canyon often exceed 100 degrees and sometimes reach 110 degrees. At this time of year, the high country is usually pleasant, with daytime highs in the seventies and lows in the forties. Thunderstorms are common from May through August.

BIG WATCHABLE WILDLIFE

Observing the abundant wildlife is a major side benefit of hiking in Hells Canyon. Many of the trail descriptions note places where large animals are likely to be seen.

The largest animal wandering this rugged landscape is the elk. Elk are found in all areas of the canyon, from bars along the Snake River to the alpine environment of the highest peaks. However, the large tan animals are far more common on the Oregon side of the canyon. The best elk viewing is in

Bighorn sheep near the mouth of the Imnaha River.

Mule deer.

the spring along the benches of the Oregon side of the canyon, between 3,000 and 5,000 feet elevation. Watch for them on the open ridgelines, where they tend to bed down.

Like the elk, mule deer range throughout the canyon. Because they feed mostly in the open, they are fairly easy to spot in the morning and evening. If you want to see large mule deer bucks, watch the high ridgetop areas. White-tailed deer are less common here than are elk and mule deer. Their range is mostly along the bottoms of the canyons below the Seven Devils Mountains.

Bighorn sheep, which were once extinct in Hells Canyon, are making a comeback. Like elk and mule deer, they range from the Snake River to the rims more than a mile above the river. Unlike mule deer and elk, however, the bighorns prefer the roughest topography they can find. Several government agencies have worked extremely hard to facilitate the reintroduction of these regal animals. Hells Canyon along with the Seven Devils and Wallowa Mountains may well be the largest contiguous area of prime bighorn habitat in the nation. As the reintroduction efforts continue, your chances of viewing these magnificent animals increase.

Mountain goat at Sheep Lake.

3

Bears in Battle Creek Canyon.

A fairly large herd of mountain goats also inhabits the rugged peaks and canyons of the Seven Devils Mountains. Mountain goats are pure white, except for their horns, eyes, and hooves, making them easy to spot on the dark cliffs. Your best chances to see mountain goats are on the north face of She Devil Mountain above Sheep Lake and near Dry Diggins Lookout. During the winter and spring, there are usually some goats on the Idaho side of the Snake River near Hells Canyon Dam.

Black bears are common throughout the area. The best viewing opportunities occur in the spring and early summer, when the bears spend much of their time on open slopes, grazing on fresh wild onions and turning over rocks to find grubs.

ACCESS

The driving directions in the Finding the Trailhead section of each description for hikes on the Oregon side of Hells Canyon and for many of the Idaho hikes begins in Joseph, Enterprise, or Baker City, Oregon. To reach the Enterprise–Joseph area, take exit 261 off Interstate 84 at La Grande, Oregon, and then follow Oregon 82 first north then east and south for 65 miles to Enterprise, Oregon. To continue to

Lord Flat aircraft parking area. JERRY LAVENDER PHOTO

Joseph, Oregon, drive east and south another 6 miles from Enterprise. Baker City is located 41 miles east of La Grande on I-84. Take exit 302 at Baker City.

For hikes in the Seven Devils Mountains and many other hikes on the Idaho side of the canyon, the main access is from Riggins, Idaho. To reach Riggins from I-84, take exit 3 and follow U.S. Highway 95 for 136 miles north to Riggins. Riggins may also be reached from Lewiston, Idaho, by driving south for 128 miles on US 95.

Many of the hikes described in this book are not easily reached by car, but do not let this deter you from enjoying them. Jet boat shuttles from either Hells Canyon Dam or Clarkston, Washington, can be easily arranged and are not very expensive. Air drop-off or pickup at one of the three back-country airstrips in the canyon is an exciting way to begin or end your hike and is not too expensive when divided among the members of a group. Flying in to begin a hike gives hikers a chance to get the best possible overall view of the country to be hiked. See appendix A for the addresses and phone numbers of the jet boat and aircraft operators.

Mouth of Bernard Creek.

How to Use This Guide

HOW THE INFORMATION FOR THIS GUIDE WAS GATHERED

The author personally hiked these trails, many of them in both directions. The mileage was very difficult to gauge exactly. Mileage from Forest Service signs and maps were taken into account whenever possible, and times were recorded while hiking. The mileage was calculated based on a knowledge of the approximate speed the author hikes over various types of trail. The mileage provided in each hike description was figured by combining the previous means as well as by pacing off the distance in some cases.

DIFFICULTY RATINGS

The trails in this book are rated as "easy," "moderate," or "strenuous," with the length or time involved not taken into account. Only the roughness of the trail, elevation change, and difficulty of following the route are considered.

The trails that are rated as "easy" will generally have gentle grades and will be easy to follow; however, there may be short sections of rocky or eroded areas. Given enough time, anyone in reasonable condition can hike easy trails.

Trails rated as "moderate" will climb or descend more steeply than do easy trails. They may climb 500 or 600 feet per mile and have fairly long sections that are rough or eroded. Following these trails may require some routefinding skills. If routefinding is required for a particular hike, the hike description will state this. Anyone in good physical condition can hike these trails with no problem. However, people in poor condition and small children may find them grueling.

Trails rated as "strenuous" are best left to expert backpackers and mountaineers. These trails may climb or descend 1,000 feet or more per mile and be very rough. Sections of these trails may be very vague or even nonexistent, so excellent routefinding skills are a requirement for safe travel. Many of these trails are not usable by parties with stock.

TRAIL MILEAGE

Distances for loop and shuttle hikes are stated one way and out-and-back hikes are stated round trip, so either figure will be the entire distance you will hike. The additional hiking options given at the end of the hike description are not taken into consideration when determining the total distance. Many hikes described in this book are internal trails, which means that they start or finish at a trail junction or drop-off point rather than at a trailhead. In these cases, you will have to add the distance to and from the junction where the hike begins and the distance of the hike to get the total distance you will cover.

MAPS

If you want one map to cover the entire Hells Canyon–Seven Devils area, use the USDA Forest Service Hells Canyon National Recreation Area map. The scale of this map is 1 inch to the mile, which is adequate for all of the well-maintained trails. If you are planning to hike the less-traveled and seldom maintained routes described in this book, the USGS 7.5-minute quad maps mentioned at the beginning of each hike description are a better choice. The larger 1:24000 scale (about 2.7 inches to the mile) of these maps makes finding your exact location much easier.

ELEVATION PROFILES

Elevation profile graphs are provided for each hike. These profiles show the major elevation changes of the hike but, because of size limitations, may not show small elevation changes.

Backcountry Safety and Hazards

BEING PREPARED

There are a few simple things you can do to improve your chances of staying healthy while you are hiking.

One of the most important is to be careful about your drinking water supply. All surface water should be filtered, chemically treated, or boiled before drinking, washing utensils, or brushing your teeth with it. The water may look clean and pure, and it may be, but you can never be sure. In many cases, there is no water along the trail, so you will need to take along all that you will need. If you use a filter, be sure it has a fairly new cartridge or has been recently cleaned before you leave on your hike. Many of the trailheads and campgrounds do not have potable water.

Check the weather report before heading into the mountains. Stormy weather with wind, rain, and even snow is possible at any time of year. The opposite is also the case much of the time, and hot sunny weather on the exposed slopes can cause quick dehydration. At these times, a broad-brimmed hat, lots of sunscreen, and light-colored, loose-fitting clothes are needed. Eat well and drink plenty of liquids.

Inform friends or relatives of your plans, including destinations and when you plan to return. If you are planning a long or difficult hike, be sure to get in shape ahead of time. This will make your trip much more pleasant as well as safer.

PASSING STOCK ON THE TRAIL

Meeting stock traffic is a common occurrence in Hells Canyon, so it is a good idea to know how to pass stock with the least possible disturbance or danger. If you meet parties with stock, try to get as far off the trail as possible. Horsemen prefer that you stand on the downhill side of the trail, but there is some question whether this is the safest place for a hiker. When possible, I like to get well off the trail on the uphill side. It is often a good idea to talk quietly to the horses and their riders, because this seems to calm many horses. If you have the family dog with you, be sure to keep it restrained and quiet. Dogs cause many horse wrecks.

FOLLOWING A FAINT TRAIL

There are many faint trails in Hells Canyon for which good map-reading and routefinding skills are required to find your way. There are a few things you can do to make this routefinding job easier.

First, read the description for the hike you plan to take before you start your hike. While hiking, try to keep track of your position on your map at all times. If properly used, an altimeter can be very useful for tracking your progress. Altimeters run on air pressure, which is always changing, so they must be set often. Anytime you reach a point where you are sure of the elevation, set your altimeter even if you set it only two or three hours ago.

GPS coordinates for the trailheads, most major trail junctions, and key points are given in each hike description. If you are proficient in the use of a GPS receiver, these coordinates can be very helpful. Remember, however, that the government scrambles GPS signals, which may cause the readings to be a little off. Usually the reading you will get on your receiver will be within 100 yards of your actual location but at times readings may be much farther off than that.

While you are hiking, watch for blazes cut into the bark of trees and for rock cairns on the ground to determine the trail's route. Logs that have been sawed off may also be an indicator of trail direction. Trees with the branches missing on one side may show that the trail passes on that side of the tree. Through thick woods, look for strips where the trees are much smaller or nonexistent; this could be the route that was once cleared for the trail.

All these things are not positive signs that you are going the right way, but when taken together with good compass and map skills, they make it much easier to follow a faint trail.

YOU MIGHT NEVER KNOW WHAT HIT YOU

Thunderstorms are common in Hells Canyon during spring and summer. On the rims of the canyon and the high ridges and peaks of the Seven Devils Mountains, it is relatively easy to see and hear a thunderstorm before it reaches your location. But in the valleys and canyons below the rims, a storm can be on you with very little advance warning. If you get caught by a lightning storm, take special precautions. Remember the following:

- Lightning can travel far ahead of the storm, so try to take cover well before the storm hits.

- Do not try to get back to your vehicle. It is not worth the risk. Instead, seek the best shelter you can find. Lightning storms usually last only a short time, and from a safe spot you might even enjoy watching the storm.

- Stay away from anything that might attract lightning, such as metal tent poles, graphite fishing rods, and metal-frame backpacks.

- Be careful not to be caught on a mountaintop or exposed ridgeline or under a solitary tree.

- If possible, seek shelter in a low-lying area, ideally in a dense stand of small, uniformly sized trees.

- Get in a crouch position with both feet firmly placed on the ground; do not lean against a tree.

- If you have a sleeping pad or a pack without a metal frame with you, put your feet on it for extra insulation against electric shock.

- Do not walk or huddle together. Instead, stay 50 feet apart; if someone does get struck, the others can give first aid.

- If you are in a tent, it is usually best to stay there in your sleeping bag with your feet on your sleeping pad.

Occasionally, a flash flood in one of the steep narrow side canyons of Hells Canyon can occur as a result of a thunderstorm. These floods, which are also known as waterspouts throughout much of the western United States, are most common when heavy rain combines with snowmelt. It is best not to camp in a narrow canyon when thunderstorms or other heavy rain is likely.

THE BUZZ BESIDE THE TRAIL

A rattlesnake's buzz is a sound you will never forget. Of the 50 states, 45 are home to at least one species of rattlesnake. Unless you will be hiking only in Alaska, Hawaii, Rhode Island, Delaware, or Maine, you need to be aware of the possibility of encountering one. Some areas of the remaining states have only a very small population of these poisonous reptiles, and other areas have none at all. Local inquiry is the best way to assess your chances of meeting a rattler on the trail.

Rattlesnakes are members of the pit viper family. Pit vipers have heat-sensing organs (pits) in their faces, which are used to detect heat. This heat detection system is probably integrated with the snake's visual senses, allowing it to *see* heat. This allows rattlers to easily strike in the dark.

Rattlesnakes inhabit a wide range of climatic zones. They are found from below sea level up to subalpine zones in the mountains of the western United States. However, they are seldom common above the transition (ponderosa pine) zone. Rattlers may be out at lower temperatures than most people think they would be. They are occasionally seen sunning themselves on warm rocks when the air temperature is only a few degrees above freezing. Conversely, the snakes seek shade or burrows when it is very hot. For a rattlesnake, the perfect temperature is about 80 degrees F.

Of the approximately 8,000 venomous snakebites in the United States each year, only 10 to 20 are fatal, and in many cases these fatalities can be at least partly attributed to other preexisting medical problems. Of these fatalities, the diamondback rattlesnake, which ranges generally south of an imaginary line drawn from Southern California to North Carolina, causes 95 percent. This is not to say that other species of rattlers do not cause much pain and an occasional death, but your chances of being killed by a snake diminish greatly as you travel north. Of the people who are bitten, about 35 percent are not injected with poison. These "dry bites" lead some people to wrongly believe that they are immune to rattlesnake venom.

Preventing bites

Do not count on rattlesnakes to rattle at your approach; they are generally shy creatures in their encounters with humans. In most cases, they will do their best to escape or to lie quietly and let the person pass without noticing them. Only about half of the snakes I have encountered have rattled before I saw them. Rattlers will sometimes strike before rattling.

Do not place your hands or feet in places that you cannot see clearly. About 65 percent of snakebites are on the hands or forearms, and another 24 percent are on the feet, ankles, and lower legs.

In areas where there is a good chance of encountering a rattler, consider wearing protective clothing, such as snakeproof gaiters or chaps and sturdy hiking boots.

During hot weather, be especially alert during the morning, evening, and night, which are the snakes' most active times.

Do not handle any snake unless you can positively identify it as being nonpoisonous. Snakes that were thought to be dead have bitten many people.

Inquisitive children have a higher than average chance of being bitten by a rattlesnake. Because of their smaller bodies, they are also more susceptible to the toxins in the venom. Warn your children of the danger, and watch them closely when you are in snake country.

First aid for snakebite

The best first-aid treatment for snakebite is to get medical help as soon as possible so that an injection of antivenin can be administered. Antivenin is the only proven treatment for snakebite. If you are within 45 minutes of medical assistance, get there as quickly as safety allows and do not bother with any other type of treatment.

Recommended first aid when medical help is far away

If you are more than 45 minutes from medical help, onsite first-aid treatment may be helpful. If there are three or more people in your party, you may want to send someone for help as you are starting the first-aid treatment, but do not leave the victim alone at this point.

A snakebite kit is necessary to adequately perform the treatment. There are two main types of snakebite kits available on the market. The most common ones include two or three rubber suction cups and a razor blade. The more advanced kits include a two-stage suction pump. The pump is capable of applying much more suction and is the preferred kit to carry. In addition to a snakebite kit, an elastic bandage is helpful in most treatments. If your snakebite or general first-aid kit does not include disinfectant or a safety razor, you should add both to it. *Before putting your snakebite kit in your pack or pocket, open it, read the instructions, and familiarize yourself with its proper use.*

Treatment must begin immediately after the bite occurs to be effective. Remember the following:

- If the wound is bleeding, allow it to continue bleeding for 15 to 30 seconds.

- If the wound is on the hand, forearm, foot, or lower leg, wrap the elastic bandage around the limb above the wound. *Wrap the bandage no tighter than you would for a sprain.*

- If you are using the pump type of kit, place the pump, with the appropriate suction cup attached, over the wound and begin the suction procedure. If a good seal cannot be achieved over the wound because of hair, it may be necessary to shave the area with the safety razor in your kit.

The suction procedure needs to start within five minutes of the bite to be effective, and it should continue for 30 minutes or more.

- *It is best not to do any cutting on the victim,* but if you must use one of the kits that require it, first disinfect the wound area and the instrument that will be used to make the incisions. Make the incisions *no deeper than* 1/8 *and no longer than* 1/4 *inch* across the puncture marks and along the long axis of the limb. If the bite is not in a large muscle, these cuts may need to be much shallower to prevent permanent tissue damage. Making these incisions too large can cut muscles and tendons, so be very careful to keep the incisions small and shallow. They need to bleed only a small amount. After making the incisions, start the suction immediately.

- After starting the suction, check for a pulse below the wound. If none can be found, loosen the elastic bandage. *Remember that it is better to have no constriction than to have too much.*

- If possible, try to keep the bitten extremity at approximately the victim's heart level, and try to keep the victim as calm as possible.

- Do not give the victim alcohol.

- After completing the treatment, cover the bite as you would any other small wound. To allow for swelling, be sure that any bandage you apply is not constrictive.

- Send someone for medical help, or get the victim to medical attention as soon as possible.

CAMPFIRE REGULATIONS

Open fires are prohibited year-round in the Snake River Corridor. This corridor covers all the land within the national recreation area that is a quarter of a mile or less from the high-water line of the Snake River. During times of low fire danger—generally from October 1 to June 15—fires are permitted if they are contained in a fire pan with sides high enough to contain all of the ashes. These dates may vary from year to year, so check with the Forest Service before your hike. If you use a fire pan, all of your ashes must be carried out with you.

Open campfires are permitted in the rest of the NRA Area during times of low fire danger. Again, check with the Forest Service for the exact dates.

ARTIFACTS

Collecting artifacts, including anything left by Native Americans or the miners and settlers that followed them, is strictly prohibited in Hells Canyon. Enjoy the artifacts, but leave them where you find them.

NORTHWEST FOREST PASS

A Northwest Forest Pass permit is required to park at many of the trailheads on the Oregon side of Hells Canyon. These permits are available at any Wallowa Whittman National Forest office.

Hells Canyon Trail Finder

	EASY	MODERATE	STRENUOUS
Along streams most of the way	4 Imnaha River Trail 37 Hells Canyon Reservoir Trail 39 Stud Creek	10 Oregon Snake River Trail South Trail 11 Oregon Snake River Trail North 40 Idaho Snake River NR Trail Temperance Creek Trail 60 Rapid River Trail 68 Allison Creek Trail	24 Temperance Creek 28 Saddle Creek Trail 43 Sheep Creek Trail
Ridgetop trails	31 Bear Mountain Trail 46 Boise Trail North	2 Cemetery Ridge Trail 7 Western Rim NR Trail North 19 Somers Point Trail 30 Western Rim NR Trail South 33 Barton Heights Trail	58 Dry Diggins Ridge Trail 66 Horse Mountain Lookout Trail
Alpine country	46 Boise Trail North 48 Heavens Gate Lookout Trail	49 Seven Devils Loop 53 Baldy Lake Trail 54 He Devil Lake Trail 55 Dry Diggins Lookout Trail 56 Sheep Lake Trail 57 Bernard Lakes Trail 61 Horse Heaven Cabin Trail 62 Six Lake Basin Trail 63 Satan Lake Route 64 Horse Pasture Basin Trail	50 Cannon Lakes Trail 51 Dog Lake Route 52 Horse Heaven Lake Route 59 Sheep Lake Climbers Route 71 He Devil Mountain 72 She Devil Mountain 73 Mount Baal 74 The Tower of Babel

Hells Canyon Trail Finder

	EASY	MODERATE	STRENUOUS
Overnight backpacking	50 Cannon Lakes Trail	7 Western Rim NR Trail North 9 Deep Creek Trail 10 Oregon Snake River Trail North 11 Oregon Snake River Trail South 30 Western Rim NR Trail South 40 Idaho Snake River Trail 49 Seven Devils Loop 53 Baldy Lake Trail 54 He Devil Lake 56 Sheep Lake Trail 57 Bernard Lakes Trail 60 Rapid River Trail 61 Horse Heaven Cabin Trail 62 Six Lake Basin Trail	1 Salmon Bar Trail 3 Eureka Wagon Road Trail 8 Deep Creek Ranch Trail 12 Camp Creek–Fingerboard Trail 14 Cat Creek Trail 22 High Trail 24 Temperance Creek Trail 28 Saddle Creek Trail 32 Battle Creek–Upper Snake River Trail 42 Bernard Creek Trail 43 Sheep Creek Trail 51 Dog Lake Route 52 Horse Heaven Lake Trail 58 Dry Diggins Ridge Trail 59 Sheep Lake Climbers Route
Lakes	50 Cannon Lakes Trail	53 Baldy Lake Trail 54 He Devil Lake Trail 56 Sheep Lake Trail 57 Bernard Lakes Trail 62 Six Lake Basin Trail 63 Satan Lake Route 64 Horse Pasture Basin Trail	51 Dog Lake Route 52 Horse Heaven Lake Route 59 Sheep Lake Climbers Route

Hells Canyon Trail Finder

	EASY	MODERATE	STRENUOUS
Mountain peaks	31 Bear Mountain Trail 48 Heavens Gate Lookout Trail 65 Sheep Rock NR Trail	33 Barton Heights Trail 57 Bernard Lakes Trail 55 Dry Diggins Lookout Trail	66 Horse Mountain Lookout Route 71 He Devil Mountain 72 She Devil Mountain 73 Mount Baal 74 The Tower of Babel
Historical features	4 Imnaha River Trail 45 Blue Jacket Mine Trail	10 Oregon Snake River Trail South 11 Oregon Snake River Trail North 13 Christmas Creek Ranch Trail 40 Idaho Snake River NR Trail 60 Rapid River Trail 68 Allison Creek Trail	3 Eureka Wagon Road Trail 5 Imnaha Trail 6 Nee-Mee-Poo Trail 8 Deep Creek Ranch Trail 14 Cat Creek Trail 20 Cougar Creek Trail 22 High Trail 24 Temperance Creek Trail 25 Sluice Creek Trail 27 Hat Creek Trail 28 Saddle Creek Trail 38 Old McGraw Creek Route 41 Granite Creek High Water Route 44 Kirkwood Ranch Trail 47 Old Timer Mountain Trail 70 Red Ledge Mine Trail
Rim to river			3 Eureka Wagon Road Trail 24 Temperance Creek Trail 27 Hat Creek Trail 43 Sheep Creek Trail

Trail User Table

Hike	Trail Number	Hiker	Biker	Stock	ATV
1 Salmon Bar Trail	1702	X		X	
2 Cemetery Ridge Trail	1731	X		X	
3 Eureka Wagon Road Trail	1732, 1713	X	X	X	
4 Imnaha River Trail	1713	X	X	X	
5 Imnaha Trail	1713	X		X	
6 Nee-Mee-Poo Trail	1727	X		X	
7 Western Rim NR Trail North	1774	X		X	
8 Deep Creek Ranch Trail	1734, 1707	X		X	
9 Deep Creek Trail	1706	X		X	
10 Oregon Snake River Trail South	1726	X		X	
11 Oregon Snake River Trail North	1726	X		X	
12 Camp Creek–Fingerboard Trail	1699	X		X	
13 Christmas Creek Ranch Trail	1726A	X		X	
14 Cat Creek Trail	1701	X		X	
15 Copper Creek–Lonepine Creek Loop	1736, 1735	X		X	
16 Copper Creek Lodge Area		X			
17 Tryon Saddle Trail	1750, 1771	X		X	
18 Deep Creek Ridge Loop	1770A, 1771, 1750	X		X	
19 Somers Point Trail	1759, 1767	X		X	
20 Cougar Creek Trail	1767	X		X	
21 Pittsburg Creek Trail	1751A	X		X	
22 High Trail	1751	X		X	
23 Salt Creek Trail	1785	X		X	
24 Temperance Creek Trail	1778	X		X	
25 Sluice Creek Trail	1748	X		X	
26 Waterspout Creek Trail	1753	X		X	
27 Hat Creek Trail	1752	X		X	
28 Saddle Creek Trail	1776	X		X	
29 Long Ridge–Freezeout Creek Loop	1749, 1757, 1774, 1763	X		X	
30 Western Rim NR Trail South	1774	X		X	
31 Bear Mountain Trail	1743	X		X	
32 Battle Creek–Upper Snake River Trail	1784, 1786	X		X	
33 Barton Heights Trail		X			
34 Thirty-Two Point Trail	1789	X		X	
35 Buck Creek Trail	1788	X		X	
36 Bench Trail	1884	X		X	
37 Hells Canyon Reservoir Trail	1890	X			
38 Old McGraw Creek Route	1879	X			
39 Stud Creek Trail	1781	X			
40 Idaho Snake River NR Trail	102	X		X	
41 Hibbs Ranch and Granite Creek High Water Route	112, 112A	X			
42 Bernard Creek Trail	58	X		X	
43 Sheep Creek Trail	53	X		X	
44 Kirkwood Ranch Trail	132	X	X	X	X
45 Blue Jacket Mine Trail		X	X	X	
46 Boise Trail North	101	X		X	

Trail User Table

Hike	Trail Number	Hiker	Biker	Stock	ATV
47 Old Timer Mountain Trail	110	X		X	
48 Heavens Gate Lookout Trail		X			
49 Seven Devils Loop	101, 124	X		X	
50 Cannon Lakes	126	X		X	
51 Dog Lake Route		X			
52 Horse Heaven Lake Route		X			
53 Baldy lake	69	X		X	
54 He Devil Lake	129	X		X	
55 Dry Diggins Lookout South	56	X		X	
56 Sheep Lake	123	X		X	
57 Dry Diggins Lookout North	57	X		X	
58 Dry Diggin Ridge	140	X		X	
59 Sheep Lake Climbers Route		X			
60 Rapid River	113	X		X	
61 Horse Heaven	214	X		X	
62 Six Lake Basin	214, 218	X		X	
63 Satan Lake Route		X			
64 Horse Pasture Basin	173	X		X	
65 Sheep Rock		X			
66 Horse Mountain Lookout		X			
67 Eckels Creek	223, 222 514	X		X	
68 Allison Creek	514	X		X	
69 Kinney Creek	211, 222 514	X		X	
70 Red Ledge Mine	219	X		X	
71 He Devil Climb		X			
72 She Devil Climb		X			
73 Mount Baal Climb		X			
74 The Tower of Babel Climb		X			

Oregon

WEST OF THE IMNAHA RIVER

Driving northeast from Enterprise through the rolling hills gives little hint of the rugged canyon country you are about to enter. Soon, glimpses of the canyons to the east start to show up, and before you reach the timber at the Wallowa Whittman National Forest Boundary, it becomes evident that you are on a plateau with a huge abyss to your east. In a few more miles, the road reaches the rim of the 4,000-foot-deep Imnaha Canyon. After following the rim for about 3 miles, you turn right on Forest Road 780 toward Buckhorn Campground and enter Hells Canyon National Recreation Area.

Just past the campground, the road forks and you must decide which hike you are going to take. To the left, rough and rocky Forest Road 788 descends into Cherry Creek Canyon to the trailheads for **Hike 1 Salmon Bar Trail** and **Hike 5 Imnaha Trail.** To the right, the route climbs to reach Cemetery Ridge Trailhead, which is the starting point for **Hike 2 Cemetery Ridge Trail** and **Hike 3 Eureka Wagon Road Trail.** On the way to Cemetery Ridge Trailhead, a side road to the right leads to Buckhorn Lookout. The view of the canyon is breathtaking from Buckhorn Lookout, making the short side trip well worth your time.

To reach **Hike 4 Imnaha River Trail,** you must either hike from any one of these trailheads or drive from Enterprise through Joseph and Imnaha to reach Cow Creek Bridge Trailhead deep in the bottom of the rugged Imnaha Canyon.

None of the trails in this region is in designated wilderness, so technically they are open to mountain bikes. But only **Hikes 3** and **4** are well adapted to wheeled travel.

Hikers on the Eureka Wagon Road.

18

West of the Imnaha River

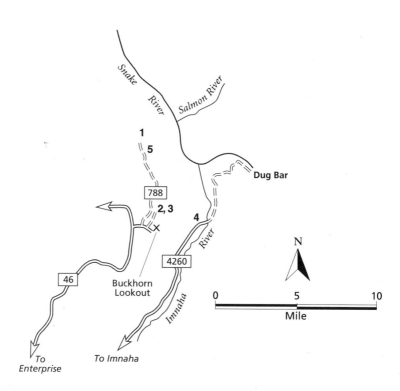

1 Salmon Bar Trail 1702

Highlights:	A hike from Cherry Creek Trailhead past the abandoned Cherry Creek Ranch and around the end of Cemetery Ridge, then descending to Salmon Bar on the Snake River, just below the mouth of the "River of No Return" (the Salmon River).
Type of hike:	Out-and-back day hike or backpack.
Total distance:	14.2 miles.
Difficulty:	Moderate to strenuous.
Best months:	April–June and September–November. Cherry Creek Road may be blocked by snow until late May some years.
Elevation gain:	510 feet.
Permits and fees:	None.
Maps:	Deadhorse Ridge USGS quad.

Finding the trailhead: From Enterprise, Oregon, head east on Oregon 82 for 3 miles to Eggleson Corner, which begins the long straightaway going into Joseph. Turn left (north) at the corner, and follow Crow Creek Road. A sign here points to Buckhorn Lookout. Follow paved Crow Creek Road 5.2 miles, and then turn right (east) on Zumwalt Road. The pavement on Crow Creek Road ends a few feet past this junction, so if you come to the end of the pavement backtrack a little.

A sign points to Tippett Corral at the junction. Zumwalt Road, which eventually becomes Forest Road 46, is chip sealed for a few more miles before becoming gravel. Follow Zumwalt Road and FR 46 32.9 miles to the junction with Forest Road 780. Turn right (northeast) onto FR 780, and drive 0.6 mile to the junction with Forest Road 788 (Cherry Creek Road). Bear left at the Y intersection, and follow FR 788 6.9 miles north to Cherry Creek Trailhead. Forest Road 788 is a rough road that requires a high-clearance vehicle. During wet weather, it may require four-wheel drive. In fall, the first 3 miles of FR 788 become very icy and may require chains, even with four-wheel drive.

The trailhead is at the point where FR 788 crosses Cherry Creek. The road is closed to motor vehicle traffic past this point. GPS coordinates at the trailhead are 45 50.206 N 116 50.523 W.

Trailhead facilities: The trailhead has parking for several cars but has no other facilities.

Camping and services: Camping is permitted at the trailhead. The closest developed campground is Buckhorn Campground, which is 7.2 miles south on FR 788 and FR 780, at Buckhorn Springs. Other services, including medical assistance, can be found in Enterprise.

For more information: USDA Forest Service at Wallowa Mountains Visitor Center in Enterprise.

Salmon Bar Trail 1702

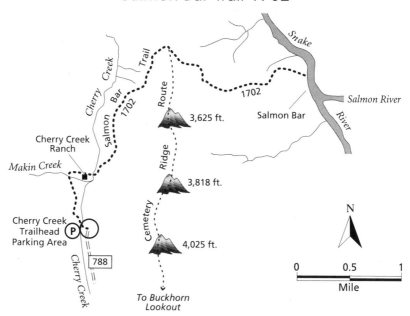

Key points:

- 0.0   Cherry Creek Trailhead.
- 1.0   Cherry Creek Ranch.
- 1.1   Trail crosses Cherry Creek.
- 1.7   Trail crosses first saddle.
- 3.1   Trail crosses main saddle and meets Cemetery Ridge cross-country route. GPS 45 51.795 N 116 49.488 W.
- 7.1   Salmon Bar. GPS 45 51.589 N 116 47.723 W.

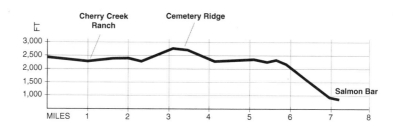

The hike: Cross Cherry Creek leaving the small parking area, and then follow the old roadbed 1 mile to Cherry Creek Ranch. The old road first climbs a little, crossing a small stream along the way, and then drops to the ranch just after crossing Makin Creek. Cherry Creek Ranch was used until recently as a wintering area for sheep.

At the ranch area, the trail first bears slightly left (northeast), then right (east), and crosses Cherry Creek again. After crossing the creek, the trail bears left (north), heading down Cherry Creek Canyon. About 0.2 mile after crossing the creek, the trail turns to the right up a side draw. It soon turns to the left, climbs out of the draw, and begins a 0.3-mile traverse to a saddle on a spur ridge. The path stays above the steep rock formations next to the creek along this traverse.

The route crosses the saddle and continues toward another saddle on Cemetery Ridge. Cemetery Ridge divides the Cherry Creek and Snake River drainages. Just before reaching this next saddle, the trail switchbacks several times to gain the last 200 feet of altitude. In the saddle, at 2,730 feet elevation, is the unmarked junction with the route along Cemetery Ridge. See Hike 2 for a description of the Cemetery Ridge Trail cross-country route, which turns to the right (south) here but may not be visible on the ground.

Crossing the saddle, Salmon Bar Trail turns slightly to the right to begin a gently descending traverse to the southeast. After traversing for 0.3 mile, the course turns east and drops more steeply, then turns right (south) to cross a gully. The track climbs a little after crossing the gully, then traverses east, crossing two more gullies to a fairly flat, rounded ridgetop at 2,400 feet elevation. Hike east-northeast on the ridgetop for a short distance; then bear right and begin to descend steeply into a small but steep canyon. You will make several switchbacks as you drop to the canyon bottom. In the canyon bottom, the trail turns left and heads down the canyon (northeast) for 0.2 mile. It then bears to the right and makes a descending traverse to the Snake River at Salmon Bar (elev. 920 feet).

When the river is not too high, Salmon Bar has a beach that is a nice spot to camp. The river level may fluctuate a couple of feet or more in a day, so be careful about camping too close to it. Snake River always has fish to be

Rafters on the Snake River.

caught. Check regulations before fishing, though, because some of the Snake's rules differ from those of the rest of the state.

Prickly pear cacti bloom along the trail in late May and in June. As usual on the lower trails in Hells Canyon, watch out for rattlesnakes. Elk are common along the trail in spring.

Options: For an alternate return hike, turn south at the unmarked junction with Cemetery Ridge cross-country route, 3.1 miles from the Cherry Creek Trailhead. Then follow the vague route along Cemetery Ridge for 2.8 miles to Imnaha Trail. Turn right (north-northwest) on Imnaha Trail and descend for 1 mile to Cherry Creek Road. Turn right on Cherry Creek Road and hike 0.7 mile to the trailhead, where you parked. You can also run a short shuttle between the trailheads. See Hikes 2 and 5 for details.

2 Cemetery Ridge Trail 1731

Highlights:	A hike down Cemetery Ridge, with ever-changing views of the canyons, from the trailhead near Buckhorn Lookout to Salmon Bar Trail.
Type of hike:	Out-and-back day hike, with shuttle and loop options.
Total distance:	17.4 miles.
Difficulty:	Moderate, requiring good routefinding skills.
Best months:	May–October.
Elevation gain:	600 feet.
Permits and fees:	None.
Maps:	Deadhorse Ridge USGS quad.

Finding the trailhead: From Enterprise, Oregon, head east on Oregon 82 for 3 miles to Eggleson Corner, which begins the long straightaway going into Joseph. Turn left (north) at the corner, and follow Crow Creek Road. A sign here points to Buckhorn Lookout. Follow paved Crow Creek Road 5.2 miles, and then turn right (east) on Zumwalt Road. The pavement on Crow Creek Road ends a few feet past this junction, so if you come to the end of the pavement backtrack a little.

A sign points to Tippett Corral at the junction. Zumwalt Road, which eventually becomes Forest Road 46, is chip sealed for a few more miles before becoming gravel. Follow Zumwalt Road and FR 46 32.9 miles to the junction with Forest Road 780. Turn right (east) on FR 780 and go 0.6 mile, passing Buckhorn Campground, to the junction with Forest Road 788 (Cherry Creek Road). Bear right at the junction, staying on FR 708, and climb 0.4 mile to the unmarked junction with Cemetery Ridge Road. Buckhorn Lookout is a short distance straight ahead, on the main road, so if you miss the junction it will be easy to backtrack. Buckhorn Lookout is a good viewpoint that is well worth visiting anyway.

Turn left (north) on Cemetery Ridge Road (which is still FR 780) and follow it 1.1 miles to the unmarked trailhead. The last mile to the trailhead may

Cemetery Ridge Trail 1731

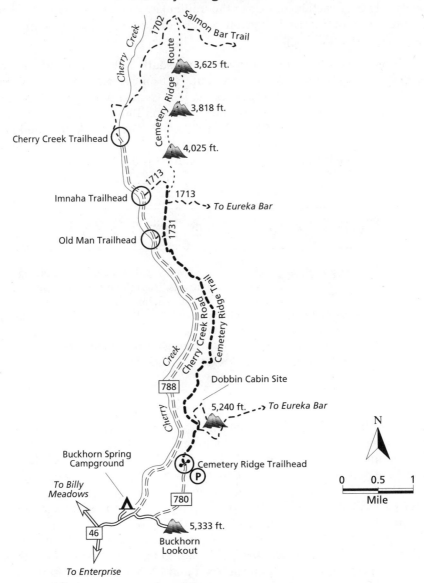

be too rough or muddy for low-clearance vehicles. This is also the trailhead for Hike 3, Eureka Wagon Road Trail. GPS coordinates at the trailhead are 45 46.101 N 116 49.090 W.

Trailhead facilities: An iron gate blocks the road at the trailhead. The trailhead has room to park several cars but has no other facilities. A horse loading ramp, campsites with tables, and a restroom are located at Buckhorn Campground, 1.8 miles to the southwest on FR 780 at Buckhorn Springs.

Camping and services: Camping is permitted at the trailhead. The closest developed campground is Buckhorn Campground, 1.8 miles to the southwest on FR 780 at Buckhorn Springs. Other services, including medical assistance, can be found in Enterprise.

For more information: USDA Forest Service at Wallowa Mountains Visitor Center in Enterprise.

Key points:
- 0.0   Cemetery Ridge Trailhead.
- 0.5   Junction with Eureka Wagon Road Trail.
- 2.7   End of roadbed.
- 4.7   Junction with Old Man Trail.
- 5.6   Junction with Imnaha Trail, to Eureka Creek Cabin and Snake River. GPS 45 49.343 N 116 49.512 W.
- 5.9   Junction with Imnaha Trail, to Cherry Creek.
- 8.7   Junction with Salmon Bar Trail. GPS 45 51.795 N 116 49.488 W.

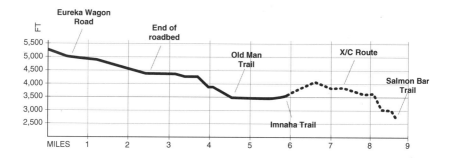

The hike: From the iron gate just past the trailhead parking area, the trail, which is actually a road at this point, heads north along the west side of Cemetery Ridge. The trail reaches a saddle at 5,050 feet elevation, 0.5 mile from the trailhead. Up to this point, Cemetery Ridge Trail and Eureka Wagon Road Trail 1732 follow the same route. (See Hike 3 for details about Eureka Wagon Road Trail.) Do not go through the saddle; instead, bear left and follow another old roadbed north for 20 yards. Here the roadbed forks again. Bear left, slightly downhill, at this fork. (The right fork heads up to the top of the ridge to the site of the old Dobbin Cabin. The 0.5-mile hike up to the cabin site makes an interesting side trip. The top of the ridge near the cabin site offers an excellent view of the canyons to the northeast.)

Following the left fork, you will cross a saddle on a spur ridge (elev. 4,915 feet) 0.8 mile from the junction with Eureka Wagon Road Trail. This area was burned in 1986 and again in 2000, and much of it is now growing up to elderberry brush with lots of room left for flowers, mainly paintbrush and wild roses. Another 1.4 miles brings you to the end of the old roadbed.

The route contours along the west side of the ridge for another 0.5 mile, then crosses the ridgeline at 4,240 feet elevation. You then continue to traverse along the east side of the ridge for another 0.5 mile, before regaining the ridgeline. From the ridgeline, follow the poor path down the ridge to the next saddle, at 3,960 feet elevation. In this saddle, bear slightly left and pick up the trail as it contours around the west side of a hump on the ridge. After passing the hump, the track regains the ridge and soon makes a switchback to the left, then another one to the right. The tread soon gets back on the ridgeline and then descends along it, passing a rock outcropping, to another saddle.

This saddle (elev. 3,520 feet), at 4.7 miles from the trailhead, holds the unmarked junction with Old Man Trail, which drops off to the left and descends steeply for 0.8 mile, losing 500 feet of elevation, to meet Cherry Creek Road.

Stay on Cemetery Ridge Trail, which heads straight ahead (north) from the junction, traversing along the right (east) side of the ridgeline. It climbs slightly at first, and then switchbacks down a subridge to the junction with Imnaha Trail, Hike 5. This first junction with Imnaha Trail (elev. 3,500 feet) is 0.9 mile from the junction with Old Man Trail. From this junction, Cemetery Ridge Trail continues 0.3 mile north, climbing slightly, to another saddle while sharing the route with Imnaha Trail. In this saddle (elev. 3,560 feet), Imnaha Trail bears to the left (north-northwest) and begins its descent to Cherry Creek Road. Cemetery Ridge Trail, which becomes simply Cemetery Ridge Route past this point, heads on along the ridge to the north.

As it leaves the saddle and second junction with Imnaha Trail, Cemetery Ridge Route climbs, following a poor path around the left side of the first two outcroppings on the ridgeline, and then regains the ridge (elev. 3,800 feet), giving you your first view of the Snake River. The route continues to follow the ridge, heading generally north and climbing. After hiking 0.8 mile from the last junction with Imnaha Trail, you will have climbed to 4,025 feet elevation. Here the Salmon River can be seen far ahead and below. Continue north along the ridge, generally descending slightly, for 0.6 mile more to a saddle above Cherry Creek Ranch. The ranch is far below to your left. The course then climbs a little and flattens out for a short distance before starting its final descent toward the junction with Salmon Bar Trail, which is 2.2 miles past the saddle above the Cherry Creek Ranch. The junction with Salmon Bar Trail is not marked, so watch closely for it as it crosses the lower end of Cemetery Ridge, in a broad saddle at 2,730 feet elevation.

There is no usable water along Cemetery Ridge Trail, so take all you will need. As is true with most ridge routes, Cemetery Ridge can be very windy and cold at times. Cemetery Ridge Trail gets most of its use during fall hunting seasons.

The lower part of this route travels through prime elk calving area. You will have a good chance of seeing these large animals. If you do, do not approach them. Watch the elk at a distance through binoculars. Getting too close to a cow elk during calving time not only is hard on the elk but also can be dangerous for you because elk will protect their calves from humans at times. Do not take your dog along in May and June when the elk are calving. Not only is it illegal to allow a dog to chase elk, but dogs can also hurt or kill calves and be injured by the mother elk in the process.

Rattlesnakes are rare along the upper portion of this trail, but they are fairly common below the junction with Old Man Trail.

Junction of Cemetery Ridge Trail and Eureka Wagon Road.

Options: An alternate return trip can be made by turning left on Salmon Bar Trail and following it 3.1 miles to Cherry Creek Trailhead. This option requires a car shuttle with a high-clearance vehicle. See Hike 1 for details.

Another shuttle option is to turn left on Old Man Trail 4.7 miles from the trailhead and descend to Cherry Creek Road. The hard-to-find junction of Old Man Trail and Cherry Creek Road is 5.1 miles north down Cherry Creek Road from its junction with FR 780 near Buckhorn Campground, and 0.5 mile south of the marked junction with Imnaha Trail. The GPS coordinates of the junction of Cherry Creek Road and Old Man Trail are 45 48.824 N 116 49.770 W.

To make a loop hike, turn right at the junction with Imnaha Trail 5.6 miles from Cemetery Ridge Trailhead and follow Imnaha Trail 3 miles to the junction with Eureka Wagon Road Trail. Turn right on the wagon road and climb south for 6.5 miles to Cemetery Ridge Trailhead. See Hikes 5 and 3 for details.

3 Eureka Wagon Road
Trail 1732, 1713

Highlights:	A hike from Cemetery Ridge Trailhead near Buckhorn Lookout to the Snake River at Eureka Bar on a historic wagon road. The road was built in the early 1900s to haul timber from the forests around the trailhead to the town site of Eureka on the river.
Type of hike:	Out-and-back backpack or long day hike, with a shuttle option.
Total distance:	15.8 miles.
Difficulty:	Moderate to strenuous.
Best months:	Late May–June and September–October.
Elevation loss:	4,220 feet.
Permits and fees:	None.
Maps:	Deadhorse Ridge USGS quad.

Finding the trailhead: From Enterprise, Oregon, head east on Oregon 82 for 3 miles to Eggleson Corner, which begins the long straightaway going into Joseph. Turn left (north) at the corner, and follow Crow Creek Road. A sign here points to Buckhorn Lookout. Follow paved Crow Creek Road 5.2 miles, and then turn right (east) on Zumwalt Road. The pavement on Crow Creek Road ends a few feet past this junction, so if you come to the end of the pavement backtrack a little.

A sign points to Tippett Corral at the junction. Zumwalt Road, which eventually becomes Forest Road 46, is chip sealed for a few more miles before becoming gravel. Follow Zumwalt Road and FR 46 32.9 miles to the junction with Forest Road 780. Turn right (east) on FR 780 and go 0.6 mile, passing Buckhorn Campground, to the junction with Forest Road 788 (Cherry Creek Road). Bear right at the junction, staying on FR 780, and climb 0.4 mile to the unmarked junction with Cemetery Ridge Road. Buckhorn Lookout is a short distance straight ahead, on the main road, so if you miss the junction it will be easy to backtrack. Buckhorn Lookout is a good viewpoint that is well worth visiting anyway.

Turn left (north) on Cemetery Ridge Road (which is still FR 780) and follow it 1.1 miles to the unmarked trailhead. The last mile to the trailhead may be too rough or muddy for low-clearance vehicles. This is also the trailhead for Hike 2, Cemetery Ridge Trail. GPS coordinates at the trailhead are 45 46.101 N 116 49.090 W.

Trailhead facilities: The trailhead has parking for several cars but has no other facilities.

Camping and services: Camping is permitted at the trailhead. The closest developed campground is Buckhorn Campground, 1.8 miles to the southwest on FR 780 at Buckhorn Springs. Other services, including medical assistance, can be found in Enterprise.

Eureka Wagon Road Trail 1732, 1713

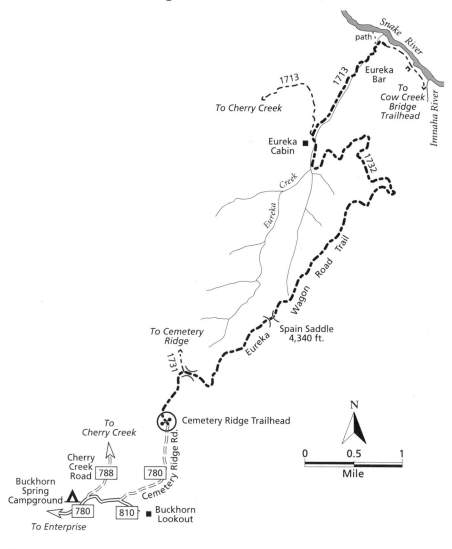

For more information: USDA Forest Service at Wallowa Mountains Visitor Center in Enterprise.

Key points:

- 0.0 Cemetery Ridge Trailhead.
- 0.5 Junction with Cemetery Ridge Trail.
- 2.1 Spain Saddle.
- 4.3 Gooseneck in the trail.
- 6.5 Junction with Imnaha Trail near Eureka Creek Cabin. GPS 45 48.528 N 116 47.343 W.
- 7.8 Trail crosses Eureka Creek for the last time near mineshaft.
- 7.9 Trail sign on Eureka Bar. GPS 45 49.337 N 116 46.530 W.

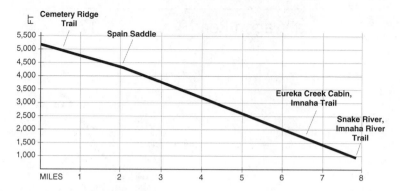

The hike: From the iron gate, a few feet past the parking area at the trail-head, the trail (road) heads north, along the left (west) side of the ridge. After following the ridge for 0.5 mile, you will reach a saddle and the junction with Cemetery Ridge Trail (elev. 5,050 feet). Up to this point, Cemetery Ridge Trail and Eureka Wagon Road Trail follow the same route. Turn right at the junction, and begin to traverse the open hillside to the southeast. After 0.4 mile, the course rounds a point and heads northeast, crossing a fenceline through a gate. It continues to descend at a fairly even grade, on mostly open slopes, for another 1.2 miles to Spain Saddle.

At Spain Saddle, elevation 4,340 feet, the route goes through another gate and travels along a partly wooded, west-facing slope for 0.6 mile, before crossing to the right side of the ridge again. After crossing to the right (east) side of the ridge, the trail continues its traverse for 1 mile along the steep open slope. These open hillsides may be covered with the large yellow flowers of arrow leaf balsamroot in May.

Past the traverse, the tread bears to the right and then makes a gooseneck turn to the left on a grassy ridgetop (elev. 3,020 feet). Watch for the cacti that bloom here in June. After passing the gooseneck turn, the track heads northwest, into and out of a draw, then crosses a ridgeline. After crossing the ridgeline, it heads southwest, continuing its descending traverse to Eureka Creek. The tread reaches the brushy creekbed of Eureka Creek (also known as Deer Creek) 6.1 miles from the trailhead.

Once at the creekbed, the route turns right (north) and goes down the east side of Eureka Creek, crossing a small side stream as it descends 0.4 mile to the Eureka Creek Cabin, at 1,740 feet elevation. Just before reaching the cabin, the trail crosses Eureka Creek. Although it is starting to deteriorate from lack of maintenance, the cabin is still used frequently. Leaving the cabin, the trace heads north and soon comes to the junction with Imnaha Trail. Imnaha Trail to the left (west) heads over Cemetery Ridge to Forest Road 788 (Cherry Creek Road). (See Hike 5 for details about Imnaha Trail.) Eureka Wagon Road Trail goes straight ahead down Eureka Creek from this junction. The trail may be very vague in the grassy area next to the junction but will soon show up again as you hike north.

Most maps show the trail going down the right (east) side of Eureka Creek—the route of the wagon road—from this junction to Eureka Bar. However,

30

the old roadbed is washed out in places and is choked with brush. The current trail starts down from the cabin on the west side of the creek. Slightly more than 0.5 mile below the cabin, the route crosses the creek for the first of seven times. Right before crossing the creek for the last time, a poor path turns to the left. This path is the remains of an old wagon road that goes a short distance to the lower end of Eureka Bar. Just after crossing Eureka Creek for the last time, you will see a mineshaft on the right side of the trail.

The tread then heads out onto the grass- and cactus-covered Eureka Bar. A trail sign a short distance onto the bar turns you to the right (southeast). There are several good campsites at Eureka Bar (elev. 950 feet), and fishing can be good for smallmouth bass and trout in the Snake River.

No water is available for the first 6 miles along this trail, so be sure you have enough with you, especially for the way back up. The lower section of this trail can be very hot in July and August. Poison ivy lines the trail from the cabin to the river. Rattlesnakes are generally found below Spain Saddle, mostly in the creekbed along Eureka Creek. On one trip, I encountered six of these snakes below the cabin, so be careful.

Options: To avoid climbing back up the wagon road to the trailhead, turn right at the trail sign on Eureka Bar and follow the trail southeast to the mouth of the Imnaha River. Then turn right on Imnaha River Trail, and hike 4.2 miles south to Cow Creek Bridge Trailhead. This hike requires a long car shuttle to Cow Creek Bridge Trailhead. See Hike 4 for information about Imnaha River Trail and driving directions to Cow Creek Bridge Trailhead.

Stamp Mill ruins at Eureka Bar.

4 Imnaha River Trail 1713

Highlights:	A hike from Cow Creek Bridge Trailhead through the exceedingly rugged Lower Imnaha River Canyon to the mouth of the Imnaha River at historic Eureka Bar on the Snake River. This gentle trail descends through the most rugged and spectacular part of the Imnaha River Canyon.
Type of hike:	Out-and-back day hike or backpack.
Total distance:	8.4 miles.
Difficulty:	Easy.
Best months:	All year.
Elevation gain:	Minimal.
Permits and fees:	None.
Maps:	Cactus Mountain and Deadhorse Ridge USGS quads.

Finding the trailhead: From Joseph, Oregon, follow the Imnaha Highway (Oregon 350) for 30 miles northeast to Imnaha, Oregon. From Imnaha, take County Road 755 north. After 6 miles, County 755 turns into Forest Road 4260 and is no longer paved. Another 14 miles of rough gravel road brings you to the Cow Creek Bridge. The bridge crosses the Imnaha River, however, not Cow Creek. As the road turns right to cross the bridge, a parking area is to the left. This is the Cow Creek Bridge Trailhead, the starting point for Imnaha River Trail. GPS coordinates at the trailhead are 45 45.822 N 116 44.820 W.

Trailhead facilities: The trailhead has parking for several cars. Stock facilities and restrooms are across the bridge. This trailhead is on private land, so please show the proper respect.

Camping and services: Camping is permitted at the trailhead. Groceries can be purchased at Imnaha; other services may be obtained in Joseph or Enterprise, Oregon.

For more information: USDA Forest Service at Wallowa Mountains Visitor Center in Enterprise.

Key points:
- 0.0 Cow Creek Bridge Trailhead.
- 0.3 Cow Creek enters river from opposite side.
- 1.9 Power lines high overhead. GPS 45 47.150 N 116 44.919 W.
- 4.0 First of three wooden footbridges.
- 4.2 Southeast end of Eureka Bar. GPS 45 49.005 N 116 45.927 W.

The hike: From the small parking area at Cow Creek Bridge Trailhead, the trail heads north, soon passing a trail sign. A bit farther along, you will go through a gate and, in another 0.2 mile,

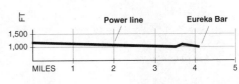

Imnaha River Trail 1713

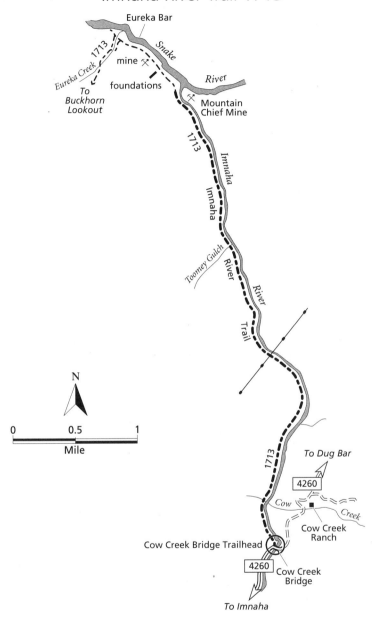

cross a very small stream. Just after the trail crosses the stream, Cow Creek enters the river from the opposite side. The route soon crosses another small stream, which flows through a culvert beneath it.

Another stream enters the river 0.7 mile farther along. This stream has a waterfall 100 feet back from the river. Half a mile farther, a set of power lines crosses the canyon and the trail. These power lines are high overhead and may not be noticed. The tread crosses another small creek at the lower end of Toomey Gulch, 1 mile past the power lines. Bighorn sheep can often be seen on the rugged canyon walls between Toomey Gulch and the Snake River. A couple hundred yards after crossing the creek, you may notice a shallow mineshaft on the left side of the trail.

Half a mile past the mineshaft, the path climbs slightly to get above the 100-foot-high cliffs that drop nearly vertically into the frothing Imnaha River. Then the course descends for 1 mile to the first of three wooden foot-bridges. One hundred yards past the first bridge the opening of the Mountain Chief Mine can be seen across the river. This 700-foot shaft goes all the way through the ridge to the Snake River. Above, to the left of the trail, is another short mineshaft, which appears to follow the same mineralized fault zone as the Mountain Chief Mine. The last two of the three wooden bridges are 50 yards farther along. Just after crossing the bridges, the tread bears to the left onto Eureka Bar, next to the Snake River. At 950 feet elevation, Eureka Bar is 4.2 miles from Cow Creek Bridge Trailhead. There are several good campsites along Eureka Bar. The cleanest water in the area comes from Eureka Creek, near the northwest end of the bar, but even it should be boiled or treated.

Eureka Bar was the site of much activity in the early 1900s, when a wagon road was cut from the timbered country around Buckhorn Springs, about 10 miles up Eureka Creek, to the town site to allow a supply of wood to be brought down. This road is now used as a trail. See Hike 3 for a description of Eureka Wagon Road Trail. The foundations on the hillside 0.1 mile northwest from the mouth of the Imnaha River are the remains of a mill that was to be used to process the copper ore from the mines. A bit farther along, the stone cellar of the Eureka Hotel sits next to the trail. The town site, of which very little remains, is 0.7 mile downstream from the mouth of the Imnaha River, at the mouth of Eureka Creek.

In 1903 the boom days of Eureka became quickly numbered with the sinking of the sternwheeler *Imnaha*. Another boat, the smaller *Mountain Gem*, was built to take its place supplying the town, but in about four more years the entire operation went under.

Imnaha River Trail gets moderate to heavy use much of the year. There may be some mountain bike and motor bike traffic as well as hiking and horse traffic. The trail is closed to motor vehicles with more than two wheels. Many large patches of prickly pear cactus inhabit the bar. It usually blooms, opening up its large, waxy yellow flowers, in late May and June. Some poison ivy is also found on Eureka Bar as well as along Imnaha River Trail. A few rattlesnakes are present, so keep your eyes and ears open.

Options: Use Imnaha River Trail as an exit route for a hike that begins at Cemetery Ridge Trailhead. See Hikes 2, 3, and 5 for details.

Imnaha River.

5 Imnaha Trail 1713

Highlights: A hike from Forest Road 788 (Cherry Creek Road)
over Cemetery Ridge to Eureka Wagon Road Trail and
Eureka Cabin.

Type of hike: Out-and-back day hike or backpack.

Total distance: 8.6 miles.

Difficulty: Strenuous.

Best months: April–June and September–November. Forest Road
788 may be blocked by snow until mid-May.

Elevation gain: 1,200 feet.

Permits and fees: None.

Maps: Deadhorse Ridge USGS quad.

Finding the trailhead: From Enterprise, Oregon, head east on Oregon 82 for 3 miles to Eggleson Corner, which begins the long straightaway going into Joseph. Turn left (north) at the corner, and follow Crow Creek Road. A sign here points to Buckhorn Lookout. Follow paved Crow Creek Road 5.2 miles, and then turn right (east) on Zumwalt Road. The pavement on Crow Creek Road ends a few feet past this junction, so if you come to the end of the pavement backtrack a little.

A sign points to Tippett Corral at the junction. Zumwalt Road, which eventually becomes Forest Road 46, is chip sealed for a few more miles before becoming gravel. Follow Zumwalt Road and FR 46 32.9 miles to the junction with Forest Road 780. Turn right (northeast) onto FR 780, and drive 0.6 mile to the junction with Forest Road 788 (Cherry Creek Road). Forest Road 788 is a rough road that requires a high-clearance vehicle. During wet weather, it may require four-wheel drive. In fall, the first 3 miles of FR 788 become very icy and may require chains, even with four-wheel drive. Bear left at the Y intersection, and follow FR 788 for 6.2 miles north to Imnaha Trailhead. A sign on the right (east) side of the road marks the trailhead. GPS coordinates at the trailhead are 45 49.583 N 116 50.059 W.

Trailhead facilities: The trailhead has limited parking but no other facilities.

Camping and services: Camping is permitted at the trailhead, but the available area is limited. The closest developed campground is Buckhorn Campground, 6.3 miles south on FR 788 and FR 780, at Buckhorn Springs. Other services, including medical assistance, can be found in Enterprise.

For more information: USDA Forest Service at Wallowa Mountains Visitor Center in Enterprise.

Key points:

0.0   Imnaha Trailhead.

1.0   Saddle on Cemetery Ridge and junction with Cemetery Ridge Trail.

1.3   Second junction with Cemetery Ridge Trail. GPS 45 49.343 N 116 49.452 W.

2.3   Crossing of Knight Creek.

Imnaha Trail 1713

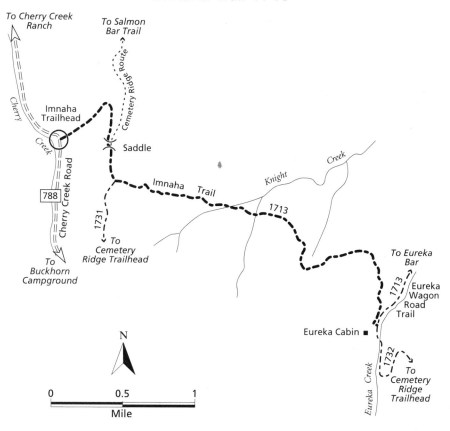

4.3 Junction with Eureka Wagon Road Trail near Eureka Creek Cabin. GPS 45 48.528 N 116 47.343 W.

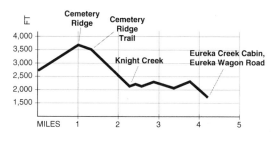

The hike: From the poorly marked trailhead, the trail heads up a draw to the northeast. It climbs the draw for 0.5 mile, then begins a series of switchbacks in which it climbs the remaining 0.5 mile to a saddle on Cemetery Ridge. At the saddle (elev. 3,560 feet) is the unmarked junction with Cemetery Ridge Trail. To the left, Cemetery Ridge Cross-Country Route (there is really no trail on Cemetery Ridge north of the junction with Imnaha Trail) follows the ridge north to Salmon Bar Trail. For the next 0.3 mile, Cemetery Ridge Trail and Imnaha Trail follow the same route. See Hike 2 for a description of Cemetery Ridge Trail.

Turn right in the saddle and join Cemetery Ridge Trail, heading south. A third of a mile from the saddle, Imnaha Trail turns to the left (east) and leaves Cemetery Ridge Trail. A sign marks this junction, which is 1.3 miles from FR 788, at 3,500 feet elevation.

After turning east at the junction, Imnaha Trail descends a series of switchbacks for 0.5 mile and then becomes hard to see in a grassy area. In this grassy area, head straight down to the east and pick up the trail again near a small rock outcropping. After passing the outcropping, the track continues to descend and soon follows a small ridge just to the left (north) of Knight Creek. The path goes down this small ridge for a short distance, then crosses Knight Creek. This crossing, at 2,070 feet elevation, is 2.3 miles from the trailhead on FR 788.

The tread then contours out of Knight Creek, rounds a small ridge, then heads back into a side draw. You cross a small stream, which may be dry, in this draw. Then the course rounds a larger but more rounded ridge, before working back into another draw, 3.3 miles from the trailhead. The trail crosses the creekbed in this draw (elev. 2,050 feet), then heads east-northeast, climbing 300 vertical feet to a rounded ridgeline. After crossing the ridge, the route descends to the southeast into Eureka Creek Canyon. It reaches the junction with Eureka Wagon Road Trail just north of the Eureka Creek Cabin, 4.3 miles from the trailhead. The elevation at the cabin is 1,740 feet. At this junction, Cemetery Ridge Trailhead is 6.5 miles to the right (south) and 3,460 vertical feet up. The Snake River at Eureka Bar is 1.4 miles to the left and 790 feet down.

Some fairly good camping spots can be found near the cabin, next to Eureka Creek, and more are available at Eureka Bar. Fishing is generally good

Eureka Cabin.

for a variety of fish in the Snake River. Check the Oregon fishing regulations before fishing. Elk, mule deer, and an occasional bighorn sheep or black bear may also be seen. Prickly pear cactus is abundant along the lower part of Imnaha Trail and blooms in late May and June. At times, especially in the spring, the bottom of Eureka Creek Canyon has a large population of rattlesnakes. Watch for them carefully. These snakes are fairly common along the whole length of Imnaha Trail, and it is normal to see one or more on this hike. Lots of poison ivy fills the brush along creekbeds.

Options: Alternate return hikes requiring a car shuttle can be made by taking Eureka Wagon Road Trail and Imnaha River Trail to Cow Creek Bridge Trailhead, slightly more than 6 miles away, or by climbing back out to Cemetery Ridge Trailhead via Eureka Wagon Road Trail. See Hikes 3 and 4 for details.

NORTHERN REGION

The northern region of Hells Canyon is dotted with abandoned homesteads. In the late nineteenth century and especially the early twentieth century, settlers attempted to scratch out a living on almost any spot of flat land. All of the homesteaders are gone now, and the remains of their hopes and dreams are slowly deteriorating. This part of the canyon is moving closer by the day to what it was a thousand years ago.

This region has the most limited road access of any region of Hells Canyon, but this should not deter the hiker from exploring this vast land with its abundant wildlife and rich history. Passenger cars can easily reach only two trailheads in this region: Hat Point Trailhead, east of Imnaha, where **Hike 27 Hat Creek Trail** begins, and Warnock Corral Trailhead, 4 miles north of Hat Point at the start of **Hike 24 Temperance Creek Trail**. High-clearance vehicles can be used to get to **Hike 6 Nee-Mee-Poo Trail**, along the Dug Bar Road, and to Dug Bar, where **Hike 11 Oregon Snake River Trail North** ends. It takes a high-clearance four-wheel-drive vehicle to negotiate Lord Flat Road north of Warnock Corral, where **Hikes 7, 17, 18,** and **19** start.

The rest of the hikes in this region are internal trails, many of which are best reached via jet boat on the Snake River. An aircraft drop-off at Pittsburg, the starting point for **Hike 11 Oregon Snake River Trail North,** is an exciting way to begin this hike along the river. Pittsburg is also the starting point for **Hike 21 Pittsburg Creek Trail.** Flying to Lord Flat is also an option.

Northern Region

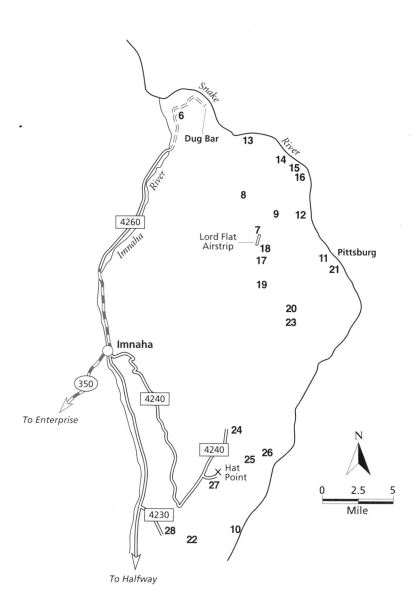

6   Nee-Mee-Poo Trail 1727

Highlights:	A hike from Dug Bar Road over Lone Pine Saddle to Dug Bar on the historic Nee-Mee-Poo Trail.
Type of hike:	Shuttle day hike.
Total distance:	5 miles.
Difficulty:	Strenuous. Some routefinding and map-reading skills are needed to follow this trail.
Best months:	March–June and September–November. This trail is free of snow nearly all year, but hiking this trail during periods of hot weather should be avoided.
Elevation gain:	860 feet.
Trailhead elevation:	1,820 feet.
Permits and fees:	None.
Maps:	USDA Forest Service Hells Canyon National Recreation Area. The USGS Cactus Mountain quad covers the area but does not show this trail.

Finding the trailhead: Drive northeast from Joseph, Oregon, following the Imnaha Highway (Oregon 350) for 30 miles to Imnaha, Oregon. From Imnaha, take County Road 755 north. After 6 miles, County 755 turns into Forest Road 4260 and is no longer paved. Another 14 miles of rough gravel road brings you to Cow Creek Bridge. Cross the Imnaha River on the bridge, and continue another 2.8 miles north to Nee-Me-Poo Trailhead, which is hard to spot. A trail sign marks the trailhead a few feet to the left of and above the road. GPS coordinates at the trailhead are 45 47.443 N 116 44.158 W.

To reach Dug Bar Trailhead, continue another 5.2 miles to the northeast on FR 4260. Dug Bar actually has two trailheads. You will reach Nee-Mee-Poo Trailhead first. A sign marks this trailhead. The GPS coordinates at the trailhead are 45 48.623 N 116 41.694 W.

Nee-Mee-Poo Trail reaches Dug Bar Road at the northwest end of Dug Bar. It is 0.6 mile from here to the southeast end of the bar and the trailhead for Oregon Snake River Trail (Hikes 10 and 11).

Trailhead facilities: The trailhead has very limited parking and no other facilities, but the trailhead at Dug Bar for Oregon Snake River Trail has several campsites, restrooms, and a boat ramp.

Camping and services: Primitive campsites are available along Dug Bar. Groceries can be purchased at Imnaha; gas and other services may be obtained in Joseph and Enterprise, Oregon.

For more information: USDA Forest Service at Wallowa Mountains Visitor Center in Enterprise.

Key points:
- 0.0   Nee-Mee-Poo Trailhead.
- 1.5   Lone Pine Saddle.
- 2.5   Big Canyon, creek, and stock tank.
- 3.2   Saddle.

Nee-Mee-Poo Trail 1727

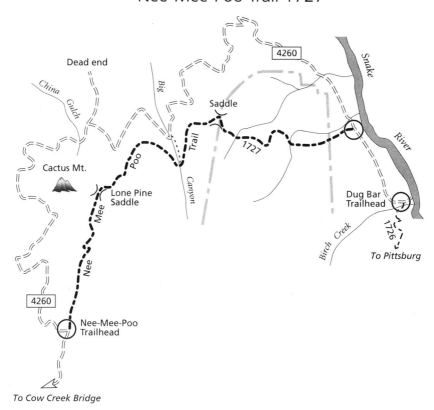

To Cow Creek Bridge

5.0   Dug Bar Road at the northwest end of Dug Bar. GPS 45 48.623 N 116 41.694 W.

The hike: This trail follows part of the historic route that the Wallowa Band of Nez Perce took in June 1877 when leaving the Wallowa Valley. The Nez Perce, under the leadership of Young Chief Joseph, were beginning their ill-fated attempt to escape to freedom. They were captured several months later in north-central Montana, only 30 miles from the Canadian border and freedom.

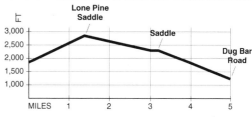

Leaving the trailhead, the route climbs steeply a few feet to a trail sign. The sign, which is held up by a rock pile, states "Nee-Mee-Poo Trail 1727, Dug Bar five miles." After passing the sign, the trail heads north, up a little ridge between two small gullies. In a short distance, the path drops into the gully on the left. The tread heads up the creekbed, passing a developed spring, then climbs steeply back up the gully to the right. Much of the route is braided from use by cattle, and it may be difficult to follow the exact trail.

The general route is fairly easy to follow, however. For the next 0.7 mile, the trail continues to climb to the north, winding its way through a couple of side gullies to a fenceline and gate (elev. 2,330 feet). Watch for lupine, which blooms here in May, as well as prickly pear cactus, which blooms in late May and June.

After crossing a couple more gullies, the trail crosses another fenceline. This fence is not as well maintained as the first one. Lone Pine Saddle, at 2,860 feet elevation, is reached 250 yards past the second fenceline. At Lone Pine Saddle, 1.5 miles from the trailhead, the view of the Snake River Canyon opens up to the north. The path crosses the saddle, then bears to the right. Do not mistake the cattle trails along the ridgeline for the main trail.

After passing Lone Pine Saddle, the trail soon crosses a little brushy draw and then rounds a point and heads southeast back into Big Canyon. You will reach the creek in Big Canyon 1 mile after crossing Lone Pine Saddle. This creek is an oasis, with blackberries and a stock tank. At times, this may be the only water source along this trail. Be sure to treat or filter the water before drinking. A poor path runs down the creek in Big Canyon to Dug Bar Road, which is only a couple hundred yards away here.

The tread traverses to the north out of Big Canyon and soon becomes braided along the steep hillside. After 0.2 mile, a fence appears to the left. The tread follows along and above the fence a couple hundred yards. It then bears to the right, rounding a ridge. At this point, another saddle comes into view to the east. The part of Nee-Mee-Poo Trail leading to the saddle can be seen 0.3 mile ahead. The route crosses the saddle (elev. 2,310 feet), goes through a gate, and begins its descent to Dug Bar.

After crossing the saddle, the route bears right and winds steeply down into a small gully. It traverses out of this gully, goes through another small gulch, then enters a larger gulch with some brush in it. The path rounds a rounded ridgeline 0.1 mile after crossing the gulch. It then crosses another small gully and soon enters a brushy larger one (elev. 1,900 feet). The course traverses nearly on the level out of the brushy gully, then drops to another saddle. The balsamroot starts to bloom in this area in mid-April. The tread makes a couple of switchbacks as it leaves the saddle, heading down to the southeast. It crosses another gully, this one with a stream, 0.2 mile after crossing the saddle. The path traverses out of this gully and soon forks. Take the left fork. It soon becomes hard to see the trail; however, it can be seen a couple hundred yards ahead. The route crosses another gully and shortly comes out on a rounded point. It then drops down the left side of the point and heads northeast to a gate in the fence, which can be seen ahead. Go through the gate, and head down the open slope to Dug Bar Road, at 1,130 feet elevation. There is a sign marking Nee-Mee-Poo Trail as it reaches Dug Bar Road.

It is much easier to hike Nee-Mee-Poo Trail in the direction described here then it is to start from Dug Bar. If you leave a car at Dug Bar, be sure to park outside the fenced area. Do not park next to the buildings at Dug Bar Ranch. The stock here has been known to knock off car mirrors and damage paint.

Dug Bar on the Snake River.

Plenty of parking is available next to the launch site below the ranch, and some is available near Nee-Mee-Poo Trail at the northwest end of the bar. Watch for an occasional rattlesnake.

Options: No other trails connect with Nee-Mee-Poo Trail.

7 Western Rim National Recreation Trail North 1774

Highlights:	Also known as Summit Ridge Trail, this is a hike along a very scenic, mostly ridgetop route from the Lord Flat Airstrip and Trailhead, atop Summit Ridge, down to and along Oregon Snake River Trail to Dug Bar Trailhead.
Type of hike:	Two-day backpack shuttle.
Total distance:	13.4 miles.
Difficulty:	Moderate, from south to north as described here; strenuous if going the other way. Some routefinding skills are required to follow this trail safely. This trail has no water for the first 4.8 miles.
Best months:	June–October south of Square Mountain (however, road access to Lord Flat may be blocked by snow until July); April–June and September–November north of Square Mountain. The lower section of trail, within a couple of miles of the junction with Oregon Snake River Trail, may be free of snow most of the year. Flowers are best in late June.
Elevation gain:	400 feet.
Permits and fees:	None.
Maps:	Lord Flat, Fingerboard Saddle, and Cactus Mountain USGS quads.

Finding the trailhead: To reach Lord Flat Airstrip and Trailhead, take Oregon 350 for 30 miles northeast from Joseph, Oregon, to the small town of Imnaha, Oregon. From Imnaha, take Hat Point Road (Forest Road 4240) east from Imnaha. After going 22 miles on the Hat Point Road, turn left (north) on Lord Flat Road (also FR 4240). Lord Flat Road (also known as Summit Ridge Trail) can be used by normal cars for about 4 miles to Warnock Corral, but then it becomes necessary to have a four-wheel-drive vehicle with high clearance. It is about 16 miles from Warnock Corral to Lord Flat. The GPS coordinates at the south end of Lord Flat Airstrip are 45 39.925 N 116 36.996 W.

Aircraft is often used to reach Lord Flat Trailhead. If you are not an experienced and daring driver with the proper vehicle, it is better to fly into Lord Flat. The best way to hike this trail one way is to place a car at Dug Bar Trailhead and fly into Lord Flat. The cost for the flight from Enterprise, Oregon, is about $130 for a planeload (2000 figure). The plane can carry at least three passengers, depending on the total weight of the people and baggage. The flight into Lord Flat is much more pleasant than four-wheeling in for several hours. It may also be possible to be picked up by plane at Dug Bar, eliminating the need for a car shuttle.

Trailhead facilities: Lord Flat has an airstrip and several good campsites. Water can be obtained from a stream about a quarter of a mile east of the south end of the airstrip.

Camping and services: Dispersed camping is allowed at Sacajawea Campground, which is located 22 miles south of the trailhead, near Hat Point Lookout. Groceries can be obtained in Imnaha. Other services are available in Joseph and Enterprise. Cellular phones work at the airstrip, but you may get better reception if you walk a couple hundred yards west to the rim of Cow Creek Canyon.

For more information: USDA Forest Service at Wallowa Mountains Visitors Center in Enterprise. Contact Spence Air Service in Enterprise for flights into Lord Flat. If you plan to fly to the trailhead in June or if there has been a wet period, call well in advance to verify airstrip conditions.

Key points:
- 0.0   Lord Flat Airstrip and Trailhead.
- 1.5   Junction with Winters Trail. GPS 45 40.853 N 116 38.037 W.
- 3.3   Fingerboard Saddle. GPS 45 42.215 N 116 38.877 W.
- 4.8   Junction with Deep Creek Ranch Trail 1734. GPS 45 42.812 N 116 39.878 W.
- 7.4   Junction with Rowley Gulch Trail 1722.
- 8.0   Trail begins its descent off Summit Ridge west of Square Mountain.
- 9.4   Tiny cabin on east side of trail.
- 11.2 Junction with Deep Creek Ranch Trail 1707.
- 11.4 Junction with Oregon Snake River Trail. GPS 45 46.847 N 116 40.979 W.
- 13.4 Dug Bar Trailhead. GPS 45 48.223 N 116 41.264 W.

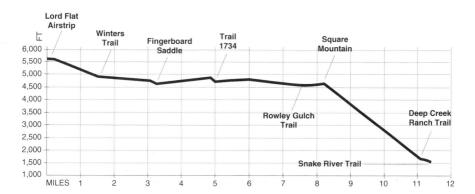

The hike: From the aircraft parking area near the south end of Lord Flat Airstrip, the trail heads north along the runway. Soon, the trail bears left of the runway and passes a small pond. It crosses the Hells Canyon Wilderness boundary 150 yards after passing the pond. From here on, the trail is closed to motor vehicles, and the ridge it follows narrows. Lots of flowers grow along this ridge, including balsamroot and lupine. The closed and abandoned four-wheel-drive road bears to the right 0.1 mile after passing the wilderness boundary. Western Rim National Recreation Trail bears slightly to the left. A sign points out the trail.

The route starts to descend off the left side of the ridge. This section of trail was recently reconstructed, and nineteen new switchbacks now ease

Western Rim National Recreation Trail North 1774
Deep Creek Ranch Trail 1734, 1707
(South half)

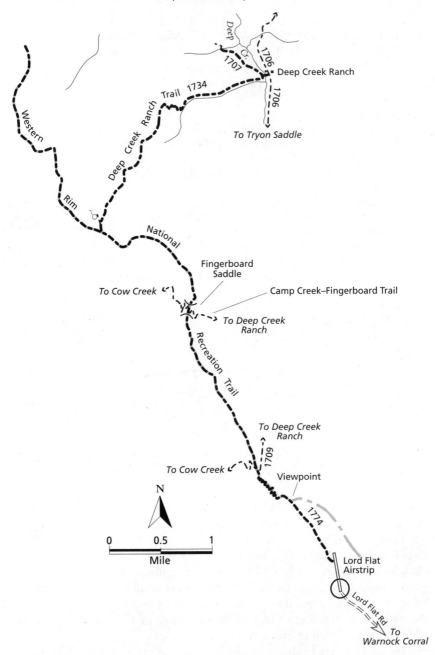

Deep Cr.

1707

1706

Deep Creek Ranch

1706

Deep Creek Ranch Trail 1734

To Tryon Saddle

Western

Rim

National

Fingerboard
Saddle

To Cow Creek

Camp Creek–Fingerboard Trail

To Deep Creek
Ranch

Recreation Trail

To Deep Creek
Ranch

1709

To Cow Creek

Viewpoint

1774

N

0   0.5   1
Mile

Lord Flat
Airstrip

Lord Flat Rd

To
Warnock Corral

Western Rim National Recreation Trail North 1774
Deep Creek Ranch Trail 1734, 1707
(North half)

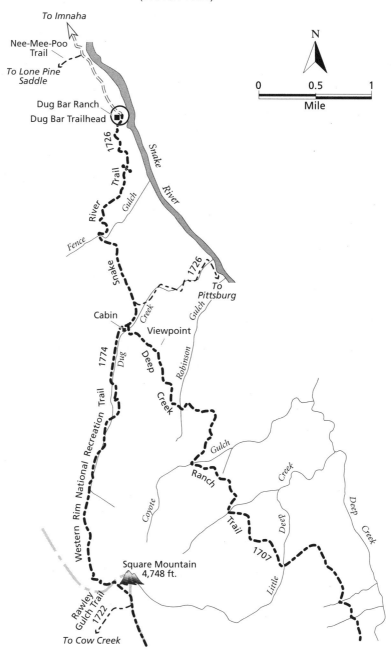

To Imnaha

Nee-Mee-Poo Trail

To Lone Pine Saddle

Dug Bar Ranch
Dug Bar Trailhead

1726

Snake River

River Trail

Gulch

Fence

Snake

1726

To Pittsburg

Cabin

Creek

Gulch

Viewpoint

1774

Dug

Deep

Robinson

Creek

Western Rim National Recreation Trail

Gulch

Ranch

Creek

Coyote

Deep Creek

Square Mountain
4,748 ft.

Trail

1707

Deep

Little

Rawley Gulch Trail 1722

To Cow Creek

N

0   0.5   1
Mile

the descent. The trail soon passes through a gate in a fenceline and then flattens out along the ridgeline. A junction with Winters Trail is 150 yards past the fence and 1.5 miles from Lord Flat, at 4,920 feet elevation. From the signed junction, Winters Trail descends to the right to meet Camp Creek–Fingerboard Trail. Cow Creek is to the left, and Western Rim Trail goes straight ahead.

Departing from the junction, Western Rim Trail traverses the right side of the ridgeline below the crest, heading northwest, on a partially timbered slope. The course crosses and recrosses the ridgeline several times in the 1.8 miles to Fingerboard Saddle. Along the ridge in this area, the trail is braided in spots and contains a few steep switchbacks. On the left side of the ridge is Cow Creek Canyon, and on the right is the Deep Creek drainage. Fingerboard Saddle (elev. 4,600 feet) contains the junction with Camp Creek–Fingerboard Trail. (See Hike 12 for a description of this trail.) Deep Creek Ranch and the Snake River are to the right, and Cow Creek is to the left.

Western Rim Trail heads north, then northwest, from Fingerboard Saddle. It generally follows the ridge but may be as much as a couple hundred feet below the crest in places. A couple of spots in this section are badly sloughed away. About 1.4 miles from Fingerboard Saddle, the tread crosses a saddle with a fenceline. The trail then goes through a gate in the fence and descends a grass-covered valley for 0.1 mile to the northwest to the junction with Deep Creek Ranch Trail 1734, at 4,710 feet elevation. This valley is one of the best places to camp along Western Rim Trail. A path from the junction leads a short distance down the valley to a spring. From the junction, Deep Creek Ranch Trail 1734 bears to the right, climbs a bit, and then drops down to Deep Creek Ranch. (See Hike 8 for the details about an alternate way to reach Dug Bar via Deep Creek Ranch Trail.)

Western Rim Trail bears left at the junction, then climbs a forested hillside to regain the ridge. Once back near the ridgeline, the trail continues to the northwest, crossing a couple of spur ridges and then generally following the ridgeline to the junction with Rowley Gulch Trail 1722. Cows graze this area, so braided trails are possible. At the junction (elev. 4,550 feet), Rowley Gulch Trail drops to the left down Rowley Gulch to Cow Creek. From the junction with Rowley Gulch Trail, you will follow the ridge for another 0.3 mile and then traverse around the left side of Square Mountain on an open slope. Where the trail bears left to start the traverse, a stock trail goes straight ahead up the mountain. Be careful to take the main trail, not the stock path. The traverse is 0.3 mile long and comes out on the ridge just west of Square Mountain. Square Mountain (elev. 4,748 feet) can easily be climbed from either end of the traverse. The short climb to the top of this phlox-covered mountain is well worth the effort. Watch for the many elk that inhabit this area.

Western Rim Trail winds down the ridge to the west for a short distance. It then turns right and drops into a grassy valley where the trail may be difficult to see. The USGS map shows several switchbacks here, but the trail now seems to head nearly straight down to the north-northwest. Before long, the valley becomes a canyon, and the trail grade steepens considerably. Here

Looking down from Square Mountain.

the trail becomes visible again. A tiny cabin once sat at 3,180 feet elevation, on the right side of the trail 1.4 miles after the trail begins its descent into the valley. (The cabin burned in 2000.) Water is available in a side canyon next to the cabin site, but it takes some bushwhacking to get to it. If you attempt to reach the water, remember that you are now down in rattlesnake country.

Below the cabin site, the trail continues to head down Dug Creek Canyon, crossing the creek several times in the 1.7 miles down the brushy canyon bottom to the junction with Deep Creek Ranch Trail 1707. The Cactus Mountain USGS quad map (1963 vintage) covers this area but does not show this section of Western Rim Trail. The trail is shown on Forest Service maps, however. (As noted above, Hike 8 provides a description of Deep Creek Ranch Trail.) Another cabin sits on the right side of the trail next to the junction. Except for the poison ivy, the area around this cabin is an excellent place to camp. Deep Creek Ranch Trail turns to the right at the junction. After passing the cabin and junction, Western Rim Trail heads north on a broad gentle slope for 0.2 mile to the junction with Oregon Snake River Trail 1726. From here, it is 2 more miles northwest to Dug Bar Trailhead along Oregon Snake River Trail. (See Hike 11 for details about Oregon Snake River Trail and directions to Dug Bar Trailhead.)

Options: Hike 8 Deep Creek Ranch Trail can be used as an alternate descent route. Following Hike 8 past the Deep Creek Ranch will add 3.8 miles to your hike.

8 Deep Creek Ranch Trail 1734, 1707

See Maps on Pages 48 and 49.

Highlights: A hike that travels from a junction with Western Rim Trail high on Summit Ridge down to the historic and now abandoned Deep Creek Ranch and then traverses the slopes of Hells Canyon from the ranch to another junction with Western Rim Trail. This is a good trail to take in spring to view elk; flowers are at their best in late spring.

Type of hike: Internal backpack, with shuttle and loop options.

Total distance: 10 miles.

Difficulty: Strenuous.

Best months: June–October.

Elevation gain: Approximately 1,000 feet.

Trailhead elevation: 4,710 feet, at the junction with Western Rim National Recreation Trail.

Permits and fees: None.

Maps: Fingerboard Saddle and Cactus Mountain USGS quads.

Finding the trailhead: Follow the "Finding the trailhead" directions in Hike 7. Then hike 4.8 miles north on Western Rim Trail to the junction with Deep Creek Ranch Trail 1734, as described in Hike 7. The GPS coordinates at the junction are 45 42.812 N 116 39.878 W.

Trailhead facilities: None.

Camping and services: Groceries can be obtained in Imnaha, Oregon. Other services are available in Joseph and Enterprise, Oregon.

For more information: USDA Forest Service at Wallowa Mountains Visitor Center in Enterprise. Contact Spence Air Service in Enterprise for flights to Lord Flat Airstrip and Trailhead.

Key points:

0.0	Junction with Western Rim National Recreation Trail on Summit Ridge.
3.5	Junction with Deep Creek Ranch Trail 1707
3.6	Deep Creek Ranch. GPS 45 44.092 N 116 37.974 W.
5.8	Ford of Little Deep Creek.
7.7	Coyote Gulch.
8.0	Robinson Ridge.
10.0	Junction with Western Rim Trail. GPS 45 46.688 N 116 41.055 W.

The hike: The area around the junction where this hike begins is a great place to camp. It has a spring located down the valley a short distance north-northwest from the junction. The path leading to this spring can easily be mistaken for the main trail, however.

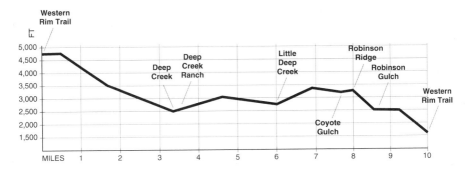

As you leave the junction, the route climbs to the north, traversing an open hillside. The tread goes through some timber 0.3 mile from the junction. It soon comes out in the open again, crosses a small subridge, and goes through more timber. Then the path starts to descend along a semiopen ridgeline, winding down the ridge for 0.7 mile. You will then make a turn to the right (elev. 4,120 feet) and begin descending a series of 22 switchbacks. The route drops 620 vertical feet in the next 0.6 mile to the creekbed. Once near the creekbed, you will continue to descend along the creek's left (north) side 1.4 miles to the junction with Deep Creek Ranch Trail 1707, at 2,470 feet elevation.

In places, the trail is in the brush along the creekbed, and in others it is a short distance up the side hill to the left of the bottom. When the trail is up on the side hill, it is in the open. Watch out for rattlesnakes in this creekbed. Just before reaching the junction with Deep Creek Ranch Trail, the trail forks. Take the left fork, and go the last few yards to the junction. An easy-to-miss trail sign hangs on a tree to the left of the trail at the junction.

At the junction, turn to the right and drop a few yards to Deep Creek. The trail here has no bridge across the creek, so the crossing through the knee-deep water is cold and wet. Usually this crossing is not dangerous, but it could be at times of very heavy runoff. Deep Creek Ranch and the junction with Deep Creek Trail 1706 are a few yards after crossing the creek. (See Hike 9 for information about Deep Creek Trail.)

The now-abandoned ranch at 2,450 feet elevation is an excellent place to camp and explore some of the history of Hells Canyon. The area close to the buildings is leased to an outfitter, so it may be best to camp well away from them. Deep Creek was once known as Deadline Creek because 1880s ranchers did not allow the Nez Perce to range their horses north of this drainage. If you camp here, be sure to watch out for rattlers as well as the other abundant wildlife.

When leaving Deep Creek Ranch, cross back over Deep Creek to the junction with Deep Creek Ranch Trail 1707. Turn right at the junction, and climb steeply to the northwest on Deep Creek Ranch Trail 1707. The course crosses a brushy draw 0.3 mile from the junction, then rounds an open slope with a good view of Deep Creek Canyon to the right. You will cross a fenceline through a gate 0.3 mile after crossing the draw. After crossing the fenceline, the path soon crosses a ridgeline covered with balsamroot, lupine, and paintbrush, then heads back into another brushy draw. It soon rounds another ridgeline, also covered with flowers, and then cuts back into another draw with a small stream in it. The tread climbs after crossing the stream, then drops slightly to cross another ridgeline. From this ridgeline, Deep Creek Trail, heading down from the ranch to the Snake River, can be seen across the canyon to the right. Deep Creek Canyon is now much steeper and more rugged than it was farther south.

The course descends along the ridge a short distance. It then turns left (southwest) and descends, making a couple of switchbacks into Little Deep Creek Canyon. The route then traverses some distance before making several more switchbacks as it drops to the canyon bottom. You will ford Little Deep Creek at 2,710 feet elevation, 2.2 miles from Deep Creek Ranch. There is a campsite to the right of the trail, beneath some large ponderosa pines, just after crossing Little Deep Creek. An abandoned homestead is located 200 yards downstream from the campsite. Watch for elk, grouse, and black bears along Little Deep Creek. There could also be a rattlesnake lurking around, so watch your step.

After leaving the campsite on Little Deep Creek, the trail climbs a few feet, then traverses to the northwest. It soon crosses a small stream, then turns left and climbs steeply. At the top of the steep climb, the route turns right and makes an ascending traverse to another ridgeline (elev. 3,260 feet). The trail then traverses west into another brushy draw with a tiny stream in it. This stream may be dry during summer and fall.

You will traverse out of this draw heading northeast. The sometimes braided tread rounds three more small ridges before reaching Coyote Gulch. Coyote Gulch, at 3,090 feet elevation, is 4.1 miles from Deep Creek Ranch and 7.7 miles from Summit Ridge. There is a possible campsite and a stream in the gulch. An old stove lying next to the trail suggests that at one time there was a homestead here.

Leaving Coyote Gulch, the route climbs to the north for 0.3 mile to the top of Robinson Ridge (elev. 3,180 feet). From the ridge, the Snake River comes into view far below to the northeast. The trail winds down the ridge, then makes several switchbacks as it descends the 720 vertical feet, to the west, into Robinson Gulch. You will climb a few feet leaving the gulch, then work your way in and out of four more small draws, before reaching another ridgeline (elev. 2,410 feet). The braided trail descends the ridge a short distance to a saddle. A short distance off the trail, to the north of the saddle, is a good viewpoint overlooking the Snake River. From the saddle, the still-braided track descends steeply to the northwest toward Dug Creek. The section of the trail between the saddle and Dug Creek is shown incorrectly on the USGS map (Cactus Mountain quad), but the Forest Service maps are correct. The path crosses Dug Creek and climbs a few feet to the junction with Western Rim Trail, at 1,720 feet elevation. At this junction, you are 10 miles from where you left Western Rim Trail. An abandoned cabin sits to the left of the trail between the creek crossing and the junction. This area makes a good place to camp, but watch out for the poison ivy and a possible Rattler.

If you want to continue to Dug Bar Trailhead, turn right and descend Western Rim Trail for a short distance to the junction with Oregon Snake River

Junction of Deep Creek Ranch Trail and Western Rim Trail. GARY FLETCHER PHOTO

Trail 1726. Turn left on Oregon Snake River Trail, and follow it for 2 miles to Dug Bar Trailhead. (See Hikes 7 and 10 for the details.)

The name "Dug" is a corruption of Douglas, the last name of T. J. Douglass. An early day rancher in the area, Douglass was found shot to death near here in the early 1880s.

Options: Use this hike as an alternate for part of Western Rim Trail, or make a loop hike by turning left on Western Rim Trail and following it for 6.4 miles up to the junction where you started this hike. See Hike 7 for a description of Western Rim Trail.

9 Deep Creek Trail 1706

Highlights:	A hike along Deep Creek from Camp Creek–Fingerboard Trail to the Snake River, via Deep Creek Ranch.
Type of hike:	Internal connector backpack, with a long loop option.
Total distance:	6.3 miles.
Difficulty:	Moderate. Most of this trail is easy to follow, but there are a few spots that require routefinding skills.
Best months:	Mid-March–June and September–early November. Snow may limit upper access until mid-June.
Elevation gain:	690 feet.
Trailhead elevation:	2,890 feet at the junction with Camp Creek–Fingerboard Trail.
Permits and fees:	None.
Maps:	Fingerboard Saddle and Cactus Mountain USGS quads.

Finding the trailhead: See Hike 12 Camp Creek–Fingerboard Trail for directions to the junction where the Deep Creek Trail begins. To reach Deep Creek Ranch and begin this hike 1.7 miles farther north, see Hike 8.

Trailhead facilities: None at the junction. Deep Creek Ranch has several good campsites.

Camping and services: See Hike 11 for the closest services; none are available even remotely close to this trail.

For more information: USDA Forest Service at Wallowa Mountains Visitor Center in Enterprise, Oregon.

Key points:
- 0.0 Junction with Camp Creek–Fingerboard Trail 1.7 miles south of Deep Creek Ranch GPS 45 42.760N 116 37.654 W.
- 1.7 Deep Creek Ranch. GPS 45 44.092 N 116 37.974 W.
- 2.1 Teaser Creek.
- 5.5 Shortcut to Thorn Spring.
- 6.3 Junction with Oregon Snake River Trail 1726. GPS 45 46.382 N 116 37.535 W.

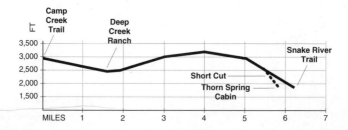

The hike: From the junction with Camp Creek–Fingerboard Trail, Deep Creek Trail heads north along the east side of Deep Creek, through old-growth

Deep Creek Trail 1706

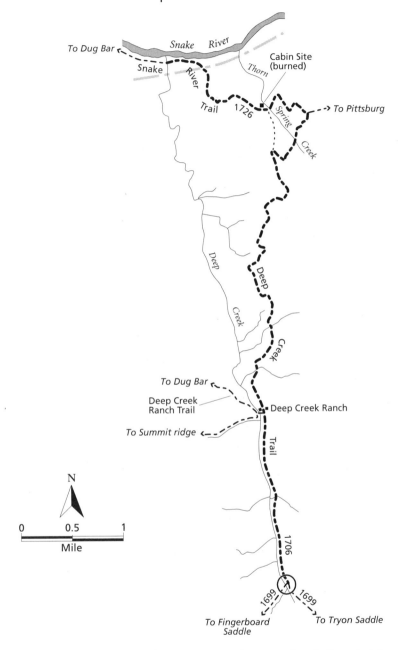

forest of large Douglas-fir. You will reach Deep Creek Ranch (elev. 2,450 feet) 1.7 miles from the junction. Just before reaching the ranch, the trail passes some apple trees and old farm machinery. Water for the ranch was piped from a spring behind the bunkhouse. There are several pieces of abandoned farm machinery sitting around the area, as well as several fruit trees.

The junction with Deep Creek Ranch Trail 1707 is at the ranch. Deep Creek Ranch Trail turns to the left and heads for Dug Bar Trailhead. (See Hike 8 for details about Deep Creek Ranch Trail.)

Deep Creek Trail heads north-northwest from the ranch buildings, crossing a meadow. There is an alternate route from here to Teaser Creek that climbs along the hillside to the right, but the route through the meadow is the better of the two. The alternate route is the one shown on the USGS map. After crossing the meadow, the trail climbs over a rise, then drops slightly through the brush to Teaser Creek. Teaser Creek is usually the last water before reaching Thorn Spring, 4.5 miles ahead. Once across Teaser Creek, the path climbs a Sumac covered hillside. It then heads on up a ridge crossing a fenceline. Watch for cactus blooming on this ridge in June.

The route comes to a small saddle 0.4 mile after crossing Teaser Creek. Deep Creek Trail turns left at the saddle. A stock trail here heads on up the ridge at the saddle, but don't take it. From the saddle, the trail traverses an open hillside that blooms with lupine in June. You will cross a couple of small gullies and a ridge covered with sumac and then enter a brushy draw. At certain times of the year, this draw has water in it but don't depend on it. Leaving the brushy creekbed, the trail crosses an open slope and another small draw, then heads up a small rounded ridge. It soon bears left off the small ridge, crosses another small draw then climbs to a ridgeline. Shortly the route bears left off this ridgeline. It traverses an open slope, and soon crosses a fenceline through a gate. You will then climb a short distance to another ridgeline. At the ridgeline there is an excellent viewpoint a few yards to the left of the trail on a rocky outcrop. From the viewpoint, the rugged Deep Creek Canyon is to the west.

After passing the viewpoint, the trail crosses a wild rose–covered hillside and heads back into another brushy draw. There is a creekbed in this draw, which will have water at the wetter times of the year. The draw also has lots of poison ivy. The trail crosses three more small draws, then heads back into a larger one. This larger draw has three subdraws in it. Just before the trail heads into the larger draw, the USGS map shows a trail turning to the left. This trail is on the map but not on the ground. Deep Creek Trail soon comes to the saddle on the ridge dividing the Deep Creek drainage and the Thorn Spring Creek drainage. At the saddle, there is a trail turning to the left and descending into the Deep Creek drainage. This trail is on the ground but not on the map; don't take it.

Deep Creek Trail crosses through the saddle, which is 5 miles from Camp Creek–Fingerboard Trail. It then heads north, descending along an open slope. From the trail an old roadbed can be seen across the draw to the east. Be sure to take the trail and not the roadbed heading down from the saddle. After descending along the slope for a short distance, the trail comes out onto a ridgeline. Dry Creek Ranch, on the Idaho side of the Snake River, can be seen while descending the slope, as can Christmas Creek Ranch on the Oregon side. The trail heads down the ridge for a short distance, passing an old plow on the way. It then switchbacks to the right and leaves the ridgeline.

There is a cross-country route for parties that are planning to head down

Thorn Spring Cabin.

river on Oregon Snake River Trail 1726, which leaves Deep Creek Trail at this switchback. The route heads on down the ridge for 0.4 mile to Thorn Spring Creek. This is a steep route. In some spots the hard slope is covered with fine gravel, making for poor footing. The entire route is in the open. Thorn Spring can be seen from the switchback. Take this route only if you are used to cross-country travel; otherwise, take the trail the rest of the way down.

From the switchback, it is 0.8 mile and 760 vertical feet down to Oregon Snake River Trail. Leaving the ridge the trail first drops into a creekbed then traverses to and crosses Thorn Spring Creek. Both creeks may be dry late in the summer. After crossing Thorn Spring Creek the trail continues to descend, making a couple of switchbacks, to the junction with Oregon Snake River Trail at 1,860 feet elevation. The trail descends a gentle grassy slope for the last 200 yards before reaching Oregon Snake River Trail. On this slope it may be very hard to see Deep Creek Trail. Just head on down the slope to Oregon Snake River Trail, which will be easy to see. (See Hike 11 for a description of Oregon Snake River Trail 1726.)

Watch for mule deer, elk, and black bear all along this trail. Rattlesnakes are possible anywhere on this trail, so watch for them too.

Options: To make a 36.4-mile lollipop loop backpack, park your car (high clearance is best) at Dug Bar Trailhead. Then hike southeast on Oregon Snake River Trail for 17.5 miles to the junction with Camp Creek–Fingerboard Trail. Then hike west for 8.3 miles over Tryon Saddle on Camp Creek–Fingerboard Trail to the junction with Deep Creek Trail where this hike began. Hike down Deep Creek as described above to the junction with Oregon Snake River Trail. Turn northwest on Oregon Snake River Trail, and follow it for 4.3 miles to Dug Bar Trailhead, where you left your car. See Hikes 11 and 12 for more information.

10 Oregon Snake River Trail South 1726

Highlights:	A hike from Saddle Creek to Pittsburg along the Oregon side of the Snake River. This hike is very rich in history as well as wildlife and flowers. When done in combination with Saddle Creek Trail and Oregon Snake River Trail North, this is the premier hike in Hells Canyon.
Type of hike:	Internal connecting trail; two- or three-day backpack.
Total distance:	21.5 miles.
Difficulty:	Easy to moderate.
Best months:	March–May and September–October. The lower elevations of Hells Canyon are generally hot during the summer. This trail may be free of snow most of the winter.
Elevation gain:	Minimal, but the trail undulates.
Permits and fees:	None if you reached the Oregon Snake River Trail via jet boat shuttle. A northwest Forest Pass is required at Freezeout Trailhead if you are hiking in via Saddle Creek Trail.
Maps:	Old Timer Mountain, Temperance Creek, Kirkwood Creek, and Grave Point USGS quads.

Finding the trailhead: Oregon Snake River Trail begins at a junction with Saddle Creek Trail 1776 a short distance west of the old Saddle Creek Ranch site. This junction can be reached by hiking Saddle Creek Trail for 11.3 miles east from Freezeout Trailhead. (See Hike 28 for a description of Saddle Creek Trail and driving directions to Freezeout Trailhead.) The GPS coordinates at the junction are 45 23.598 N 116 37.499 W.

You can also reach the mouth of Saddle Creek by jet boat. Nearly all of Oregon Snake River Trail can be accessed by jet boat from Hells Canyon Dam or Clarkston, Washington. To reach the starting point described here, jet boat service is available only from Hells Canyon Dam. From Clarkston, Washington, it is possible to boat only as far as Rush Creek Rapids.

Trailhead facilities: Campsites are available at the mouth of Saddle Creek.

Camping and services: Some groceries can be obtained in Imnaha, Oregon; the closest place for gas and other services is Joseph or Enterprise, Oregon.

For more information: USDA Forest Service at Wallowa Mountains Visitor Center, Enterprise. Contact Beamer's Hells Canyon Tours and Excursions for jet boat transportation from Clarkston, Washington. For boat transportation from Hells Canyon Dam, contact Hells Canyon Adventures in Oxbow, Oregon. For air transportation to or from the Pittsburg Airstrip, contact Spence Air Service in Enterprise. Contact Hells Canyon Outdoor Supply in Oxbow for car shuttles.

Oregon Snake River Trail South 1726
(South half)

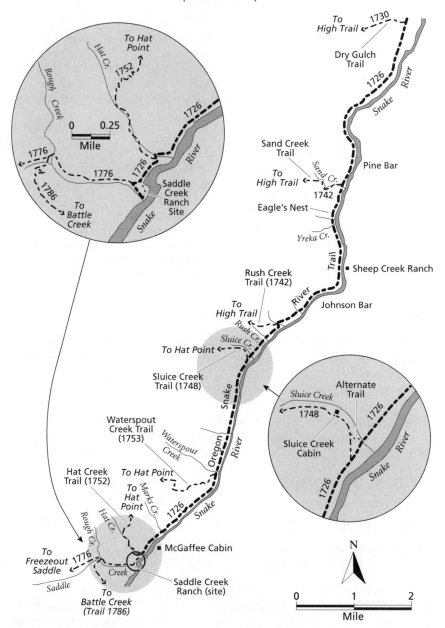

Key points:

0.0   Junction of Saddle Creek Trail and Oregon Snake River Trail near mouth of Saddle Creek.

0.4   Junction with Hat Creek Trail 1752.

2.7   Junction with Waterspout Creek Trail 1753.

Oregon Snake River Trail South 1726
(North half)

4.3   Junction with Sluice Creek Trail 1748. GPS 45 26.693 N 116 35.199 W.

5.2   Junction with Rush Creek Trail 1742.

8.0   Eagle's Nest.

8.5   Junction with Sand Creek Trail 1742. GPS 45 29.340 N 116 33.388 W.

12.0   Junction with Dry Gulch Trail 1730.

12.8   Temperance Creek Ranch. GPS 45 32.414 N 116 31.901 W.

13.8   Junction with Salt Creek Trail 1785.

15.7   Cougar Creek Bridge.

21.2   Junction with Pittsburg Creek Trail 1751A.

21.5   Pittsburg Ranch Ranger Station. GPS 45 37.833 N 116 28.664 W.

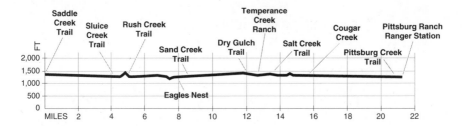

The hike: When you arrive at the mouth of Saddle Creek, take the time to read the historical signboard before beginning your hike down the Snake River. From the junction with Saddle Creek Trail, at 1,420 feet elevation, Oregon Snake River Trail climbs to the north over a small rise. You then descend slightly to meet a poor path coming from the ranch site. The course then climbs some concrete steps and makes several switchbacks before traversing back into Hat Creek Canyon. Just before crossing Hat Creek is the junction with Hat Creek Trail 1752. (See Hike 27 for the details about Hat Creek Trail.)

Once across Hat Creek the route heads downstream along its north side then turns north along the Snake River. Along the river the path climbs and descends several times never gaining or losing much elevation. There are a couple of spots in this section, which may flood if the river is very high. One mile from Hat Creek the trail switchbacks up a rise across the river from the old McGaffee Cabin. Yellowbells bloom along this section of trail in March, as they do in many places in the canyon. After topping the rise the path, which is chipped out of the cliffs in places, drops back closer to the river. You will soon pass the sign marking Marks Creek, which seldom has water in it at this point. Oregon Snake River Trail enters the burn area of the August 1996 Salt Creek fire 0.7 mile after passing Marks Creek. It stays generally in the burn area for the rest of the way to Pittsburg Ranch Ranger Station. Most of the burn area was grassland, which recovers very quickly, so evidence of the burn will be minimal. In fact the grass and most flowers do better after being burned.

The junction with Waterspout Creek Trail 1753 is reached 0.2 mile after entering the burn. See Hike 26 for a description of the Waterspout Creek Trail. This junction is 2.7 miles from Saddle Creek. Oregon Snake River Trail crosses Waterspout Creek, then generally stays close to the river, passing several rapids in the next 1.6 miles to the junction with Sluice Creek Trail 1748. (See Hike 25 for information about Sluice Creek Trail.) There is a good campsite a few yards up the Sluice Creek Trail. A short distance farther along there is an unmarked junction with an alternate to the Sluice Creek Trail. Another 20 yards and you will ford Sluice Creek. After crossing Sluice Creek the path climbs a few feet to a relatively flat area with a short rough abandoned airstrip on it.

The route heads northeast along the airstrip, to ford Rush Creek 0.2 mile farther along. Rush Creek Rapids, the rapids that stop most jet boaters from continuing farther up the river, is to the right. The trail soon begins to climb. It climbs about 150 feet, making a couple switchbacks, crosses Pony Creek

Gully, then comes to the junction with Rush Creek Trail 1742, at 1,500 feet elevation.

The poorly maintained Rush Creek Trail climbs northwest to meet Trail 1741 then descends back to the river as Sand Creek Trail. Trail 1741 climbs on up to meet High Trail, about 5 miles from Oregon Snake River Trail. From Oregon Snake River Trail near this junction, Hat Point, the highest point on the Oregon Rim of Hells Canyon can be seen, far above to the west-southwest.

Leaving the junction with Rush Creek Trail, you will descend very gently for 0.4 mile, then drop steeply for a short distance. Johnson Bar is across the river in Idaho. The trail has been chipped out of the cliff 1.4 mile past the junction with Rush Creek Trail. Sheep Creek Ranch can be seen across the river at this point. There is a campsite next to the river 0.9 mile farther along at Yreka Creek; however during times of very high water, this section of the trail and the campsite may flood.

The Eagle's Nest section of trail is reached 0.3 mile after passing Yreka Creek. This is one of the most spectacular sections of Oregon Snake River Trail. At the Eagle's Nest the route is cut into the cliff above the river, with rock overhanging it for a short distance. Stone and mortar walls have been built along the river side of the tread for safety. Sand Creek and the junction with Sand Creek Trail 1742 are reached 0.5 mile after passing the Eagle's Nest. There is a cabin (which is not open to the public) and a good campsite next to the signed junction. Sand Creek is 8.5 miles from Saddle Creek.

The trail passes Pine Bar 0.6 mile after leaving the Junction with Sand Creek Trail. Pine Bar, across the river, is interesting because it is about the only place along the river that a large number of Ponderosa Pines grow. The growth of pine trees here is made possible by a different chemical content in the soil. Soon the path goes through a notch in the rocks as it continues on down river.

You will cross Quartz Creek, which will probably be dry, 1.1 mile farther along, and reach the junction with Dry Gulch Trail 1730 in another 1.6 miles. There is a fenceline on the right side of the trail for some distance before reaching the junction. Dry Gulch Trail climbs to the west, gaining 2,600 feet elevation in 3.5 miles to join High Trail.

Oregon Snake River Trail is vague and somewhat braided in this section. You will cross a ditch, go through a gate, and head down toward the buildings at Temperance Creek Ranch 0.4 mile after passing the junction with Dry Gulch Trail. The path soon goes through another gate, then follows a wide roadbed to the ranch.

Temperance Creek Ranch was the last operating sheep ranch on the Oregon side of Hells Canyon. It discontinued operation in 1996. The trail goes past the buildings, crosses Temperance Creek and comes to the junction with Temperance Creek Trail 1778. This junction, at 1,320 feet elevation, is 12.8 miles from Saddle Creek, and there are 8.7 miles left to go to Pittsburg. (See Hike 24 for a description of Temperance Creek Trail.) In the spring watch for the many elk that inhabit the area around Temperance Creek Ranch.

Oregon Snake River Trail crosses Hominy Creek 0.5 mile after leaving Temperance Creek Ranch. After crossing Hominy Creek the route passes Suicide Point, the high rocky mountain on the Idaho side of the river. (For more information about Suicide Point, see Hike 40 Idaho Snake River National Recreation Trail 102.) Half a mile past Hominy Creek the trail crosses Salt Creek and comes to the junction with Salt Creek Trail 1785. (See Hike 23 for details about Salt Creek Trail.) There are several possible campsites at Salt Creek.

You will cross Two Corral Creek 0.3 mile past Salt Creek. There is a good campsite next to the river shortly after crossing Two Corral Creek; however, this campsite may flood during very high water. One and one half miles past the campsite the trail crosses a wooden bridge over Cougar Creek. At Cougar Creek the historic Kirkwood Ranch is across the river. (See Hike 44 for more information about this historic place.) Chukar Partridge are common along this section of trail. Muir Creek is crossed 1.6 miles farther along. Kirby Creek Lodge can be seen across the river near Muir Creek. Another 0.8 mile is the Durham Creek crossing.

A short distance past Durham Creek the trace is chipped out of the cliffs again. A little farther along you will hike past China Rapids, then climb over a rise. Upper Pittsburg Landing at the northern end of Idaho Snake River Trail can be seen across the river as the course climbs to the top of the rise. The route soon passes a tin building then crosses Pittsburg Creek. A few more yards bring you to the junction with Pittsburg Creek Trail 1751A. At the junction, 2 miles after crossing Durham Creek, Saddle Creek is 21.2 miles behind you. (See Hike 21 for a description of Pittsburg Creek Trail.)

The short (only 850 feet) Pittsburg Landing Strip is between the trail and the river at the junction. Pittsburg Ranch Ranger Station is reached 0.3 mile after passing the junction. There was a ferry across the Snake River here from 1891 to 1933. To continue north on Oregon Snake River Trail, see Hike 11.

Most wildflowers bloom along the river beginning in late March and continue through June. Fishing for catfish and bass is good to excellent all along the river; there are also some trout and sturgeon to be caught. Check the Oregon Sports Fishing Regulations before fishing. There are several special rules for fishing the Snake River. Elk are the most common large animals along this trail; you will likely see some of them as well as some Mule Deer and possibly a Black Bear. Bald Eagles are fairly common in winter and spring, as are Canada Geese

Be careful when you're close to this large, deep, powerful river. Many lives have been lost in it. Very occasionally there is a huge water discharge from Hells Canyon Dam. When water flow over the dam is exceptionally high, a few small sections of the trail may be flooded and some campsites may be under water. Check with Idaho Power or the Forest Service for discharge rates and forecast. Jet boat transportation may not be available above Rush Creek Rapids during times of high river flow.

Rattlesnakes are common all along this trail. If you hike this trail during hot weather remember that these snakes will be more active during the cooler parts of the day and at night. Hikers who are out during the early morning, late afternoon, and early evening have a better chance of encountering

The Eagle's Nest.

them. During cooler weather the snakes are active all day. Rattlers are generally in hibernation from early November to mid March. Black Widow and Brown Recluse (Fiddler) spiders also inhabit the canyon. Thunderstorms and their resulting flash floods (known locally as waterspouts) are possible at times especially in the side draws. You are a long ways from medical help in the canyon so be extra careful.

Open campfires are prohibited all along the Snake River Corridor, which includes all land within one fourth mile of the river Check with the Forest Service for the present restrictions.

Options: Combine this hike with Hikes 28 and 11 to make a 56.8-mile backpack from Freezeout Trailhead to Dug Bar. Allow five to seven days to make this trip.

Check out the hike descriptions for the many side trails mentioned above. Many of these side trails offer great out-and-back day hikes from a camp along Oregon Snake River Trail.

11 Oregon Snake River Trail North 1726

Highlights:	A hike along the Oregon side of the Snake River from Pittsburg to Dug Bar, passing many historic sites along the way.
Type of hike:	Three- or four-day backpack, from an internal start.
Total distance:	25.3 miles.
Difficulty:	Moderate.
Best months:	March–June and September–November.
Elevation gain:	Approximately 5,000 feet.
Permits and fees:	None.
Maps:	Grave Point, Lord Flat, Wolf Creek, and Cactus Mountain USGS quads.

Finding the trailhead: Fly or jet boat to Pittsburg, or hike in along Oregon Snake River Trail. The cost for a flight from Enterprise, Oregon, to Pittsburg is about $145 per planeload (2000 figure). For a description of the southern section of Oregon Snake River Trail, see Hike 10. The GPS coordinates at Pittsburg Ranch Ranger Station are 45 37.833 N 116 28.664 W

To reach Dug Bar Trailhead, which is at the end of this hike, follow Oregon 350 from Joseph, Oregon, for 30 miles northeast to Imnaha. Then take County Road 735, which becomes Forest Road 4260, for 28 miles north along the Imnaha River and over Cactus Mountain to Dug Bar. The last 8 miles of FR 4260 (Dug Bar Road) become very rough and muddy at times and may require a four-wheel-drive vehicle. Check locally for road conditions. Dug Bar Trailhead can also be reached by chartered flight from Enterprise and by jet boat from Clarkston, Washington. Cost to fly to Dug Bar is $140.00 (2000 price).

Trailhead facilities: Pittsburg has an aircraft landing strip and some unimproved campsites.

Camping and services: Some groceries can be obtained in the tiny town of Imnaha, but for gas and other services, the closest place is Joseph or Enterprise.

For more information: USDA Forest Service at Wallowa Mountains Visitor Center in Enterprise. Contact Beamer's Hells Canyon Tours in Clarkston, Washington, or Hells Canyon Adventures in Oxbow, Oregon, for jet boat transportation. For air transportation to Dug Bar or Pittsburg, contact Spence Air Service in Enterprise. The Imnaha Store and Tavern in Imnaha will have information about the Dug Bar Road conditions.

Key points:
0.0   Pittsburg Ranch Ranger Station and Airstrip.
2.3   Junction with High Trail 1751. GPS 45 38.743 N 116 30.619 W.
4.9   Junction with Trail 1770 near Somers Place.

7.8   Junction with Camp Creek–Fingerboard Trail 1699. GPS 45 41.267 N 116 31.909 W.

9.8   Junction with Lookout Creek Trail 1737.

10.7   Junction with Lonepine Creek Trail 1735. GPS 45 43.499 N 116 32.221 W.

12.3   Junction with path to the Copper Creek Lodge.

14.7   Roland Creek.

16.5   Dorrance Ranch and junction with Christmas Creek Ranch Trail 1726A.

18.4   Junction with Deep Creek Trail 1706. GPS 45 46.382 N 116 37.535 W.

21.0   Deep Creek.

23.3   Junction with Western Rim National Recreation Trail 1774. GPS 45 46.847 N 116 40.979 W.

25.3   Dug Bar Trailhead. GPS 45 48.223 N 116 41.264 W.

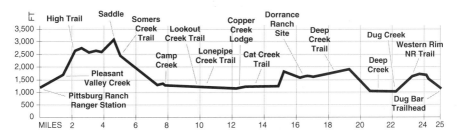

The hike: Leaving the Pittsburg Ranch Ranger Station the trail begins its longest climb. The route climbs to the northwest, passing a developed spring in 0.4 mile. The spring (elev. 1,400 feet), which is the water source for the Pittsburg Ranch, is some distance below the trail to the right. From here the RV Park at Pittsburg Landing can be seen across the Snake River to the east. The path soon flattens out, crosses several draws then climbs again to a ridgeline at 1,600 feet elevation. You then traverse west to Pleasant Valley Creek. There are some possible campsites at Pleasant Valley Creek, but there is a lot of Poison Ivy here. The trail from Pittsburg to Pleasant Valley Creek is braided in places, but is fairly easy to follow. Watch for Elk in this area.

The tread crosses Pleasant Valley Creek and climbs, sometimes steeply, for 0.8 mile to the junction with High Trail 1751 at 2,610 feet elevation. (See Hike 22 for a description of High Trail.) High Trail turns to the left at the signed junction, 2.3 miles from Pittsburg. Past the junction Oregon Snake River Trail climbs to a ridgeline making a couple of switchbacks along the way. It then descends for 0.6 mile to Davis Creek. There is a waterfall in Davis Creek to the left of the trail. You then round another ridge to McCarty Creek. McCarty Creek is intermittent; you may be able to hear water flowing below but not see any. The McCarty Creek drainage is one of the few areas of thick forest that was heavily burned in the August 1996 Salt Creek Fire. There are quite a few Wild Rose bushes in this area.

After crossing McCarty Creek you will cross a couple of small gullies then work your way up a draw toward a saddle. The trail is steep and braided in places as it heads up the left side of the draw. It also makes several switchbacks as it climbs to the saddle. This saddle, at 3,090 feet elevation, is the highest point on the Oregon Snake River Trail and a great place to stop for

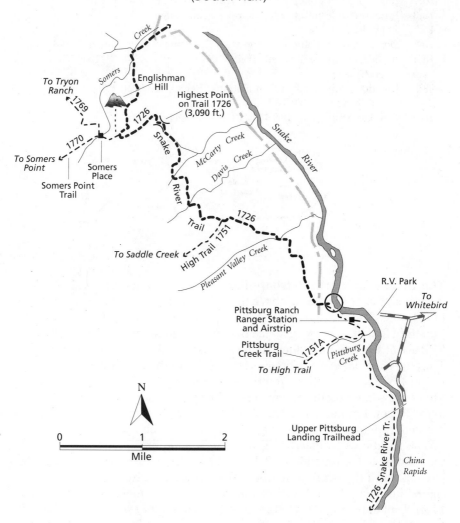

Oregon Snake River Trail North 1726
(South half)

Creek

Somers

To Tryon
Ranch

1769

Englishman
Hill

1726

Highest Point
on Trail 1726
(3,090 ft.)

Snake

River

1770

To Somers
Point

Somers
Place

Somers Point
Trail

McCarty Creek

Davis Creek

Snake

River

Trail

1726

High Trail 1751

To Saddle Creek

Pleasant Valley Creek

R.V. Park

To
Whitebird

Pittsburg Ranch
Ranger Station
and Airstrip

Pittsburg
Creek Trail

1751A

Pittsburg
Creek

To High Trail

N

0   1   2
Mile

Upper Pittsburg
Landing Trailhead

1726 Snake River Tr.

China
Rapids

lunch and admire the view. After crossing the saddle the tread makes five switchbacks as it descends into the Somers Creek drainage. These switchbacks were recently constructed, and an easy grade.

One half mile past the last switchback, after crossing a couple of little gullies is the junction with the Somers Creek Trail 1770. This junction (elev. 2,490 feet) is 4.9 miles from Pittsburg. From the junction Somers Creek Trail heads west for 0.3 mile to the abandoned and now burned Somers Ranch. The flat areas around the burned ranch buildings make an excellent campsite. From the ranch Somers Creek Trail continues another 4.5 miles to join Somers Point Trail, gaining well over 3,000 vertical feet along the way. See

Oregon Snake River Trail North 1726
(North half)

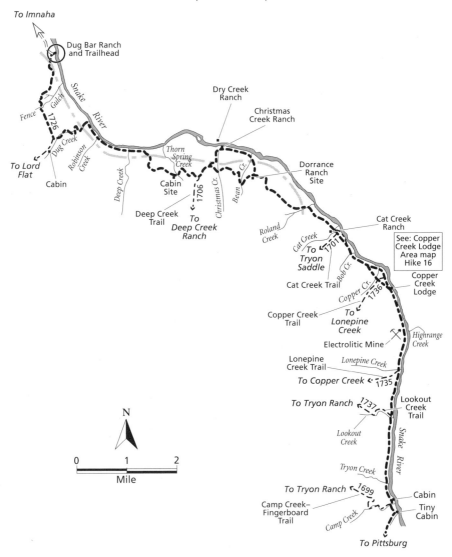

Hike 19 for details about Somers Point Trail.

Also from the same junction, an unmarked route to Englishman Hill heads to the north. This route traverses around the left side of the highest point on the ridgeline then reaches the ridge a quarter mile from the junction. From there it follows the ridge another 0.2 mile to the point called Englishman Hill. Excellent views of the canyons below can be had at Englishman Hill; the flowers out here in the spring can also be great.

Leaving the junction with Somers Creek Trail, Oregon Snake River Trail turns to the right (north). It descends making several switchbacks to the bottom of a draw. The path follows the draw down passing a spring and making more switchbacks. It soon crosses a small stream, then heads on down along the right side of the brook. The brush in this draw was nearly completely burned in the Salt Creek Fire, but will re-grow in a few years. Soon the small stream you have been following flows into Somers Creek. A short distance farther along the trail crosses Somers Creek. This crossing is a knee-deep ford in the spring. The route then makes a switchback and re-crosses Somers Creek. Just past the second crossing Hog Creek flows in from the west to join Somers Creek. The tread passes the wilderness boundary sign 275 yards after the second crossing.

You will soon enter an open area with good campsites and an old stove on the left side of the trail. This area is the abandoned site of the Whitter Place. Turkeys were raised here in the early 1900s. A man was once shot and killed here, then buried next to the creek. There is a fence along the left side of the trail here for a short distance, then the trail turns left and crosses Somers Creek for the last time. The fenceline also crosses the creek and the trail follows it down, staying on its left. Half a mile after the last crossing, the tread reaches a tiny cabin near the Snake River, at 1,160 feet elevation. A short side path leads from the cabin down to the river and a campsite.

Here the trail turns left (north) and soon begins to climb. The route climbs steeply, making four switchbacks and gaining 210 feet in the 0.2 mile to the top of a rise. It then descends making five more switchbacks in the 350 yards to the junction with the Camp Creek–Fingerboard Trail 1699. (See Hike 12 for a description of Camp Creek–Fingerboard Trail.)

Leaving the junction with Camp Creek–Fingerboard Trail, which is an abandoned roadbed on the south side of Camp Creek, Oregon Snake River Trail crosses Camp Creek and leads on down the river. It soon passes another small cabin. Tryon Creek is reached 0.5 mile from Camp Creek. Along Tryon Creek between the trail and the river there are some low stone walls on both sides of the creek. These walls were here before white men came to the canyon. Their use has yet to be determined.

The Oregon Snake River Trail bears left and heads a few yards back into the Lookout Creek Canyon 1.5 miles after crossing Tryon Creek and 9.8 miles from Pittsburg. The route crosses Lookout Creek to the junction with Lookout Creek Trail 1737. The rough and very steep Lookout Creek Trail heads west up Lookout Creek Canyon. It then climbs steeply to the south to the junction with High Bench Trail 1735.

Leaving the junction with Lookout Creek Trail, Oregon Snake River Trail heads back out to the river. It soon passes Lookout Creek Rapids, and a fenceline with a gate. The trail makes a switchback to the left then one to the right, climbing slightly, 0.7 miles farther along. There is another long rapid in the river here. Another 0.2 mile brings you to the junction with Lonepine Creek Trail 1735. Lonepine Creek Trail is not visible on the ground but there is a sign marking the junction. (See Hike 15 Copper Creek–Lonepine Creek Loop, for a description of Lonepine Creek Trail.)

Oregon Snake River Trail crosses Lonepine Creek, which may be dry, shortly after passing the junction. It soon crosses another fenceline through a gate. There is a rusting stove and a rock dugout below the trail, 0.2 mile after passing the fenceline. Another quarter mile brings you to the abandoned Electrolitic Mine. Copper was mined here in the early twentieth century. The 400-foot tunnel has a bat door covering its entrance. This door protects a nursery colony of big-eared bats from disturbance during critical times of the year.

A few feet past the mine you will cross another fenceline through a gate and pass Highrange Rapids. The route is chipped out of the side of the cliff 0.3 mile after passing the Electrolitic Mine. Another 0.4 mile along the path you cross another fenceline through a gate. The route then traverses a ledge with cliffs both above and below to another gate. Just past the gate, 12.3 miles from Pittsburg, the trail forks. The fork to the right is the river level trail to Copper Creek Lodge, which is a couple hundred yards ahead. The left fork, which is the main trail, climbs to a bench above the lodge, making seven turns and switchbacks as it climbs.

Once on the low bench the trail heads northwest, passing a developed spring, which is the water source for the Copper Creek Lodge. A short distance after passing the spring is a junction with another trail to the lodge and a fenceline. (See Hike 16 for a description of the short but interesting trails in the Copper Creek Lodge area.) Just after crossing the fenceline is the junction with Copper Creek Trail. The Copper Creek Trail turns to the left. (See Hike 15 for information about Copper Creek Trail.) Oregon Snake River Trail continues northwest for 300 more yards to another junction. At the signed junction a trail to the right heads back to Copper Creek Lodge.

Once past the third and last trail heading to the lodge, Oregon Snake River Trail continues on to the northwest to Bob Creek. There is another trail junction just before reaching Bob Creek. The vague and hard-to-follow trail, which turns to the left (southeast) at this junction, connects with Copper Creek Trail. A sign points to Tryon Creek at this junction.

An excellent campsite can be found next to the river 0.1 mile after crossing Bob Creek. Next to the campsite the trail climbs to a low bench. The junction with the trail to Cat Creek Ranch is reached a quarter mile after passing the campsite. The trail to the ranch bears to the right, and may be used as an alternate to the main Snake River Trail.

A quarter mile farther along is the junction with Cat Creek Trail 1701. (See Hike 14 for a description of Cat Creek Trail.) Cat Creek Trail turns to the left (south). A short distance more and the tread crosses Cat Creek just above the ranch. There is a trail next to the crossing that turns right and leads down to the ranch. Bob and Cat Creeks were named for the many bobcats a pair of sheep men killed in the area.

After crossing Cat Creek, Oregon Snake River Trail heads on to the northwest. It passes a rusting old plow and crosses a couple of old fencelines in the 0.8 mile to Roland Creek and the Roland Bar Rapids. The trail crosses Roland Creek (elev. 1,140 feet), then turns left (west) and begins to climb. You will climb for 0.4 mile, gaining 560 vertical feet on this fairly steep section of trail. The path then crosses a couple of small gullies and descends slightly to Bar Creek Spring. At the spring there are a couple of stock tanks on the right side of the trail. After passing the spring, the route climbs for a couple hundred yards to the abandoned and burned Dorrance Ranch and the junction with the trail to Christmas Creek Ranch. You are now 16.5 miles from Pittsburg. (See Hike 13 for a description of Christmas Creek Ranch Trail 1726A.) Jim Tryon and Lou Knapper, early ranchers in the area, named Christmas Creek in commemoration of Christmas Day 1888. The trail junction and sign are just after passing the ranch at 1,660 feet elevation.

At the junction Oregon Snake River Trail bears to the left, and heads west and south for 0.3 mile to Bean Creek. The route stays mostly level to Bean Creek, but descends slightly just before reaching the crossing. After crossing Bean Creek you will climb gently for 0.2 mile to a ridgeline. The path then rounds the head of a gully and traverses to another rounded ridgeline (elev. 1,730 feet). After crossing the ridge the path descends, making a couple of switchbacks. It then traverses in and out of several small draws to Christmas Creek. You will cross Christmas Creek at 1,540 feet elevation.

The tread soon crosses a couple more small gullies as it climbs very slightly to the second junction with Christmas Creek Ranch Trail. At this signed junction, 1.3 miles from Bean Creek, Christmas Creek Ranch Trail turns to the right. From the junction (elev. 1,610 feet), Oregon Snake River Trail heads to the southwest, climbing 250 feet in the 0.3 mile to the junction with Deep Creek Trail 1706. This junction is 18.4 miles from Pittsburg. (See Hike 9 for a description of Deep Creek Trail.) Deep Creek Trail is difficult to see here, but there is a sign marking the junction.

Past the junction with Deep Creek Trail you will cross a couple more ridges in the 0.4 mile to Thorn Spring Creek. Dry Creek Ranch can be seen across the river from this section of trail. There is a stock tank next to the trail at Thorn Spring and an abandoned cabin site a few yards past the creek crossing (elev. 1,850 feet). At Thorn Spring Creek an alternate route to Deep Creek Trail leaves Oregon Snake River Trail. This cross-country route, described in Hike 9, is not visible on the ground. Mock Orange (Syringa) blooms next to the cabin site in June. Their blooms resemble true citrus blooms in both appearance and fragrance.

Once past the Thorn Spring cabin site the route climbs gently for 0.5 mile to the top of a rise (elev. 1,920 feet). It then begins its descent down Trail Gulch. The path descends Trail Gulch for 1.2 miles, making many switchbacks and dropping 880 feet in elevation. At the bottom of Trail Gulch you will be close to the Snake River once more.

Along the river the tread bears left, and heads west for 0.3 mile to Deep Creek. There is a campsite on the river side of the trail, and a fenceline with gate, just before the crossing. Fording Deep Creek is generally no problem, but during times of heavy runoff it could be difficult.

The mouth of Deep Creek is the site of the 1887 Chinese Massacre. In late May of that year, 32 Chinese miners were shot here in an attempt to steal the gold they supposedly mined during the previous winter. Most of

74

Snake River Trail near Copper Creek Lodge.

their bodies were disposed of in the river and began floating past Lewiston a few days later.

Another campsite is reached 0.5 mile after crossing Deep Creek. After passing the campsite the trail crosses Robinson Creek and winds its way through the outcroppings along the river for 0.7 mile to Dug Creek. Miners used this section of the canyon, and evidence of their presence can be seen in several spots.

You will cross Dug Creek and turn left (southwest) at a trail sign. The route then heads up Dug Creek for 0.8 mile, crossing the creek seven times. Along the creek there are many signs of earlier use in the form of old fences and household relics. The path gains about 500 vertical feet in elevation, while ascending along Dug Creek. After crossing Dug Creek for the last time the trail climbs to the southwest up a small ridge for 500 yards to the junction with Western Rim National Recreation Trail 1744 (also known as Summit Ridge Trail). See Hike 7 for a description of Western Rim Trail. The junction, 23.3 miles from Pittsburg at 1,660 feet elevation, is in a small gully. There are several campsites close by, up the Western Rim Trail.

At the junction Oregon Snake River Trail turns to the right (northwest), and continues to climb. It climbs for 0.4 mile gaining 200 vertical feet, to the ridge dividing the Dug Creek drainage and Fence Gulch. The trail is braided in this section but easy to follow. After crossing the ridge the tread descends slightly and crosses the small stream in Fence Gulch. The route climbs slightly leaving Fence Gulch then begins to descend, crossing several small draws. Four-tenths mile after crossing Fence Gulch the trail crosses a fenceline on a ridge top (elev. 1,520 feet). It then descends more steeply for three-quarters of a mile to Dug Bar Ranch and Trailhead. Dug Bar Ranch and Trailhead is 25.3 miles from Pittsburg, at 1,090 feet elevation.

A short distance before reaching the trailhead the trail forks. Take the steeper right fork and cross another fenceline by climbing over it on some steps. Then follow the trail around the right side of the ranch buildings to the trailhead. There is a side trail to the Nez Perce Crossing a few yards before reaching the trailhead. Nez Perce Crossing is the point where the Nez Perce Indians crossed the Snake River as they were trying to escape from the army in June 1877.

Open campfires are prohibited all along the Snake River Corridor, which includes all land within a quarter mile of the river. Check with the Forest Service for the current restrictions.

Most wildflowers bloom along the river beginning in late March and continue through June. Fishing for catfish and bass is good to excellent all along the river; there are also some trout and sturgeon to be caught. Check the Oregon sports fishing regulations before fishing. There are several special rules for fishing the Snake River. Elk are the most common large animals along this trail; you will likely see some of them as well as some Mule Deer and possibly a Black Bear. Bald Eagles are fairly common in winter and spring, as are Canada Geese. Rattlesnakes and Poison Ivy are fairly common all along this trail.

Options: Use this route as a continuation of your hike along the Snake River. See Hike 10 for details about the southern section of Oregon Snake River Trail.

Check out the hike descriptions for the many side trails mentioned above. Many of these side trails offer great out-and-back day hikes from a camp along Oregon Snake River Trail. From Dug Bar Trailhead, the route up to Deep Creek along Oregon Snake River Trail makes an excellent day hike.

12 Camp Creek–Fingerboard Trail 1699

Highlights:	A hike from the Snake River up to the historic Tryon Ranch then over Tryon Saddle and up the West Fork of Deep Creek to Fingerboard Saddle and the junction with Western Rim National Recreation Trail.
Type of hike:	Internal connecting backpack, with out-and-back and loop options.
Total distance:	10.9 miles.
Difficulty:	Moderate to strenuous.
Best months:	March–June and September–November up to Tryon Ranch; May–October above the ranch.
Elevation gain:	5,210 feet.
Permits and fees:	None.
Maps:	Lord Flat and Fingerboard Saddle USGS quads.

Finding the trailhead: See Hike 11 for driving directions to Dug Bar Trailhead; from this trailhead, hike 17.5 miles southeast along Oregon Snake River Trail to the signed junction with Camp Creek–Fingerboard Trail 1699. The GPS coordinates at the junction are 45 41.267 N 116 31.909 W.

The best way to reach the trail junction where this hike begins is by jet boat from Dug Bar or Clarkston, Washington. This hike ends at a junction with Western Rim Trail 3.3 miles north of the Lord Flat Airstrip and Trailhead. See Hike 7 for directions to Lord Flat and details about this part of Western Rim Trail.

Trailhead facilities: The junction of Camp Creek Trail and Oregon Snake River Trail has some campsites but no other facilities.

Camping and services: See Hikes 7 and 11 for the closest services; none are available even remotely close to this trail. Cell phone service is generally available from Fingerboard Saddle.

For more information: USDA Forest Service at Wallowa Mountains Visitor Center in Enterprise, Oregon. Contact Beamers Hells Canyon Tours for information about jet boat transportation.

Camp Creek–Fingerboard Trail 1699

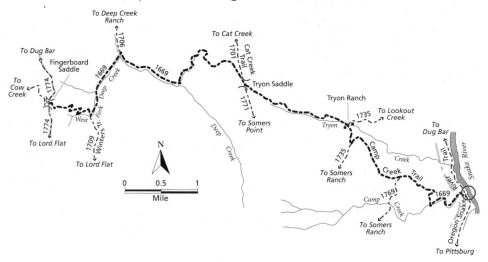

Key points:

- 0.0 Junction with Oregon Snake River Trail 17.5 miles southeast of Dug Bar Trailhead.
- 1.8 Unmarked junction with Trail 1769.
- 3.2 Tryon Ranch. GPS 45 42.010 N 116 33.834 W.
- 5.2 Tryon Saddle GPS 45 42.447 N 116 35.585 W.
- 5.4 Junction with Cat Creek Trail 1701.
- 8.3 Junction with Deep Creek Trail 1706.
- 9.4 Junction with Winters Trail 1709. GPS 45 42.046 N 116 38.148 W.
- 10.9 Fingerboard Saddle. GPS 45 42.215 N 116 38.877 W.

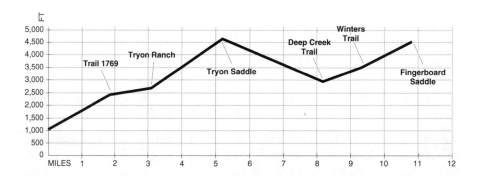

The hike: Camp Creek–Fingerboard Trail heads west from Oregon Snake River Trail. A few feet into the hike the route crosses Camp Creek, and begins to follow an old roadbed, up the north side of the stream. You will cross Camp Creek again and cross the Hells Canyon Wilderness Boundary (elev. 1,400 feet) 0.3 mile after leaving Oregon Snake River Trail.

The trail recrosses Camp Creek 300 yards farther along. One hundred yards past the crossing the trail forks. Take the left fork and head on up Camp Creek. The track soon crosses the creek again, and 100 yards farther along it crosses it for the last time at 1,640 feet elevation. The path makes a switchback to the right at the crossing.

After the last crossing the trail climbs up a side draw for a quarter mile, then makes a switchback to the right. You then wind your way up the open hillsides and ridges for 0.8 mile to an unmarked junction with Trail 1769. Trail 1769, which is fairly easy to follow but rough in spots, heads south for 3.5 miles to Somers Ranch. Just before reaching the junction Tryon Creek Ranch comes into view in the distance to the northwest. Bear right at the junction, leaving the roadbed (elev. 2,450 feet).

The trail continues to climb west for another quarter mile more then flattens out and traverses for 0.7 mile to the northwest, to the junction with Trail 1735. This rough and sometimes obscure trail heads south from the junction and leads to Somers Ranch via Hog Creek. Bear right and head northwest at the junction.

The route soon winds around the end of a rise, and then heads to the southwest passing some rusting farm equipment. A short distance past the equipment the trail crosses a gully and joins a roadbed heading north. Another 0.2 mile is the gate in the fence surrounding Tryon Ranch. A short distance past the gate is a trail junction, with a sign. Tryon Saddle is to the left (westnorthwest), and the rough path to Lookout Creek is straight-ahead (north). The ranch house is to the left at the junction. Tryon Creek Ranch, at 2,640 feet elevation and 3.2 miles from Oregon Snake River Trail, is still in use by the Forest Service. If this is to be an out-and-back hike from a campsite on Oregon Snake River Trail, the ranch is a good place to turn around.

Turn left at the junction; pass the ranch house and head up the left (south) side of Tryon Creek. Seventy-five yards past the ranch house the trail goes through a gate and enters a brushy area along Tryon Creek. A short distance farther along it crosses Tryon Creek. After the crossing, the path bears slightly away from the creek. You will cross a side gully 0.2 mile after crossing Tryon Creek. The hillside above the trail, as it enters the gully, is covered with Balsamroot. Balsamroot is in full bloom, with its large yellow flowers, in mid-May in this area.

The tread crosses another fenceline, 0.4 mile after crossing the side gully. Soon it makes six tiny switchbacks. Four-tenths of a mile past the switchbacks there is a spring (elev. 3,920 feet), on the left side of the trail. This is the last water for some distance. After passing the spring the course heads on up the now-dry creekbed, then makes 11 switchbacks as it climbs to Tryon Saddle. The saddle, at 4,650 feet elevation, is 0.7 mile past the spring, and 5.2 miles from Oregon Snake River Trail. The trail between the ranch and the saddle gets very muddy and slippery during wet weather.

In the saddle that may be nearly covered with Phlox is the signed junction with Trail 1771. Trail 1771 turns to the left at the junction. (See Hike 17 for a description of this part of Trail 1771.) Turn right (north) at the junction and follow the trail as it contours along the open slope. This slope blooms with Paintbrush and Lupine in May. You will reach the junction with Cat Creek Trail 1701 300 yards after leaving the junction with Trail 1771 in Tryon Saddle. Cat Creek Trail turns to the right. (See Hike 14 for details about Cat Creek Trail.)

From the junction with Cat Creek Trail, the route continues to traverse the open slope for another 0.3 mile before heading west out a rounded ridge. Shortly the route begins to descend, making a couple of switchbacks. The path heads down a subridge to the north, makes 13 more switchbacks, then traverses an open slope before entering the timber. There was a sow and yearling Black Bear in this timber, when we hiked this trail. The tread leaves the timber in about 100 yards, it makes a left turn, then a right turn, and drops the last few feet to the bottom of the draw. Once in the bottom of the draw the trail bears left and heads on down to the southwest. The bottom of the draw has brush in it but the sides are mostly open.

The route crosses a creek 0.3 mile after heading down the draw. You will cross the same creek five more times before reaching Deep Creek. This section of trail is very rocky in places. After the sixth and last crossing the trail heads northwest down Deep Creek Canyon, staying on the right (northeast) side of Deep Creek. The junction with Deep Creek Trail 1706 is reached 0.9 mile more down this heavily timbered canyon bottom. See Hike 9 for a description of Deep Creek Trail, which is straight ahead (north-northwest) at the junction. The junction, elevation 2,890 feet, is 3.1 miles from Tryon Saddle and 8.3 miles from Oregon Snake River Trail.

Turn to the left at the signed junction, and ford Deep Creek. After crossing Deep Creek the route climbs to the southwest along the West Fork of Deep Creek. You will cross the West Fork of Deep Creek about 0.8 mile after crossing Deep Creek. In another quarter mile the path recrosses the West Fork and soon comes to the junction with Winters Trail 1709, at 3,470 feet elevation.

Winters Trail is an alternate route if you are heading for the Lord Flat Trailhead and Airstrip. The 1.6-mile Winters Trail may be rough and a little difficult to follow in places, but it saves considerable distance if you are heading for Lord Flat.

To continue on Trail 1699, which you have been following all the way from the Snake River, turn right at the junction and begin the steep climb toward Fingerboard Saddle. Most of the next 1.5 miles of this trail has been rebuilt fairly recently and is in good condition. You will make ten switchbacks as you climb the open flower-covered slopes to Fingerboard Saddle. At Fingerboard Saddle, elevation 4,560 feet, is the junction with Western Rim Trail. If you turn left on Western Rim Trail it is 3.3 miles to the Lord Flat Trailhead and Airstrip. To the right it is 9.9 miles to Dug Bar Trailhead. (See Hike 7 for a description of Western Rim Trail.)

Watch for rattlesnakes all along this trail.

Options: Use the first 3.2 miles of this hike, up to the Tryon Ranch, as a side trip from a base camp along Oregon Snake River Trail.

A loop can be made by turning left on Trail 1769, 1.8 miles from Oregon Snake River Trail, and following it to Somers Ranch. From the ranch hike

The author's niece at Fingerboard Saddle.

east on Somers Creek Trail 1770 for 0.2 mile to the junction with the Oregon Snake River Trail. Turn left on Oregon Snake River Trail and follow it for 2.9 miles north to Camp Creek and the junction with the Camp Creek–Fingerboard Trail, to complete the 8.9-mile loop.

13 Christmas Creek Ranch Trail 1726A

Highlights:	A 1.8-mile alternate trail, off Oregon Snake River Trail 1726, passing the abandoned Christmas Creek Ranch. This description is in the downriver direction. The trail on the ground is not in exactly the same place that it is on the USGS quad map.
Type of hike:	Internal alternate for a section of Oregon Snake River Trail.
Total distance:	1.8 miles.
Difficulty:	Moderate, but requires routefinding skills.
Best months:	March–May and September–mid-November.
Elevation gain:	530 feet.
Permits and fees:	None.
Maps:	Wolf Creek USGS quad.

Finding the trailhead: Christmas Creek Ranch Trail 1726A is an alternate route for a section of Oregon Snake River Trail 1726. This description begins 8.8 miles southeast of Dug Bar Trailhead, just above the abandoned Dorrance

Christmas Creek Ranch Trail 1726A

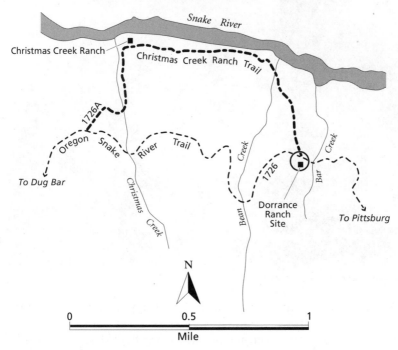

Ranch, and ends 7.2 miles southeast of Dug Bar Trailhead at another junction with Oregon Snake River Trail. (See Hike 10 for a description of Oregon Snake River Trail.) The GPS coordinates at the southeast end of this trail where the hike description begins are 45 46.494 N 116 36.130 W.

Trailhead facilities: Dorrance Ranch has a couple of possible campsites but no other facilities.

Camping and services: Some groceries can be obtained in the tiny town of Imnaha, Oregon, but the closest place for gas and other services is Joseph or Enterprise, Oregon.

For more information: USDA Forest Service at Wallowa Mountains Visitor Center in Enterprise.

Key points:
- 0.0   Junction with Oregon Snake River Trail at Dorrance Ranch site.
- 1.3   Christmas Creek Ranch.
- 1.8   Junction with Oregon Snake River Trail 1726. GPS 45 46.574 N 116 37.241 W.

The hike: From the junction with Oregon Snake River Trail at Dorrance Ranch, Christmas Creek Ranch Trail heads north around a small knob on the ridgeline. It then bears slightly left and descends

Dorrance Ranch.

steeply down the sloping ridge. You will descend the ridge for a quarter of a mile then turn to the left. Then the path continues to descend, now less steeply, along the hillside to the northwest. The trail crosses Bean Creek 0.4 mile after leaving the ridgeline.

Soon after crossing Bean Creek, the tread crosses another tiny stream as it traverses west-northwest. The trail continues to traverse generally to the west for another 0.7 mile to the abandoned and burned Christmas Creek Ranch. After crossing Bean Creek, the trail becomes very faint in places. The route crosses a fenceline just before reaching the ranch.

Leaving the ranch, at 1,080 feet elevation, the trail climbs along the east side of Christmas Creek for a quarter of a mile. It then crosses the creek (elev. 1,360 feet). After crossing the creek the path climbs to the west for a couple hundred yards to a ridgeline. It then turns left on the ridge and continues to climb for 300 yards to the junction with Oregon Snake River Trail. You will cross a fenceline about 100 yards before reaching the junction. The elevation at the junction is 1,610 feet. From here it is 7.2 miles northwest (right) to Dug Bar Trailhead.

Options: This trail is an alternate route for a section of Oregon Snake River Trail; no other trails connect with it.

14 Cat Creek Trail 1701

Highlights:	A moderate 4-mile round-trip hike to an abandoned and now burned cabin site or a strenuous 6.8-mile connecting trail between Oregon Snake River Trail 1726 and Camp Creek–Fingerboard Trail 1699 at Tryon Saddle. The section of this trail above the cabin requires excellent routefinding and map reading skills to follow safely.
Type of hike:	Internal connecting backpack, with out-and-back and loop options.
Total distance:	6.9 miles to Tryon Saddle; 4 miles round-trip to the cabin site.
Difficulty:	Moderate up to the cabin site; strenuous with much routefinding needed above the cabin site.
Best months:	March–June and September–November up to the cabin; June–October above the cabin. Late June and September–October are the best times to hike to Tryon Saddle.
Elevation gain:	3,850 feet.
Permits and fees:	None.
Maps:	Wolf Creek and Lord Flat USGS quads.

Finding the trailhead: If you plan to hike to the junction where Cat Creek Trail meets Oregon Snake River Trail, follow Oregon 350 from Joseph, Oregon, for 30 miles northeast to Imnaha. Then take County Road 735, which becomes Forest Road 4260, for 28 miles north along the Imnaha River and over Cactus Mountain to Dug Bar Trailhead. The last 8 miles of FR 4260 become very rough and muddy at times and may require a four-wheel-drive vehicle. Check locally for road conditions. From Dug Bar Trailhead, hike 11.5 miles southeast on Oregon Snake River Trail to the junction with Cat Creek Trail. (See Hike 11 for a description of Oregon Snake River Trail North.) The trail begins at a trail sign 200 yards up Cat Creek from the abandoned Cat Creek Ranch. The GPS coordinates at the junction of Oregon Snake River Trail and Cat Creek Trail are 45 45.628 N 116 33.996 W.

An easier way to get to the starting point is to take a jet boat from Dug Bar or Clarkston, Washington.

Trailhead facilities: Cat Creek Ranch has some possible campsites but no other facilities.

Camping and services: Overnight accommodations are available at Copper Creek Lodge 0.8 mile southeast of the junction where this hike began, along Oregon Snake River Trail. Copper Creek Lodge makes an excellent base camp for exploring this part of Hells Canyon.

For more information: USDA Forest Service at Wallowa Mountains Visitor Center in Enterprise, Oregon. Contact Beamers Hells Canyon Tours for a jet boat shuttle and information about Copper Creek Lodge.

Cat Creek Trail 1701

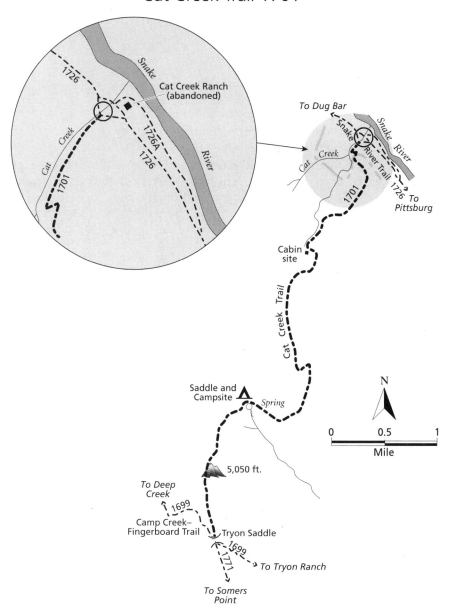

Key points:

- 0.0   Junction with Oregon Snake River Trail 1726 11.5 miles southeast of Dug Bar Trailhead.
- 2.0   Cabin site.
- 5.4   Saddle and campsite.
- 6.9   Tryon Saddle. GPS 45 42.447 N 116 35.585 W.

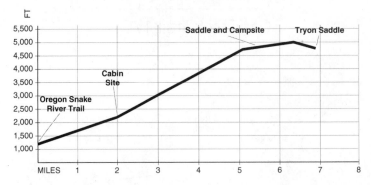

The hike: From the trail sign and junction with Oregon Snake River Trail, at 1,200 feet elevation, Cat Creek Trail heads southwest, through a meadow on the left side of Cat Creek. After going up the meadow for 0.1 mile, you make a switchback to the left and climb away from the creek. The path makes three more switchbacks as it works its way to the top of a small ridge. From the ridge a waterfall can be seen in the distance, to the west, up the Main Fork of Cat Creek, from the switchbacks.

The course turns right and continues to climb along the left side of the ridgeline, winding its way up, and crossing the ridgeline several times. In 0.4 mile a small saddle, at 1,710 feet elevation, is reached. Above the saddle the track continues to work its way up the ridge for another 0.6 mile to the point where the ridge flattens out. You then head southwest, on the grass covered flats for 0.2 mile to the point where the ridge begins to steepen again. Here the trail bears to the right, and begins a traverse along a hillside. After traversing for 0.4 mile the trail nearly reaches a creekbed.

You will find a fork in the route just before reaching the creekbed. The fork to the right (south) crosses the creek and goes a short distance to an abandoned cabin site. The remains of the cabin, 2 miles from Oregon Snake River Trail, is the turnaround point if this is an out-and-back hike from a base camp along the Snake River. The flat area around the cabin site is the best campsite along the lower part of this trail.

To continue on Cat Creek Trail, bear left at the fork and head up the side of the creekbed. For the next 3 miles the route may tax your routefinding skills. You work your way up the creekbed, crossing it several times, for 1.8 miles. Then at about 3,800 feet elevation, the route bears left to climb to a ridgeline. After winding up to the ridge you will bear right and follow the ridge south and west to a saddle. From the saddle the route, which again becomes a path, traverses around the north side of a high point on the ridge. As you make this traverse you may notice a small spring in a patch of brush below the trail. Shortly after passing the spring the path reaches another saddle. This saddle provides the best campsite on Cat Creek Trail above the cabin site. The campsite in the saddle is 5.4 miles from Oregon Snake River Trail, at 4,780 feet elevation.

Leaving the saddle the trail climbs southwest along the rounded ridgeline for 0.4 mile. You then head south along the broad ridge, climbing gently for another 0.5 mile to reach its highest point at 5,050 feet elevation. There

Cat Creek Ranch.

is a large cairn with a steel post in it, to the left of the trail at its highest point. A white metal triangle is attached to the steel post.

Once you have passed the high point the path begins to descend. The route stays slightly to the right of ridgeline much of the time as it descends the flower-covered slopes to the junction with Camp Creek–Fingerboard Trail at the north end of Tryon Saddle. Tryon Saddle, at 4,650 feet elevation, has some small, flat spots that are big enough to set a tent on, but it makes a very poor place to camp. The nearest water is several hundred feet down on either side, and the saddle can be very windy at times.

Options: To make a 20.7-mile loop backpack, turn right in Tryon Saddle, on Camp Creek–Fingerboard Trail, and descend 2.9 miles to the junction with Deep Creek Trail. Then turn right (north) on the Deep Creek Trail and follow it for 6.3 miles to the junction with Oregon Snake River Trail. Turn right on Oregon Snake River Trail and follow it east-southeast for 4.6 miles to the junction with Cat Creek Trail, where this hike began. For more information about the trails used to make this loop, see Hikes 12, 9, and 11.

15 Copper Creek–Lonepine Creek Loop 1736, 1735

Highlights: A hike heading up Copper Creek to the historic Rankin Cabin, then backtracking to Copper Creek Trail, following it up Copper Creek and across the benches to reach Lonepine Creek Trail, descending the rugged Lonepine Trail to Snake River Trail, and following the river back to the starting point.

Type of hike: Internal loop day hike from a base camp.

Total distance: 6.3 miles.

Difficulty: Moderate to Rankin Cabin; strenuous past the cabin. Good map reading and routefinding skills are required. Descending back down to the Snake River on Lonepine Creek Trail is a very steep and hard-to-follow route.

Best months: Mid-February–May and September–mid-November. Wildlife and flowers are best in April and May.

Elevation gain: Approximately 2,000 feet.

Permits and fees: None.

Maps: Lord Flat USGS quad covers the area but shows the location of the trail somewhat incorrectly.

Finding the trailhead: Follow the driving directions in Hike 11 to Dug Bar Trailhead. Then hike 12.7 miles southeast along Oregon Snake River Trail to Copper Creek Lodge. Copper Creek Trail leaves Oregon Snake River Trail 300 yards northwest of the lodge. A sign at this junction marks Oregon Snake River Trail but no sign points out Copper Creek Trail. The GPS coordinates at the junction with Oregon Snake River Trail are 45 45.013 N 116 33.016 W.

An easier way to reach Copper Creek Lodge is by jet boat from Clarkston, Washington, or Dug Bar.

Trailhead facilities: Copper Creek Lodge near the beginning of this hike has all the facilities for a great canyon stay, or you can camp at Bob Creek, 1 mile northwest of the starting point on Oregon Snake River Trail.

Camping and services: Copper Creek Lodge has cabins and a dining room; reservations are required.

For more information: USDA Forest Service at Wallowa Mountains Visitor Center in Enterprise, Oregon. For jet boat transportation and lodging at Copper Creek Lodge, contact Beamers Hells Canyon Tours in Clarkston.

Key points:

- 0.0   Junction with Oregon Snake River Trail 300 yards northwest of Copper Creek Lodge.
- 0.3   Junction with Rankin Cabin Trail.
- 0.7   Trail goes through notch on ridge.
- 1.8   Trail crosses fenceline.

Copper Creek–Lonepine Creek Loop 1736, 1735

3.1 Trail crosses Lonepine Creek.
3.6 Junction with Lonepine Creek Trail 1735. GPS 45 43.382 N 116 32.869 W.
4.6 Junction with Oregon Snake River Trail. GPS 45 43.499 N 116 32.221 W.
6.2 Copper Creek Lodge.

The hike: Heading south from Oregon Snake River Trail, Copper Creek Trail climbs up Copper Creek. Copper Creek is dry here most of the time, however. The course climbs gently up the creekbed for 0.2 mile to the junction

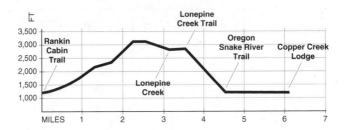

with Rankin Cabin Trail, at 1,320 feet elevation. At this junction Rankin Cabin Trail heads on up the creek to the southwest. There is another path that turns to the right and climbs out of the creekbed. This path soon fades out.

Copper Creek Trail turns left at the junction then climbs steeply along a hillside. You will climb generally east for 0.3 mile to a ridgeline, where the path goes through a notch, at 1,570 feet elevation. The trail is faint in this area. After going through the notch the trail turns right (southwest) and soon regains the ridgeline. Once on the ridgeline the route works its way up for about 0.5 mile, gaining approximately 620 feet elevation. The trail in this area does not follow the route marked on the USGS map; however, it is placed nearly correct on Forest Service maps. After climbing the ridge the tread turns off to the left (southeast). Shortly you will cross a small gully, then traverse to a gate in a fenceline. This gate (elev. 2,390 ft.) is 1.8 mile from the junction with Oregon Snake River Trail.

After going through the gate the route climbs into and up another gully for a short distance. You then turn left and climb out to a rounded ridgeline. The trace climbs the rounded ridge, heading southwest for 0.4 mile, gaining 250 feet elevation. It then bears to the left off the ridgeline, and crosses the top of a bowl. The trail soon reaches the top of a flat ridge at 3,040 feet elevation. At this ridgeline the trail generally rejoins the route marked on the USGS map.

Cross the flat ridge then descend to Lonepine Creek. The route makes a switchback as it descends the steep side hill to the crossing. Where the trail crosses Lonepine Creek there is a path to the right. This path climbs 50 yards to an abandoned cabin.

Once across Lonepine Creek the trail soon crosses another fenceline through a gate as it traverses a steep hillside. The junction with Lonepine Creek Trail 1735 is reached 0.4 mile after crossing Lonepine Creek. This junction, at 2,880 feet elevation, is southwest of and slightly lower than it is shown on the USGS map. From here on, Copper Creek Trail becomes very hard to follow. Hikers with good map reading and routefinding skills can follow it on to Tryon Ranch, but this is recommended only for expert hikers.

Lonepine Creek Trail is also very vague at the junction. Turn left (east) at the signed junction, and head straight down a ridgeline. The route descends the ridgeline for a quarter of a mile, then bears slightly left and continues descending along the north-facing slope. The course stays north of the ridgeline for 0.5 mile then the grade moderates. From here you will descend a grass-covered slope to the junction with Oregon Snake River Trail. The last

Lonepine Creek Canyon.

quarter mile of the route on the grassy slope may not be visible on the ground. There is a sign marking the junction with Oregon Snake River Trail.

This 1,760-foot descent in 1 mile makes this route one of the steepest in the canyon. Only persons who are proficient at following a faint path and do not mind doing some scrambling should use the Lonepine Creek Trail section of this loop. This trail could be dangerous to novice hikers because there is some exposure in places. Be sure to take along a good map.

Turn left on Oregon Snake River Trail and follow it for 1.6 miles north to the Copper Creek Lodge area, where this hike started. See Hike 11 for a description of this section of Oregon Snake River Trail.

Options: For a shorter trip, hike to Rankin Cabin and back. See Hike 16 for the details.

16 Copper Creek Lodge Area

Highlights:	Various short hikes to interesting historical sites in three directions. The trails mentioned here do not have significant elevation gain or loss. The Forest Service generally does not maintain these trails, but the trails get enough use to be fairly easy to follow. Watch for rattlesnakes and poison ivy.
Type of hike:	Short day hikes from a base camp.
Total distance:	Varies with hike.
Difficulty:	Easy to moderate.
Best months:	February–June and September–November.
Elevation gain:	Varies with hike.
Permits and fees:	None.
Maps:	Lord Flat and Wolf Creek USGS quads cover the area but do not show all the trails.
Starting point:	Copper Creek Lodge.

Finding the trailhead: Copper Creek Lodge is located next to the Snake River 12.7 miles southeast of Dug Bar Trailhead. See Hike 10 for driving directions to Dug Bar Trailhead. Then hike 12.7 miles southeast on Oregon Snake River Trail to the lodge. Copper Creek Lodge can also be reached by jet boat from Clarkston, Washington.

Trailhead facilities: Beamers Hells Canyon Tours of Clarkston runs Copper Creek Lodge. The lodge, 70 miles upriver from Clarkston, offers lodging in private cabins, meals in the dining room, and jet boat transportation, all by reservation only. Copper Creek Lodge is a great spot to begin or end an extended hike in Hells Canyon or to stay a few days and explore the surrounding country.

Camping and services: Copper Creek Lodge has cabins and a dining room; reservations are required. The closest medical services are in Lewiston,

Copper Creek Lodge Area

Idaho, 70 miles downriver by jet boat. Some groceries can be obtained in the tiny town of Imnaha, Oregon, but the closest place for gas and other services is Enterprise, Oregon.

For more information: USDA Forest Service at Wallowa Mountains Visitor Center in Enterprise. Contact Beamers Hells Canyon Tours in Clarkston for information about jet boat shuttles and lodge reservations. Beamers will also pick you up at Dug Bar.

Rankin Cabin

The round trip up Copper Creek to Billy Rankin's stone cabin can be made in a couple of hours. To hike to the cabin, take the left fork in the trail at the west end of the lodge area by the stock pen. Climb gently on this trail for 250 yards to the junction with Oregon Snake River Trail 1726; then turn right and go through the gate. Just past the fenceline, Copper Creek Trail 1736 turns to the left. (See Hike 15 for a description of Copper Creek Trail.) Follow Copper Creek Trail, heading southwest up the brushy draw, for 500 yards.

Copper Creek Lodge.

At this point, Copper Creek Trail turns to the left. Stay on the path in the creekbed and continue 500 yards more to the cabin, passing a developed spring on the way.

Rankin Pump
Another good short hike from the lodge is to Rankin's old water pump. To go to the pump, take the right fork of the trail at the west end of the lodge area. Follow this trail for 250 yards to a fenceline and gate. Go through the gate and follow the trail another 0.2 mile to its junction with Oregon Snake River Trail. Turn right on Oregon Snake River Trail and head downriver another 150 yards. The pump will be to your right on the riverbank, but it is hard to see from the trail. Powered with a gasoline engine, this pump was used in Billy Rankin's mining operation.

Cat Creek Ranch Trail
Cat Creek Ranch Trail 1726A is a 0.3-mile alternate route to Oregon Snake River Trail approximately 1 mile northwest of Copper Creek Lodge. The ranch trail bears right off Oregon Snake River Trail 0.4 mile after crossing Bob Creek and descends gently through the old fields of Cat Creek Ranch. At the northwest end of the fields, the trail bears left to the abandoned buildings that were Cat Creek Ranch. Past the buildings, it climbs a few yards to rejoin Oregon Snake River Trail.

Options: For longer hikes in this extremely interesting area, see Hikes 11, 14, and 15.

17 Tryon Saddle Trail 1750, 1771

Highlights:	A hike that travels down off Summit Ridge and across Deep Creek, then climbs the ridge between Deep Creek and the Snake River and follows the flower-covered ridge north to Tryon Saddle.
Type of hike:	Out-and-back day hike or backpack, with a loop option.
Total distance:	11 miles.
Difficulty:	Moderate, but much of the trail is not well maintained and Deep Creek must be forded. Some parts of this trail are not suitable for stock.
Best months:	Mid-June–October.
Elevation gain:	300 feet.
Permits and fees:	None.
Maps:	Lord Flat USGS quad.

Finding the trailhead: To Reach Lord Flat, drive east and north from Joseph, Oregon, on Oregon 350 (Imnaha Highway or Little Sheep Creek Highway) for 30 miles to Imnaha, Oregon. Take Hat Point Road (Forest Road 4240) east from Imnaha. After going 22 miles on Hat Point Road, turn left (north) on Lord Flat Road. Lord Flat Road (also known as Western Rim National Recreation Trail or Summit Ridge Trail) can be used by normal cars for about 4 miles to Warnock Corral; then it becomes necessary to have a four-wheel-drive vehicle with high clearance. It is about 15 miles from Warnock Corral to the junction where this hike begins. The sign at the junction calls this Hog Creek Trail. The GPS coordinates at the junction are 45 39.223 N 116 36.194 W.

Aircraft is often used to reach Lord Flat Trailhead. If you are not an experienced and daring driver with the proper vehicle, it is best to fly into Lord Flat. If you fly in, it will be necessary to hike 1 mile south from the airstrip to reach the junction with Hog Creek Trail where this hike starts.

Trailhead facilities: No facilities are available at the junction where this hike begins.

Camping and services: The closest campsites are next to the airstrip at Lord Flat. Groceries can be obtained in Imnaha. For gas and other services, the closest place is Joseph. Cell phone service is available in many spots along Western Rim Trail and at Lord Flat.

For more information: USDA Forest Service at Wallowa Mountains Visitor Center in Enterprise, Oregon. Contact Spence Air Service in Enterprise for information about flying into Lord Flat.

Key points:
- 0.0   Junction with Western Rim Trail (Lord Flat Road) 1 mile south of Lord Flat Airstrip and Trailhead.
- 1.5   Crossing of Deep Creek.

Tryon Saddle Trail 1750, 1771

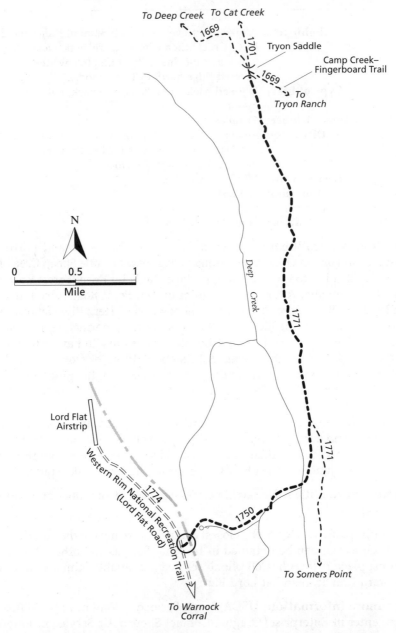

2.2   Junction with Trail 1771, on ridgeline.
5.5   Tryon Saddle. GPS 45 42.474 N 116 35.585 W.

The hike: As you leave the junction with Western Rim Trail the route, which is often called the Glass Eye Trail, heads northeast. In a short distance you will pass the Hells Canyon Wilderness Boundary, then descend gently

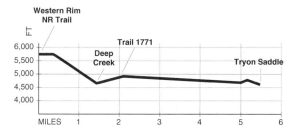

through a small meadow. There is a spring to the right of the path a quarter of a mile after leaving the junction. The tread continues to descend along the small stream that begins at the spring. Trilliums grow in the damp shade along the stream. One mile from the junction with Western Rim Trail the course crosses the stream, and soon recrosses it. The stream you have been following soon joins Deep Creek. The path drops a bit more and crosses Deep Creek 1.5 miles from Western Rim Trail, at 4,640 feet elevation.

Deep Creek must be forded because there is no bridge. The crossing is generally not difficult here, but it is cold and wet. During spring melting time in May and June, this ford can be dangerous. Once across Deep Creek, the path climbs steeply for a short distance. The grade soon moderates, as the trail heads north along the east slope of Deep Creek Canyon. You will reach the ridgeline at 4,940 feet elevation, in a saddle 0.7 mile after crossing Deep Creek.

On the Phlox covered ridgeline Hells Canyon comes into view to the east. The junction with Trail 1771 is reached on the ridgeline. To the right (south) Trail 1771 is in poor condition as it heads to Somers Point.

Foggy evening at Tryon Saddle.   Jerry Lavender photo

Turn left on the ridgeline and head north on Trail 1771. Much of this ridgeline was burned in 1996 and 2000. In June the ridge may be nearly covered with Paintbrush, Balsamroot, and many other flowers. You will make a couple short but steep switchbacks, to get below a rim 0.9 mile after leaving the saddle where you reached the ridge. Past the switchbacks the track climbs steeply, then flattens out on the narrow ridgeline. The path begins its gradual descent toward Tryon Saddle 0.4 mile farther along. As you follow the ridge watch for Elk.

The route reaches Tryon Saddle 5.5 miles after leaving Western Rim Trail. In the saddle, at 4,650 feet elevation, is the junction with Camp Creek–Fingerboard Trail 1699. (See Hike 12 for a description of Camp Creek–Fingerboard Trail.)

Options: Retracing your steps back up the ridge and across Deep Creek makes the easiest return. An alternate loop hike can be done by following Camp Creek–Fingerboard Trail west for 5.7 miles to Fingerboard Saddle and the junction with Western Rim Trail. (See Hike 12 for details.) Turn left (south) on Western Rim Trail and follow it for 3.3 miles southeast to Lord Flat. (See Hike 7 for a description of Western Rim Trail.)

18 Deep Creek Ridge Loop 1770A, 1771, 1750

Highlights:	A hike from Summit Ridge across Deep Creek Canyon, with a spectacular view of Hells Canyon, and then a return by a different route.
Type of hike:	Lollipop-loop day hike from a base camp.
Total distance:	9.2 miles.
Difficulty:	Strenuous. Good routefinding and map reading skills are required to follow this trail safely.
Best months:	Late June–September.
Elevation gain:	Approximately 1,600 feet.
Trailhead elevation:	5,600 feet.
Permits and fees:	None.
Maps:	Lord Flat USGS quad.

Finding the trailhead: To Reach Lord Flat, drive east and north from Joseph, Oregon, on Oregon 350 (Imnaha Highway or Little Sheep Creek Highway) for 30 miles to Imnaha, Oregon. Take Hat Point Road (Forest Road 4240) east from Imnaha. After going 22 miles on Hat Point Road, turn left (north) on Lord Flat Road. Lord Flat Road (also known as Western Rim National Recreation Trail or Summit Ridge Trail) can be used by normal cars for about 4 miles to Warnock Corral; then it becomes necessary to have a four-wheel-drive vehicle with high clearance. It is about 16 miles from Warnock Corral to Lord Flat.

Deep Creek Ridge Loop 1770A, 1771, 1750

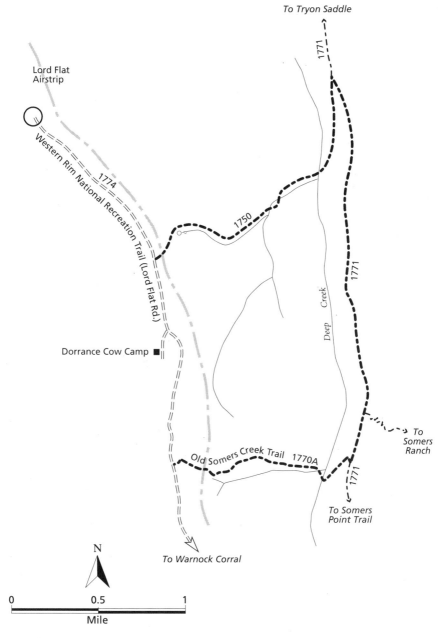

Aircraft is often used to reach the Lord Flat Airstrip and Trailhead. If you are not an experienced and daring driver with the proper vehicle, it is best to fly into Lord Flat. The flight in is much more pleasant than four-wheeling in for several hours. The GPS coordinates at the south end of Lord Flat Airstrip are 45 39.925 N 116 36.996 W.

Trailhead facilities: Primitive campsites are available next to Lord Flat Airstrip.

Camping and services: The east side of Lord Flat Airstrip has several primitive campsites. Cell phones work at the airstrip, but you may get better reception if you walk a couple hundred yards west to the rim of Cow Creek Canyon.

For more information: USDA Forest Service at Wallowa Mountains Visitor Center in Enterprise, Oregon. For flights into Lord Flat, contact Spence Air Service in Enterprise. If you plan to fly to Lord Flat in June or if there has been a wet weather period, call well in advance to check on airstrip conditions.

Key points:
0.0	South end of Lord Flat Airstrip.
1.0	Junction with Trail 1750. GPS 45 39.223 N 116 36.194 W.
1.5	Dorrance Cow Camp.
2.2	Junction with Old Somers Creek Trail 1770A. GPS 45 38.212 N 116 36.145 W.
3.2	Crossing of Deep Creek.
3.4	Ridge and junction with Trail 1771.
3.7	Unmarked trail to right leading to Somers Point Trail.
5.9	Junction with Trail 1750.
6.7	Crossing of Deep Creek.
8.2	Junction with Western Rim Trail. GPS 45 39.223 N 116 36.194 W.
9.2	Lord Flat Airstrip.

The hike: Departing from the south end of Lord Flat Airstrip the route heads south on Western Rim Trail, which is a four-wheel-drive road here. The track crosses flower-covered ridgetop meadows for 1 mile to the junction with Trail 1750. At the junction, continue south on Western Rim Trail.

Half a mile past the junction with Trail 1750, the route forks. The right fork goes a short distance to Dorrance Cow Camp, which has a cabin and a developed spring. Bear left at the fork and continue to hike south on Western Rim Trail.

After hiking 0.7 mile past the trail to Dorrance Cow Camp, you will reach the junction with Old Somers Creek Trail 1770A. The junction is 2.2 miles from Lord Flat Airstrip and just before Western Rim Trail crosses a fenceline.

Old Somers Creek Trail begins as a closed four-wheel-drive road. At the junction (elev. 5,840 feet), turn left and head east. The route climbs very gently for a quarter of a mile to the top of a rise through a meadow. The meadow may be nearly covered with blooming Mule's Ear in late June. Shortly after passing the top of the rise you will come to the Hells Canyon Wilderness Boundary, where the four-wheel-drive road becomes a trail.

The path now descends to the east through open forest and meadows. A couple hundred yards after passing the wilderness boundary you will notice a tiny stream and a broken down fenceline to your right. This stream may or may not have water in it depending on the season. The route descends the slope on the north side of the streambed for 0.6 mile, to the point where the path forks. Bear right at the fork and cross the broken fenceline, then descend to Deep Creek, making a couple of switchbacks along the way.

At the Deep Creek crossing (elev. 5,320 feet) it is very easy to lose the trail. Angle upstream as you ford Deep Creek and look for the vague path as it climbs out the other side. The hard-to-follow route climbs a short distance to the southeast after crossing Deep Creek. It then makes a switchback to the left (northeast). Once past the switchback the route becomes easier to follow again. A short distance after passing the switchback the trail forks. The fork to the left is a now-abandoned section of trail. Bear right at the fork and continue to climb to the northeast. The USGS Lord Flat quad map shows the abandoned section of trail as it crosses Deep Creek, making the map somewhat incorrect for a short distance here.

The route continues to climb to the northeast, and makes a couple more switchbacks just before reaching the ridgeline. On the ridgeline, at 5,580 feet elevation, is the unmarked junction with Trail 1771. Trail 1771 south of this junction is a very vague path that leads south about 2.7 miles to a junction with Somers Point Trail. (See Hike 19 for a description of Somers Point Trail.)

On the ridgeline the view to the east is breathtaking. The road to Pittsburg Landing can be seen in the distance across the Snake River in Idaho. Turn left and head north along the ridgeline on Trail 1771. Flowers cover this semiopen ridge in late June and July. A short distance north of the junction the route enters an area that was burned several years ago. Approximately 0.3 mile from the junction where you reached the ridgeline is another unmarked junction.

At this junction a very vague path turns to the right (east). This path is the continuation of the Old Somers Creek Trail. (From this junction Old Somers Creek Trail descends steeply for about 3 miles to the abandoned and now burned Somers Ranch. Another 0.2 mile past the Somers Ranch Old Somers Creek Trail reaches a junction with Oregon Snake River Trail. The section of the Old Somers Creek Trail east of Trail 1771 is a very rough and steep hike.)

Continue north along the ridge from the junction. The route generally follows the ridgeline for the next 2.2 miles, losing 500 feet in elevation, to a junction with Trail 1750. The path along this ridge is rough and vague in spots, but as long as you stay close to the ridgeline you shouldn't lose the route.

At the junction with Trail 1750, turn left (south-southwest), and descend back into Deep Creek Canyon. The part of this hike from here to

Dorrance Cow Camp.

the junction with Western Rim Trail is also described in Hike 17. The route descends for 0.8 mile then fords Deep Creek. Once across the creek it is a 1.5-mile climb up to Western Rim Trail. At the junction turn right and retrace your steps for 1 mile to the northwest to Lord Flat Airstrip.

Options: Make this loop as a day hike from a base camp at Lord Flat Airstrip. The rim of Cow Creek Canyon to the west of the airstrip is an excellent place to look for wildlife. Bears and Elk are often viewed from the rocky outcroppings along the rim.

19 Somers Point Trail 1759, 1767

Highlights:	A hike along a flower-covered ridge overlooking Hells Canyon, from Summit Ridge to Somers Point.
Type of hike:	Out-and-back day hike or backpack.
Total distance:	7.6 miles.
Difficulty:	Moderate. Some routefinding skills are required to follow this route.
Best months:	Mid-June–September.
Elevation loss:	Approximately 500 feet.
Permits and fees:	None.
Maps:	Temperance Creek USGS quad.

Finding the trailhead: To Reach Lord Flat, drive east and north from Joseph, Oregon, on Oregon 350 (Imnaha Highway or Little Sheep Creek Highway)

Somers Point Trail 1759, 1767

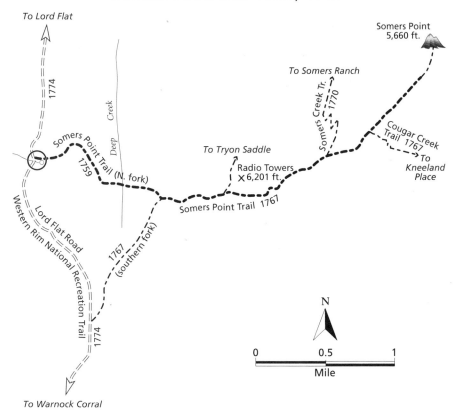

for 30 miles to Imnaha, Oregon. Take Hat Point Road (Forest Road 4240) east from Imnaha. After going 22 miles on Hat Point Road, turn left (north) on Lord Flat Road. Lord Flat Road (also known as Western Rim National Recreation Trail or Summit Ridge Trail) can be used by normal cars for about 4 miles to Warnock Corral; then it becomes necessary to have a four-wheel-drive vehicle with high clearance. It is about 11.7 miles from Warnock Corral to the junction with the northern fork of Somers Point Trail where this hike begins. GPS coordinates at the junction are 45 36.618 N 116 35.601 W.

Trailhead facilities: The junction has water available from a spring but has no other facilities.

Camping and services: Groceries can be obtained in Imnaha. The closest place for gas and other services is Joseph. Cell phone service is available in many spots along Western Rim Trail

For more information: USDA Forest Service at Wallowa Mountains Visitor Center in Enterprise, Oregon.

Key points:

- 0.0 Junction of Western Rim Trail and northern fork of Somers Point Trail 1759.
- 0.9 Crossing of Deep Creek.
- 1.2 Junction with southern fork of Somers Point Trail 1767. GPS 45 36.372 N 116 34.497 W.
- 1.7 Junction with Trail 1771. GPS 45 36.377 N 116 33.936 W.
- 2.6 Junction with Somers Creek Trail 1770. GPS 45 36.708 N 116 33.077 W.
- 3.0 Junction with Cougar Creek Trail 1767. GPS 45 36.857 N 116 32.585 W.
- 3.8 Somers Point.

The hike: Somers Point Trail climbs to the east as it leaves Western Rim Trail. At first the route follows an abandoned four-wheel-drive road that is reverting to a trail. After climbing through the woods for a short distance the tread enters a meadow. The path may be vague as it crosses the flower-covered meadow. The route

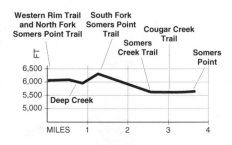

crosses a portion of the meadow (heading east) then follows the meadow's southern edge along the timber for a short distance. It then bears right (southeast) and re-enters the timber. After going through the timber for 150 yards you will enter another narrower meadow. Continue to the southeast through the center of this meadow and re-enter the woods (elev. 6,070 feet). Back in the woods the path heads to the southeast for a short distance; it then turns to the east and descends to Deep Creek, crossing another sloping meadow along the way.

The route crosses Deep Creek at 5,920 feet elevation, 0.9 mile from the junction with Western Rim Trail. There is usually no water along the Somers Point Trail after crossing Deep Creek. Once across the creek the path climbs to the east through woods and a sloping meadow to a rounded ridgetop. Atop the ridge the route turns right (south) and traverses the ridgetop meadow to the junction with the southern fork of Somers Point Trail 1767. There is a cairn and sign marking the junction at 6,160 feet elevation.

The southern fork of Somers Point Trail, which is another abandoned four-wheel-drive road at this point, heads southwest to connect with Western Rim Trail. This route reaches Western Rim Trail about 1.4 miles south of the point where the northern fork of Somers Point Trail left it.

Turn left and hike east along the ridgeline. For the next 1.8 miles you will be following Somers Point Trail 1767. Along the ridgeline the view of Hells Canyon really opens up to the right. When we hiked this trail in late June, we spotted cougar tracks in the mud along this ridgeline. In 0.5 mile you will come to the junction with Trail 1771. This is the end of the abandoned four-wheel-drive road. At the top of the hill to the east-northeast of this junction are some radio towers.

Trail 1771 turns left and descends a ridge to the north for 2.7 miles to the junction with Old Somers Creek Trail, then continues on to Tryon Saddle. (For a further description of Trail 1771, see Hikes 17 and 18.)

104

Near Somers Point.

Continue east from the junction with Trail 1771, and begin to descend along the semiopen slope. Paintbrush, Larkspur, and Lupine cover this slope in late June. About 0.4 mile from the junction with Trail 1771 the route re-enters the woods. It makes a couple of descending switchbacks as it drops to a low point on the ridgeline at 5,740 feet. The route then climbs over a small rise to the junction with Somers Creek Trail 1770. This junction is 2.6 miles from Western Rim Trail, at 5,620 feet elevation.

Somers Creek Trail turns to the left and switchbacks down to Somers Creek, then descends the creekbed to the abandoned (and now burned) Somers Ranch. It is approximately 4.5 miles and a 3,200-foot drop to Somers Ranch along Somers Creek Trail. Somers Creek Trail meets the Oregon Snake River Trail 0.3 mile below Somers Ranch. (See Hike 11 for details about Oregon Snake River Trail.)

Continue to the east-northeast from the junction on the Somers Point Trail, following the semiopen ridgeline. Many of the trees along this ridge were burned in the 1996 Salt Creek Fire. About 0.4 mile after passing the junction with Somers Creek Trail you will reach the junction with Cougar Creek Trail (also known as Kneeland Trail). At this junction Cougar Creek Trail, which is the continuation of Trail 1767, turns to the right (southwest). A sign marks the junction, but Cougar Creek Trail is hard to spot as it leaves Somers Point Trail. You are now 3 miles from Western Rim Trail, at 5,660 feet elevation. (For a description of the Cougar Creek Trail, see Hike 20.)

Departing from the junction with Cougar Creek Trail, Somers Point Trail heads to the northeast along the open rounded ridgeline. This ridge is a real flower garden in early summer. Lupine, Phlox, Cat's Ear Lilies, and many other flowers form a colorful foreground for the spectacular view of the canyons. Somers Point Trail fades past the junction. About 0.6 mile from the junction it ends completely a short distance to the left of the ridgeline. The spot where the trail ends is sometimes used as a makeshift campsite. From the end of the trail hike northeast, through the burnt timber and open meadows to the ridgeline for a fantastic view of Hells Canyon. Penstemon and Paintbrush color the rocks on the rim of Somers Point.

Options: For a loop hike, turn right on Cougar Creek Trail and follow it for 2 miles down to the Kneeland Place and the junction with High Trail 1751. Turn left on High Trail, and hike 6.5 miles northeast to the junction with Oregon Snake River Trail 1726. Turn left on Oregon Snake River Trail, and head northwest for 2.6 miles to the junction with Somers Creek Trail near Somers Ranch. From Somers Ranch, follow Somers Creek Trail back up to its junction with Somers Point Trail mentioned earlier. Allow three or four days to make this loop. See Hikes 22 and 11 for more information.

20 Cougar Creek Trail 1767

Highlights:	A steep connecting trail, from High Trail near the site of the abandoned Kneeland Place to a junction with Somers Point Trail 0.9 mile southwest of Somers Point. Cougar Creek Trail (also known as Kneeland Trail) can be hiked as a side trip off High Trail as described here or as a connecting route to reach High Trail from Western Rim Trail.
Type of hike:	Internal, out-and-back day hike from a base camp.
Total distance:	4.2 miles.
Difficulty:	Strenuous.
Best months:	May–October; however, access to Somers Point Trail from Summit Ridge may be blocked by snow until mid-June.
Elevation gain:	1,640 feet.
Permits and fees:	None.
Maps:	Temperance Creek USGS quad.

Finding the trailhead: To reach the junction of Cougar Creek Trail and High Trail where this hike begins, hike, jet boat, or fly to Pittsburg Ranch Ranger Station. See Hikes 10 and 11 for more information about getting to Pittsburg Ranch Ranger Station. From Pittsburg Ranch, hike southeast on Oregon Snake River Trail for 0.3 mile to the junction with Pittsburg Creek Trail. Turn right and hike southwest on Pittsburg Creek Trail for 2.1 miles to the junction with High Trail. (See Hike 21 for details about Pittsburg Creek Trail.) Turn left on High Trail and go 2.6 miles southwest to the junction with Cougar Creek Trail, where this description begins. (See Hike 22 for a description of High Trail.) The GPS coordinates at the junction of Cougar Creek Trail and High Trail are 45 36.351 N 116 31.449 W.

See Hike 19 for details about reaching the upper end of Cougar Creek Trail, where this hike ends.

Trailhead facilities: Kneeland Place, near the junction where this hike begins, has campsites and a spring, making it a good spot for a base camp.

Camping and services: See Hikes 11 and 19 for the closest services; none are available even remotely close to this trail.

For more information: USDA Forest Service at Wallowa Mountains Visitors Center in Enterprise, Oregon. For jet boat transportation to Pittsburg, contact Beamers Hells Canyon Tours in Clarkston, Washington, or Hells Canyon Adventures in Oxbow, Oregon. For flights to Pittsburg, contact Spence Air Service in Enterprise.

Key points:
- 0.0 Junction with High Trail near Kneeland Place.
- 0.1 Site of abandoned Kneeland Place and large spring.
- 0.7 First crossing of Cougar Creek.

Cougar Creek Trail 1767

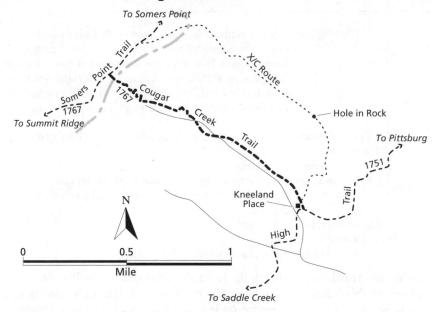

0.9   Second crossing of Cougar Creek.

2.1   Junction with Somers Point Trail. GPS 45 36.857 N 116 32.585 W.

The hike: Leaving the signed junction on High Trail, Cougar Creek Trail climbs gently to the northwest. A short distance from the junction, it passes the site of the old Kneeland Place. Only the rock cellar remains of the house at the Kneeland Place. Just past the cellar a large spring flows from beneath a grove of Thorn Brush. Both the cellar and spring are to the left of the trail.

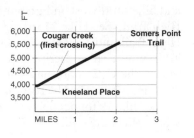

After passing the spring the trail enters the timber. This area was burned in the 1996 Salt Creek Fire but most of the trees survived. The trail, which is a bit vague in the open area from the junction to past the spring, becomes obvious after entering the timber.

The path climbs through the timber along the right side of Cougar Creek for 0.6 mile, then crosses it. The creek is usually dry at this crossing (El. 4,480 ft), as the water flows beneath the surface here. Two-tenths of a mile farther along the trail crosses Cougar Creek again (elev. 4,600 ft). In the spring when there is lots of water the trail may be covered by a couple inches of water for a few yards just below this crossing.

After crossing the creek the second time the now rough and rocky trail climbs steeply, making several switchbacks. The trail makes a switchback in the creekbed 0.7 mile farther up. There is a spring, which flows during wet weather on the left side of the trail in this switchback. Its water runs

down the trail for a short distance. The route makes several more switchbacks as it climbs the last 400 vertical feet to the ridgeline, then drops a few feet to the junction with Somers Point Trail, at 5,660 feet elevation. (See Hike 19 for a description of Somers Point Trail.)

Buttercups bloom along the trail in April and many other woodland flowers can be enjoyed through the spring and summer. The old Kneeland Place is a good campsite; there are few other acceptable spots along this trail. From midsummer through fall there may be no water above the spring at the Kneeland Place. Rattlesnakes are possible but not common along this trail, and ticks seem to be prevalent in the spring.

Options: For climbers and advanced hikers, an alternate off-trail route climbs the ridge north of the Kneeland Place. This scenic but strenuous route passes a large hole through the rock in the ridgeline (elev. 4,900 ft) that can be seen from the Kneeland Place. The route generally stays slightly to the left (southwest) of the ridgeline as it climbs. When the top of the ridge, south of Somers Point, is reached at 5,630 feet, head northwest then west on nearly flat ground to get to Somers Point Trail. Returning from this route, it is best to take Cougar Creek Trail back down to the Kneeland Place.

21 Pittsburg Creek Trail 1751A

Highlights: A steep internal hike, on a seldom-maintained trail, from the Oregon Snake River Trail near Pittsburg to High Trail. Pittsburg Creek Trail is much easier to follow than the north end of High Trail and is often used as an alternate for that route.

Type of hike: Internal connector; day hike or backpack.

Total distance: 2.1 miles.

Difficulty: Strenuous.

Best months: March–May and September–mid-November.

Elevation gain: 1,760 feet.

Permits and fees: None.

Maps: Grave Point, Kirkwood Creek, and Temperance Creek USGS quads. This trail is in the corners of three quad maps.

Finding the trailhead: Pittsburg Creek Trail begins at a junction with Oregon Snake River Trail 1726 0.3 mile south of Pittsburg Ranch Ranger Station. Hike, jet boat, or fly to Pittsburg Ranch Ranger Station. See Hikes 10 and 11 for more information about getting to Pittsburg Ranch Ranger Station. From Pittsburg Ranch, hike southeast on Oregon Snake River Trail for 0.3 mile to the junction with Pittsburg Creek Trail. The GPS coordinates at the junction are 45 37.667 N 116 28.403 W.

Trailhead facilities: Pittsburg Ranch Ranger Station has an airstrip and possible campsites.

Camping and services: The closest groceries are in Imnaha, Oregon. The closest place for gas and other services is Joseph, Oregon.

For more information: USDA Forest Service at Wallowa Mountains Visitor Center in Enterprise, Oregon. For air taxi to Pittsburg, contact Spence Air Service in Enterprise. For jet boat transportation to Pittsburg, contact Beamers Hells Canyon Tours in Clarkston, Washington, or Hells Canyon Adventures in Oxbow, Oregon.

Key points:

0.0 Junction with Oregon Snake River Trail 0.3 mile southeast of Pittsburg Ranch Ranger Station.

0.7 Hells Canyon Wilderness Boundary.

2.1 Junction with High Trail 1751. GPS 45 37.059 N 116 30.152 W.

The hike: From the junction with Oregon Snake River Trail, Pittsburg Creek Trail descends a few feet and crosses Pittsburg Creek. Once on the south side of the creek, it bears right and heads upstream along the blackberry-covered streambed. The trail crosses the creek three

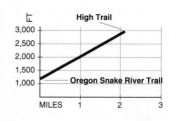

Pittsburg Creek Trail 1751A

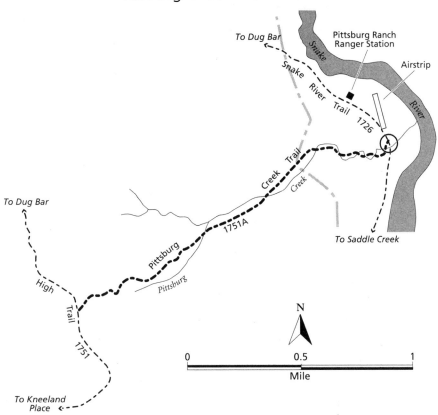

more times before reaching the wilderness boundary 0.7 mile from the junction with Oregon Snake River Trail. Just after the fourth creek crossing the trail climbs well above the creekbed. As it climbs a waterfall can be seen to the left in Pittsburg Creek.

After passing the wilderness boundary sign the course gets somewhat closer to the creek again. Soon it re-crosses the creek for the fifth time. At this crossing the tread actually goes right up the creek for a short distance. Once across it climbs out of the creekbed and heads up a small side gully. From the top of the small gully the path continues to climb and soon crosses the creek again. At this point (elev. 1,890 feet), the trail leaves the route marked on the Kirkwood Creek USGS Map. The route climbs well to the right of Pittsburg Creek, then winds its way, steeply up a small ridge, for 500 vertical feet, to the junction with High Trail 1751, at 2,970 feet elevation. (See Hike 22 for a description of High Trail.)

There is some Poison Ivy along Pittsburg Creek, and Rattlers can be encountered anywhere along this trail. Cactus bloom along this trail in late May and June and both feral and wild roses grow along the trail.

Climbing Pittsburg Creek Trail.

Options: Use Pittsburg Creek Trail and High Trail to reach a base camp at the old Kneeland Place. Then hike to Somers Point. See Hikes 22, 20, and 19 for details.

22 High Trail 1751

Highlights:	A hike along the bench lands high above the Snake River from Saddle Creek to a junction with Oregon Snake River Trail. High Trail is probably the best springtime elk viewing route in Hells Canyon.
Type of hike:	Long internal backpack with an extended shuttle hike option.
Total distance:	38.8 miles.
Difficulty:	Strenuous. Good routefinding and map reading skills are required to follow this trail north of the Pittsburg Trail junction.
Best months:	April–October
Elevation gain:	Approximately 4000 feet.
Permits and fees:	A Northwest Forest Pass is required if you are parking at Freezeout Trailhead.
Maps:	Hat Point, Old Timer Mountain, Temperance Creek, and Lord Flat USGS quads.

Finding the trailhead: Drive east and north from Joseph, Oregon, on Oregon Highway 350 (also known as Imnaha Highway or Little Sheep Creek Highway) for 30 miles to Imnaha, Oregon. From Imnaha, head south on County Road 727 for 12.5 miles to the junction with Forest Road 4230. Turn left on to FR 4230 and follow it 2.8 miles to its end at Freezeout Trailhead. Then hike east as described in Hike 28 on Saddle Creek Trail for 5.3 miles to the junction with High Trail. The GPS coordinates at the junction are 45 22.849 N 116 42.994 W.

Trailhead facilities: Some marginal campsites can be found near the junction with Saddle Creek Trail.

Camping and services: Camping is allowed at Freezeout Trailhead, which is 5.3 miles west of the junction where High Trail begins. There are no services close to this route. The closest groceries are in Imnaha. The closest place for gas and other services is Joseph.

For more information: USDA Forest Service at Wallowa Mountains Visitor Center in Enterprise, Oregon, or Larry Snook at the Sports Corral in Joseph.

Key points:
0.0	Junction with Saddle Creek Trail 5.3 miles east of Freezeout Trailhead.
4.6	Crossing of Twobuck Creek.
8.3	Cabin and North Fork of Hat Creek.
8.5	Second junction with Hat Creek Trail 1752.
8.7	Junction with Sluice Creek Trail 1748. GPS 45 25.885 N 116 38.142 W.
15.4	Junction with Trail 1741.
20.7	Junction with Dry Gulch Trail 1730. GPS 45 31.457 N 116 34.465 W.
21.9	Wisnor Place and junction with Temperance Creek Trail 1778. GPS 45 31.901 N 116 35.260 W.

High Trail 1751
(South half)

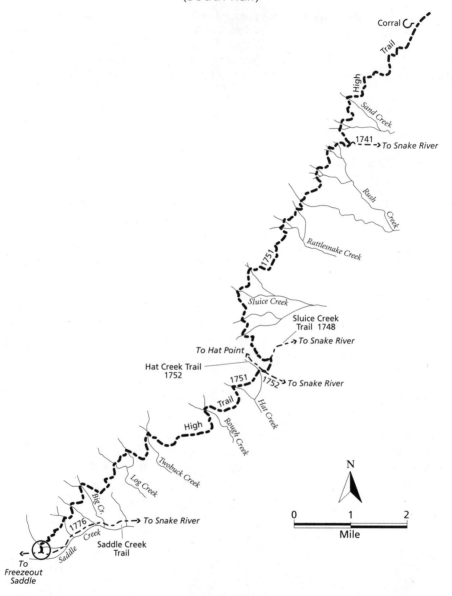

24.8	Hominy Saddle.
29.6	Junction with Salt Creek Trail 1785. GPS 45 35.347 N 116 32.554 W.
32.3	Junction with Cougar Creek Trail 1667 near the Kneeland Place.
34.9	Junction with Pittsburg Creek Trail 1751A. GPS 45 37.059 N 116 30.152 W.
38.8	Junction with Oregon Snake River Trail 1726. GPS 45 38.743 N 116 30.619 W.

High Trail 1751
(North half)

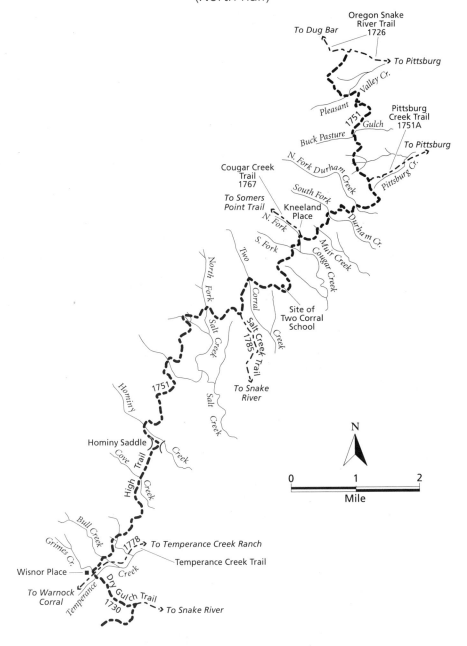

To Dug Bar

Oregon Snake
River Trail
1726

To Pittsburg

Valley Cr.

Pleasant

Gulch

1751

Pittsburg
Creek Trail
1751A

Buck Pasture

To Pittsburg

N. Fork Durham Creek

Pittsburg Cr.

Cougar Creek
Trail
1767

South Fork

To Somers
Point Trail

Kneeland
Place

N. Fork

Durham Cr.

S. Fork

Muir Creek

Cougar Creek

North Fork

Two

Corral

Site of
Two Corral
School

Salt Creek

Salt Creek Trail
1785

Creek

To Snake
River

1751

Salt
Creek

Hominy

Hominy Saddle

Creek

Cove Creek

High Trail

N

Bull Creek

0   1   2
Mile

Grimes Cr.

1778

To Temperance Creek Ranch

Temperance Creek Trail

Wisnor Place

Creek

To Warnock
Corral

Dry Gulch Trail

Temperance

1730

To Snake River

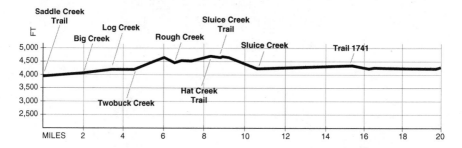

The hike: High Trail heads north from the junction with Saddle Creek Trail, through the old burn area of the Freezeout fire. You will cross five streambeds, some of which may be dry, in the first 2 miles before reaching Big Creek. In the last streambed before reaching Big Creek there is a spring a short distance below the trail. The route drops steeply for a short distance, just before crossing Big Creek (elev. 4,030 ft).

After crossing Big Creek the track crosses three more draws, some with small streams, before reaching Log Creek. It crosses Log Creek at 4,175 feet elevation, then climbs slightly to a rounded ridgeline. The trace then crosses the ridgeline and descends very gently, making a couple of switchbacks before reaching Twobuck Creek, 4.6 miles from Saddle Creek Trail. Be especially watchful for Elk between Log Creek and Twobuck Creek. These large animals are very common here in the winter and spring.

The tread crosses a long, flat topped, ridge 1.4 mile after crossing Twobuck Creek. On the ridge (elev. 4,620 ft), there is a path turning to the right (south). This path goes to a campsite farther out the ridge. High Trail bears left and heads north-northwest into Rough Creek Canyon. The route descends a couple hundred feet as it traverses to Rough Creek, 0.5 mile after crossing the long ridge. You cross the two forks of Rough Creek, 6 miles into the hike, then turn to the east. At Rough Creek the trail leaves the old burn area mentioned above.

The course traverses out of Rough Creek Canyon and gently ascends to the next ridgeline. Crossing the ridgeline the tread turns left and heads northwest, staying nearly level for 0.3 mile along the timbered slope, to Hat Creek. You cross Hat Creek then head northeast, through the timber, for 0.6 mile to the North Fork of Hat Creek. Just after crossing the creek there is a cabin on the right side of the trail. A short distance past the cabin is the first junction with Hat Creek Trail 1752. (See Hike 27 for details about Hat Creek Trail.)

For the next 0.1 mile High Trail and Hat Creek Trail follow the same route. Head east at the junction to the second junction with Hat Creek Trail. Several excellent campsites are located next to the trail between the junctions. The second junction with Hat Creek Trail is 8.5 miles from Saddle Creek Trail, at 4,690 feet elevation. At the second junction High Trail bears to the left (north). The junction with Sluice Creek Trail 1748 is reached 0.2 mile after passing the second junction with Hat Creek Trail. (See Hike 25 for a description of Sluice Creek Trail.) At the junction with Sluice Creek Trail, High Trail turns to the left (northwest), entering the burn area of the 1996

116

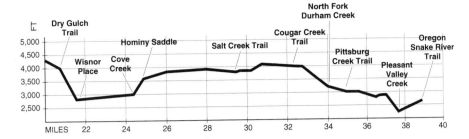

Salt Creek Fire. This was a fast-moving fire that burned most of the grass and small brush but left much of the timber intact or only partially burned. In fact, this fire generally improved the range conditions.

The trace winds in and out of the draws in the head of the Sluice Creek drainage for the next 3.2 miles. In this section there is timber on the north slopes, but the south slopes are mostly open. There are several small stream crossings but few campsites along these rugged slopes and the track is braided in a few spots. This braiding was caused by stock, mostly sheep. The trail descends about 400 vertical feet to the crossing of the Main Fork of Sluice Creek, then traverses out of the Sluice Creek drainage to a broad ridgeline.

The course crosses the broad ridgeline into the Rattlesnake Creek drainage. Rattlesnake Creek is a northern fork of Sluice Creek. You will then traverse an open slope to another ridgeline. From this ridge the route heads generally north crossing a small draw. The remains of a small structure sit to the left of the trail 150 yards after crossing the draw. The structure may have been a tent platform or a cabin. The path crosses a couple more tiny draws then comes out on a ridge at 4,280 feet elevation.

After crossing the ridge the track cuts back into another draw through the partially burned timber. It crosses a couple more small draws then traverses back out on a more open slope. You will cross one more side draw before reaching the ridgeline dividing the Rattlesnake Creek and Rush Creek drainages. The Rush Creek drainage was more severely burned than were the Sluice Creek and Rattlesnake Creek drainages. After you cross the divide, most of the trees you will see were killed in the fire.

Through the Rush Creek drainage, the path generally stays close to the steep cliffs and rock pinnacles that form the east face of Summit Ridge. The route crosses seven draws with intermittent streams in them in the 2 miles to the junction with Trail 1741. While crossing the heavily burned headwaters of the Rush Creek drainage, High Trail stays at a fairly constant elevation of between 4,200 and 4,300 feet. About halfway across the drainage it crosses a broad open ridge. I saw many Elk in this area when I checked out this trail in November.

The junction with Trail 1741 is reached on another broad ridge just before leaving the Rush Creek drainage. Trail 1741 descends to the east to meet Rush Creek and Sand Creek Trails. (Rush Creek and Sand Creek Trails share the same trail number: 1742.) Both Rush Creek Trail and Sand Creek Trail descend to join Oregon Snake River Trail along the Snake River.

High Trail heads northwest from the junction with Trail 1741, climbing gently to cross a ridgeline. The course then traverses six draws in the next 3.6 miles as it crosses the rugged head of the Sand Creek drainage. As you hike out of the Sand Creek drainage, the terrain becomes slightly less rugged. A short walk down the ridge to the southeast of the trail as you leave the Sand Creek drainage offers some great viewpoints. If you are here in the spring watch for the many Elk that inhabit these grass covered slopes and benches.

After leaving the Sand Creek drainage the path traverses more gently along thinly timbered slopes. You will pass an abandoned sheep corral then descend a small rounded ridge to a saddle. If you walk a few yards to the left of the trail, in the saddle, you will get a birds eye view of the Wisnor Place in Temperance Creek Canyon, far below to the north.

From the saddle High Trail rounds a high point on the ridgeline to the junction of Dry Gulch Trail 1730, at 3,980 feet elevation. Dry Gulch Trail turns right at the junction and descends for 3 miles to meet Oregon Snake River Trail. A short side trip out Dry Gulch Trail allows a view of the Snake River and Temperance Creek Ranch.

High Trail turns left (west) at the junction with Dry Gulch Trail. The braided path now begins its steep descent into Temperance Creek Canyon. The tread makes nine switchbacks, then turns to the northwest on the open slope, just above a brush-choked draw. As you get closer to the bottom of Temperance Creek Canyon the path enters open partly burned woods. The route fords Temperance Creek at 2,840 feet elevation. Just after crossing the creek the vague route forks. Bear right at the fork and head north. You will cross a meadow then climb slightly to the Wisnor Place and the junction with Temperance Creek Trail. The Wisnor Place is 1.2 miles from the junction with Dry Gulch Trail and 21.9 miles from Saddle Creek Trail. (For a description of Temperance Creek Trail, see Hike 24.)

The abandoned cabin at the Wisnor Place is becoming quite rundown, but the area around it makes a great campsite. Water is available from Grimes Creek behind the cabin and from Temperance Creek. From the Wisnor Place a side hike on an unmaintained path up the ridge to the northwest is well worth the effort. Grimes Creek has a waterfall a short distance up this path. The unmaintained path crosses Grimes Creek just above the falls and continues on up the ridges and benches to offer some great views of the canyons below. Watch for agates along the side path.

High Trail crosses Temperance Creek Trail next to the Wisnor Cabin, then crosses Grimes Creek and heads north-northeast. The course traverses an open slope to cross Bull Creek 0.3 mile from the Wisnor Place. After crossing Bull Creek the path bears left for a few yards, makes a switchback to the right, and then climbs to a ridgeline before continuing its traverse. The route crosses a couple of tiny streams (which may be dry) and rounds a couple of ridges before reaching Cove Creek, 2.2 miles from the Wisnor Place. After crossing Cove Creek the tread climbs fairly steeply up a draw for 0.7 mile to Hominy Saddle, at 3,576 feet elevation. Leaving Hominy Saddle the course traverses northwest into lightly wooded Hominy Creek Canyon. The route crosses Hominy Creek then climbs and traverses to a ridgeline.

From the ridge 0.9 mile north of Hominy Saddle the track heads back into a draw, crossing a semiopen slope with some burnt timber. The trace crosses the draw, then traverses out on an open slope to a rounded ridgeline (elev. 3,760 ft.), which it crosses to reenter the timber. The tread traverses through the timber heading north-northwest, and crossing a couple of small draws, to the South Fork of Salt Creek, which it crosses at 3,780 feet elevation. Once across the creek the course heads east out onto another rounded ridgeline. It rounds the ridge and enters an area of almost completely burned timber. Once through the burned area the trail works in and out of several draws at the head of the North Fork of Salt Creek. You then head generally east on an open slope to another rounded ridge and the junction with Salt Creek Trail 1785. This junction, at 3,880 feet elevation, is 29.6 miles from Saddle Creek Trail. (See Hike 23 for details about Salt Creek Trail.)

Leaving the junction with Salt Creek Trail, High Trail quickly reenters the timber and crosses a brushy gully. The timber here is only lightly burned with most of the mature trees surviving. Many Dogtooth Violets (also known as Glacier Lilies) bloom here in mid-April. The trail crosses a tiny stream, which may be dry, and soon reaches Two Corral Creek. There used to be a trail up Two Corral Creek to Somers Point Trail, but it is now abandoned. After passing Two Corral Creek the trace leaves the timber and crosses more open slopes with only scattered trees. It traverses in and out of a couple draws, which may be covered with Buttercups and Yellowbells in early spring, to broad open ridge. This ridge is the site of the old Two Corral School (also known as Pittsburg School #69). The remains of the school are hard to find, however. Classes were held here from 1908 to 1920.

After passing the old school site the trail heads northwest back into the draw at the head of the South Fork of Cougar Creek, crossing a couple of small gullies along the way. On the ridge between these small gullies there is a rusting wood stove lying just below the trail. Another quarter of a mile through the woods is the North Fork of Cougar Creek. Watch for Dogtooth Violets along this stretch of the route. The junction with the Cougar Creek Trail 1767 (also known as Kneeland Trail) is reached 0.1 mile after the crossing. A rusting old hay rake sits next to the sign at the junction. The site of the abandoned Kneeland Place and a good campsite is a few yards up Cougar Creek Trail from the junction. (See Hike 20 for a description of Cougar Creek Trail.) The elevation at the junction is 3,990 feet.

Departing from the junction with Cougar Creek Trail, you will soon cross another rounded open ridge and then cut back into Muir Creek, which will probably be dry. A short distance before reaching the ridge the trail appears to fork. The path that goes straight ahead is just a stock path, so bear to the left. There is another stock path here that heads some distance to the southeast, out the ridge between Cougar Creek and Muir Creek, for a good side trip. This ridge is a likely place to see Elk in the spring. It also has many wild flowers.

High Trail crosses another ridgeline then cuts back again, through thin timber, to the South Fork of Durham Creek. It then traverses out to another ridgeline, which it descends for a short distance. The route then turns to the

Saddle Creek Canyon from High Trail.

left (northeast) and begins its steep descent to the North Fork of Durham Creek. Where the trail turns off the ridge it leaves the older route marked on the Temperance Creek USGS quad map. The old trail, which is no longer used, soon becomes very vague. Turn left off the ridge and wind down through the many steep switchbacks to the North Fork of Durham Creek (elev. 3,200 ft). Then traverse east on the open slope to another ridge. What appears to be a ditch crosses this ridge just below the trail. This "ditch" is an abandoned section of Pittsburg Creek Trail. The depth with which it is worn into the ground indicates heavy stock use in the past. Bear left at the ridgeline and descend to the northwest through thin timber for a quarter of a mile to the junction with Pittsburg Creek Trail 1751A. (See Hike 21 for a description of Pittsburg Creek Trail.) At the junction (elev. 2,970 ft) Pittsburg Creek Trail bears to the right (northeast) and is the much more heavily used trail. Pittsburg Creek Trail is used as a shortcut down to Pittsburg on the Snake River.

High Trail goes straight ahead (north) at the signed junction, but it receives limited use past here. Past the junction the tread soon crosses a gully, climbs a few feet to a small flat area, then reaches a ridgeline at 2,970 feet elevation. The vague course then descends through the ponderosa pine timber and crosses a couple small gullies. After crossing the second tiny gully the trace begins to climb gently on an open slope. This slope gets a good bloom of Balsamroot in late April and early May. The tread crosses several more small draws and ridges on slopes that bloom profusely with Woodland Stars in late April, to the ridge that divides Pittsburg and Buckpasture Creeks. On the ridge the track bears left and descends slightly through scattered timber. It then winds down and crosses a couple of gullies at the head of Buckpasture Gulch. The trail is obscure to follow in places as it descends into the Buckpasture Creek drainage. The Upper Buckpasture drainage was almost completely burned in the 1996 Salt Creek Fire.

As the route leaves the Buckpasture Creek drainage it first climbs a bit, then traverses a steep open slope covered with Woodland Star and Balsamroot. There is also some Sumac on this slope. The tread crosses a spur ridge and shortly comes to the ridge dividing the Buckpasture and Pleasant Valley Creek drainages at 2,800 feet elevation. Leaving the ridge it descends, heading northwest for 0.2 mile, before starting a series of switchbacks, taking it down the open hillside to Pleasant Valley Creek. The trail crosses Pleasant Valley Creek 37.7 miles from the junction with Saddle Creek, at 2,240 feet elevation, then enters a small area of burnt timber.

Leaving the timber the route climbs steeply for 0.5 mile, gaining 400 feet elevation. Then it traverses an open slope for another 0.5 mile to the junction with Oregon Snake River Trail 1726, at 2,610 feet elevation. This junction is the north end of High Trail 1751. (See Hike 11 for a description of Oregon Snake River Trail.)

Options: High Trail can be used as an alternate route for the one mentioned in Hikes 10 and 11 when making the long backpack from Freezeout Trailhead to Dug Bar. Using High Trail adds about 10 extra miles, but it allows you to hike along the benches rather than along the river for about half of the total distance to Dug Bar Trailhead.

23 Salt Creek Trail 1785

Highlights:	A hike from a junction with High Trail to the Snake River and a junction with Oregon Snake River Trail. Salt Creek Trail first follows a ridge, with views of nearby benches and lots of elk, and then descends steeply to the junction with Oregon Snake River Trail at the mouth of Salt Creek.
Type of hike:	Internal connector; backpack.
Total distance:	3.4 miles.
Difficulty:	Strenuous.
Best months:	March–May and September–mid-November.
Elevation loss:	2,560 feet.
Permits and fees:	None.
Maps:	Temperance Creek USGS quad.

Finding the trailhead: Salt Creek Trail begins at a junction with High Trail 29.6 miles south of Saddle Creek. You can reach the junction by following the driving directions in Hike 28, then hiking 5.3 miles east to the junction with High Trail and following that trail to the junction. The closest way to reach Salt Creek Trail from a road is via Somers Point Trail and Cougar Creek Trail. Using these two trails brings you to High Trail 2.7 miles north of the junction with Salt Creek Trail. See Hikes 19, 20, and 22 for details. The GPS coordinates at the junction are 45 35.347 N 116 32.554 W.

Salt Creek Trail 1785

Salt Creek Trail ends at a junction with Oregon Snake River Trail 1726 13.8 miles north of Saddle Creek and 33 miles southeast of Dug Bar Trailhead. See Hikes 10 and 11 for a description of Oregon Snake River Trail.

The lower end of Salt Creek Trail may also be reached by jet boat from Hells Canyon Dam boat launch.

Trailhead facilities: None.

Camping and services: See Hike 19 for the closest services; none are available even remotely close to this trail. Cell phones sometimes work along the upper part of this trail but do not count on it.

For more information: USDA Forest Service at Wallowa Mountains Visitor Center in Enterprise, Oregon, or Hells Canyon Visitor Center 1 mile north of Hells Canyon Dam next to the launch site. For jet boat transportation, contact Hells Canyon Adventures in Oxbow, Oregon.

Key points:
- 0.0 Junction with High Trail 29.6 miles north of Saddle Creek Trail.
- 2.6 Trail begins steep descent off ridge.
- 3.3 Salt Creek Cabin.
- 3.4 Junction with Oregon Snake River Trail 1726. GPS 45 33.248 N 116 31.687 W.

The hike: Salt Creek Trail leaves High Trail on a rounded ridge at 3,880 feet elevation. From the signed junction Salt Creek Trail heads southeast and soon begins to descend into a small valley. At times this valley is covered with Buttercups and Shooting Stars. This part of the trail is difficult to see, but the route is not hard to follow. The trail begins to traverse out

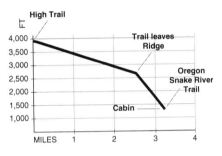

of the right side of the valley about 0.5 mile from the junction with High Trail. It traverses, dropping gently out to a ridgeline just above an old corral. There is some rusting farm equipment near the corral (elev. 3,400 ft).

After passing the corral the route crosses a draw that is choked with Thorn Brush below the trail. The trail then climbs very slightly to the top of a rounded ridge. It then descends along the open, sometimes steep hillside, crossing a couple more small draws to a pocket close to the top of the ridge, at 3,080 feet elevation. There was once another corral in this little flat pocket. Balsamroot, Yellow Bells, and Lupine add color to these slopes. The bloom starts in mid April.

The trail is vague leaving the pocket. It descends to the east, winding down for a short distance, then bears slightly to the right and traverses the open hillside. There are several stock trails that traverse nearly level from the pocket. These stock trails fade out in a short distance. The route reaches a ridgeline 0.6 mile after leaving the pocket. You then descend along the left side of the ridgeline to a saddle. The path crosses through the saddle and traverses around a high point on the ridge to another saddle, at 2,610 feet elevation.

Once across this second saddle the trail begins its steep descent toward the Snake River. It twists and drops steeply for 0.9 mile to Salt Creek Cabin, losing 1,250 feet in elevation. The old cabin is on the right side of the trail. After the trail passes the cabin, the junction with Oregon Snake River Trail

Salt Creek Cabin.

1726 is another 0.1 mile. (See Hike 10 for a description of Oregon Snake River Trail.)

Options: Use the upper 2.5 miles of Salt Creek Trail as a side trip while you are backpacking along High Trail.

24 Temperance Creek Trail 1778

Highlights:	A hike from Warnock Corral on Summit Ridge down through the rugged Temperance Creek Canyon to Temperance Creek Ranch on the Snake River, passing a long abandoned homestead along the way.
Type of hike:	Shuttle day hike or out-and-back backpack.
Total distance:	11.2 miles.
Difficulty:	Strenuous.
Best months:	Mid-June–September to the Wisnor Place; March–May and September–November below there. September is the best month for hiking the entire trail.
Elevation loss:	5,530 feet.
Permits and fees:	None.
Maps:	Hat Point, Old Timer Mountain, and Temperance Creek USGS quads. Only a small part of this trail is on the Old Timer Mountain quad.

Temperance Creek Trail 1778

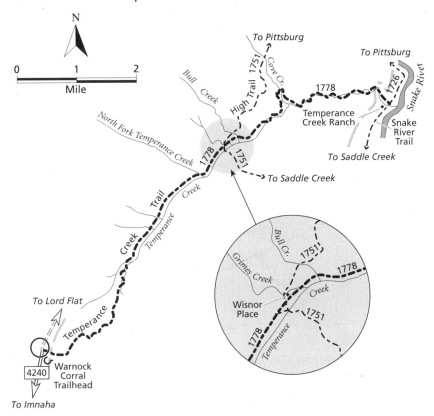

Finding the trailhead: To reach Warnock Corral, drive east and north from Joseph, Oregon, on Oregon Highway 350 (also known as Imnaha Highway or Little Sheep Creek Highway) for 30 miles to Imnaha, Oregon. Then take Hat Point Road (Forest Road 4240) east from Imnaha. After going 22 miles on Hat Point Road, turn left (north) on Lord Flat Road. Lord Flat Road can be used by cars without four-wheel drive for the 4.3 miles to Warnock Corral. The trail leaves from the south end of the grass-covered parking area. The GPS coordinates at the trailhead are 45 28.989 N 116 38.935 W.

A jet boat pickup from Temperance Creek Ranch at the end of this hike can be arranged.

Trailhead facilities: The trailhead has horse facilities, restrooms, and a few unimproved campsites.

Camping and services: The trailhead has a few primitive campsites. The closest groceries are in Imnaha. The closest place for gas and other services is Joseph. Cell phone service is generally available from the rim of the canyon 0.4 mile east of the trailhead.

For more information: USDA Forest Service at Wallowa Mountains Visitor Center in Enterprise, Oregon. For jet boat pickup, contact Hells Canyon Adventures in Oxbow, Oregon, or Beamers Hells Canyon Tours in Clarkston, Washington.

Key points:
    0.0   Warnock Corral Trailhead.
    5.5   North Fork of Temperance Creek.
    6.3   Wisnor Place and junction with High Trail. GPS 45 31.901 N 116 35.260 W.
    8.4   Cove Creek.
    11.2   Temperance Creek Ranch. GPS 45 32.414 N 116 31.901 W.

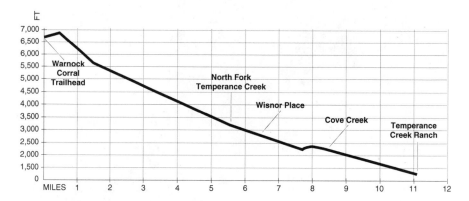

The hike: Leaving Warnock Corral Trailhead the trail heads east through recently burned lodgepole pine woods. It climbs gently for 0.4 mile to the top of a rise on the rim of Hells Canyon at 6,850 feet elevation. Just after crossing the rise the path bears left and traverses an open slope. After traversing 250 yards the trail forks. There is a sign at the fork. Bear right (northeast) at the sign and begin to descend into the canyon.

The trace makes 31 switchbacks in the next mile as it descends to a timbered saddle at 5,550 feet elevation. This section of trail offers the best views of the canyon and the Seven Devils Mountains across it. The Snake River can be seen from a couple of spots. Wildflowers cover the open slopes in early summer. There is a possible campsite in the saddle but no water.

The trail is steep in spots above the saddle but after crossing it the steep descent becomes constant. After crossing the saddle the trail winds and switchbacks down a gully. The timber in this gully is partially burned but many green trees remain. The route descends the steep gully for 1.6 miles, crossing Temperance Creek, which is a small intermittent, stream here, four times. Then the grade moderates some and continues on down the canyon, with the creek to the right of the trail.

The track crosses the North Fork of Temperance Creek (elev. 3,160 ft.) 5.5 miles from the trailhead. As the course enters an open meadow 0.6 mile past the North Fork of Temperance Creek it forks. The trail to the right is a shortcut to High Trail 1751. Bear left (northeast) at the fork and continue another

Wisnor Place.

0.2 mile to the Wisnor Place and the junction with High Trail at 2,880 feet elevation. (See Hike 22 for a description of High Trail.)

Leaving the Wisnor Place the route descends for a short distance and crosses Grimes Creek, which will probably be dry here. You will ford Bull Creek 0.3 mile from the Wisnor Place as the track enters the timber. The timber here was partly burned in the 1996 Salt Creek Fire. One mile below the Wisnor Place after crossing another small stream the route fords Temperance Creek. This is the first of the 18 times you will have to ford Temperance Creek between the Wisnor Place and Temperance Creek Ranch.

After being close to or in the creek for another 0.2 mile the trace begins to climb. The path climbs, fairly steeply in spots and making a couple of switchbacks, to cross three spur ridges before descending into Cove Creek Canyon. On these rocky spurs are good viewpoints of the canyons below. A few cacti line the trail on these rocky slopes. The USGS Temperance Creek quad map shows this part of the trail incorrectly. The course makes a couple more switchbacks before reaching Cove Creek. You will cross Cove Creek then turn right to descend along its north side.

The track follows Cove Creek to the southeast for 0.1 mile then bears east along Temperance Creek. Temperance Creek rushes over a small falls shortly after the trail rejoins it. In the next 1.9 miles to the Hells Canyon Wilderness Boundary, the route fords Temperance Creek 12 times. Many spots along this section are densely lined with Poison Ivy. After passing the Wilderness Boundary you will have to ford Temperance Creek four more times before reaching Temperance Creek Ranch and the junction with Oregon Snake River Trail 1726. At the junction (elev. 1,320 feet), you are 4.9 miles from the Wisnor Place and 11.2 miles from Warnock Corral Trailhead.

The lower section may be very hot during the summer. Rattlesnakes and creek crossings can be a problem in the section below the Wisnor Place.

Options: To make a long but rewarding backpack, use Temperance Creek Trail as an access route to High Trail or Oregon Snake River Trail; then follow one of those trails to Dug Bar Trailhead. High Trail joins the Oregon Snake River 23 miles before reaching Dug Bar Trailhead. See Hikes 10, 11, and 22 for more information.

25 Sluice Creek Trail 1748

Highlights:	A hike from a junction with Oregon Snake River Trail up Sluice Creek Canyon to a junction with High Trail on the broad benches below Hat Point.
Type of hike:	Internal connector with a loop option.
Total distance:	4.2 miles.
Difficulty:	Strenuous.
Best months:	April–May and September–October.
Elevation gain:	3,230 feet.
Permits and fees:	None.
Maps:	Old Timer Mountain and Hat Point USGS quads.

Finding the trailhead: Sluice Creek Trail is an internal trail that begins at the junction with the Oregon Snake River Trail, 4.3 miles down river from Saddle Creek, and 42.5 miles upriver from the Dug Bar Trailhead. The easiest way to get to this junction is by jet boat from Hells Canyon Dam. If you are going to hike to the junction of the Sluice Creek Trail and the Oregon Snake River Trail the easiest way is to park at the Freezeout Trailhead and hike from there. From Freezeout Trailhead take the Saddle Creek Trail for 11.1 miles to its junction with the Oregon Snake River Trail. See Hike 28 for driving directions to Freezeout Trailhead and a trail description of Saddle Creek Trail.

At the junction turn left (north) on the Oregon Snake River Trail and hike 4.3 miles to the junction with the Sluice Creek Trail where this hike begins. For a description of this section of the Oregon Snake River Trail see Hike 10. The GPS coordinates at the junction of the Sluice Creek Trail and Oregon Snake River Trail are 45 26.693 N 116 35.199 W.

The junction with High Trail at the upper end of this hike is 3.8 miles east of Hat Point Trailhead. (See Hike 27 and Hike 22 for more information.)

Trailhead facilities: Some possible campsites are close to the Snake River, but there are no other facilities.

Camping and services: The closest groceries are in Imnaha, Oregon. The closest place for gas and other services is Joseph, Oregon.

For more information: USDA Forest Service at Wallowa Mountains Visitor Center in Enterprise, Oregon, or Hells Canyon Visitor Center 1 mile north

Sluice Creek Trail 1748

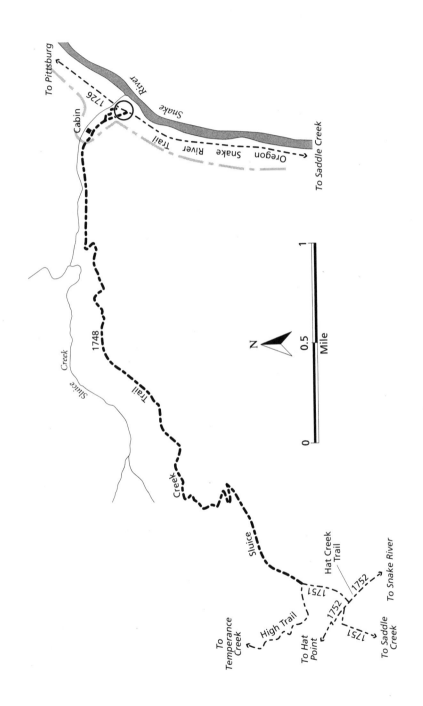

of Hells Canyon Dam next to the launch site. For jet boat transportation, contact Hells Canyon Adventures in Oxbow, Oregon.

Key points:
 0.0 Junction with Oregon Snake River Trail 4.3 miles north of Saddle Creek.
 0.3 Cabin.
 4.2 Junction with High Trail 1751. GPS 45 25.885 N 116 38.142 W.

The hike: From the signed junction with Oregon Snake River Trail, Sluice Creek Trail climbs to the northwest, passing a campsite. Next to the campsite another trail bears to the right. This short trail also connects with Oregon Snake River Trail next to Sluice Creek. After passing the campsite the route enters the brushy canyon bottom of Sluice Creek. Up the canyon bottom 0.2 mile, there is an abandoned cabin next to the trail.

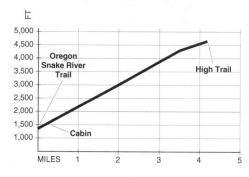

Passing the cabin the trail continues up the brushy canyon bottom for a short distance. It then bears slightly to the left and leaves the brush for an open slope. For the next 2.1 miles the route ascends the open slope, making a few switchbacks as it climbs to the west-southwest. This area was burned in the August 1996 Salt Creek Fire, so what little timber there was in the

Sluice Creek Cabin.

130

small draws is now dead snags. After climbing to 3,300 feet elevation, about 2.5 miles from Oregon Snake River Trail, the route begins a series of switchbacks. In these switchbacks the trail climbs 900 vertical feet in just over 1 mile. On this slope most of the timber escaped the fire and is still green.

At the top of the switchbacks the trail bears to the right and continues to climb, at a somewhat gentler grade, along an open ridge. After climbing along the ridge for 0.6 mile the tread reaches the junction with High Trail at 4,590 feet elevation.

There is a great campsite on High Trail 0.2 mile to the left (southwest).

Options: To make a loop, turn left at the junction with High Trail and hike 0.2 mile to the junction with Hat Creek Trail 1752. Turn left again on Hat Creek Trail and descend for 3.6 miles to Oregon Snake River Trail. Then follow Snake River Trail for 3.9 miles back to the mouth of Sluice Creek, completing the loop.

26 Waterspout Creek Trail 1753

Highlights:	A steep connecting route between Hat Creek Trail and Oregon Snake River Trail below Hat Point Lookout. Most of this trail passes through the burn area of the August 1996 Salt Creek Fire. Because there were very few trees to burn, the fire did little but improve the range conditions here. The name *Waterspout* is a local word for a flash flood in a steep creekbed.
Type of hike:	Internal connector.
Total distance:	2.4 miles.
Difficulty:	Strenuous.
Best months:	April–May and September–October.
Elevation loss:	2,560 feet.
Permits and fees:	None.
Maps:	Old Timer Mountain USGS quad.

Finding the trailhead: From Joseph, Oregon, take Oregon 350 for 30 miles northeast to the small town of Imnaha, Oregon. From Imnaha, drive east on Hat Point Road (Forest Road 4240) for 22 miles to the junction with Forest Road 315. Turn right (east) on FR 315, and follow it for 2 miles to Hat Point Lookout and Trailhead. The trail begins at a small parking area a short distance before reaching the main Hat Point Lookout parking area. Hike down Hat Creek Trail to the east for 5 miles to the junction with Waterspout Creek Trail (as described in Hike 27). The GPS coordinates at the junction are 45 24.692 N 116 37.281 W.

The trail ends at a junction with Oregon Snake River Trail. This junction is 2.7 miles downriver (north) from Saddle Creek or 44.1 miles upriver from Dug Bar Trailhead. The junction is just south of Waterspout Creek. (See Hike 10 for a description of Oregon Snake River Trail.)

Waterspout Creek Trail 1753

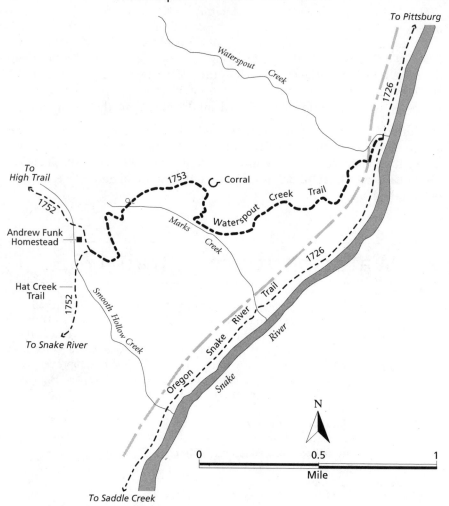

Trailhead facilities: The abandoned Andrew Funk Homestead has some possible campsites.

Camping and services: The closest groceries are in Imnaha, Oregon. The closest place for gas and other services is Joseph.

For more information: USDA Forest Service at Wallowa Mountains Visitors Center in Enterprise, Oregon. For jet boat transportation, contact Hells Canyon Adventures in Oxbow, Oregon.

Key points:
- 0.0 Junction with Hat Creek Trail 1752 5 miles east of Hat Point near Andrew Funk Homestead.
- 1.0 Corral.
- 2.4 Junction with Oregon Snake River Trail. GPS 45 24.989 N 116 35.831 W.

Nonpoisonous bull snake, aka gopher snake.

The hike: As you leave the signed junction with Hat Creek Trail you will traverse an open slope heading southeast. Soon the route rounds the ridgeline and begins to descend to the northwest into Marks Creek Canyon. The track descends along an open slope for 0.3 mile then switchbacks down to Marks Creek. Marks Creek may be dry, so don't depend on it for water. Shortly after crossing Marks Creek the path crosses another small draw. There is

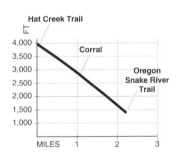

a wet weather spring in this draw a short distance to the left of, and above the trail.

After passing the draw the course heads east on a sloping bench to an abandoned sheep corral. Parts of this bench were once cultivated as were many of the benches in Hells Canyon. The trail turns right at the corral (elev. 2,860 ft.) and drops back down to Marks Creek. It then turns left along the creekbed and descends to another lower bench. On this lower sloping bench the route bears left and descends the slope for about three-quarters of a mile. It then winds and switchbacks steeply down a small ridge south of Waterspout Creek to the junction with Oregon Snake River Trail, at 1,400 feet elevation.

The infrequently maintained and lightly used Waterspout Creek Trail is steep for much of its length. Sheep have heavily used the bench areas in past years and the trail is braided in spots so some routefinding may be required to follow it. Possible campsites are available on both of the benches along the trail but water may be a problem at times. Even considering these difficulties descending this trail is probably easier than continuing down Hat Creek Trail to the Snake River if that is your destination.

Options: Several extended loop backpacks are possible by combining Waterspout Creek Trail with other trails in the area. See Hikes 27, 28, 22, and 10 for details. A jet boat pickup can be arranged if you wish to make this a one-way hike.

27 Hat Creek Trail 1752

Highlights:	A hike from Hat Point Lookout to the Snake River in the deepest part of Hells Canyon. This trail accesses High Trail and Waterspout Creek Trail.
Type of hike:	Long out-and-back day hike or backpack, with loop and jet boat shuttle options.
Total distance:	14.2 miles.
Difficulty:	Moderate from Hat Point to High Trail; strenuous beyond there. Some routefinding is required between the junction with High Trail and the junction with Oregon Snake River Trail.
Best months:	Mid-June–October. The lower part of Hat Creek Trail between High Trail and the Snake River is generally free of snow from April through mid-November. The best time to hike the entire length of Hat Creek Trail is as soon as you can reach Hat Point by car in the spring (usually mid-June).
Elevation loss:	5,430 feet.
Permits and fees:	None.
Maps:	Hat Point and Old Timer Mountain USGS quads.

Finding the trailhead: From Joseph, Oregon, take Oregon 350 for 30 miles northeast to the small town of Imnaha, Oregon. From Imnaha, drive east on Hat Point Road (Forest Road 4240) for 22 miles to the junction with Forest Road 315. Turn right (east) on FR 315, and follow it for 2 miles to Hat Point Lookout and Trailhead. The trail begins at a small parking area a short distance before reaching the main Hat Point Lookout parking area. The trail can also be reached by descending from the lookout on a short switchbacking path. The GPS coordinates at the trailhead are 45 26.183 N 116 39.786 W.

Trailhead facilities: The trailhead has ample parking, restrooms, picnic tables, horse facilities, and a lookout tower to climb.

Camping and services: Dispersed camping is available at Sacajawea Campground, which is a short distance northwest of Hat Point Lookout, and at Saddle Camp, which is approximately 5 miles southwest of the trailhead on Hat Point Road (FR 4240).

Hat Creek Trail 1752

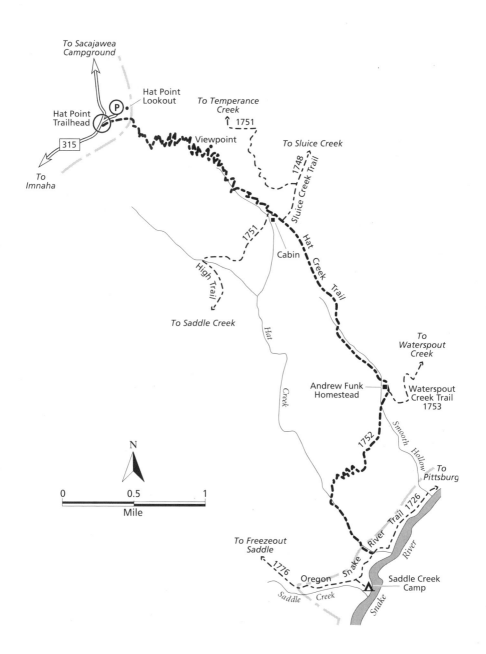

To Sacajawea
Campground

Hat Point
Lookout

Hat Point
Trailhead

315

To
Imnaha

Viewpoint

To Temperance
Creek

1751

To Sluice Creek

1748

Sluice Creek Trail

1751

Cabin

Hat Creek Trail

High Trail

To Saddle Creek

Hat

Creek

To
Waterspout
Creek

Andrew Funk
Homestead

Waterspout
Creek Trail
1753

1752

Smooth Hollow

To
Pittsburg

N

0   0.5   1
Mile

Snake River Trail 1726

Snake

River

To Freezeout
Saddle

1776

Oregon

Saddle Creek
Camp

Saddle Creek

Snake

For more information: USDA Forest Service at Wallowa Mountains Visitor Center in Enterprise, Oregon. For jet boat pickup, contact Hells Canyon Adventures in Oxbow, Oregon.

Key points:
0.0 Hat Point Lookout and Trailhead.
2.0 Viewpoint.
3.6 Second junction with High Trail 1751. GPS 45 25.663 N 116 38.250 W.
4.9 Andrew Funk Homestead.
5.0 Junction with Waterspout Creek Trail 1753. GPS 45 24.692 N 116 37.821 W.
7.1 Junction with Oregon Snake River Trail 1726. GPS 45 23.742 N 116 37.346 W.

The hike: From Hat Creek Trailhead, head east and traverse the open slope passing the Hells Canyon Wilderness Boundary. In the next 2 miles the trail makes 29 switchbacks. You work your way down passing through stands of timber as well as some open slopes.

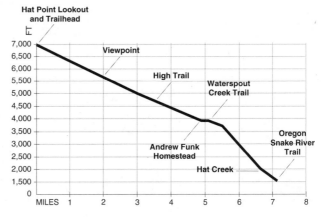

These open slopes will be flower-covered in early summer. There is a viewpoint 20 yards to the left of the trail as it makes a switchback to the right 2 miles down from the lookout. The elevation at the viewpoint is 5,640 feet. High cliffs drop away below the viewpoint, and the rock close to them is unstable, so be careful as you look at the tremendous view. Looking down Sluice Creek Canyon (northeast) from the viewpoint, you can see Johnson Bar on the Idaho side of the Snake River. A herd of mountain goats was transplanted into the canyon just north of this viewpoint in the summer of 2000

The route continues to switchback down after passing the viewpoint. You will cross a small stream 0.5 mile below the viewpoint. After crossing the stream the path makes a switchback to the left and re-crosses the same stream again. After crossing the stream the second time there is a fork in the trail. Bear right at the fork. The left fork is a steeper alternate trail that rejoins the main trail just before reaching the junction with High Trail. A short distance past the fork, the trail again crosses the same stream. The stream is often dry at this point. The tread makes six more switchbacks as it descends the remaining 0.7 mile to the junction with the High Trail 1751. Just before reaching the junction a cabin can be seen below to the right of the trail.

Turn left at the junction, and join High Trail for a short distance; then turn to the right at a second junction and continue your descent toward the

Snake River. Near the junction with High Trail is the best place to camp along Hat Creek Trail. The area, at 4,700 feet elevation, is relatively flat, and water is available a short distance south, next to the cabin mentioned above. Camping here under the large Ponderosa Pines is an excellent place to take a rest day and explore the benches nearby. Watch for Elk in this area especially in the spring.

Turning right off the High Trail, Hat Creek Trail begins its descent into Smooth Hollow. The country below the junction is mostly open, with brush in the draws. From here to the river the country north of the trail was burned in the huge 1996 Salt Creek Fire. Fire in this grass-covered area is not necessarily a bad thing, because the grass usually comes back better then ever after a fire. The trail crosses a creek 0.6 mile below the junction with the High Trail. It then descends along the right side of the creek for 0.5 mile.

The tread then recrosses the creek next to the old Andrew Funk Homestead. The Funk Homestead was patented in 1909. Hogs were raised here as well as Percheron draft horses. These large horses seem to be an odd thing to raise in this steep country, but it seems they were able to get along just fine. Not much of the homestead is left today, just a corral and scattered farm machinery.

The junction with Waterspout Creek Trail 1753 is reached 0.1 mile after passing the old homestead. (See Hike 26 for a description of Waterspout Creek Trail.) At the junction (elev. 3,960 ft), Waterspout Creek Trail turns to the left. Waterspout Creek Trail seems to get more use than the Hat Creek Trail does at this point. From here on down to Oregon Snake River Trail, Hat Creek Trail gets little use and is hard to see in some spots. Leaving the signed junction the route drops to the south and crosses the creek. The area along the creek is covered with Thorn Brush. Because of very limited maintenance downed brush may cover the trail for a short distance in this area. Once through the brush the path traverses out of Smooth Hollow, heading south to a notch in the ridgeline. Crossing the ridgeline the tread begins to descend beneath dark cliffs, south toward another ridgeline. You will make a couple of switchbacks as you work your way south for 0.4 mile to the next ridgeline. At the top of the second ridgeline (elev. 3,080 ft), the trail begins its steep descent into Hat Creek Canyon. The poor path makes 23 switchbacks as it drops the 1,080 vertical feet to the canyon bottom. While descending the switchbacks a waterfall in Hat Creek can be seen, dropping over the cliffs to the west.

Once in the bottom of Hat Creek Canyon the trail becomes somewhat choked with brush. The vague path crosses Hat Creek nine times as it winds and switchbacks down the canyon bottom for 0.5 mile to the junction with Oregon Snake River Trail 1726. This section may seem to be more than half a mile because of the brush and the many creek crossings. There is much Poison Ivy along this section of trail. The elevation at the junction with Oregon Snake River Trail is 1,520 feet.

Watch out for Rattlesnakes, especially along the canyon bottom in Hat Creek Canyon. Rattlers have been seen all the way up to Hat Point but are more common in the lower areas.

Viewpoint next to Hat Creek Trail.

Options: An alternate return trip can be made by taking Oregon Snake River Trail a short distance south to Saddle Creek Trail and then climbing up the easier Saddle Creek Trail to Freezeout Saddle. From Freezeout Saddle, take Western Rim Trail on up to Jim Spring Trailhead on Hat Point Road. A short car shuttle will need to be made from Jim Spring Trailhead to Hat Point Lookout to make this loop trip. See Hikes 10, 28, and 30 for details about this 19-mile loop hike. Allow three days to hike this loop.

If you are feeling less ambitious, a jet boat pickup can be arranged at the mouth of Saddle Creek.

SOUTHERN REGION

From Saddle Creek to McGraw Creek, the southern region of Hells Canyon on the west side of the Snake River provides the hiker with ever-changing views, rugged landscapes, and bountiful wildlife viewing opportunities. Road access here is considerably better than it is in the northern region.

Driving south from Imnaha, up the beautiful Imnaha River Canyon, the junction with Forest Road 4230 is reached in 12.5 miles. If you turn left and follow FR 4230 east for 2.8 miles, you will reach Freezeout Trailhead. **Hike 28 Saddle Creek Trail** starts from Freezeout Trailhead and climbs over Summit Ridge through Freezeout Saddle before making its long descent to the Snake River in the deepest part of Hells Canyon. To make a loop hike, take **Hike 29 Long Ridge–Freezeout Creek Loop** from Freezeout Trailhead to the top of Summit Ridge and back.

About 20 miles farther south along the Imnaha River on Forest Road 39 is the junction with Forest Road 3962. Turning left (east) on FR 3962 and following it and Forest Road 3965 for 10 miles brings you to the trailhead for **Hike 36 Bench Trail.** Bench Trail descends and contours along the slopes of Hells Canyon for 11.5 miles to Hells Canyon Reservoir Trailhead. Seven tenths of a mile north of the trailhead for Bench Trail on FR 3965 is Buck Creek Trailhead and Campground and the starting point for **Hike 35 Buck Creek Trail.** Be sure to stop at the viewpoints along FR 3956 and take in the awesome grandeur of Hells Canyon and the Seven Devils Mountains to the east. Be sure to watch for bighorn sheep in the canyon and even along the road. I once had five rams run along this road ahead of my car. Continuing north on FR 3965, you soon reach the unmarked trailhead for **Hike 34 Thirtytwo Point Trail,** and a little farther along the road is gated and closed to become **Hike 30 Western Rim National Recreation Trail South.**

Along Hells Canyon Reservoir, north of Oxbow, in the bottom of the canyon are Hells Canyon Reservoir Trailhead and the beginning of **Hike 37 Hells Canyon Reservoir Trail.** Hells Canyon Reservoir Trail is the access route to **Hike 38 Old McGraw Creek Route** and the end of **Hike 36 Bench Trail.** If you cross the Snake River at Oxbow and drive north, you will cross Hells Canyon Dam in 21 miles. A little over a mile after crossing back into Oregon on the dam is Hells Canyon Visitors Center and the trailhead for **Hike 39 Stud Creek Trail.**

Southern Region

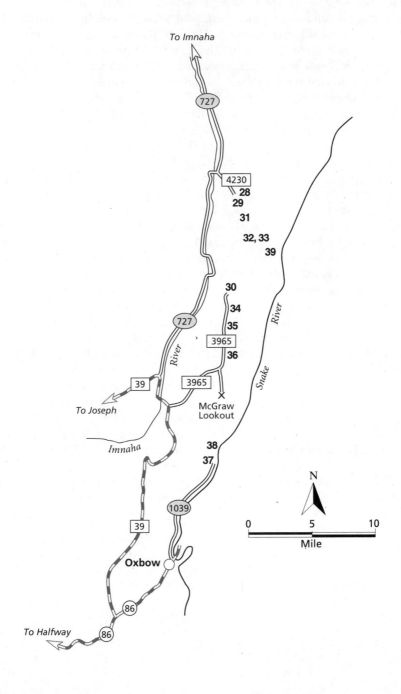

To Imnaha

727

4230
28
29

31

32, 33
39

30
34
35
3965
36

727

River

Snake River

39
3965

To Joseph

X
McGraw
Lookout

Imnaha

38
37

N

0   5   10
Mile

1039

39

Oxbow

86

To Halfway   86

28 Saddle Creek Trail 1776

Highlights: A hike from Freezeout Trailhead over the flower-covered Freezeout Saddle with a descent through rugged Saddle Creek Canyon to the Snake River. Saddle Creek Trail is the easiest trail route to the southern parts of Oregon Snake River Trail 1726 and High Trail 1751.

Type of hike: Out-and-back backpack, with jet boat shuttle, loop, and extended backpack options.

Total distance: 22.6 miles.

Difficulty: Strenuous.

Best months: April–June and September–October.

Elevation gain: 1,870 feet.

Permits and fees: Northwest Forest Pass.

Maps: Sheep Creek Divide, Hat Point, and Old Timer Mountain USGS quads.

Finding the trailhead: Drive east and north from Joseph, Oregon, on Oregon 350 (also known as Imnaha Highway or Little Sheep Creek Highway) for 30 miles to Imnaha, Oregon. From Imnaha, head south on County Road 727 for 12.5 miles to the junction with Forest Road 4230. Turn left onto FR 4230, and follow it 2.8 miles to its end at Freezeout Trailhead. The GPS coordinates at the trailhead are 45 22.505 N 116 45.703 W.

Trailhead facilities: The trailhead has parking for several horse trailers and several cars. It also has an informational sign, a stock loading ramp, and restrooms.

Camping and services: Camping is permitted at the trailhead. Groceries can be obtained in Imnaha. The closest place for gas and other services is Joseph. Cell phone service can be had at Freezeout Saddle.

For more information: USDA Forest Service at Wallowa Mountain Visitors Center in Enterprise, Oregon. For jet boat pickup, contact Hells Canyon Adventures in Oxbow, Oregon.

Key points:
- 0.0 Freezeout Trailhead.
- 3.3 Freezeout Saddle. GPS 45 22.870 N 116 44.204 W.
- 5.3 Junction with High Trail. GPS 45 22.849 N 116 42.994 W.
- 7.0 Crossing of Big Creek.
- 8.7 First crossing of Saddle Creek.
- 10.6 Junction with Battle Creek–Upper Snake River Trail. GPS 45 23.603 N 116 38.227 W.
- 11.1 Junction with Oregon Snake River Trail. GPS 45 23.598 N 116 37.499 W.
- 11.3 Campsite at mouth of Saddle Creek, on the Snake River. GPS 45 23.493 N 116 37.411 W.

Saddle Creek Trail 1776

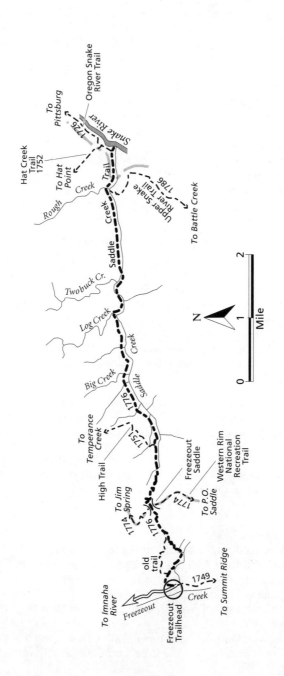

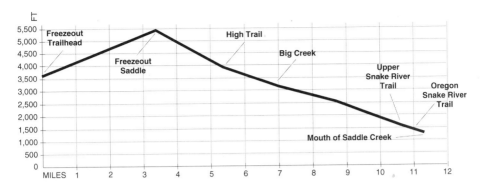

The hike: Two trails start at Freezeout Trailhead, both behind the informational sign at the left (northeast) side of the parking area. The trail to the left is Saddle Creek Trail; the trail to the right continues up Freezeout Creek to Summit Ridge. (See Hike 29 if you wish to head up Freezeout Creek.) There is a trail sign a few feet up the Saddle Creek Trail, showing the distances to Freezeout Saddle, Summit Ridge, and the Snake River.

The trail winds and switchbacks its way up the first 0.5 mile to the junction with an old section of Saddle Creek Trail. At the junction bear to the right on the now reconstructed trail. The route then traverses to the southwest for 0.6 mile before crossing a stream. Just after the crossing the tread turns to the north and climbs along the streambed. In a short distance you will recross the stream. After the second crossing the path climbs steadily, making 19 switchbacks in the next 0.8 mile, as it climbs an open slope. Above these switchbacks the course traverses to the northeast to the bottom of another set of eight switchbacks. The tread climbs these switchbacks to another junction with the old section of Saddle Creek Trail mentioned above.

Here the path flattens out for a short distance and crosses a gully with some trees in it. Soon you will cross another gully and start a set of six more switchbacks. One hundred yards after the switchbacks there is a fork in the trail. Take the left fork and climb the last two switchbacks to Freezeout Saddle and the junction with Western Rim National Recreation Trail 1774 at 5,448 feet elevation. (See Hike 30 for a description of Western Rim Trail.) The right fork is a shortcut for parties heading south on Western Rim Trail.

From the saddle the rugged old burn area of the upper Saddle Creek Canyon can be seen ahead and below. Watch for Elk in this area; they are abundant here in the spring. After crossing the saddle the route enters the burn area, as it starts its steep descent toward the Snake River. The tread makes 18 switchbacks as it works its way steeply down to the first stream crossing at 4,250 feet elevation. Another 0.3 mile and a couple more switchbacks bring you to the junction (elev. 3,920 feet) with High Trail. (See Hike 22 for details about High Trail.) The junction with High Trail is 5.3 miles from Freezeout Trailhead. There is a campsite on a small flat-topped ridge just past the junction.

The path bears slightly to the right at the campsite and drops down the right side of a small ridge. It soon makes a couple more switchbacks as it gets very close to Saddle Creek. Two-tenths mile farther along you will make four more switchbacks, while you continue to descend through this heavily burned, but recovering area. The trail crosses several small dry gullies, then makes a couple more switchbacks before crossing a small stream. In the next quarter of a mile the trail makes two more switchbacks then crosses another small stream. Watch for the Yellow Bells that bloom in this area in early spring. The route fords Big Creek 300 yards after crossing the last small stream. The elevation where the trail crosses Big Creek is 3,120 feet, and it is 7 miles from Freezeout Trailhead. After being in a completely burned area for 3.5 miles, some green pine trees are now starting to show up, along the trail.

The canyon narrows 300 yards after crossing Big Creek. The route makes two switchbacks as the canyon narrows, and then it follows a ledge in the side of the canyon wall for a short distance. Soon the tread bears to the left into a small side canyon and crosses a small stream. It then returns to the main canyon, continuing to descend and making a couple more switchbacks in the 0.8 mile to a crossing of Log Creek. The trail fords Log Creek at 2,580 feet elevation, 8.1 miles from the trailhead.

After crossing Log Creek you climb slightly and go through a notch. Then the course descends again making six switchbacks in the 0.6 mile to the first crossing of Saddle Creek (elev. 2,300 feet). The trail fords Saddle Creek through the usually knee-deep, cold water. This crossing could be difficult during times of heavy runoff. Now you are mostly out of the burn area. The path follows the south side of Saddle Creek for 0.3 mile then recrosses it to the north side. After crossing Saddle Creek the second time the trail traverses above the creekbed, along an opener slope. It then climbs slightly on a ledge, but soon flattens out and starts to descend again. Between here and the junction with Upper Snake River Trail 1786, the route follows ledges for short distances three more times. Be careful of the Poison Ivy found in the creek bottom along this section of trail.

You will reach the junction with Upper Snake River Trail 10.6 miles from Freezeout Trailhead, at 1,650 feet elevation. USGS maps show this junction on the other side of Rough Creek from where it is, but newer Forest Service maps show it correctly. From this junction, Upper Snake River Trail heads south to Battle Creek. (See Hike 33 for a description of the Battle Creek–Upper Snake River Trail.) Just past the junction the trail crosses Rough Creek. Saddle Creek Trail crosses a fenceline, through a gate three hundred yards after crossing Rough Creek. On the right side of the path, just past the gate there are some rock walls, which were once part of a ranching operation.

The junction with Oregon Snake River Trail 1726 is a quarter of a mile past the gate. (See Hike 10 for details about Oregon Snake River Trail.) The junction has no sign, but a short distance farther along is a sign to the left of the trail. Just past the sign there is an outhouse on the left and a few yards more is a flat area with old farm machinery and an information signboard. The sign, next to the Snake River at 1,400 feet elevation and 11.3 miles from Freezeout Trailhead, describes the ranching operation that once occupied this site. A good campsite often used by rafters is located at the mouth of Saddle Creek.

Freezeout Saddle.

Be careful of Rattlers and Poison Ivy along the lower section of this trail. The lower part of this hike may be very hot during the summer.

Options: This trail can be used in combination with Oregon Snake River Trail (Hikes 10 and 11) to make extended trips, possibly including a jet boat ride or a rafting trip to exit the canyon. Saddle Creek Trail can also be hiked uphill to make the loop hike suggested in the Options section of Hike 27.

29 Long Ridge–Freezeout Creek Loop 1749, 1757, 1774, 1763

Highlights:	A hike from Freezeout Trailhead to Summit Ridge and back on lightly used trails. Both flowers and wildlife are abundant on this loop.
Type of hike:	Long loop day hike or backpack.
Total distance:	13.1 miles.
Difficulty:	Strenuous. Some routefinding is required on parts of this rarely maintained loop.
Best months:	June–October.
Permits and fees:	Northwest Forest Pass.
Maps:	Jaynes Ridge and Squirrel Prairie USGS quads.
Elevation gain:	3,300 feet.

Long Ridge–Freezeout Creek Loop
1749, 1757, 1774, 1763

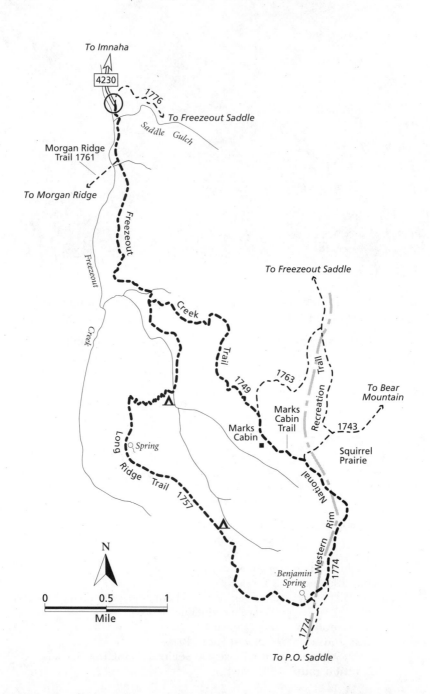

Finding the trailhead: Drive east and north from Joseph, Oregon, on Oregon 350 (also known as Imnaha Highway or Little Sheep Creek Highway) for 30 miles to Imnaha, Oregon. From Imnaha, head south on County Road 727 for 12.5 miles to the junction with Forest Road 4230. Turn left onto FR 4230, and follow it 2.8 miles to its end at Freezeout Trailhead. The GPS coordinates at the trailhead are 45 22.505 N 116 45.703 W.

Trailhead facilities: The trailhead has parking for several horse trailers and several cars. It also has an informational sign, a stock loading ramp, and restrooms.

Camping and services: Camping is permitted at the trailhead. Groceries can be obtained in Imnaha. The closest place for gas and other services is Joseph.

For more information: USDA Forest Service at Wallowa Mountain Visitors Center in Enterprise, Oregon.

Key points:
0.0	Freezeout Trailhead.
0.6	Junction with Morgan Ridge Trail.
2.1	Junction with Long Ridge Trail 1757. GPS 45 21.185 N 116 45.219 W.
3.0	Creek crossing and campsite.
3.8	Trail reaches top of Long Ridge, at top of steep switchbacks.
6.7	Benjamin Spring. GPS 45 19.087 N 116 43.554 W
6.9	Junction with Western Rim Trail 1774.
8.2	Junction with Marks Cabin Trail 1763. GPS 45 20.091 N 116 43.713 W.
8.5	Marks Cabin. GPS 45 20.118 N 116 44.026 W
8.7	Junction with Freezeout Creek Trail 1749. GPS 45 20.387 N 116 44.114 W.
11.0	Second junction with Long Ridge Trail.
13.1	Freezeout Trailhead.

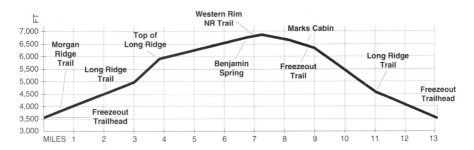

The hike: From behind the large sign at Freezeout Trailhead, the trail climbs 50 yards to a fork. Turn hard right at the fork and head southeast passing another path to the right. This path goes back to the parking lot. A short distance past the path the trail crosses a small creek, at the bottom of Saddle Gulch. After crossing the creek the route heads on up Freezeout Creek Canyon, through an open forest of Douglas-fir and ponderosa pine. The signed junction with Morgan Ridge Trail 1761 is reached 0.4 mile after the creek crossing.

Bear left at the junction with Morgan Ridge Trail and soon cross a creek. Then climb up a small ridge. On this ridge the tread is wide and braided. After climbing the ridge for 0.3 mile, making several switchbacks, the trail levels out some. It then traverses along the right side of the ridge and continues to climb. As you climb there are more openings in the timber. The route crosses a draw and shortly leaves the timber. As it leaves the timber the trail bears to the left and crosses a steep open side hill. This slope is flower covered in late spring. The path descends a little on the open slope and soon enters the timber again. In the timber you will cross a creek, then climb steeply, for a short distance to the junction with Long Ridge Trail 1757. The junction with Long Ridge Trail, at 4,570 feet elevation, is 2.1 miles from Freezeout Trailhead.

At the signed junction bear to the right (really straight ahead to the south) on Long Ridge Trail. The route crosses a small draw then bears left to climb a ridge. You will wind up the ridge for a short distance, climbing steeply and gaining a couple hundred feet elevation. The grade then moderates and the trail continues up the now rounded ridge through the timber for 0.3 mile. There are several possible campsites along this ridge but no water. The trail then leaves the ridgeline and traverses the forested slope heading southeast then south to a creek crossing at 4,990 feet elevation. There is a good campsite to the left of the trail just after crossing the creek.

In the next 0.8 mile the path makes 33 switchbacks as it climbs to the top of Long Ridge. This is the steepest part of Long Ridge Trail. The average grade in this section is 20 percent, but some spots are considerably steeper. Once on the top of the ridge, at 5,810 feet elevation and 3.8 miles from the trailhead, the route heads south traversing the mostly open slope to the right of the ridgeline.

The trail passes a developed spring with a water trough 0.5 mile after beginning the traverse. Shortly after passing the spring the path bears around the slope and heads southeast. You will enter timber that shows the signs of a long ago forest fire 0.8 mile after passing the spring. Another 0.3 mile brings you to a well-developed campsite (elev. 6,330 feet). There is a flattened area to the left of the trail that makes an excellent tent site. Water from another developed spring can be obtained a short distance farther along the trail.

Just after passing the spring the trail becomes vague. It bears left and climbs through the burnt timber almost to the rounded ridgeline. There are many stock trails here and following the trail can be difficult. As you near the ridge bear right, staying in the open area to the right of the thick stand of young pine trees and head southeast to a long abandoned roadbed. Then follow the roadbed south-southeast to a tiny pond and another spring. A short distance after passing the pond the roadbed forks. Bear left at the fork and head east 0.2 mile to another fork in the road. At this fork bear left and climb slightly to the northeast before heading east-southeast again on the faint path. Another quarter of a mile brings you to Benjamin Spring at 6,800 feet elevation and 6.7 miles from the Freezeout Trailhead.

There are two ponds to the right of the trail at Benjamin Spring. A log fence about 100 yards north of the ponds surrounds the developed spring.

The area around Benjamin Spring blooms profusely with White Mule's Ear in July. Elk are common on these ridge top meadows in summer. Campsites are plentiful along Summit Ridge near the spring.

An alternate route for Western Rim Trail passes next to the spring. Turn left (northeast) on this vague trail and hike for 0.2 mile to the junction with Western Rim National Recreation Trail 1774. (See Hike 30 for a description of Western Rim Trail, which was once called Summit Ridge Trail.)

The section of Long Ridge Trail from the developed campsite to Benjamin Spring is difficult to follow exactly. If you lose the trail in this area, head east and very slightly south from the campsite. Do not enter the thick timber, and do not descend. You will reach Western Rim Trail in about 1.5 miles. Western Rim Trail is an abandoned roadbed in this area.

Turn left (north) on Western Rim Trail and soon go through a gate. Here the route enters a stretch of old-growth timber as it heads north along the ridge. The roadbed climbs gradually for 0.4 mile to the top of a rise at 6,880 feet elevation. It then descends for 250 yards to a benchmark. The benchmark is on the right side of the trail. Near the benchmark the trail turns to the left. It soon begins to descend toward the junction with Marks Cabin Trail 1763. The junction (elev. 6,740 ft) is reached 0.6 mile after passing the benchmark. (To continue north on Western Rim Trail, see Hike 30. Squirrel Prairie a short distance north of the junction on Western Rim Trail makes a good campsite.)

Turn left on Marks Cabin Trail, which is also an abandoned roadbed and hike to the northwest. You will pass through a gate 0.2 mile after the leaving Western Rim Trail. Another 0.1 mile brings you to Marks Cabin. The well-maintained cabin is a few feet to the left of the trail. Marks Cabin is

Benjamin Spring.

locked and closed to the public. There is a spring next to the cabin. At Marks Cabin you are 8.5 miles into this loop hike.

The route continues north-northwest past the cabin and descends 0.2 mile to the junction with Freezeout Creek Trail 1749 (elev. 6,480 ft.). The trail to the right is a continuation of Marks Cabin Trail that connects back up with Western Rim Trail in 1.4 miles.

Hike straight ahead (northwest) at the junction, and begin to descend the steep Freezeout Creek Trail. The path crosses a fenceline, through a gate 0.2 mile after leaving the junction with Marks Cabin Trail. You will then make ten switchbacks as you descend the next 0.4 mile through the timber. The route then traverses an open slope and crosses a small ridgeline before reaching a tiny spring. Balsamroot, Paintbrush, Lupine, White Top, and many other flowers carpet this slope in late June. Past the spring the tread descends through a brushy old burn area. Below the burn area the route heads northwest along a rounded ridgeline for 0.4 mile. It then descends off the ridge and makes six switchbacks as it drops on down to the junction with Long Ridge Trail. This junction with Long Ridge Trail is the point where you turned off Freezeout Creek Trail 2.1 miles after you began this hike. Bear right at the junction and retrace your steps back to Freezeout Trailhead.

Options: Bear Mountain Trail makes an excellent side trip from a campsite at Squirrel Prairie. See Hike 31 for a description of this trail.

30 Western Rim National Recreation Trail South 1774

Highlights:	A hike from P.O. Saddle Trailhead, along Summit Ridge with its fantastic views, to Jim Spring Trailhead on Hat Point Road. Much of this trail follows the old Summit Ridge Road, which is reverting nicely to a trail. Watch for mule deer, elk, an occasional black bear, and abundant wildflowers along this trail.
Type of hike:	Shuttle; day hike or backpack.
Total distance:	15.1 miles.
Difficulty:	Easy south of junction with Bear Mountain Trail; moderate from there to Hat Point Road.
Best months:	Mid-June–September.
Elevation gain:	2,780 feet total.
Permits and fees:	Northwest Forest Pass.
Maps:	Puderbaugh Ridge, Jaynes Ridge, Squirrel Prairie, and Hat Point USGS quads.

Finding the trailhead: To reach P.O. Saddle Trailhead (which is really 1.1 miles south of P.O. Saddle). take Oregon 350 (also known as Imnaha Highway or Little Sheep Creek Highway) east from Joseph, Oregon. Follow OR 350 for 8 miles to the junction with Forest Road 39 (Wallowa Mountain

Loop Road). Turn right on FR 39 and follow it 41 miles to the junction with Forest Road 3962. Turn left on FR 3962 and drive east for 5.5 miles to the junction with Forest Road 3965. Turn left on FR 3965 and follow it east and north for 7.5 miles to the campground and trailhead. An iron gate blocks FR 3965 to motor vehicle use north of this point. Even if the gate is open, continuing farther by car is prohibited. The GPS coordinates at the iron gate are 45 13.827 N 116 46.342 W.

Jim Spring Trailhead, on the north end of this section of Western Rim National Recreation Trail (also known as Summit Ridge Trail) is 17 miles east of Imnaha, Oregon, on Hat Point Road (Forest Road 4240). The GPS coordinates at Jim Spring Trailhead are 45 23.933 N 116 43.960 W.

Trailhead facilities: A campground and horse facilities can be found on a side road a short distance west of FR 3965, 0.1 mile before reaching the iron gate. A path also connects the campground with FR 3965 at the gate.

Camping and services: In addition to the campsites near the trailhead mentioned in the trailhead facilities section above, there is a campground at Buck Creek Trailhead 2.3 miles to the south on FR 3965. Gas, groceries, and medical services can be obtained in Joseph. Cell phone service is available at many high points along Western Rim Trail.

For more information: USDA Forest Service at either Wallowa Mountains Visitor in Enterprise, Oregon, or Pine Ranger Station in Halfway, Oregon.

Key points:

0.0	P.O. Saddle Trailhead.
1.1	P.O. Saddle. GPS 45 14.333 N 116 45.704 W.
2.5	Saulsberry Saddle. GPS 45 15.251 N 116 45.306 W.
4.9	Himmelwright Spring.
5.3	Jensen Spring.
5.4	Junction with Battle Creek Trail 1784. GPS 45 17.810 N 116 44.416 W.
7.1	Lookout Mountain. GPS 45 18.748 N 116 43.681 W.
7.6	Benjamin Spring.
8.9	Junction with Marks Cabin Trail 1763. GPS 45 20.091 N 116 43.713 W.
9.1	Junction with Bear Mountain Trail 1743. GPS 45 20.265 N 116 43.414 W.
10.1	Second junction with Marks Cabin Trail.
13.0	Junction with Saddle Creek Trail 1776, in Freezeout Saddle. GPS 45 22.870 N 116 44.204 W.
15.1	Trailhead on Hat Point Road near Jim Spring. GPS 45 23.933 N 116 43.960 W.

Western Rim National Recreation Trail South 1774
(South half)

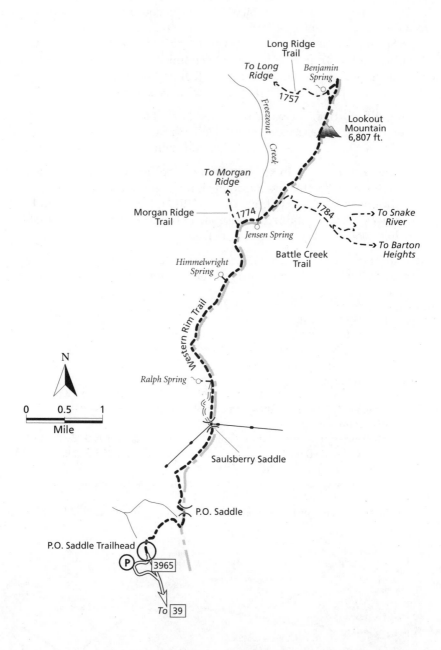

Long Ridge Trail

To Long Ridge

Benjamin Spring

1757

Freezeout Creek

Lookout Mountain 6,807 ft.

To Morgan Ridge

Morgan Ridge Trail

1774

To Snake River

1784

To Barton Heights

Jensen Spring

Battle Creek Trail

Himmelwright Spring

Western Rim Trail

Ralph Spring

Saulsberry Saddle

P.O. Saddle

P.O. Saddle Trailhead

P 3965

To 39

N

0   0.5   1
Mile

Western Rim National Recreation Trail South 1774
(North half)

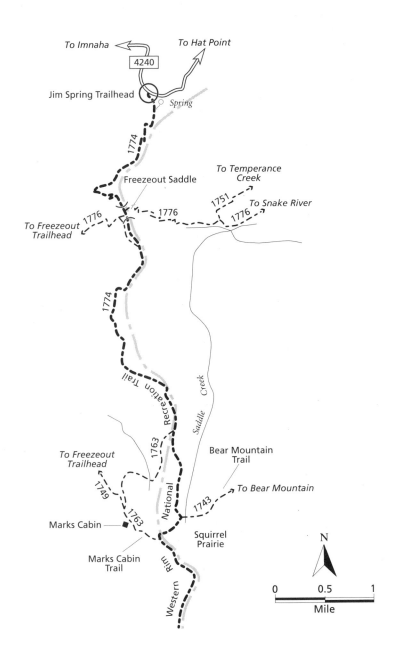

The hike: The trail starts as closed FR 3965 at the iron gate 1.1 miles south of P.O. Saddle. Even if this gate is open, the road is closed to motor vehicle use north of this point. A short distance after passing the gate the road forks. Take the left fork (actually straight ahead) and continue to descend gently. Soon the road crosses a small gully, climbs a few feet then begins to descend again. The route crosses a creek (elev. 5,710 ft) 0.9 mile after passing the gate. Once across the creek you climb gently for 0.2 mile to P.O. Saddle and the first view of the canyon to the east. The abandoned roadbed climbs for 0.5 mile after passing P.O. Saddle, gaining 230 feet of elevation. Then it flattens and begins to descend gradually toward Saulsberry Saddle. The saddle is reached 0.8 mile after starting the descent.

An old sign on a large tree on the right side of the trail marks Saulsberry Saddle. The power lines coming up from Hells Canyon Dam cross Summit Ridge and the trail in the saddle. At the saddle the trail bears right off the road. There is also another road that bears farther to the right and goes out to one of the power line towers. Western Rim Trail is to the right of the main road but still traverses the left (west) side of the ridge. Leaving Saulsberry Saddle the path traverses an open side hill, which is covered with flowers in June. Then it goes through a finger of trees, and climbs through a sloping meadow, before rejoining the road, 0.7 mile from the saddle.

A few yards after rejoining the road, the trail (road) enters dense forest of Spruce and Lodgepole Pine timber at the Hells Canyon Wilderness Boundary. There are two signs on trees on each side of the road marking the wilderness boundary.

You may notice an unmarked trail junction 0.2 mile past the wilderness boundary. The trail to the left goes a quarter mile west to Ralph Spring. Western Rim Trail goes straight ahead through the forest. It soon heads slightly right of the ridgeline, where views of Hells Canyon, to the right (east), can be had through the openings in the trees. You will stay quite close to the ridgeline for the next 1.5 miles, through timbered sections and open areas, to a point where the ridge broadens. Where the ridge broadens out the ground is nearly covered with White Mule's Ear. The middle of June until early July is the normal blooming time for these beautiful flowers. Shortly after the ridge broadens you reach the junction with the side trail to Himmelwright Spring. There is a sign on the left side of the trail, on a large fir tree marking the junction. Himmelwright Spring is about 150 yards to the left of the trail. This is a developed spring, and water is normally available.

Just past the trail to Himmelwright Spring, the track, which is still a closed road, enters a very old burn area. Much of the old burn area is now grown up to Lodgepole Pine. The trail bears to the right, passing another junction with a closed road.

This road is Morgan Ridge Trail, which descends north-northwest to meet Freezeout Creek Trail near Freezeout Trailhead. A sign marks the junction, but it is hard to spot under the limbs of a fir tree to the left of the trail

Western Rim Trail descends gently to the northeast from the junction and soon reaches Jensen Spring (elev. 6,270 ft), at the head of Freezeout Creek. Parts of the trail in the 0.4 mile between Himmelwright Spring and Jensen

Spring may be wet and muddy in June but are usually dry by mid-July. There is a pond to the right of the trail at Jensen Spring. Next to the spring you will go through a gate and cross Freezeout Creek.

The route soon passes through another old gate and reaches the junction with Battle Creek Trail 1784 in another 0.3 mile. At the signed junction, 5.4 miles from P.O. Saddle Trailhead, at 6,350 elevation, Battle Creek Trail turns to the right (east). (See Hike 32 for details about Battle Creek Trail and Hike 33 for a description of Barton Heights Trail, which is a side trip off Battle Creek Trail.)

After passing the junction with Battle Creek Trail, Western Rim Trail climbs gently for 0.6 mile to the top of a rise, then flattens on the top of the ridgeline. It soon climbs a bit more then drops slightly through a small saddle on the ridge. From the saddle the trail climbs more steeply through scattered Sub-Alpine Fir trees, for 0.5 mile to the top of Lookout Mountain, 6,807 feet above sea level. There used to be a lookout on the top of Lookout Mountain a few yards to the right of the trail, but now there are only radio towers. There is an excellent view of the canyon and the Seven Devils Mountains from Lookout Mountain.

Leaving Lookout Mountain the trail descends slightly for 0.3 mile to a junction. At the junction the main trail bears to the right. The trail to the left goes to Benjamin Spring and Long Ridge. (See Hike 29 for details about Long Ridge Trail 1757.) Benjamin Spring (elev. 6,750 ft) is approximately 0.2 mile from the main trail. The spring is contained in a log corral, and there are a couple of ponds below it. A plastic pipe coming from the spring generally has a good flow of water. As always, filter or boil the water before use. The trail past the spring rejoins the main trail a short distance farther along but may be difficult to see.

Soon after passing the trails to Benjamin Spring, Western Rim Trail goes through a gate. Here it enters a stretch of old-growth timber as it heads north along the ridge. The route climbs gradually for 0.4 mile to top a rise at 6,880 feet elevation. It then descends for 250 yards to a benchmark. The benchmark is on the right side of the trail. Near the benchmark the route turns to the left and soon begins to descend toward the junction with Marks Cabin Trail 1763. The junction at 6,740 feet elevation is reached 0.6 mile after passing the benchmark and 8.9 miles from P.O. Saddle Trailhead. Marks Cabin Trail bears to the left (west) at the junction. (See Hike 29 for a description of this section of Marks Cabin Trail.)

At the junction Western Rim Trail turns to the right and climbs over a small ridge. It then descends through a forest of small Lodgepole Pines and old stumps for 0.3 mile to the junction with Bear Mountain Trail 1743. At the junction (elev. 6,600 ft), Bear Mountain Trail heads to the east. Western Rim Trail turns to the left (northwest). This junction is the end of the old roadbed that you have been following for most of the 9.1 miles from the trailhead. There is a campsite on Bear Mountain Trail a short distance from the junction, in Squirrel Prairie, just across Saddle Creek. (See Hike 31 for a description of Bear Mountain Trail.) A colony of red diggers inhabit the meadow around the junction.

155

Seven Devils Mountains from Summit Ridge.

Leaving the junction with Bear Mountain Trail, Western Rim Trail climbs gently to the northwest. One mile from the Bear Mountain Trail junction is the second junction with Marks Cabin Trail. Marks Cabin Trail turns to the left but may not be visible on the ground. There is a sign marking this ridgetop junction (elev. 6,760 ft).

Shortly after passing the second Marks Cabin Trail junction the trail begins to descend. Soon it goes through a gate and begins to drop more steeply on an open slope. This slope is covered with blooming Balsamroot and many other flowers in June. The path descends the open slope for 0.9 mile. It then bears to the north and passes through scattered groves of fir trees. The timber becomes thicker and larger as the trail descends toward Freezeout Saddle. You will reach the south end of the broad saddle 2.4 miles after passing the second Marks Cabin Trail junction.

A short distance out onto the saddle the trail forks. Bear right at the fork. The trail to the left connects with Saddle Creek Trail as it drops to the west toward Freezeout Trailhead. From the fork Western Rim Trail heads north, just left of the ridgeline, to a junction with Saddle Creek Trail 1776. (See Hike 28 for a description of Saddle Creek Trail.) There is a sign marking the junction, 13 miles from P.O. Saddle Trailhead, at 5,448 feet elevation. Saddle Creek Trail crosses Western Rim Trail at this junction. The view from the junction is spectacular. Saddle Creek Canyon is to the right, and Freezeout Canyon is to the left. The whole west side of the saddle is generally covered with flowers in June. Watch for Elk that are abundant in this area.

From the junction with Saddle Creek Trail, Western Rim Trail climbs to the northwest on an open slope. It makes a couple of switchbacks then climbs to a spur ridge. On the spur ridge the trail turns to the right, then climbs to the northeast to regain the main ridge. This section of trail has been recently reconstructed and is in excellent shape. On the main ridge the route continues to climb, sometimes on the ridge, but mostly on the slope to the left of the ridgeline. The path makes several switchbacks as it climbs to Jim Spring Trailhead on Hat Point Road. It crosses a small stream a quarter of a mile before reaching the trailhead. There is a sign marking Jim Spring Trailhead. You are now 15.1 miles from P.O. Saddle Trailhead, at 6,550 feet elevation.

Water is available at fairly regular intervals along most of the trail, but there is no water from the junction with Bear Mountain Trail to the stream just before reaching Jim Spring Trailhead on Hat Point Road. Rattlesnakes are usually not seen along this trail but there is always a possibility of them mainly in late summer. There are campsites all along this trail except for the section north of the second junction with Marks Cabin Trail.

Options: Take a side trip to Barton Heights from a campsite near Jensen Spring (see Hike 32 for details), or hike to Bear Mountain (see Hike 31) as a side trip from a camp at Squirrel Prairie.

31 Bear Mountain Trail 1743

Highlights:	A hike from Western Rim Trail to Bear Mountain, and possibly another 0.7 mile to Black Mountain, along a ridgetop trail. Some of the best views of Hells Canyon are along this route. Most of this trail passes through an area that was burned many years ago, so it is more open than it may have once been.
Type of hike:	Internal, out-and-back day hike.
Total distance:	5 miles.
Difficulty:	Easy to Bear Mountain; strenuous from there to Black Mountain.
Best months:	June–October.
Elevation gain:	670 feet to Bear Mountain; 1,090 feet to Black Mountain.
Permits and fees:	None.
Maps:	Squirrel Prairie USGS quad.

Finding the trailhead: From Joseph, Oregon, take Oregon 350 for 30 miles northeast to the small town of Imnaha. From Imnaha, take Hat Point Road (Forest Road 4240) 17 miles east to Jim Spring Trailhead. A sign on the right side of the road marks the trailhead, but it is sometimes missed. From the trailhead, hike south on Western Rim National Recreation Trail for 6 miles to the junction with Bear Mountain Trail. A sign marks the junction. The GPS coordinates at the junction are 45 20.265 N 116 43.414 W.

If you want to reach this junction from the south, follow the driving directions in Hike 30 to P.O. Saddle Trailhead. Then hike north on Western Rim Trail for 9.1 miles (as described in Hike 30) to the junction with Bear Mountain Trail.

Bear Mountain Trail 1743

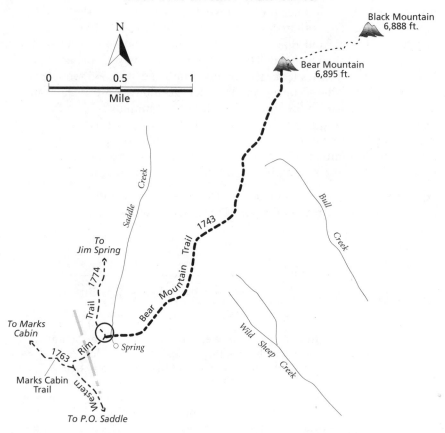

Trailhead facilities: Good campsites can be found near the junction with Western Rim Trail.

Camping and services: Gas, groceries, and medical services can be obtained in Joseph. Cell phone service is available at many high points along the route.

For more information: USDA Forest Service at Wallowa Mountains Visitor Center in Enterprise, Oregon.

Key points:
0.0   Junction with Western Rim Trail 9.1 miles north of P.O. Saddle Trailhead.
0.1   Trail crosses Saddle Creek.
0.2   Top of rounded ridge.
2.5   Summit of Bear Mountain. GPS 45 21.859 N 116 41.878 W.
3.2   Summit of Black Mountain.

The hike: From the junction, Bear Mountain Trail heads east across the meadow and drops slightly to cross Saddle Creek, at 0.1 mile. The

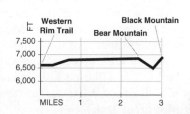

USGS map shows a pond here, below the trail, but at present there is no pond. After crossing the creek the course becomes better defined as it climbs to the east through a stand of small Lodgepole Pines. Soon the small timber thins out, and the route bears slightly to the left to traverse an open slope. This area may be muddy in June because there are several wet-weather springs here.

The path soon comes out on a rounded ridgetop at 6,820 feet elevation. Here the view of the Seven Devils Mountains opens up to the east. The trail continues to head northeast, generally following the rounded ridge, through a forest of silver snags with small Lodgepole Pine and Sub-Alpine Fir growing up between them. About 0.3 mile along the ridge, Freezeout Saddle can be seen to the left (northwest), and the Wallowa Mountains are in view far to the west.

The route becomes vague 1.4 miles after leaving Western Rim Trail, as it works its way through the blow downs. The course stays very near to the ridgeline here, crossing an area that was burned more recently. A short distance more and the path reaches a small saddle on the ridgeline. Leaving the saddle you will traverse slightly left of the ridge for 0.2 mile, before regaining the ridgeline, in another small, recently burned area. A few yards after regaining the ridge the tread drops off a few yards to the left again. The trail is very hard to see in this area; if you lose it here, just follow the ridge to the northeast, allowing for the rock outcroppings. The route regains the ridge again a quarter of a mile farther along, then climbs fairly steeply, just to the left of the ridgeline, for the last couple hundred yards to the summit of Bear Mountain.

Looking east from Bear Mountain Trail.

The view from the summit of Bear Mountain, at 6,895 feet elevation, is impressive. The Seven Devils Mountains and the most rugged part of Hells Canyon are to the east. Dry Diggins Lookout can be seen in the distance to the northeast, and Hat Point Lookout is in the distance to the north. The Snake River in the bottom of the canyon is in view 5,500 feet below the point where you are standing.

From the summit of Bear Mountain the path leading up Black Mountain can be seen. To continue to Black Mountain follow the ridge down steeply to the east-northeast, for 0.3 mile, to the saddle between Bear Mountain and Black Mountain. The elevation at the saddle is 6,460 feet, making this a 435-foot descent. Then follow the path, climbing steeply to the northeast, to the summit at 6,880 feet elevation.

The flowers along this ridge trail are at their peak bloom in late June. Elk are common here in summer, and it is sometimes possible to see Bighorn Sheep. There is a Red Digger colony at the junction with Western Rim Trail. No water is available after crossing Saddle Creek. Watch out for lightning storms along this high exposed ridge and especially on Bear Mountain and Black Mountain.

Options: Hike Bear Mountain Trail as a side trip while you are backpacking along Western Rim Trail.

32 Battle Creek–Upper Snake River Trail 1784, 1786

Highlights:	A rough trail from the western rim of Hells Canyon to the Snake River and then following the river to the mouth of Saddle Creek. This hike is through some of the most rugged terrain in Hells Canyon.
Type of hike:	Internal backpack, with jet boat shuttle and loop options.
Total distance:	13.9 miles.
Difficulty:	Strenuous.
Best months:	Mid-June–October.
Elevation gain:	Approximately 2,500 feet.
Permits and fees:	Northwest Forest Pass if you are parking at P.O. Saddle Trailhead.
Maps:	Squirrel Prairie and Hat Point USGS Quads.

Finding the trail: Follow the driving directions in Hike 30 to P.O. Saddle Trailhead. Then hike north on Western Rim National Recreation Trail (a closed road) for 5.4 miles to the junction with Battle Creek Trail, as described in Hike 30. The GPS coordinates at the junction are 45 17.810 N 116 44.416 W.

Trailhead facilities: Camping and horse facilities are available at P.O. Saddle Trailhead, which is 5.4 miles south of the junction where this hike begins.

Battle Creek–Upper Snake River Trail 1784, 1786

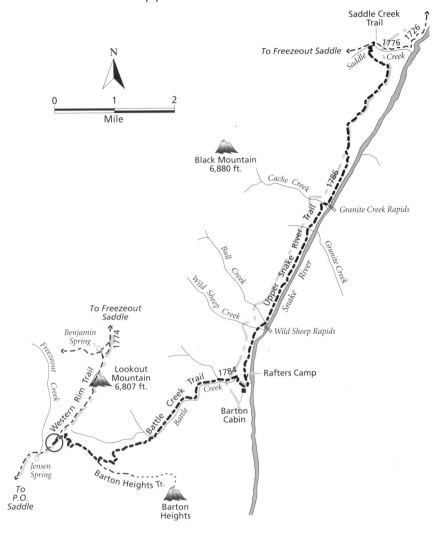

Camping and services: The closest campground is at P.O. Saddle Trailhead. Gas and groceries can be obtained in Oxbow, Halfway, or Joseph, Oregon. Cell phones work at many spots along Western Rim Trail.

For more information: USDA Forest Service at Pine Ranger Station in Halfway, Oregon; Hells Canyon Visitor Center near Hells Canyon Dam; or Wallowa Mountains Visitor Center in Enterprise, Oregon. For jet boat transportation, contact Hells Canyon Adventures in Oxbow, Oregon.

Key points:
- 0.0   Junction with Western Rim Trail.
- 1.4   Junction with Barton Heights Trail. GPS 45 17.548 N 116 43.524 W.
- 3.0   Trail reaches Battle Creek.

5.5	Barton Cabin and junction with Upper Snake River Trail 1786. GPS 45 18.698 N 116 40.566 W.
6.9	Wild Sheep Rapids and Wild Sheep Campsite.
9.8	Cache Creek. GPS 45 21.526 N 116 39.206 W.
13.9	Junction with Saddle Creek Trail 1776. GPS 45 23.603 N 116 38.227 W.

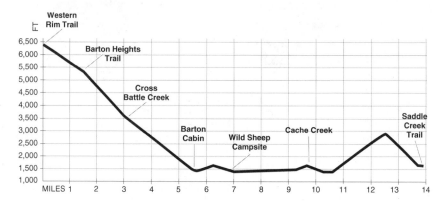

The hike: From the junction with Western Rim Trail, at 6,350 feet elevation, Battle Creek Trail heads northeast, passing the Hells Canyon Wilderness Boundary. The route first drops gently then becomes steeper as it descends an open slope with a view of the Seven Devils Mountains to the east. Two tenths of a mile from the junction the tread makes the first of several switchbacks. Balsamroot graces these slopes with its showy yellow flowers in late June. The path continues to descend fairly steeply for a little over a mile then flattens out some. Paintbrush and many other flowers color this ridge as the route heads southeast to the junction with Barton Heights Trail. The junction is in a saddle on the ridgeline 1.4 miles from Western Rim Trail at 5,350 feet elevation. (See Hike 33 for details about hiking out to Barton Heights.)

At the junction with Barton Heights Trail, Battle Creek Trail turns to the left (north) to begin its steep descent into Battle Creek Canyon. You will wind and switchback your way down to a usually dry creekbed. The steep, rough, winding tread then descends down the creekbed to Battle Creek. Don't depend on your GPS here; readings are hard to get in this tight canyon

Cross Battle Creek at 3,600 feet elevation, then work your way down through the fir woods and talus slopes along it. The Squirrel Prairie quad map shows the trail incorrectly here. In a couple of the talus slopes the route has been recently reconstructed and is in good condition; the rest of it is rough and overgrown. You will cross a small stream, which may be dry, 0.5 mile after crossing Battle Creek. A short distance past the stream there is a tiny campsite to the left of the trail. A couple tenths of a mile past the campsite, the path crosses another small stream that may be dry in late summer.

As you continue your descent the timber thins out and the slopes become more open. The trace crosses a larger stream (elev. 2,800 feet) 1.1 miles after crossing Battle Creek. The canyon this unnamed stream has cut between the rock cliffs above is very rugged and is worth taking a few minutes to admire. The best viewpoint is a few yards after crossing the stream. Dry Diggins Lookout, far in the distance to the northeast, can be seen with binoculars from this part of Battle Creek Trail. There is no tower at the lookout, only a square building atop the ridge.

Shortly after crossing the stream. the course descends a series of small switchbacks. Just past the switchbacks watch for a shallow cave to the left of the trail. Below the cave the track follows Battle Creek fairly closely, staying in the brush most of the time. Poison Ivy is thick and sometimes shoulder high, along this part of the route. You may see a couple of pieces of rusting mine equipment sitting next to the trail in the brush. This is about all that remains now of the abandoned gold mine that once operated here.

The route soon bears to the east, crossing a tiny stream that may be dry and a slightly larger creek. It then contours above the Battle Creek on a semi-open side hill before descending to the creekbed again. The route then crosses Battle Creek three times in quick succession. These crossings can be knee-deep at times. After the third crossing the path descends a grassy bench studded with Hackberry trees to the Barton Cabin and the junction with Upper Snake River Trail.

The historic Barton Cabin, built by Ralph Barton in 1932, has a metal roof and is in fairly good shape; however, the rodent population makes it more pleasant to camp next to the cabin than to stay in it. The cabin, 5.5 miles from Western Rim Trail, at 1,510 feet elevation, is a couple hundred yards from the Snake River.

From Barton Cabin on, the route now follows Upper Snake River Trail 1786. The path first descends east toward the river, then turns left to cross Battle Creek for the last time. Shortly after crossing the creek the trail enters an open grassy area. This grassy bench is used by many rafting parties as a campsite. It is very easy to lose the route in this open area. About halfway across the open area the trail splits. The right fork, which is the far more used route, goes to more campsites and a place where rafters beach their boats. To continue on Upper Snake River Trail you will need to bear left at the fork, on the vague path.

The course soon begins to ascend a steep slope through the rock outcroppings, making several switchbacks as it climbs. You will climb a couple hundred feet above the river then traverse the slopes as you head north. Soon the vague trace crosses a brushy draw filled with Poison Ivy. The tread passes a viewpoint a couple hundred yards after crossing the draw, it then begins to descend. You will make four switchbacks as you descend. Mock Orange and Wild Roses line the trail in spots. One and three tenths miles from Barton Cabin the path crosses Wild Sheep Creek (which may be dry). Shortly after crossing Wild Sheep Creek, you will enter the Wild Sheep Campsite. This is another place where it is easy to lose the route because of several side trails that lead to campsites.

As you enter the Wild Sheep Campsite, head to the right (northeast) and descend gently toward the river. The route leaves the camping area fairly close to the river. This section of Upper Snake River Trail is used by rafters to scout Wild Sheep Rapids, one of the two most difficult rapids in Hells

Canyon, so the path is well beaten here. Just after passing Wild Sheep Rapids the track crosses Bull Creek.

After crossing Bull Creek the trail climbs well above the river then descends back close to it several times in the next 2 miles. Then it begins to climb steadily as you pass the mouth of Granite Creek. Granite Creek, which drains a large part of the Seven Devils Mountains, rushes into the Snake River from the Idaho side. Just before reaching the mouth of Granite Creek a flat-topped outcropping to the right of the trail offers an excellent view of that creek's mouth and the river above Granite Creek Rapids. From the viewpoint the route continues to climb to another viewpoint, this one above and slightly south of Granite Creek Rapids. Here the trail is nearly 400 feet above the roaring Snake River. A few wooden steps aid the climb and descent in this area.

After passing this viewpoint the trail begins to descend toward Cache Creek. When you reach Cache Creek you are 4.3 miles from Barton Cabin and 9.8 miles from Western Rim Trail. The path descends along the south side of Cache Creek for a short distance, then crosses it to continue toward the river. If you need water, Cache Creek is usually a good place to get it. The tread gets close to the river at the mouth of Cache Creek. Here the Snake River rolls and thunders over Granite Creek Rapids. Granite Creek Rapids and Wild Sheep Rapids are the most difficult rapids to run in Hells Canyon.

At the mouth of Cache Creek the course turns left and heads north-northeast along the low bench above the river for about 0.5 mile. Some campsites are available in this section. The path then begins to climb again. The route climbs to 2,900 feet elevation (about 1,600 feet above the river), before descending to meet Saddle Creek Trail 1776, 8.4 miles from Barton Cabin and

Barton Cabin.

13.9 miles from Western Rim Trail, where this hike begin. The elevation at the junction with Saddle Creek Trail is 1,650 feet. From the junction it is 10.6 miles to the left (southwest) over Freezeout Saddle to Freezeout Trailhead. To the right it is 0.7 mile to the mouth of Saddle Creek on the Snake River. (See Hike 28 for a description of Saddle Creek Trail.)

Watch for Rattlesnakes all along this trail and especially along Battle Creek and the Snake River. Bears are common and Bighorn Sheep are sometimes seen.

Options: It is possible to take a jet boat to the mouth of Battle Creek and hike from there to Saddle Creek along Upper Snake River Trail or to arrange to be picked up at the mouth of either Battle Creek or Saddle Creek.

If you want to make a loop, hike up Saddle Creek Trail to Freezeout Saddle. Turn left on Western Rim Trail and follow it back to the junction where you started this hike. See Hikes 28 and 30 for a description of these trails. Allow about four days to make this loop.

For a really long but very rewarding backpack, continue on Oregon Snake River Trail 1726 for the 46.8 miles from the mouth of Saddle Creek to Dug Bar Trailhead. This hike would require a car shuttle to Dug Bar. See Hikes 10 and 11 for a description of Oregon Snake River Trail.

33 Barton Heights Trail

Highlights:	A hike that consists of 0.7 mile of trail then 1.1 miles of cross-country ridge travel, from the junction with Battle Creek Trail to Barton Heights. Barton Heights affords an excellent view of the inner gorge of Hells Canyon. The jagged heights of the Seven Devils Mountains are across the canyon, and the Snake River can be seen below. From a rocky outcrop a few yards to the north of the highest point, Hells Canyon Dam and the river more than 4,000 feet below Barton Heights come into view.
Type of hike:	Internal, out-and-back day hike.
Total distance:	3.6 miles.
Difficulty:	Moderate, but good routefinding skills are required.
Best months:	Mid-June–October.
Elevation gain:	595 feet.
Permits and fees:	Northwest Forest Pass.
Maps:	Squirrel Prairie USGS quad.

Finding the trailhead: Barton Heights Trail is a side trail off Battle Creek Trail 1784. It leaves Battle Creek Trail 1.4 miles east of Western Rim National Recreation Trail. See Hike 32 for a description of Battle Creek Trail and Hike 30 for details about Western Rim Trail. The GPS coordinates where Barton Heights Trail leaves Battle Creek Trail are 45 17.548 N 116 43.524 W. A sign at the junction marks the trail.

Barton Heights Trail

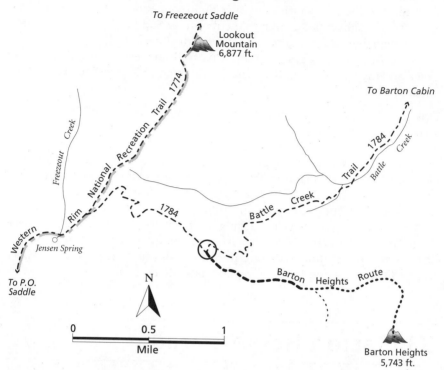

To Freezeout Saddle

Lookout Mountain 6,877 ft.

To Barton Cabin

1774

1784

Freezeout Creek

National Recreation Trail

Rim

Western

Trail

Battle Creek

1784

Battle Creek

Jensen Spring

To P.O. Saddle

N

Barton Heights Route

0   0.5   1
Mile

Barton Heights 5,743 ft.

Trailhead facilities: Campsites are available along Western Rim Trail.

Camping and services: The closest campground is at P.O. Saddle Trailhead. Gas and groceries can be obtained in Oxbow, Halfway, or Joseph, Oregon. Cell phone service is available at many spots along Western Rim Trail.

For more information: USDA Forest Service at Wallowa Mountains Visitor Center in Enterprise, Oregon, or Hells Canyon Dam Visitors Center.

Key points:
- 0.0   Junction with Battle Creek Trail 1.4 miles east of Western Rim Trail.
- 0.7   Trail, which is now a faint path, bears to the right off the ridge; route leaves path.
- 1.5   Rocky point on ridge north of Barton Heights.
- 1.8   Barton Heights. GPS 45 17.126 N 116 41.877 W.

The hike: From the junction with Battle Creek Trail, Barton Heights Trail heads southeast along the ridgeline. Shortly the path begins to climb. After climbing 100 feet in a quarter of a mile, it begins to descend. Some of this descent is fairly steep and rocky. The trail drops for 300 hundred yards then flattens out on the ridgeline

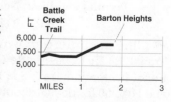

Hells Canyon Dam from Barton Heights.

at about 5,300 feet elevation. The route then follows the ridge for a short distance before bearing off slightly to the right. Soon the path bears farther to the right and heads down through some trees. This is the point where it is easy to lose the route to Barton Heights. Do not follow the path downhill; it is a side trail that heads down to a campsite. Stay above the trees and brush, never getting more than 100 yards from the ridgeline.

The route soon rounds two small bald knobs on the ridgeline as it heads east. Stay in the open just to the right of both knobs. There are some trees and brush along the ridge between the knobs, but it is fairly easy to work your way through. After passing the second knob, head generally east for about 0.3 mile, through the timber, along the now rounded and poorly defined ridge to a rocky point. This point is on the same ridge as Barton Heights, and a quarter of a mile north of it. Hike south from the rocky point along the ridge to Barton Heights. Be sure to take close note of the route after passing the second knob because it can be very confusing on the return trip. There is a sign marking the highest point of Barton Heights at 5,743 feet elevation.

Be sure to take a topographical map and compass along when doing this hike. The "approximate route" marked on the USGS map is very close to the route you will want to take. There is no water along this route. The wildflowers are best along this trail in June.

Options: The hike to Barton Heights can be done in one long day hike from P.O. Saddle Trailhead. This makes an 18-mile round trip from your car.

34 Thirtytwo Point Trail 1789

Highlights:	A hike from the unmarked Thirtytwo Point Trailhead on a lightly used trail down into Hells Canyon to the junction with Bench Trail.
Type of hike:	Out-and-back day hike, with shuttle options.
Total distance:	16 miles.
Difficulty:	Strenuous.
Best months:	Late June–October.
Elevation gain:	1,770 feet.
Permits and fees:	Northwest Forest Pass.
Maps:	Puderbaugh Ridge and White Monument USGS quads.

Finding the trailhead: To reach Thirtytwo Point Trailhead, take Oregon 350 (also known as Imnaha Highway or Little Sheep Creek Highway) east from Joseph, Oregon. After following OR 350 for 8 miles, turn right on Forest Road 39 (Wallowa Mountain Loop Road). Follow FR 39 for 41 miles to the junction with Forest Road 3962. Turn left and follow FR 3962 east for 5.5 miles to the junction with Forest Road 3965. Turn left on FR 3965 and drive east and north for 6.9 miles to the Thirtytwo Point Trailhead. The

Thirtytwo Point Trail 1789 • Buck Creek Trail 1788

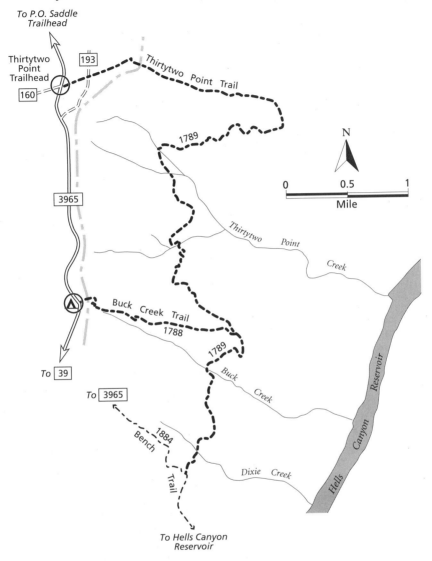

unsigned trailhead is on the right (east) side of the road, directly across from Forest Road 160. It is marked as Forest Road 190 and begins as a blocked four-wheel-drive road, heading east-northeast. The GPS coordinates at the trailhead are 45 13.343 N 116 46.090 W.

If you miss the trailhead, you will come to the iron gate at P.O. Saddle Trailhead in 0.6 mile. The iron gate closes FR 3965 to motorized travel beyond this point.

Trailhead facilities: The trailhead has parking for a couple of cars but has no other facilities.

Camping and services: Buck Creek Trailhead, which is 1.7 miles south of Thirtytwo Point Trailhead on FR 3965, has a campground. The closest place for gas, groceries, and medical services is Joseph.

For more information: USDA Forest Service at Wallowa Mountains Visitor Center in Enterprise, Oregon, or Pine Ranger Station in Halfway, Oregon.

Key points:
- 0.0   Thirtytwo Point Trailhead.
- 0.7   Wilderness Boundary.
- 2.7   Second trail sign.
- 3.9   Trail crosses fork of Thirtytwo Point Creek.
- 6.4   Junction with Buck Creek Trail 1788. GPS 45 11.676 N 116 44.289 W.
- 8.0   Junction with Bench Trail 1884. GPS 45 10.725 N 116 44.741 W.

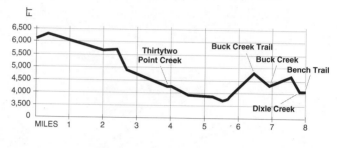

The hike: From the trailhead, the route climbs east-northeast in a nearly straight line for 0.2 mile to a fork. Bear left (really straight ahead) at the fork. One hundred fifty yards past the fork is a junction with closed FR 193. Bear right (also almost straight ahead) at this junction and climb a few feet more in the 0.4 mile to the top of a rise. This rise, at 6,230 feet elevation, is the highest point on Thirtytwo Point Trail. The trail is vague from the junction to the top of the rise, as it climbs to and follows the top of a poorly defined ridgeline through thick timber.

The path bears to the right at the top of the rise, then passes the Hells Canyon Wilderness Boundary sign. Now you begin to descend into the canyon, along a ridge. Just before leaving the timber the tread turns left, goes 30 yards, then turns right again on a slope covered with low brush. Here the trail begins to drop steeply. It makes a couple switchbacks then traverses back out onto a brushy ridge, which it descends. You soon make another switchback to the left, then one to the right on a semiopen slope. The trail is sometimes difficult to see on this slope, which may be covered with Brown's Peony, Paintbrush, Lupine, and many other flowers in early summer. You will make seven more switchbacks as you head down the ridge to a saddle, at 5,600 feet elevation.

After passing the saddle the faint tread climbs a few feet then traverses along the right side of the ridge. You soon cross the ridge in another small saddle, then climb a few feet just to the left of the ridgeline. The route soon regains the top of the ridge and follows it for 150 yards. Then the trail turns off the left side of the ridge. It makes three switchbacks before traversing back out onto the ridgeline. The ridge in this area is timbered on the left and open on the right. A trail sign is located on the open hillside, 50 yards to the right of the trail, 0.2 mile after regaining the ridgeline. There is another trail sign

0.3 mile down the ridge from this sign. It is very important that you find the second sign because this is the point that the trail leaves the ridge that it has been following. The second sign is at 4,940 feet elevation and is 2.7 miles from the trailhead.

At the second sign the route, which will probably not be visible on the ground, drops to the west-southwest. After heading west-southwest for 0.2 mile the trail crosses a small ridge through a saddle. The point where the trail crosses this ridge is 100 yards to the right (north) of the lowest point of the saddle. USGS maps show the location of the trail incorrectly here. After crossing the small ridge head west for a short distance, on the level, to the top of another small rise. From here the faint but visible path starts to descend through thin timber.

After descending for 0.2 mile you will cross a brushy draw, then traverse out onto a small steep ridgeline. Once across this ridgeline the trail crosses a lightly timbered slope for 0.4 mile. It then makes a switchback to the left and one to the right as it drops to a creek crossing (elev. 4,240 ft). Just after crossing the creek, 3.9 miles from the trailhead, there is a sign that says Thirtytwo Point Creek. You will cross another creek a short distance past the sign. These creeks are both forks of Thirtytwo Point Creek. The path makes a couple of switchbacks as it climbs out of the creekbed, then levels out and soon begins to descend through a timbered, brushy area to another creek crossing.

From this creek crossing the now fairly easy to follow tread crosses five more small creeks (some of which may be dry) as it winds its way through mostly timbered country, for 2.2 miles south to the junction with the Buck Creek Trail 1788. (See Hike 35 for a description of Buck Creek Trail.) There is an old 2-mile trail marker on a tree on the left side of the trail 0.2 mile before reaching the junction. The junction with Buck Creek Trail is on the top of a semiopen ridge at 4,730 feet elevation, 6.4 miles from the Thirtytwo Point Trailhead.

Leaving the junction with Buck Creek Trail, Thirtytwo Point Trail descends to the southeast for 0.3 mile. It then turns right and flattens for a short distance, before dropping to the southwest and entering the timber. You then descend through the timber for another 0.4 mile to Buck Creek. The route crosses Buck Creek (elev. 4,280 ft), then climbs for 0.5 mile to a ridgeline (elev. 4,600 ft). The USGS quad map shows the position of the trail incorrectly between Buck Creek and this ridge. There is a trail sign 10 yards west of the trail as it crosses the ridge. After crossing the ridge the trail descends generally south for 0.3 mile, then turns to the west. It heads west for a short distance then drops south again, entering the timber. The USGS map again shows the trail incorrectly as it descends through the timber to cross Dixie Creek at 4,040 feet elevation. The route climbs slightly after crossing Dixie Creek. One tenth of a mile past the crossing there is a campsite a few yards to the right of the trail.

Past the campsite the route descends slightly for about a quarter of a mile to the junction with Bench Trail 1884. Bench Trail to the right (west) is a bit difficult to spot, but it is obvious straight ahead to the south. This

Balsamroot.

is the end of Thirtytwo Point Trail, 8 miles from the trailhead, at 4,040 feet elevation.

Much of this trail is hard to follow, and the maps of the area are incorrect in spots. Good routefinding skills are very necessary to follow this trail safely. There is no water along the trail above Thirtytwo Point Creek. Rattlesnakes are a possibility along this trail. Watch for Bighorn Sheep while descending the ridge between the trailhead and Thirtytwo Point Creek.

Options: Return via the same route, or climb out on either Buck Creek Trail or Bench Trail. These last two possible return routes require a short car shuttle or a walk along FR 3965. See Hikes 35 and 36 for details.

It is also possible to combine Thirtytwo Point Trail with part of Bench Trail and hike down to Hells Canyon Reservoir. See Hike 36 for more information about Bench Trail.

35 Buck Creek Trail 1788

See Map on Page 169

Highlights: A hike from Buck Creek Trailhead to the junction with Thirtytwo Point Trail deep in Hells Canyon.

Type of hike: Out-and-back day hike or backpack, with shuttle and loop options.

Total distance: 3.8 miles.

Difficulty: Strenuous.

Best months: Late June–October.

Elevation loss: 1,270 feet.

Permits and fees: Northwest Forest Pass.

Maps: Puderbaugh Ridge and White Monument USGS quads.

Finding the trailhead: To reach Buck Creek Trailhead, take Oregon 350 (also known as Imnaha Highway or Little Sheep Creek Highway.) east from Joseph, Oregon. After following OR 350 approximately 8 miles, turn right on Forest Road 39 (Wallowa Mountain Loop Road.) Follow FR 39 for 41 miles to the junction with Forest Road 3962. Turn left and follow FR 3962 east for 5.5 miles to the junction with Forest Road 3965. Turn left on FR 3965 and drive 5.2 miles east and north to Buck Creek Trailhead and Campground. The campground is on the left side of the road, and the trailhead is on the right. The GPS coordinates at the trailhead are 45 11.879 N 116 45.816 W.

Trailhead facilities: The trailhead has a campground, horse facilities, and restrooms.

Camping and services: Buck Creek Trailhead has a campground. The closest place for gas, groceries, and medical services is Joseph.

For more information: USDA Forest Service at Wallowa Mountains Visitor Center in Enterprise, Oregon, or Pine Ranger Station in Halfway, Oregon.

Key points:
- 0.0   Buck Creek Trailhead.
- 0.1   Viewpoint.
- 1.9   Junction with Thirtytwo Point Trail. GPS 45 11.676 N 116 44.289 W.

The hike: As you leave the trailhead, the tread heads east-northeast and soon begins to descend. After 0.1 mile it makes a switchback to the right. Just to the left of the trail at the switchback is a viewpoint with an excellent view of the canyon country below. A short distance farther along the path makes another switchback, this one to the left, and heads down a semiopen slope that is covered with balsamroot in the early summer. The route descends nearly to the creekbed of Buck Creek (which may be dry), then traverses back out onto the ridgeline, at approximately 5,000 feet elevation, making

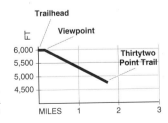

Buck Creek Trailhead.

a couple more switchbacks along the way. After regaining the ridge, the trail generally follows its rocky top on down to the junction with Thirtytwo Point Trail 1789 at 4,730 feet elevation.

The Buck Creek Trail is steep and rocky in places but is generally easy to follow. There is usually no water available along this trail. Watch for the Bighorn Sheep, which inhabit this section of Hells Canyon.

Options: An alternate return trip can be made by turning left at the junction with Thirtytwo Point Trail and climbing back out to Thirtytwo Point Trailhead, making a 8.3-mile hike. This would involve a short car shuttle or a 1.7-mile walk back along FR 3965 to Thirtytwo Point Trailhead. See Hike 34 for a description of Thirtytwo Point Trail.

36 Bench Trail 1884

Highlights:	A hike from Bench Trailhead high on Summit Ridge to Hells Canyon Reservoir. Bench Trail roughly follows the route of the 1883–84 Bonneville expedition.
Type of hike:	Shuttle day hike or backpack, with a loop option.
Total distance:	11.5 miles.
Difficulty:	Strenuous. Good map reading and routefinding skills are essential to follow this trail safely.
Best months:	Late June–October
Elevation gain:	750 feet.
Permits and fees:	Northwest Forest Pass.
Maps:	Puderbaugh Ridge, White Monument, and Homestead USGS quads.

Finding the trailhead: To reach Bench Trailhead, take Oregon 350 (also known as Imnaha Highway or Little Sheep Creek Highway) east from Joseph. After following OR 350 approximately 8 miles, turn right on Forest Road 39 (Wallowa Mountain Loop Road.) Follow FR 39 for 41 miles to the junction with Forest Road 3962. Turn left and head east on FR 3962, and follow it for 5.5 miles to the junction with Forest Road 3965. Turn left on FR 3965 and drive east and north for 4.5 miles to Bench Trailhead. The sign marking the trailhead is on a side road 100 yards to the right (east) of FR 3965 and can be seen from the main road. The GPS coordinates at the trailhead are 45 11.436 N 116 45.913 W.

To make a car shuttle between the trailheads, backtrack the 10 miles to FR 39. Turn left (south) and follow FR 39 for 21miles to the junction with Oregon 86. Turn left (northeast) on OR 86, and drive for 9 miles to Oxbow, Oregon. From Oxbow, head north along the west side of Hells Canyon Reservoir on County Road 1039 for 8.7 miles to Hells Canyon Reservoir Trailhead.

For driving directions from Baker City to Hells Canyon Reservoir Trailhead, see Hike 37.

Bench Trail 1884

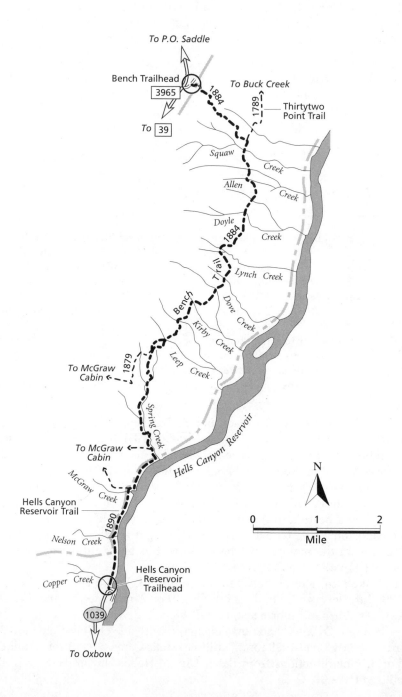

Trailhead facilities: The trailhead has parking for several cars but has no other facilities. Buck Creek Campground is 0.7 mile north of Bench Trailhead on FR 3962.

Camping and services: There is a campground at Buck Creek Trailhead, which is 0.7 mile north of Bench Trailhead on FR 3965. Gas, groceries, and medical services can be obtained in Joseph, Oregon, and Baker City, Oregon.

For more information: USDA Forest Service at Pine Ranger Station in Halfway, Oregon, or Wallowa Mountains Visitor Center in Enterprise, Oregon.

Key points:

0.0	Bench Trailhead.
2.0	Junction with Thirtytwo Point Trail. GPS 45 10.725 N 116 44.741 W.
3.1	Doyle Creek.
6.1	Leep Creek.
6.2	Junction with McGraw Creek Trail. GPS 45 07.978 N 116 46.474 W.
8.7	Junction with Hells Canyon Reservoir Trail. GPS 45 06.456 N 116 46.578 W.
11.5	Hells Canyon Reservoir Trailhead. GPS 45 04.793 N 116 47.118 W.

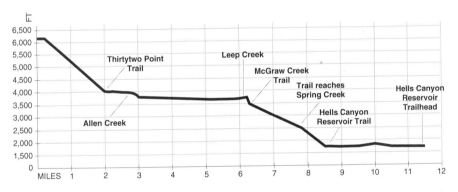

The hike: From the trailhead sign on the east side of FR 3965 the trail heads northeast, staying nearly level for a short distance. The route passes the Hells Canyon Wilderness Boundary sign, then soon bears right and begins to descend. You will wind down the ridgeline for 0.2 mile, then turn right and drop off the ridge on a slope that may be covered with Paintbrush and Balsamroot. These red and yellow flowers bloom in July here. The path soon crosses the ridgeline again and continues to head down, switchbacking across the ridge several times. Where the ridge splits, the trail follows the right (south) ridgeline. After going down the south ridgeline, the trail turns right off the ridge and soon comes to what looks like an unmarked junction. At this junction turn to the left and follow the rock cairns into the timber and brush. There are also some blazes marking the trail in this area. Another 0.2 mile brings you to the junction with Thirtytwo Point Trail 1789 at 4,040 feet elevation. The trail may be hard to see in the small meadow just before reaching the junction. Head east and down across the meadow. There is a sign on a tree marking this junction, two miles from the trailhead.

Bench Trail turns right at the junction and heads south through an old burn area that is growing up with young Ponderosa Pines and brush. It crosses Squaw Creek 0.1 mile from the junction. After crossing Squaw Creek the route climbs slightly and continues south along the benches. You soon leave the burn area to enter a forest of larger trees. The trail may be a bit hard to see in places; watch for cut logs. Half a mile after crossing Squaw Creek you will cross Allen Creek (elev. 3,960 ft). There is a sign marking Allen Creek, but the stream may be dry in late summer and fall. After crossing Allen Creek the course soon crosses a small ridge. The ridgetop is mostly open, and there is a campsite to the right of the trail. There is no water, however. A couple hundred yards farther along the tread crosses the North Fork of Doyle Creek. Doyle Creek is crossed 0.2 mile after crossing the north fork. There is a sign marking Doyle Creek, 3.1 miles from the trailhead, at 3,880 feet elevation.

The timber begins to thin soon after crossing Doyle Creek, and the view of the canyon to the left opens up. Hike across the open benches for 0.7 mile before reentering the timber and crossing the North Fork of Lynch Creek. The trail may be a little difficult to see just before the crossing, but soon shows up again. Another 150 yards through the timber and the route crosses Lynch Creek. Lynch Creek may be dry in fall. After crossing Lynch Creek you will traverse a timbered slope for 0.2 mile before leaving the timber again. Another 0.2 mile along is Dove Creek, which may also be dry in late summer and fall. Shortly after crossing Dove Creek there is a sign to the right of the trail that says Kirby Creek. The sign is in a strange place, because there is no creek here and Kirby Creek is some distance to the south. A short distance past the sign the trail crosses a broad ridgeline. After crossing the ridge the path enters a brushy draw and crosses the North Fork of Kirby Creek. Shortly after crossing the North Fork of Kirby Creek you will cross a small ridge. Here the country you are traversing becomes more rugged. Far below to the left Hells Canyon Reservoir can be seen. The parking area and boat ramp you can see on the Idaho side of the reservoir is Big Bar Recreational Site.

Half a mile after crossing the North Fork of Kirby Creek you will cross Kirby Creek, in a brushy draw. There is a sign at the crossing that calls this stream Bar Creek. Kirby Creek crossing (elev. 3,670 ft) is 5.3 miles from the trailhead. After crossing Kirby Creek the trail rounds several small ridges, and crosses several small streams, in the 0.8 mile to Leep Creek. On the steep side hills in this area the trail is in rather poor condition. It has slid away in several spots and is braided in some others, making the exact route a bit difficult to follow. By remembering that this section of trail does not gain or lose much elevation you should be able to stay close to the right route. After crossing Leep Creek (elev. 3,700 ft), which may be dry in late summer and fall, the route climbs a few yards to a ridgeline. On the ridge is a fence, with a gate to let trail traffic through. Just past the gate the trail forks. The main route bears to the right at the fork, and descends steeply, making a couple of switchbacks, in the 0.3 mile to the junction with McGraw Creek Trail (Old McGraw Creek Route) at 3,450 feet elevation. The left fork of the trail also makes the descent to this junction passing a spring and stock water trough on the way. At the junction, marked with a signpost, McGraw Creek Trail turns to the right. The sign pointing to the right says West McGraw Creek; the sign pointing to the left says Snake River. Bear to the left and stay on Bench Trail.

From the junction Bench Trail drops off the ridgeline to the southwest for a short distance, then heads south toward Spring Creek, continuing its descent. It makes several switchbacks as it works its way down to a flatter area next to the creek.

This section of trail was badly braided and hard to follow, but parts of it have now been reconstructed. The route descends and crosses Spring Creek then traverses above the creekbed to the junction with another new section of trail that is replacing the Old McGraw Creek Route. At the junction bear left and descend to the junction with Hells Canyon Reservoir Trail 1890.

Turn right on Hells Canyon Reservoir Trail and hike 2.8 miles south to Hells Canyon Reservoir Trailhead. (See Hike 37 for more information about Hells Canyon Reservoir Trail.)

The condition of Bench Trail generally becomes poorer south of Lynch Creek. The USGS quads show it correctly, but the actual trail may be a challenge to follow. For people with good routefinding skills the route is not hard to stay on, but for the novice it is very easy to lose your way.

An encounter with a Rattlesnake is possible along almost any part of this trail. Be especially watchful for them in the area below the junction with Mc-Graw Creek Trail. The lower sections of this trail may be very hot in summer.

Options: Turn left at the junction with Thirtytwo Point Trail 2 miles from Bench Trailhead. Then hike north for 1.6 miles to the junction with Buck

McGraw Divide.

Creek Trail. Turn left on Buck Creek Trail and climb 1.9 miles west to Buck Creek Trailhead. You can make a car shuttle between Buck Creek Trailhead and Bench Trailhead or hike south along FR 3965 for 0.7 mile. See Hikes 34 and 35 for information about these trails. Good fishing for warmwater game fish can be had in Hells Canyon Reservoir.

37 Hells Canyon Reservoir Trail 1890

Highlights:	A hike along the west side of Hells Canyon Reservoir, from the trailhead to Spring Creek. The first flowers begin to bloom along this trail about the first of March. Watch for bald eagles along the reservoir in winter and spring and for bighorn sheep all year. This trail is the access route for the Old McGraw Creek Route and the exit route for Bench Trail 1884.
Type of hike:	Out-and-back day hike with loop option.
Total distance:	6 miles.
Difficulty:	Easy.
Best months:	March–June and September–November.
Elevation gain:	Minimal.
Permits and fees:	None.
Maps:	Homestead USGS quad.

Finding the trail: Head east from Interstate 84 at Baker City on Oregon 86. Follow OR 86 for 70 miles to Oxbow, Oregon. From OR 86 at Oxbow, drive north along the west side of the Hells Canyon Reservoir on County Road 1039. After going 8.7 miles, CR 1039 ends at the trailhead, which is located to the right at the end of the road, next to the reservoir. The GPS coordinates at the trailhead are 45 04.793 N 116 47.118 W.

Trailhead facilities: The trailhead has parking for several cars as well as some unimproved campsites.

Camping and services: The trailhead has several unimproved campsites. Gas and groceries can be had at Pine Creek, which is 2 miles southwest of Oxbow on OR 86. For medical services, your best bet is to head for Halfway, Oregon, another 15 miles to the southwest on OR 86.

For more information: USDA Forest Service at Pine Ranger Station in Halfway or at Wallowa Mountains Visitor Center in Enterprise, Oregon.

Key points:
- 0.0 Hells Canyon Reservoir Trailhead.
- 1.0 Nelson Creek.
- 2.0 McGraw Creek and junction with Old McGraw Creek Route. GPS 46 06.082 N 116 46.868 W.
- 2.8 Junction with Bench Trail. GPS 45 06.456 N 116 46.578 W.
- 3.0 Spring Creek.

Hells Canyon Reservoir Trail 1890
Old McGraw Creek Route 1879

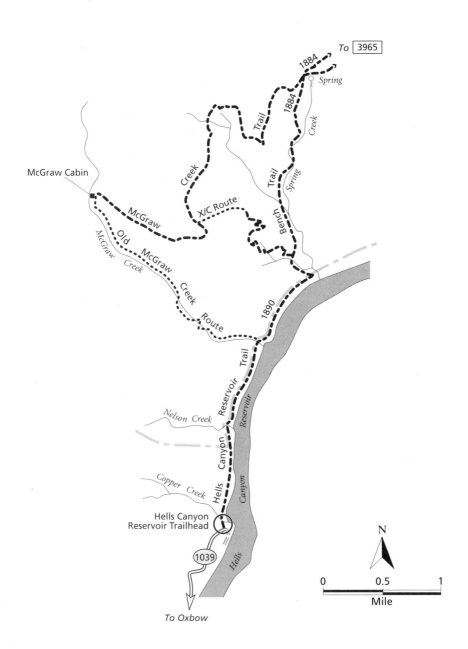

To 3965

1884

1884

Spring

Trail

Creek

Trail

Spring Creek

McGraw Cabin

Creek

X/C Route

Bench

McGraw

Old McGraw Creek Route

McGraw Creek

1890

Reservoir Trail

Reservoir

Nelson Creek

Hells Canyon

Canyon

Copper Creek

Hells Canyon
Reservoir Trailhead

Hells

1039

To Oxbow

N

0   0.5   1
Mile

The hike: From the sloping, grass-covered parking area and wilderness registration box, the trail heads northwest 0.1 mile, crossing an area that was heavily damaged by a waterspout, to Copper Creek. It crosses the creek and in a few yards comes to a trail sign. The sign points the hiker ahead 2 miles to McGraw Creek and 3 miles to Bench Trail. From the sign the trail heads northeast a short distance,

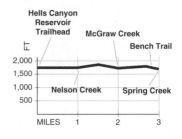

climbing slightly. It then rounds a rocky point and heads to the north along the reservoir.

One mile from the trailhead the path climbs gently into a side draw and crosses Nelson Creek. Past Nelson Creek the route climbs slightly back out to a rocky outcropping, overlooking the reservoir. Half a mile after crossing Nelson Creek a dripping spring can be heard but not seen above the trail to the left. This spring may not be flowing during the drier parts of the year. The tread crosses a fence line 0.1 mile after passing the spring. At 1.9 miles there is a shallow cave to the left of the trail. Soon the path rounds a rocky point and heads into McGraw Creek Canyon. It crosses McGraw Creek and comes to the unmarked junction with Old McGraw Creek Route, a few yards after the crossing. The creekbed of McGraw Creek was scoured by a waterspout in 1997, and there is no evidence of Old McGraw Creek Route at the junction. (See Hike 38 for details about Old McGraw Creek Route.)

After passing the junction with Old McGraw Creek Route, Hells Canyon Reservoir Trail heads east for a short distance along the north side of McGraw

Waterspout debris at mouth of McGraw Creek.

Creek, back to the reservoir. The route climbs gently, through a rockslide covered with green lichen, and soon rounds another rocky point. The course cuts its way through a patch of blackberries a short distance before reaching the junction with Bench Trail 1884. (See Hike 36 for a description of Bench Trail.) This junction is shown slightly incorrectly on Forest Service maps. At the junction bear right on the less-used trail. Another 0.2 mile and the trail reaches Spring Creek, the end of your hike.

From here north the trail has not been maintained for many years and is closed to stock traffic. The route is difficult to follow and has slid away or been washed out in many places. There are some slopes that drop off steeply into the reservoir, which could be dangerous for children. Poison Ivy is common along this trail, and Rattlesnakes are always a possibility, except during the coldest time of the year.

Options: Use Old McGraw Creek Route and Bench Trail to make a very strenuous, 12.5-mile, lollipop loop hike. See Hikes 38 and 36 for details. This optional loop is not suitable for stock.

38 Old McGraw Creek Route 1879

See Map on Page 181

Highlights:	A hike from Hells Canyon Reservoir Trail passing a historic cabin to a junction with Bench Trail, watching for deer, elk, and bighorn sheep as you go.
Type of hike:	Internal connector day hike or backpack, with a loop option.
Total distance:	6 miles.
Difficulty:	Strenuous. Good map reading, routefinding, and scrambling skills are necessary to navigate this route safely. Do not take stock on the part of this route in McGraw Creek Canyon between Hells Canyon Reservoir Trail and McGraw Cabin.
Best months:	April–June and September–November.
Elevation gain:	Approximately 2,000 feet.
Trailhead elevation:	1,715 feet.
Permits and fees:	None.
Maps:	Homestead and Puderbaugh Ridge USGS quads. USGS maps show this trail incorrectly between Hells Canyon Reservoir Trail and McGraw Cabin.

Finding the trailhead: Follow the driving directions in Hike 37 to Hells Canyon Reservoir Trailhead. Then hike 2 miles north on Hells Canyon Reservoir Trail to the unmarked junction with Old McGraw Creek Route. This canyon was hit by a waterspout on January 1, 1997, so the path is hard to see at the junction. The GPS coordinates at the junction with Hells Canyon Reservoir Trail are 45 06.082 N 116 46.868 W.

Trailhead facilities: A couple of possible campsites can be found on the waterspout debris near the junction.

Camping and services: The Hells Canyon Reservoir Trailhead has several primitive campsites. Gas and groceries can be obtained at Pine Creek, which is 2 miles southwest of Oxbow on OR 86. For medical services, your best bet is to head for Halfway, Oregon, another 15 miles to the southwest on OR 86.

For more information: USDA Forest Service at Pine Ranger Station in Halfway, or Wallowa Mountains Visitor Center in Enterprise, Oregon.

Key points:
- 0.0 Junction with Hells Canyon Reservoir Trail 2 miles north of Hells Canyon Reservoir Trailhead.
- 0.4 Turnaround point for casual hikers. GPS 45 06.123 N 116 47.224 W.
- 2.0 McGraw Cabin.
- 4.0 Old 4-mile trail marker on tree.
- 6.0 Junction with Bench Trail. GPS 45 07.978 N 116 46.474 W.

The hike: From the junction with the Hells Canyon Reservoir Trail the route path heads west, up Mc-Graw Creek Canyon. Steep black canyon walls, broken with talus slopes are above, and McGraw Creek rushes to your left. The very vague route climbs the waterspout de-

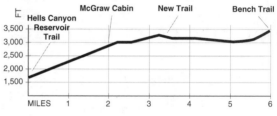

bris for 0.2 mile, then turns right at a rock cairn. You then climb a few feet out of the creekbed bear left (west) on a vague path through the sumac and other brush. Watch for Bighorn Sheep on the cliffs above as you work your way up the canyon.

The route traverses steep slopes and rocky ledges for another 0.2 mile to a point where it is washed out again. This is the turnaround point for all but experienced and agile cross-country hikers. During periods of heavy runoff McGraw Creek may be difficult to cross. The January 1, 1997, waterspout obliterated most of the trail for the next 1.2 miles. House-size boulders line the creek as it flows over many small but beautiful waterfalls.

If you continue your hike through this very rough area you will be able to climb out of the north side of the creekbed for the last time about 1.6 miles from the junction with Hells Canyon Reservoir Trail, at approximately 2,500 feet elevation. The fairly steep path then climbs along an open hillside for 0.2 mile, before flattening out to traverse a mostly open slope. Patches of Sumac and Thorn Brush dot this slope. Shortly you will come alongside a fence. The remains of an old apple orchard can be seen across the fence to the left. McGraw Cabin soon comes into view ahead. The square cabin with a pyramid roof is in fair condition. There is a gate in the fence next to the cabin. The cabin, at 2,760 feet elevation, is 2 miles from Hells Canyon Reservoir Trail.

Passing the cabin, the tread continues along the fence line to the north-northeast for 100 yards to a fork. Turn right at the fork. The left fork heads on up into McGraw Creek Canyon but is not maintained and soon becomes difficult to follow. After turning right you will climb to the east on an open grassy slope. The route climbs for 0.4 mile then flattens out on a bench. At one time hay must have been cut on this bench, because there is a rusty old mower sitting beside the trail.

The trail stays nearly level for 0.2 mile as it crosses the bench. If you are hiking this trail in the spring, watch for Elk, from here to the junction with Bench Trail. They are very abundant here at that time of the year, as are Mule Deer. The route crosses a fenceline. After crossing the fenceline on the far side of the flat bench, you climb a slope covered with quartzite boulders and limestone outcroppings. The course makes a left turn a quarter of a mile after crossing the fenceline. It soon bears to the right again and heads on to the east. You will make a turn to the left and cross a ridgeline at 3,320 feet elevation, 0.5 mile after crossing the fenceline.

Once across the ridge the tread heads northwest and descends slightly. As you descend you may notice a vague cross-country route to your right (east-northeast). This route leads to a newly constructed section of trail. The newly constructed section is a replacement for the part of the route you have been hiking that washed out in the 1997 flood. For more information about this new section of trail, see the options section below.

The rugged dark rimrocks of the McGraw Divide are straight ahead to the west, and to the northeast the twisted light gray and tan limestone formations underlying the bench you are on are exposed. The route descends gently for 0.5 mile, over mostly open slopes to the northwest to a small grove of pine trees (elev. 3,190 ft). There is a small stream in the grove, which may be dry by summer. The old 4-mile trail marker is on a large pine next to the stream. The flat area at the north end of the grove is an excellent campsite. The trail heads north from the creek crossing, and soon bears northeast then northwest. It crosses a small ridgeline 0.2 mile after crossing the creek.

After crossing the ridgeline the path drops fairly steeply for a short distance and goes through a small grove of Douglas-fir. Just after passing the fir grove, you cross a small streambed and turn to the right (north). The tread then climbs over a small rise and winds its way back to the west, to a small stream crossing. After crossing the small stream the route rounds another point to a larger stream. The trail is hard to see in this area. It passes a prospect hole shortly after crossing the larger stream. The prospect hole is below the trail to the right (elev. 3,080 ft). After passing the prospect hole the tread soon crosses another streambed.

Across the streambed, which may or may not have water in it, the trail contours to the east for 0.3 mile. It then turns left and crosses a ridgeline next to a mud hole. From here to the junction with Bench Trail, the vague route is very difficult to follow exactly. It contours to the northeast for 0.6 mile, to another stream crossing (elev. 3,110 ft). The course then continues to contour for another 0.1 mile, around another ridge to a gully. Here the route turns steeply up, climbing the right side of the gully to the junction

Waterfall in McGraw Creek.

with the Bench Trail 1884, at 3,450 feet elevation and 6 miles from the junction with Hells Canyon Reservoir Trail where this hike started. The Bonneville Expedition is thought to have made camp near this junction in the winter of 1833–34.

Both elk and cattle heavily use this area. Their trails cross and parallel the main trail, making it nearly impossible to tell whether you are on the right trail.

Options: Turn around at 0.4 mile from Hells Canyon Reservoir Trail, or make a loop hike by descending Bench Trail south to Hells Canyon Reservoir Trail and then following that trail southwest to the junction with Old McGraw Creek Route and Hells Canyon Reservoir Trailhead. See Hike 36 for a description of Bench Trail.

To reach McGraw Cabin via a much easier route, follow Hells Canyon Reservoir Trail to the junction with Bench Trail. Turn left on Bench Trail and climb west for a short distance to the junction with the newly constructed section of trail that replaces Old McGraw Creek Route. Bear left at the junction and hike west to Old McGraw Creek Route as described above. Turn left on Old McGraw Creek Route and follow it for about 0.7 mile to the cabin.

39 Stud Creek Trail 1781

Highlights:	A hike along the turbulent waters of the Snake River below Hells Canyon Dam as you watch the slopes above for mountain goats and bighorn sheep.
Type of hike:	Out-and-back day hike.
Total distance:	2.4 miles.
Difficulty:	Easy.
Best months:	March–November.
Elevation gain:	Minimal.
Permits and fees:	None.
Maps:	Squirrel Prairie USGS quad.

Finding the trailhead: To reach Hells Canyon Dam Visitor Center and Boat Launch, head east from Interstate 84 at Baker City on Oregon 86. Follow OR 86 for 70.5 miles to the bridge over the Snake River at Copperfield Park. Cross the bridge and turn left on the Idaho Power Company Road. Follow the Idaho Power Company Road, which becomes Forest Road 454, for 21 miles north along Hells Canyon Reservoir to Hells Canyon Dam. Cross the dam and continue north on the Oregon side of the river for 1.2 miles to the Hells Canyon Visitor Center and Boat Launch. The GPS coordinates at the trailhead and boat launch are 45 15.252 N 116 41.836 W.

Trailhead facilities: The trailhead has a visitor center, restrooms, a picnic table, a boat ramp, and adequate parking.

Camping and services: Camping is available at the Idaho Power Company Park 16.2 miles north of the trailhead on FR 454. Gas and groceries can be had at Pine Creek, which is 2 miles southwest of Oxbow on OR 86. For medical services, your best bet is to head for Halfway, Oregon, another 15 miles to the southwest on OR 86.

For more information: USDA Forest Service at Hells Canyon Dam Visitor Center next to the trailhead.

Key points:

0.0   Hells Canyon Dam Boat Launch and Trailhead.
1.2   Stud Creek. GPS 45 15.982 N 116 41.379 W.

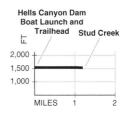

The hike: Register at the register box and begin your hike to Stud Creek on the boardwalk trail. A few yards into the boardwalk, steps climb to the left. These steps lead to a rock shelter that was used by early Native Americans. The boardwalk soon ends, and nine wooden steps take the trail to a ledge above the river. Desert parsley and larkspur as well as poison ivy line the trail as it passes beneath overhanging rocks. Soon you pass an area where the tread is elevated a few feet to prevent damage and allow passage during times of high water.

Stud Creek Trail 1781

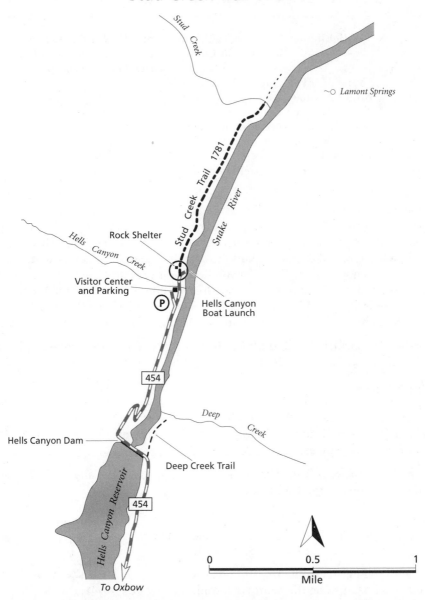

The course winds up and down to get past the rock outcroppings, never gaining or losing much elevation. Sometimes wooden steps and switchbacks ease the grade. In spots the trail has been chipped out of the cliffs. In April, Shooting Stars bloom between the boulders as you hike north. Barton Heights rises 4,000 feet above the river ahead. As you hike, watch to your right across the river in Idaho for the mountain goats that inhabit the cliffs. Occasionally bighorn sheep can also be seen on the Oregon side of the river.

Barton Heights from Stud Creek Trail.

One mile from the trailhead the trace enters the alluvial fan of Stud Creek. Balsamroot and Woodland Stars add color to the fan below the scrubby Hackberry trees and scattered pines. The path crosses a small stream, then crosses Stud Creek. After crossing Stud Creek, the trail quickly fades. Walk a few yards farther and take a break next to the river. An occasional rattlesnake may be encountered along this trail.

The small patches of brush across the river above the bar are Lamont Springs, where the Idaho Snake River Trail used to begin. At one time there may have been a ford across the river here to connect with the trail on the Idaho side, but do not try to ford the river now.

Options: Drive back across Hells Canyon Dam and park at a small parking area a couple hundred yards south of it. Then walk back along the road to the east end of the dam and the trailhead for Deep Creek Trail. Register at the trail register box and descend the trail, which includes 259 metal steps, to the mouth of Deep Creek. Do not leave this trail as you descend because the steep cliffs and churning water below are very dangerous. Do not confuse this trail with the other Deep Creek Trails.

Idaho

NORTHERN REGION

Measured from the summits of the peaks in the Seven Devils Mountains, Hells Canyon is probably the deepest canyon in North America. The 8,000 feet of local vertical relief in this region make for the widest variety of flora and fauna to be found in Hells Canyon. The huge difference in elevation also makes for some of the most challenging trails. All of the hikes in this region except **Hike 45 Blue Jacket Mine Trail** interconnect.

In the bottom of the canyon, **Hike 40 Idaho Snake River National Recreation Trail** winds its way through the arid landscape along the Snake River. Hiking along the river from Upper Pittsburg Landing to Kirkwood Ranch and back is a great early starter for your hiking season.

Hike 42 Bernard Creek Trail and **Hike 43 Sheep Creek Trail** connect the Idaho Snake River Trail with the alpine terrain of the Seven Devils Mountains. Far above the river, **Hike 49 Seven Devils Loop** encircles the highest peaks of the range. **Hikes 50** through **54** and **Hike 56** are internal trails leading from the loop to the alpine lakes of the region. **Hike 55 Dry Diggins Lookout Trail** and **Hike 57 Bernard Lakes Trail** are also side trips off the loop, and they lead to Dry Diggins Lookout, the best viewpoint in the Hells Canyon Wilderness. The area around the lookout is a likely place to spot mountain goats grazing on the nearly perpendicular cliffs.

Most of **Hike 46 Boise Trail North** follows an abandoned roadbed along the northern ridgeline of the Seven Devils. Much of this hike is through ridgetop meadows, allowing for spectacular views of Hells Canyon to the west, the high peaks of the Seven Devils to the south, and Salmon River Canyon to the east. The first few miles of **Hike 60 Rapid River Trail** make an excellent springtime hike because of the trail's easy access and relatively low elevation.

He Devil Mountain over Sheep Lake. GARY FLETCHER PHOTO

Northern Region

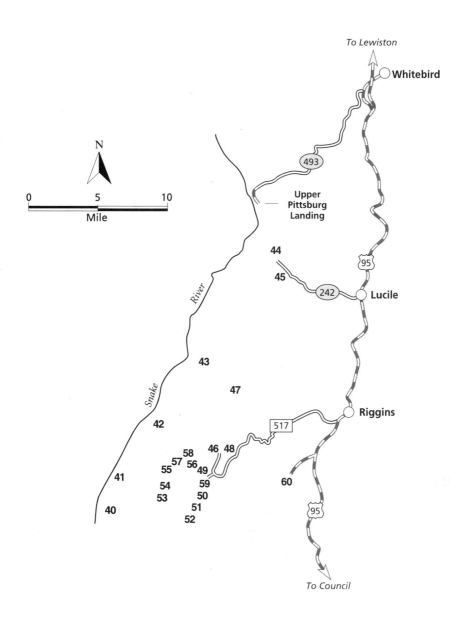

N

0   5   10
Mile

To Lewiston

Whitebird

493

Upper
Pittsburg
Landing

44

45

242   Lucile

95

River

43

47

Snake

42

Riggins

517

46 48

58
57 56
55   49
54   59
53   50
51
52

40

41

60

95

To Council

40 Idaho Snake River National Recreation Trail 102

Highlights:	A hike through the deepest part of Hells Canyon, along the Idaho side of the Snake River from the drop-off point at Butler Bar to the Upper Pittsburg Landing Trailhead.
Type of hike:	3- to 5-day backpack with jet boat shuttle.
Total distance:	30.1 miles.
Difficulty:	Moderate, but good routefinding skills are necessary to follow the first 3.1 miles from Butler Bar to Granite Creek.
Best months:	March–June and September–November.
Elevation gain:	Approximately 4,500 feet.
Trailhead elevation:	1,420 feet, at Butler Bar.
Permits and fees:	None.
Maps:	Squirrel Prairie, Hat Point, Old Timer Mountain, Temperance Creek, and Kirkwood Creek USGS quads or USDA Forest Service Travel Opportunity Guide for Hells Canyon National Recreation Area.

Finding the trailhead: The south end of Idaho Snake River Trail at Butler Bar is best reached by using jet boat transportation from Hells Canyon Dam Boat Launch. For jet boat transportation from Hells Canyon Dam to Butler Bar, contact Hells Canyon Adventures in Oxbow, Oregon. The GPS coordinates at Butler Bar are 45 19.189 N 116 40.405 W.

To reach Hells Canyon Dam Visitor Center and Boat Launch, head east from Interstate 84 at Baker City on Oregon 86. Follow OR 86 for 70.5 miles to the bridge over the Snake River at Copperfield Park. Cross the bridge and turn left on Idaho Power Company Road. Follow Idaho Power Company Road, which becomes Forest Road 454, for 21 miles north along Hells Canyon Reservoir to Hells Canyon Dam. Cross the dam and continue north on the Oregon side of the river for 1.2 miles to Hells Canyon Visitor Center and Boat Launch.

To reach drop-off points along the river below Johnson Bar, check with Beamers Hells Canyon Tours or Hells Canyon Adventures.

Upper Pittsburg Landing Trailhead, the end of this hike, is reached by taking County Road 493 from White Bird, Idaho. Go west on CR 493 from White Bird for 16 miles, over Pittsburg Saddle to Pittsburg Landing. The trailhead, at Upper Pittsburg Landing, is 1 mile to the left at the first junction after

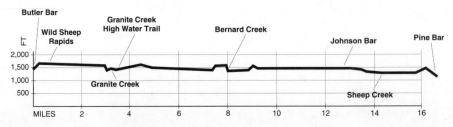

hitting the pavement.

Trailhead facilities: Hells Canyon Visitor Center and Boat Launch has restrooms and adequate parking. Campsites and restrooms are also located at Pittsburg Landing, at the end of this hike.

Camping and services: An Idaho Power Campground is located 14 miles south of Hells Canyon Dam on FR 454. Groceries and gas can be purchased in Pine Creek, Oregon, on OR 86 2 miles west of Oxbow. Other services can be obtained in Halfway, Oregon.

An RV park is located 1 mile north of Upper Pittsburg Landing at Pittsburg Landing. From the park, gas and groceries can be obtained in White Bird, Idaho, 16 miles to the east.

For more information: USDA Forest Service at Hells Canyon Dam Visitor Center, Hells Canyon National Recreation Area office in Riggins, Idaho, or Wallowa Mountains Visitor Center in Enterprise, Oregon. Hells Canyon Adventures in Oxbow will have information about water level and jet boat transportation. Bret Armocost, the owner of Hells Canyon Adventures, is also a good source for trail information. For car shuttle information, contact Scotty's Hells Canyon Outdoor Supply in Oxbow. For air transportation to or from Big Bar Airstrip, contact Spence Air Service in Enterprise.

Key points:
  0.0   Butler Bar.
  0.9   Wild Sheep Rapids.
  3.1   Granite Creek Bridge and junction with Little Granite Creek Trail. GPS
        45 20.789 N 116 39.249 W.
  3.4   Junction with Granite Creek High Water Trail. GPS 45 21.117 N 116
        38.997 W
  4.8   Three Creek.
  8.0   Bernard Creek Bridge and McGaffee Cabin. GPS 45 24.073 N 116 36.714 W.
 14.3   Sheep Creek Bridge and Sheep Creek Ranch. GPS 45 28.140 N 116
        33.239 W.
 16.6   Pine Bar.
 20.8   Temperance Creek Ranch across Snake River from trail.
 22.3   Suicide Point.
 24.6   Kirkwood Ranch. GPS 45 34.083 N 116 29.891 W.
 30.1   Upper Pittsburg Landing Trailhead. GPS 45 37.033 N 116 27.775 W.

The hike: The trail once started a few more miles upriver from Butler Bar at Lamont Springs, but the section above Butler Bar is fragmented and hard to follow. The condition of the trail generally gets better the farther downriver you go. The trail is seldom maintained and may be hard to follow above

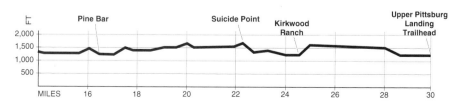

Idaho Snake River National Recreation Trail 102
(South half)

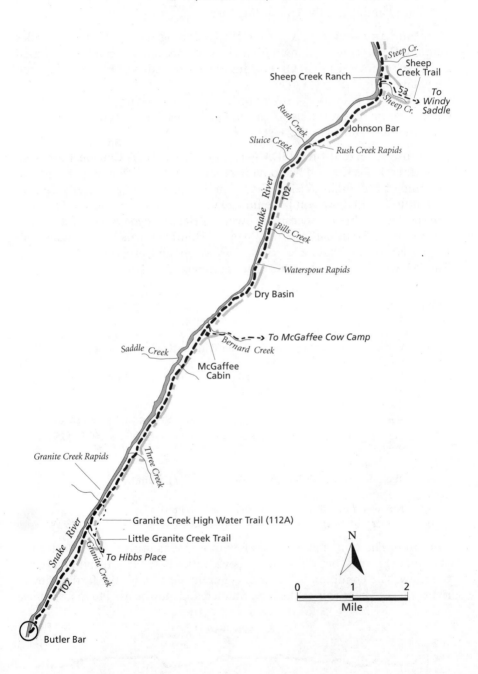

Steep Cr.

Sheep Creek Trail

Sheep Creek Ranch

53

To Windy Saddle

Sheep Cr.

Rush Creek

Johnson Bar

Sluice Creek

Rush Creek Rapids

Snake River

102

Bills Creek

Waterspout Rapids

Dry Basin

To McGaffee Cow Camp

Bernard Creek

Saddle Creek

McGaffee Cabin

Granite Creek Rapids

Three Creek

Granite Creek High Water Trail (112A)

Little Granite Creek Trail

Snake River

To Hibbs Place

Granite Creek

102

N

0   1   2
Mile

Butler Bar

Idaho Snake River National Recreation Trail 102
(North half)

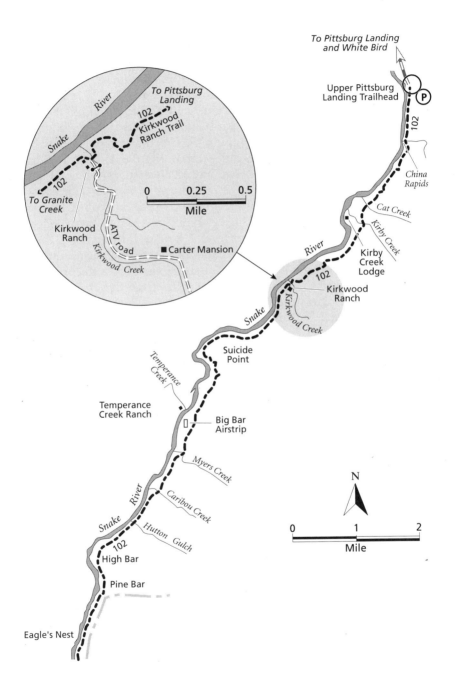

To Pittsburg Landing and White Bird

Upper Pittsburg Landing Trailhead

P

102

China Rapids

Cat Creek

Kirby Creek

Kirby Creek Lodge

River

102

Kirkwood Ranch

Snake

Kirkwood Creek

Suicide Point

Temperance Creek

Temperance Creek Ranch

Big Bar Airstrip

Myers Creek

Snake River

Caribou Creek

Hutton Gulch

102

High Bar

Pine Bar

Eagle's Nest

N

0   1   2
Mile

Inset

Snake River

To Pittsburg Landing

102

Kirkwood Ranch Trail

102

To Granite Creek

Kirkwood Ranch

ATV road

Kirkwood Creek

Carter Mansion

0   0.25   0.5
Mile

Granite Creek but is maintained yearly below there. Trail traffic is light above Granite Creek, moderate from Granite Creek to Kirkwood Ranch, and heavy below there. Light horse traffic can be expected.

Jet boat drop-off or pickup may not be possible between Wild Sheep Rapids and Johnson Bar in the spring, if water flow is too high. At normal water levels, getting around the low spot in the trail just below Granite Creek is no problem. However, if the water is high, it can be very difficult and possibly dangerous. There is a route around this low spot in the trail, but it is difficult and hard to follow. (See Hike 41 for a description of Granite Creek High Water Trail.) *Don't wade if the water level is too high.*

Leaving the drop-off point at Butler Bar, at 1,420 feet elevation, the vague route climbs to the northeast. The path climbs 300 feet, then flattens out and begins a traverse. Wild Sheep Rapids, the first major rapids below Hells Canyon Dam, is below the trail 0.9 mile from Butler Bar. Past the rapids the route works its way along a slope that may be covered with blooming Balsamroot in late April, for 0.6 mile, before returning to river level. It soon bears to the right and climbs away from the river again. Watch for cairns marking the trail in this section. The tread follows a wide sloping ledge for a short distance, 450 feet above river level, 1.2 miles farther along. Past the ledge the trail drops, sometimes in switchbacks, to the campsite next to Granite Creek. Bear to the right (east) in this open area and cross the bridge over Granite Creek. Granite Creek Bridge is 3.1 miles from Butler Bar.

Just over the bridge is the junction with Little Granite Creek Trail 112. The old Hibbs Ranch is 1 mile up Little Granite Creek Trail. Idaho Snake River Trail bears to the left after passing the junction and heads down along Granite Creek. This section may be brushed in with Poison Ivy. A quarter of a mile after crossing the bridge, the track drops down very close to the river, beneath some cliffs. At this point the trail becomes impassable during high water. Your jet boat captain will be able to tell you if the water is too high to get through this area. There is a trail around this section, but it is difficult to follow and extremely strenuous. (See Hike 41 for a description of the difficult route around the low section of Idaho Snake River Trail and details about hiking to Hibbs Ranch.)

After being next to the river for a short distance you will climb again, passing the downstream junction with Granite Creek High Water Trail and Granite Creek Rapids. The path continues downriver, passing the 25-mile mark, for 1.3 miles to Three Creek. The 25-mile mark, which indicates the distance to Pittsburg Landing, is on a pine tree on the right side of the trail. In 1889 Frank and Alberta Hiltsley moved to Three Creek. They raised hay on 5 acres they cleared on the bench north of the creek. Frank was drowned in 1912 as he was crossing the Snake River in a rowboat.

The route crosses a small muddy stream a short distance after crossing Three Creek. There is a campsite a little over a mile after crossing Three Creek. Saddle Creek enters the river from the Oregon side 1 mile after passing the campsite. Another mile ahead, after crossing a small rise, the trail reaches McGaffee Cabin.

This cabin was built about 1905 and is on the National Register of Historic Places. The cabin is in fairly good condition and at present the public is allowed to use it. Bill Hiltsley and his wife first settled this site in 1901. The land and cabin were sold to Frank McGaffee in 1915. Lenora Barton and Bud Wilson each owned the site for a time before it was sold to the Forest Service and became public land. There was once an extensive orchard here, including plum, pear, walnut, apricot, apple, cherry, and peach trees.

The tread crosses Bernard Creek on a bridge a short distance past the cabin. Bernard Creek, which was once called Squaw Creek, is 8 miles from the drop-off point at Butler Bar. The junction with Bernard Creek Trail 58 is reached just after crossing the bridge. Bernard Creek Trail is not visible on the ground here. (See Hike 42 for details about Bernard Creek Trail.)

After passing the junction, Idaho Snake River Trail contours along the river, on ledges a couple of times, for 0.6 mile, then begins to climb. It climbs 200 feet, then flattens out and starts to descend gently below Dry Basin. The trail takes 0.4 mile to get back close to the river, where it follows a small ledge for a short distance.

Along the ledge, on the right side of the trail, is a round vertical hole in the rock. This hole was caused by a hard rock being swirled around in a depression in the softer rock strata and wearing a deep hole. There are many of these holes along the river; some of them still have the hard rock inside of them.

In the next 0.4 mile the trail climbs to a bench above Waterspout Rapids. It soon descends off the bench, crosses Bills Creek, and passes Bills Creek Rapids. Just past Bills Creek are the remains of a stone cabin to the left of the trail. Silas Bullock built the cabin around 1912. Sluice Creek enters the river from the Oregon side 1.4 miles past Bills Creek. By looking southwest up Sluice Creek Canyon, Hat Point Lookout can be seen on the skyline. Rush Creek joins the Snake River 0.5 mile below Sluice Creek. It also enters from the Oregon side. At the mouth of Rush Creek is Rush Creek Rapids. The bottom of Rush Creek Rapids is considered to be the head of navigation by most jet boaters. The route enters the south end of Johnson Bar at Rush Creek Rapids.

Seven-tenths of a mile down Johnson Bar, there is a small fenced area to the left of the trail. A rusting hay rake sits beside the fence. The remains of a stone cabin, built in 1915 by Ralph Barton and Silas Bullock, are to the right of the trail here. At the north end of Johnson Bar, 0.8 mile farther along, is the Johnson Bar Camp used by rafters and jet boaters. Across the river a gauging station can be seen. Leaving the campsite at Johnson Bar the path first climbs a little, drops, then climbs again, making two switchbacks.

Past Johnson Bar Camp 0.7 mile, the course crosses a bridge over Sheep Creek. Past the bridge it climbs a few feet to Sheep Creek Ranch. Bill McLeod settled this area in 1884. There is a house, barn, and some other outbuildings at the ranch. The house was first built by Bill McGaffee and his brother Fred and later was rebuilt by Ace Barton. Sheep Creek Ranch, which now belongs to the Forest Service, is being used as a lodge by Snake River Adventures. It is 14.3 miles from the drop-off point at Butler Bar.

Bear left along the edge of the lawn area and pick up the trail again. The junction with Sheep Creek Trail 53 is at the north end of the lawn. (See Hike 43 for a description of Sheep Creek Trail.) Sheep Creek Trail turns right and goes between the house and the barn. A short distance ahead Idaho Snake River Trail comes to a mailbox and a sign marking the end of navigation. As far as the Army Corps of Engineers is concerned, this is the head of navigation, but many boaters go on up a bit farther. Just past the mailbox and sign the trail may be underwater for a few feet when the river is high, but this spot is easy to get around.

A quarter of a mile farther along, the track follows a ledge for a few yards, then crosses Steep Creek. On the Oregon side of the river, 0.6 mile past Steep Creek crossing, an exceptional bit of trail work can be seen. Here Oregon Snake River Trail 1726 has been cut out of a cliff. It is not on a ledge but is actually cut into a nearly vertical rock face. This section of Oregon Snake River Trail is called the Eagles Nest. The route now climbs a bit then follows a ledge for a short distance. It then drops slightly to another creek crossing. After crossing this creek the tread climbs over a rise, with the aid of 12 concrete steps.

The course then descends to Pine Bar, passing an outhouse and a table, which are some distance below the trail to the left. At Pine Bar a large number of ponderosa pine trees grow clear down to the river. The high alum content in the soil in this area supposedly allows these trees to prosper in this dry harsh climate. Watch for otters along the shore as you leave Pine Bar. At the north end of Pine Bar the route climbs slightly, to cross High Bar. It crosses High Bar for 0.6 mile then begins a descending traverse on an open hillside. The trace has dropped to river level again 0.6 mile after leaving High Bar. It soon climbs for 0.2 mile, then flattens out, and Temperance Creek Ranch, on the Oregon side of the river, comes into view far ahead.

The path continues its traverse for 0.6 mile, crossing a creek along the way. It then bears to the right back into a side canyon and climbs. A tunnel, and a pipe leading to it, can be seen across this side canyon. This pipe was used to divert water from Myers Creek to irrigate the hay fields on Big Bar. The trail keeps climbing up the side canyon and soon crosses Myers Creek. After crossing the creek the route climbs the ridge on the north side of the canyon. Then it drops steeply for a short distance to Big Bar. A 1,100-foot-long airstrip and a cabin can be seen to the left and below on Big Bar, as the trail descends. Air transportation can be arranged from Enterprise, Oregon, to and from this airstrip ($145 as of 2000). Six-tenths of a mile after crossing the ridge, Temperance Creek Ranch is directly across the river from the trail. Old farm machinery is scattered around, well above the river, on Big Bar.

On Big Bar the route is fairly flat for 0.6 mile except for crossing a couple small gullies. It then begins to climb toward Suicide Point. You will cross a large gully, then climb for 0.5 mile to a rocky point overlooking the river. The tread then winds in and out of steep rocky gullies for another 0.2 mile to Suicide Point. Suicide Point is the most spectacular point along Idaho Snake River Trail. From the point it is more than 300 feet nearly straight down to the Snake River. Cutting the trail out to this point took a tremendous amount of trail crew work. Try to allow some time to enjoy the view from here, but be careful to stay back from the cliff and keep children and animals restrained. Suicide Point, at 1,620 feet elevation, is 22.3 miles from the drop-off point at Butler Bar.

Leaving Suicide Point the path descends, making a couple of switchbacks. It soon climbs again, crosses a rise and then traverses an open slope. Soon the slope gets steeper, and the trail works its way along several ledges, as it drops back to river level. The course passes through a gate 2 miles after passing Suicide Point. Another 0.3 mile brings you to Kirkwood Ranch and the junction with Kirkwood Ranch Trail, on Kirkwood Bar. (See Hike 44 for more information about Kirkwood Ranch and the trail leading down to it from the Kirkwood Corrals far above to the east.)

At the ranch Idaho Snake River Trail crosses Kirkwood Creek, at 1,220 feet elevation, and passes a restroom to reach a campsite. The route heads north from the restroom to a gate in the northeast end of the pasture that the camp is in. You will go through the gate and pass the 6-mile marker before starting to climb. The track climbs 470 feet in the next 0.6 mile, making six switchbacks along the way. Then the course flattens out and traverses a steep hillside covered with Balsamroot, Paintbrush, and many other flowers. It crosses a gully and rounds a rocky point before reaching the 5-mile mark. Half a mile after passing the 5-mile mark the path passes through a notch. It then heads back into a side canyon, drops a little and crosses Kirby Creek.

A short distance farther, Kirby Creek Lodge can be seen, far below to the left, next to the river. Kirby Creek Lodge sits on the only spot of private ground along this trail. The route continues to traverse to mile mark 4, then starts to descend. It winds its way down nearly to river level, then traverses a gentle slope, covered with Hackberry bushes, boulders, and cactus. The path soon crosses a small stream, then begins to climb gently on an open slope.

After crossing the open slope the tread heads back into a side canyon and soon crosses the brushy canyon bottom. Then the route rounds a point and descends a little, along a very steep hillside above the river. It soon drops back into a small side canyon. In the canyon bottom the trail turns left and heads down. You will soon bear right and go through a gate. The route then winds its way down another 100 vertical feet before flattening out again. Half a mile after flattening out the trail crosses a creek. It goes through another gate 0.2 mile farther along. Here the path is cut out of a rock face only a few feet above the river. The trail climbs for a short distance, then flattens and drops again, passing a side trail to the left, to Upper Pittsburg Landing Trailhead. Upper Pittsburg Landing Trailhead, at 1,190 feet elevation, is 30.1 miles from Butler Bar.

Rattlesnakes are common all along the trail; there is a good chance you will see one, so be cautious, especially with children and pets. Watch out for Poison Ivy, which is abundant in many places. People drown in the Snake River almost every year. This is a large, powerful, and sometimes very cold river. Take all the precautions necessary to keep yourself and your children safe.

Idaho Snake River Trail.

Open fires are prohibited all year in the Snake River Corridor. This corridor covers all the land within the National Recreation Area that is a quarter of a mile or less from the high-water line of the Snake River. During times of low fire danger—generally from about October 1 to June 15—fires are permitted if they are contained in a fire pan. These dates may vary from year to year so check with the Forest Service before you leave on your hike. A fire pan must have sides high enough to contain all of the ashes. If you use a fire pan, all of your ashes must be carried out with you.

Fishing in the Snake River can be good for a variety of fish all along this trail. The larger side streams also contain trout. Check Idaho fishing regulations before fishing. Watch for River Otters in the river; these playful critters are fairly common here. Deer and Elk may be seen all along the trail. Elk are most common in winter and spring. Occasionally a Mountain Goat is seen along the south part of this hike, and they are fairly common along Granite Creek. Black Bears are common around Granite Creek.

Options: The Bernard Creek Trail and Sheep Creek Trail into the Seven Devils Mountains mentioned in the hike description make good side trips. Hiking up the river (in the opposite direction from which this description is written) from Upper Pittsburg Landing to Kirkwood Ranch and back makes a wonderful 11-mile, springtime hike.

The short Mexican Hat Trail, a 0.7-mile hike along the paved road north of Upper Pittsburg Landing Trailhead, is an interesting walk past some well-preserved petroglyphs.

41 Hibbs Ranch and Granite Creek High Water Route 112, 112A

Highlights:	A short hike to the abandoned Hibbs Ranch from a campsite along Idaho Snake River Trail, or a very steep alternate route around a section of Idaho Snake River Trail that floods during times of high water.
Type of hike:	Out-and-back day hike to the ranch; one-way if using the High Water Route while following Idaho Snake River Trail.
Total distance:	1.8 miles round trip to the ranch; 2.1 miles one way if using the High Water Route.
Difficulty:	Moderate to the Hibbs Ranch; very strenuous, with much routefinding skill required, on the High Water Route.
Best months:	March–November.
Elevation gain:	400 feet to the ranch; 790 feet along the High Water Route.
Permits and fees:	None.
Maps:	Squirrel Prairie USGS quad covers the area but does not show this trail. Forest Service maps show it somewhat incorrectly.

Finding the trailhead: The junction where this hike begins is 27 miles south of Upper Pittsburg Landing Trailhead along Idaho Snake River Trail 102. See Hike 40 for a description of Idaho Snake River Trail. The GPS coordinates at the junction are GPS 45 20.789 N 116 39.249 W.

Trailhead facilities: There are some good campsites along Idaho Snake River Trail close to Granite Creek

Camping and services: See Hike 40 for the closest services. None are available even remotely close to this trail.

For more information: USDA Forest Service at Hells Canyon Dam Visitor Center, Hells Canyon National Recreation Area office in Riggins, Idaho, or Wallowa Mountains Visitor Center in Enterprise, Oregon. Hells Canyon Adventures in Oxbow, Oregon, will have information about water level and jet boat transportation. Bret Armocost, the owner of Hells Canyon Adventures, is also a good source for trail information. For car shuttle information, contact Scotty's Hells Canyon Outdoor Supply in Oxbow. For air transportation to or from Big Bar Airstrip, contact Spence Air Service in Enterprise.

Key points:

0.0   Junction with Idaho Snake River Trail near mouth of Granite Creek.

0.3   Junction with High Water Route 112A. GPS 45 20.505 N 116 39.064 W.

1.3   Trail crosses last ridge.

2.1   Junction with Idaho Snake River Trail 102. GPS 45 21.117 N 116 38.997 W.

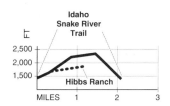

201

Hibbs Ranch and Granite Creek
High Water Route 112, 112A

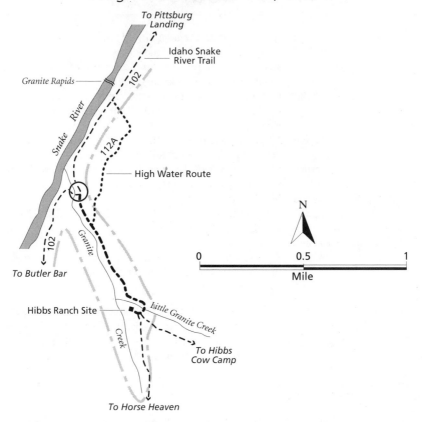

The hike: The High Water route starts off along Little Granite Creek Trail. Little Granite Creek Trail heads southeast from the junction with Idaho Snake River Trail, crossing a grassy and flower-covered meadow. You will pass a sign shortly after leaving the junction. The sign indicates that Devils Farm Trail and Hibbs Ranch are 1 mile ahead and it is 14 miles to Windy Saddle. Soon the route leaves the meadow and goes through an area of dense brush. This part of the trail is maintained fairly often, but the brush, much of it Poison Ivy, grows very quickly, crowding out the trail much of the time. The path leaves the brush, and enters a burned area 0.2 mile from the junction. A short distance into the burn area you will come to the unmarked and very difficult to spot junction with Granite Creek High Water Route. There is a burned but still somewhat legible 14-mile mark on a dead tree just to the left of the trail at the junction. To continue on to Hibbs Ranch, see the Options section below.

If your purpose for this hike is to get around high water that is covering Idaho Snake River Trail, turn left at this junction. The route heads north, climbing steeply for the first couple hundred yards. Then the route becomes

Low section of Snake River Trail.

less steep and crosses a rockslide. Watch for cairns marking the route. After crossing the slide the vague path makes a switchback to the right, then one to the left. A couple hundred yards past the switchbacks the nearly invisible trace flattens on a ledge with a cairn, at 1,840 feet elevation. It soon starts to climb again, crossing a couple more rockslides to a ridgeline with another cairn (elev. 1,970 feet). At this ridgeline the route bears to the right and continues to climb. It soon crosses a small steep ridge, then a jagged spur, and another small steep ridge. On the next ridgeline a small fairly flat spot, almost a saddle can be seen. The route crosses over the flat spot, which is approximately 1 mile from Little Granite Creek Trail at 2,230 feet elevation, then drops very steeply into the next canyon. Upon reaching the canyon bottom the route bears left and heads straight down the steep rocky canyon to Idaho Snake River Trail.

The High Water Route is very hard to follow. Do not be surprised if you lose the route and have to backtrack to find it again. In places, it is not visible on the ground for some distance. The part of the route that heads down the canyon bottom once had many switchbacks, but now most of them have been washed out. Watch out for rattlesnakes all along this route. Unstable rocks are a problem in the canyon bottom section. Use this route only when it is necessary and then only if you are a very advanced and agile hiker, with excellent routefinding skills. Do not take stock on the High Water Route. Traffic on this route is very light.

Options: If you continue to the southeast from the junction with the High Water Route 112A and cross Little Granite Creek, it is about 0.6 mile to the site of Hibbs Ranch. There is not much left of the ranch today, just a little rusting farm machinery and the remains of a foundation. The route to the ranch is brushed out fairly often but may be overgrown at times. From the ranch site it is about 7 miles southeast and 5,500 feet up to Hibbs Cow Camp and the junction with Seven Devils Loop. This part of Little Granite Creek Trail is not often maintained and can be very hard to follow. See Hike 49 for a description of Seven Devils Loop. Devils Farm Trail, which heads south-southeast up Granite Creek from the ranch, is also in very poor condition and is difficult to follow.

42 Bernard Creek Trail 58

Highlights:	A hike from a junction with Idaho Snake River Trail near McGaffee Cabin up the steep Bernard Creek Trail to a saddle on the north end of Dry Diggins Ridge near McGaffee Cow Camp. The trail then descends the steep and vague path down to a junction with Sheep Creek Trail. Excellent routefinding and map reading skills are required to follow this route, but the views and the solitude make all the difficulties worthwhile.
Type of hike:	Out-and-back backpack with loop options.
Total distance:	18.6 miles.
Difficulty:	Strenuous, with routefinding skills required.
Best months:	May–June and September–October.
Elevation gain:	4,560 feet.
Permits and fees:	None.
Maps:	Old Timer Mountain USGS quad.

Finding the trail: Bernard Creek Trail begins at a junction with Idaho Snake River Trail 8 miles north of the Butler Bar drop-off point and 22.1 miles south of Upper Pittsburg Landing Trailhead. (See Hike 40 for a description of Idaho Snake River Trail 102.) The unmarked junction is about 20 feet north of the bridge over Bernard Creek. The GPS coordinates at the junction are 45 24.073 N 116 36.714 W.

Jet boat transportation to Bernard Creek from Hells Canyon Dam can be arranged.

Trailhead facilities: Undeveloped campsites are available at the mouth of Bernard Creek.

Camping and services: See Hike 40 for the closest services; none are available even remotely close to this trail. Cell phone service is sometimes available in the saddle 5.9 miles from Idaho Snake River Trail and along the ridge just north of there.

For more information: USDA Forest Service at Hells Canyon Dam Visitor Center, Hells Canyon National Recreation Area office in Riggins, Idaho, or Wallowa Mountains Visitor Center in Enterprise, Oregon. Hells Canyon Adventures in Oxbow, Oregon, will have information about water level and jet boat transportation.

Key points:

0.0	Junction with Idaho Snake River Trail.
0.3	First crossing of Bernard Creek.
0.7	Second crossing of Bernard Creek.
3.2	Corral.
4.3	Ridgeline. GPS 45 23.955 N 116 34.460 W.
5.4	Trail junction near McGaffee Cow Camp. GPS 45 24.227 N 116 33.430 W.

Bernard Creek Trail 58

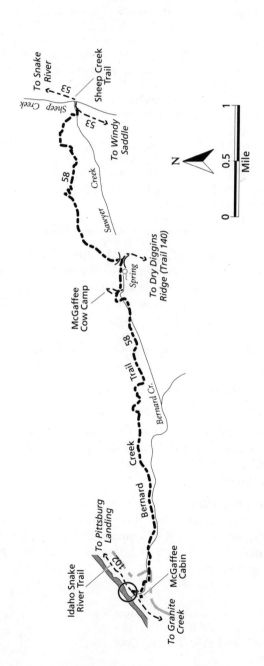

5.9   Junction with Dry Diggins Ridge Trail 140. GPS 45 24.242 N 116 33.014 W.

9.3   Junction with Sheep Creek Trail 53. GPS 45 24.710 N 116 31.420 W.

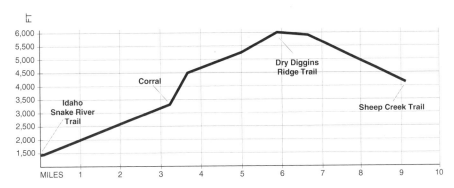

The hike: The USGS quad map shows the junction of Bernard Creek Trail and Idaho Snake River Trail as it used to be. Now the route leaves Idaho Snake River Trail just north of the bridge over Bernard Creek. Bernard Creek Trail may be badly overgrown with brush at the junction and hard to see.

Head southeast from the junction up a shallow draw. Soon a vague path marked sparingly with rock cairns will appear. After hiking about a quarter of a mile you will reach the first crossing of Bernard Creek. Usually this ford is not a problem, but during times of very high water it could be. The ford is normally about knee deep.

Once across the creek the cairn-marked path heads east through a semi-open area dotted with cactus and small hackberry trees. Sego Lilies bloom along the trail here in June. Seven-tenths of a mile into the hike the tread drops a few feet into the brush-choked creekbed and recrosses Bernard Creek. This crossing at 1,750 feet elevation is also about knee deep. There may be no water available for the next 4 miles along the trail, so it is a good idea to fill your water bottles, with filtered water, at this crossing.

The course heads southeast after the second crossing, climbing steadily up the creekbed. During the wetter times of the year a couple of tiny streams cross the trail as you ascend the brushy creekbed. Three-tenths of a mile above the second crossing of Bernard Creek the brush starts to thin out as the route climbs out of the creekbed. The path continues to climb fairly steeply crossing rockslides and a few spots of thick brush.

At 2.1 miles from Idaho Snake River Trail the route makes a couple of small switchbacks as it climbs farther away from the creek. The path soon works its way through some rock outcroppings then becomes very vague as it crosses a small draw. Climb out of the draw, heading east just below a grove of short Sumac, to a small ridgeline. Bear slightly left along the ridge and climb a little more to reach a bench spotted with patches of Elderberry and Mock Orange. Continue east on the bench to a small steel post and wire corral 3.2 miles from Idaho Snake River Trail, at about 3,300 feet elevation. There are no streams on this bench, although there are some shown on the USGS quad map.

At the corral look up to the east-northeast; you should to be able to spot the trail high above on a grassy slope. You will also see a shallow brushy draw. Head for the draw. As you reach the steeper slope the path shows up again, switchbacking its way up through the short sumac, just to the right of the draw. The braided route climbs about 300 vertical feet up through the sumac then crosses the draw. Just after crossing the now very shallow draw turn right and continue to climb to the east-northeast for about 100 vertical feet. After crossing the draw the trail becomes very vague. There are also several game trails here to add to the confusion. Recross the shallow draw above the brush and climb to the southeast to a small semiflat brushy area on the north side of a grove of fir trees at 4,000 feet elevation. Head east along the edge of the grove of trees for 100 yards or so and the path will show up again. The route then makes three switchbacks as it climbs the steep grassy slope to a ridgeline, at 4,470 feet elevation.

A few yards below the trail on the ridgeline is a rock outcropping that offers excellent views of the canyons to the west and the waterfalls in Bernard Creek to the south. Dry Diggins Lookout is far above to the southwest. The route climbs along the ridge to the northeast for a short distance, then bears slightly right to continue its climb up the slope. For the next 0.2 mile the grade moderates some. Then it crosses a small draw through Wild Rose bushes and enters the timber. Shortly the course begins to climb along the left side of another draw through thickening timber. Soon it is in the bottom of the draw. It then makes a turn to the right to climb out on the other side. Above this shallow draw the route turns left and continues to wind up through the timber. The route may be brushy in spots here but is fairly easy to follow. At about 5,200 feet elevation, 4.8 miles from Idaho Snake River Trail, the draw you are climbing becomes much wetter. Small springs show up and water runs down the trail well into the summer. The Old Timer Mountain USGS quad map shows the trail incorrectly in this area. The path crosses a small creek at 5,540 feet elevation then climbs northeast and east to an unmarked trail junction at 5,700 feet elevation, 5.4 miles from Idaho Snake River Trail.

Turn left at the junction and walk 20 yards to the north. Then turn right off the path and climb a grassy slope through the Ponderosa Pines for 20 yards to another vague path. Turn right (south) on this path. If you turn left on this path McGaffee Cow Camp is about 200 yards to the north. Soon after turning right the trail becomes more obvious again. The course continues to climb to the southeast for 0.4 mile to a saddle and the junction with Dry Diggins Ridge Trail 140, at 5,980 feet elevation.

As you approach the saddle the tread fades out again. A small, hard-to-spot sign on a tree at the south end of the saddle points south up Dry Diggins Ridge to Windy Saddle. This saddle, which makes a fairly good campsite, is the junction with Dry Diggins Ridge Trail, although neither trail may be visible on the ground here. Water is available by hiking a short distance back down the route you came up to an open slope, then descending a short distance to the south into a draw with a stream in it. If this is an out-and-back hike, this is a good place to turn around. (See Hike 58 for a description of Dry Diggins Ridge Trail.)

To continue your hike to the junction with Sheep Creek Trail, turn left in the saddle and walk to the north, staying slightly left (west) of the rounded ridgeline. Soon the vague tread shows up as it traverses the slope slightly west of the ridgeline. After being on the west side of the ridgeline for about 0.4 mile the route bears slightly right, to follow the top of the ridge for a short distance. Soon the course bears to the right again and begins to descend off the east side of the ridge. The vague tread then descends moderately along a semiopen slope that blooms with balsamroot, lupine, and sego lilies in early July.

The route makes its first descending switchback 1.2 miles after leaving the saddle. You will make 15 switchbacks in the next 0.8 mile. Two-tenths of a mile after the last of the switchbacks, at approximately 4,600 feet elevation, the route turns to the right (east) off what appears to be the main trail. A game trail heads straight ahead (north-northwest) here so it is very easy to miss this turn. Watch for cut logs marking the correct route. After making the turn the vague tread descends to the east down a shallow draw for 0.2 mile. It then turns right and traverses the wooded slope for a quarter of a mile to Sawyer Creek. The now more obvious trace drops steeply for a few feet just before crossing Sawyer Creek. It then climbs steeply for a short distance to the junction with Sheep Creek Trail 53 at 4,100 feet elevation, 9.3 miles from Idaho Snake River Trail. (See Hike 43 for details about Sheep Creek Trail.)

Many Black Bears (all colors) inhabit the area along this trail so take the appropriate precautions. Poison Ivy grows in profusion along the lower section of this trail.

High above the Snake River on Bernard Creek Trail.

Options: If you turn left on Sheep Creek Trail, it is 8.3 miles back down to Sheep Creek Ranch on Idaho Snake River Trail, where a jet boat can pick you up if you have made arrangements ahead of time.

It is also possible to make a loop back to the saddle you crossed 3.9 miles back. To make this loop, turn right on Sheep Creek Trail and follow it for 5.9 miles southeast to the junction with Seven Devils Loop. Turn right on the loop and hike 5 miles west to the junction with Dry Diggins Ridge Trail. Then turn right again on Dry Diggins Ridge Trail and walk the 4 miles back to the saddle and the junction with Bernard Creek Trail. See Hikes 43, 49, and 58 for more information about these trails.

43 Sheep Creek Trail 53

General description:	A hike from the arid depths of Hells Canyon to the alpine ridge between the Snake and Salmon Rivers. This challenging route requires excellent routefinding skills to follow safely. It also takes a lot of endurance.
Type of hike:	Internal backpack, with shuttle, out-and-back, and loop options.
Total distance:	14.7 miles.
Difficulty:	Strenuous.
Best months:	September and early October are the best times to hike this entire trail. Snow may limit access to Windy Saddle Trailhead until early July, and July and August are very hot in the lower elevations. At the lower elevations (below 3,000 feet), the trail is usually free of snow March through November.
Elevation gain:	6,500 feet.
Permits and fees:	None.
Maps:	Old Timer Mountain and He Devil USGS quads.

Finding the trailhead: Sheep Creek Trail begins at a junction with Idaho Snake River Trail 14.3 miles north of the Butler Bar drop-off point and 15.8 miles south of Upper Pittsburg Landing Trailhead. (See Hike 40 for a description of Idaho Snake River Trail 102.) Jet boat transportation to Sheep Creek from Hells Canyon Dam or Lewiston, Idaho, can be arranged. The GPS coordinates at the junction are 45 28.140 N 116 33.239 W.

Windy Saddle Trailhead, where this hike ends, can be reached by car from Riggins, Idaho. Drive 1 mile south from Riggins on U.S. Highway 95 to the junction with Squaw Creek Road. Turn west on Squaw Creek Road (County Road 517) and follow it for 16.5 miles to Windy Saddle Trailhead. County Road 517 makes a left turn at a junction slightly less than 2 miles after leaving US 95 and becomes Forest Road 517 at the Nez Perce National Forest Boundary, approximately 4 miles from US 95. Road signs point to Seven Devils Campground at the junction with US 95 and at other intersections along

Sheep Creek Trail 53

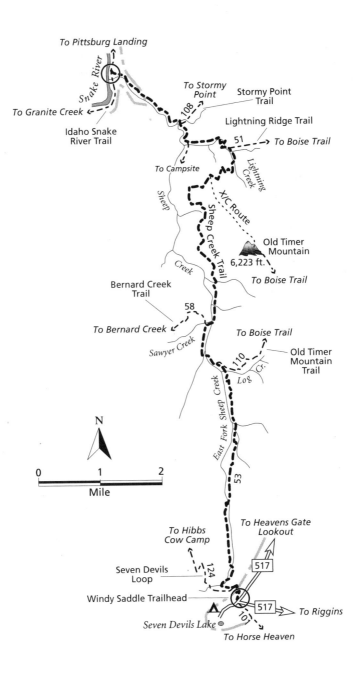

To Pittsburg Landing

Snake River

To Stormy Point

Stormy Point Trail

Lightning Ridge Trail

To Granite Creek

108

51 → To Boise Trail

Idaho Snake River Trail

To Campsite

Lightning Creek

Sheep

XJC Route

Sheep Creek Trail

Old Timer Mountain 6,223 ft.

Creek

To Boise Trail

Bernard Creek Trail

58

To Bernard Creek

Sawyer Creek

To Boise Trail

110

Old Timer Mountain Trail

Log Cr.

N

East Fork Sheep Creek

0   1   2
Mile

53

To Hibbs Cow Camp

To Heavens Gate Lookout

Seven Devils Loop

124

517

Windy Saddle Trailhead

517 → To Riggins

Seven Devils Lake

10

To Horse Heaven

the way. Seven Devils Campground is .05 mile past the trailhead. The GPS coordinates at the trailhead are 45 20.818 N 116 30.864 W.

Trailhead facilities: Check with Snake River Adventures about the lodging facilities at Sheep Creek Ranch.

Camping and services: See Hike 40 for the closest services; none are available even remotely close to the lower part of this trail.

Campsites are available at Windy Saddle Trailhead and at Seven Devils Lake 0.5 mile to the southwest. Other services, including gas and groceries, can be obtained in Riggins, 16.5 miles to the east. Cell phone service is sometimes available in Windy Saddle and gets better as you head north up the road toward Heavens Gate Lookout.

For more information: USDA Forest Service at Hells Canyon Dam Visitor Center, Hells Canyon National Recreation Area office in Riggins, or Wallowa Mountains Visitor Center in Enterprise, Oregon. Hells Canyon Adventures in Oxbow, Oregon, will have information about water level and jet boat transportation, as will Beamer's Hells Canyon Tours in Clarkston, Washington.

Key points:
- 0.0 Sheep Creek Ranch.
- 1.8 Junction with Stormy Point Trail 108 (to Low Saddle). GPS 45 27.495 N 116 31.920 W.
- 3.4 Unmarked junction with Lightning Ridge Trail 51. GPS 45 27.059 N 116 30.923 W.
- 4.8 Unmarked junction with cross-country route to Old Timer Mountain. GPS 45 26.082 N 116 31.318 W.
- 8.3 Junction with Bernard Creek Trail 58. GPS 45 24.710 N 116 31.420 W.
- 9.1 Junction with Old Timer Mountain Trail 110. GPS 45 24.247 N 116 31.312 W.
- 14.2 Junction with Seven Devils Loop 124. GPS 45 21.242 N 116 30.878 W.
- 14.7 Windy Saddle Trailhead. GPS 45 20.818 N 116 30.864 W.

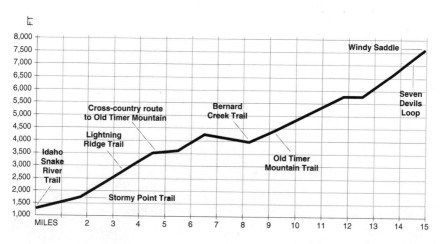

The hike: Leaving the junction with Idaho Snake River Trail, Sheep Creek Trail heads east between the ranch house and an outbuilding. A sign at the ranch points to Low Saddle and Windy Saddle as you begin your hike up the north bank of Sheep Creek. Soon the tread crosses a ditch on a tiny wooden bridge then passes through a gate. The creekbed is quite brushy here with lots of Poison Ivy trying to invade the path. Shooting Stars and Bleeding Hearts grow in the damper areas and on the drier slopes Larkspur and Paintbrush bloom as the course climbs.

One mile from Sheep Creek Ranch the route makes the first of four switchbacks as it climbs to round a ridge well above Sheep Creek. After rounding the ridge the tread switchbacks back into the creekbed of Clarks Fork. You then climb gently along Clarks Fork for a couple hundred yards before fording the stream. Just after crossing Clarks Fork is the junction with Stormy Point Trail 108, at 1,770 feet elevation. Stormy Point Trail has not been maintained for years. It is in very poor condition and is extremely difficult to follow. It is about 5 miles up Stormy Point Trail to Low Saddle.

Sheep Creek Trail turns right at the junction with Stormy Point Trail, descends to cross a gully, and then resumes its climb. The path makes two tiny switchbacks before topping a rise. It then descends back into the creekbed of Sheep Creek. To the right of the trail 0.3 mile past the junction with Stormy Point Trail, there is a campsite between the tread and the creek. The few Douglas-fir trees that grow here show the scars of a fire. Dogtooth Violets, Yellowbells, and Buttercups bloom between the partly blackened trees.

Four-tenths of a mile past the junction with Stormy Point Trail, Sheep Creek Trail leaves Sheep Creek to ascend along Lightning Creek. An unmaintained path turns to the right just above the confluence of Sheep Creek and Lightning Creek. This path heads on up Sheep Creek and dead ends. Bear left where the trail appears to fork and head up Lightning Creek. The route becomes vague as you climb along Lightning Creek. You will cross Lightning Creek several times as you ascend the 1.2 miles to the unmarked and obscured junction with Lightning Ridge Trail 51. Lightning Ridge Trail turns left (east) at the junction. This junction, at 2,640 feet elevation, was marked with a steel fence post driven into the ground upside down when I hiked this trail. Lightning Ridge Trail, which climbs out of the canyon to connect with Boise Trail, has not been maintained for years and is very difficult to follow.

At the junction Sheep Creek Trail bears slightly right (southeast) and quickly crosses the North Fork of Lightning Creek. A couple hundred yards after crossing the North Fork the route crosses Lightning Creek. Once across Lightning Creek the trace makes 15 switchbacks as it climbs to a semiopen ridgeline at 3,360 feet elevation. The path turns left (south) up the ridge for a couple hundred yards, then bears right to cross a draw. After crossing the draw the path reaches another ridgeline at 3,560 feet elevation.

This ridgeline, which is 4.8 miles from Sheep Creek Ranch, is the point where a cross-country route that goes over the top of Old Timer Mountain to Boise Trail leaves Sheep Creek Trail. A small rock cairn marks the junction with the cross-country route. (See the Options section of Hike 47 for a description of this rough, steep cross-country route.)

Sheep Creek Trail crosses the ridgeline staying nearly level, then cuts back traversing an open slope into another draw. As the trace nears the bottom of this draw you will reenter the timber. The path continues its traverse through the timber to another ridgeline where it leaves the thick timber. This nearly level traverse continues for about another 0.7 mile, then the route enters thicker timber and begins to climb. The vague tread climbs for 0.9 mile to another open ridgeline, at 4,300 feet elevation, then descends open and lightly timbered slopes for another 0.7 mile to a creek crossing. This stream may be dry so don't depend on it for water. The course then traverses the mostly timbered slope for another 0.5 mile to Old Timer Creek. Four-tenths of a mile after crossing Old Timer Creek the trail fords Sheep Creek. This ford could be difficult during heavy runoff but is usually not a problem.

Once across Sheep Creek the path climbs steeply for a short distance to the junction with Bernard Creek Trail 58. At the junction a sign points right (northwest) to McGaffee Cow Camp and Dry Diggins Ridge. The sign also incorrectly says this is Trail 110. (See Hike 42 for a description of Bernard Creek Trail.) The junction with Bernard Creek Trail, at 4,060 feet elevation, is 8.3 miles from Sheep Creek Ranch, and you have 6.3 uphill miles to go to Windy Saddle Trailhead.

Turn left at the junction and head south, climbing gently through the timber. Half a mile after leaving the junction with Bernard Creek Trail the route fords the West Fork of Sheep Creek. Just before reaching the ford there is a great campsite on the right side of the trail. A few feet after crossing the West Fork the trail crosses the East Fork of Sheep Creek. Both of these crossings are usually not difficult, but they could be during high-water times.

After crossing the forks of Sheep Creek the trace climbs steeply for 0.3 mile, making a couple of switchbacks to the junction with Old Timer Mountain Trail 110. This junction, at 4,460 feet elevation, is 9.1 miles from Sheep Creek Ranch. Old Timer Mountain Trail bears to the left (east) to climb steeply up to Boise Trail near The Narrows. (See Hike 47 for details about Old Timer Mountain Trail.)

The vague Sheep Creek Trail heads southeast from the junction, climbing for 0.3 mile to Log Creek. The brushed-in, hard-to-follow path climbs steeply leaving Log Creek. Soon the grade moderates a little as you cross the steep slope. In openings Clarkia blooms in July. The route stays nearly level for the next 0.6 mile to a creek crossing. It is easy to lose the trail at this washed-out crossing. Head upstream a few yards along the creek before making the crossing and the trail will show up on the other side in the brush. Shortly the course crosses another stream, then climbs steeply making eight switchbacks to a small ridgeline. This semiopen ridge is brightly spotted with Paintbrush in July.

The trace climbs up the ridge making several more switchbacks, then flattens as it traverses the slope heading south. Soon the path is close to the East

Campsite near Clark's Fork.

Fork of Sheep Creek again. The route crosses the East Fork at 5,850 feet elevation, 12.2 miles from Sheep Creek Ranch. Head upstream a few yards at the crossing to pick up the trail.

After crossing the creek the path climbs steeply through the brush and makes a switchback before flattening out some at 6,130 feet elevation. The tread then continues to climb moderately through semiopen woods. Huckleberry bushes crowd the trail between the trees as you climb. The track crosses the East Fork of Sheep Creek again 13.5 miles from Sheep Creek Ranch, at 6,700 feet elevation. Two-tenths of a mile after the crossing there is a small spring on the left side of the trail. Just past the spring the route crosses a tiny stream. Both the spring and the tiny stream may be dry by late summer. You will cross a couple more tiny streams and an open slope with a great view to the north down the canyon before reaching the junction with Seven Devils Loop 124. (For a description of Seven Devils Loop, see Hike 49.) This junction, at 7,280 feet elevation, is 14.2 miles from Sheep Creek Ranch. Turn left at the junction and hike 0.5 mile, gaining 326 feet to Windy Saddle Trailhead.

Options: Turn right on Seven Devils Loop and hike west for 5 miles to the junction with Dry Diggins Ridge Trail. Turn right on Dry Diggins Ridge Trail and follow it for 4 miles to the junction with Bernard Creek Trail. From this junction, you can either take Bernard Creek Trail to the east and hook back up with Sheep Creek Trail or take it to the west and descend to Idaho Snake River Trail. If you descend to Idaho Snake River Trail and hike north along it to Sheep Creek Ranch, you will have made a 35-mile loop. See Hikes 49, 58, 42, and 40 for details.

44 Kirkwood Ranch Trail 132

Highlights:	A hike from the trailhead high above Hells Canyon to the historic Kirkwood Ranch Living History Museum on the banks of the Snake River. This trail was once a road and is sometimes used by ATVs.
Type of hike:	Out-and-back day hike or backpack, with a shuttle option.
Total distance:	10.2 miles.
Difficulty:	Strenuous
Best months:	Late June and September–October. If you plan to hike this trail in June, be sure to check with the Forest Service first to make sure the road to the trailhead is open.
Elevation loss:	3,400 feet.
Permits and fees:	None.
Maps:	Kirkwood Creek USGS quad.

Kirkland Ranch Trail 132 • Blue Jacket Mine Trail

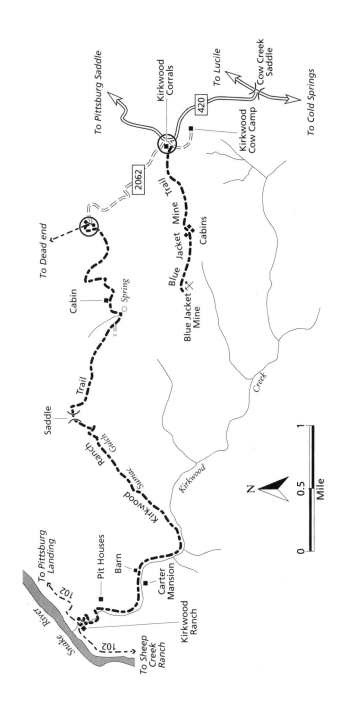

To Pittsburg Saddle

Kirkwood Corrals

To Lucile

Cow Creek Saddle

To Cold Springs

420

Kirkwood Cow Camp

2062

Blue Jacket Mine Trail

Cabins

To Dead end

Cabin

Spring

Blue Jacket Mine

Creek

Saddle

Ranch Trail

Kirkwood Sunrise Gulch

Kirkwood Creek

N

0.5

Mile

0

1

To Pittsburg Landing

Pit Houses

Barn

Carter Mansion

Kirkwood Ranch

102

Snake River

102

To Sheep Creek Ranch

Finding the trailhead: From the small town of Lucile, 8.5 miles north of Riggins, Idaho, on U.S. Highway 95, head west crossing the bridge over the Salmon River on County Road 242. Follow CR 242 for 8 miles to Cow Creek Saddle. From the saddle, drive northwest on Forest Road 420 for 1 mile to Kirkwood Corrals. No sign marks the corrals, which are on the left side of the road. Just past the corrals, turn left on Forest Road 2062 and follow it 1.2 miles northwest to the iron gate blocking the road. Park here and begin your hike. The GPS coordinates at the gate are 45 34.088 N 116 25.938 W.

Trailhead facilities: The trailhead has parking for two or three cars at the gate but has no other facilities.

Camping and services: Primitive camping is allowed in the national forest around the trailhead. Gas, groceries, and other services can be obtained in Riggins.

For more information: USDA Forest Service at the Hells Canyon National Recreation Area office in Riggins. For jet boat shuttle information, contact Hells Canyon Adventures in Oxbow, Oregon, or Beamer's Hells Canyon Tours in Clarkston, Washington.

Key points:
    0.0   Iron gate 1.2 miles northwest of Kirkwood Corrals on FR 2062.
    1.1   Cabin.
    2.2   Saddle. GPS 45 34.130 N 116 27.815 W.
    4.3   Carter Mansion.
    5.1   Kirkwood Ranch. GPS 45 34.083 N 116 29.891 W.

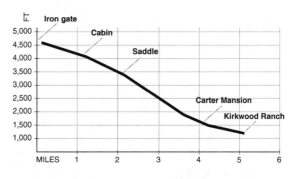

The hike: Go through the iron gate and walk straight ahead on the roadbed. About 100 yards after passing the gate the track forks. Turn left (southwest) at the fork and begin your descent along an open slope. Shortly you will enter the timber as you cross the bottom of a draw. The track forks 0.2 mile into the timber. Bear left and follow the main fork. Asters bloom in the openings between the trees here in July. Soon the side trail that forked off to the right rejoins the main trail.

The course gets back out in the open 0.6 mile from the trailhead. Here it forks again; bear left following the main trail. Soon the route makes a hard turn to the left; another side route leaves the main trail here but bear left and continue on the main trail. The course works its way around the head of a basin and soon reaches the remains of a cabin, on the right side of the trail. The elevation at the cabin is 4,030 feet, and you are now 1.1 miles from the trailhead. The side trail that left the route at the hard left turn rejoins the main trail next to the cabin.

As the tread leaves the cabin it heads west, then south for 0.2 mile through the trees and Thorn Brush to a spring. Soon after passing the spring the route forks again. Bear right at this fork staying on the main trail. As you descend this open ridge Hat Point Tower across the canyon in Oregon comes into view in the distance to the southwest. The side route that forked off a short distance back soon reenters the main trail. Coneflowers bloom along this section of trail in July.

About 2.2 miles from the trailhead the first glimpse of the Snake River shows up far below to the right of the trail, as you reach a saddle. In the saddle, at 3,380 feet elevation, the trace turns to the left. The track now makes a steep descent making three switchbacks as it drops to the bottom of Sumac Gulch. Watch for Chukars as you descend the switchbacks. At the bottom of the gulch the route turns left to continue its descent. Sumac Gulch is aptly named because Sumac bushes nearly cover its slopes in spots. The bottom of the gulch is wet in spots and very brushy. Some of the bushes are Poison Ivy so be careful what you touch.

Sumac Gulch joins Kirkwood Creek Canyon 3.7 miles from the trailhead, at about 1,900 feet elevation. The route then descends along Kirkwood Creek, which is far less steep than Sumac Gulch. Hackberry trees show up beside the tread and the Poison Ivy continues to flourish.

The track passes a metal barn 4.2 miles from the trailhead. A short distance past the barn the Carter Mansion sits to the left of the trail across Kirkwood Creek. The Carter Mansion is really just a house that was owned by Dick Carter, whose main occupation at the time was making moonshine. There is a path with a bridge across the creek just below the mansion. A side trail to some pit house remains turns to the right off the now much improved trail 0.4 mile past the mansion. The side trail rejoins the main route a couple hundred yards farther along.

After passing the pit houses the course soon crosses Kirkwood Creek. When I hiked this trail in July 1999, this crossing was made via a tricky single log with a rope hand line. Shortly the trail recrosses the creek but this time it is on a flattened single log bridge with a wooden handrail. One hundred fifty yards after crossing the bridge the track goes through a gate. From here on the trail is closed to motor vehicle use.

After passing the gate the path crosses another single log bridge and enters the lawn area at Kirkwood Ranch. The junction with Idaho Snake River Trail 102 is reached just after passing the buildings at the ranch. Camping is allowed in the field across Kirkwood Creek from the ranch next to the Snake River. The elevation at Kirkwood Ranch is 1,220 feet, and you are now 5.1 miles from the trailhead.

Native Americans heavily used Kirkwood Bar. Early visitors to the bar found extensive artifacts proving this use. In 1885 the Kirkwoods moved to this site. Several other parties owned Kirkwood Bar after the Kirkwoods moved out, and in 1932 Len Jordan bought it. Jordan, who was later to become governor of Idaho and a U.S. Senator, lived here for 11 years. The Kirkwood ranch now belongs to the Forest Service and is used as a living history museum. Be sure to take the time to go through the museum.

Kirkwood Ranch.

Options: If you do not want to hike back up this steep trail, a jet boat pick-up can be arranged to carry you to Pittsburg Landing, which is 6 miles down-river from Kirkwood Ranch. You can also hike along Idaho Snake River Trail to Upper Pittsburg Landing Trailhead. For a description of Idaho Snake River Trail, see Hike 40. Either option would require a car shuttle to Pittsburg Landing.

45 Blue Jacket Mine Trail

See Map on Page 217

Highlights:	A short hike on an abandoned mine road from Kirkwood Corrals, passing abandoned cabins, to the site of the Blue Jacket Mine. This trail offers excellent flowers and possible wildlife viewing early or late in the day. The last 150 yards of this route are on private land, so permission to pass could be revoked at any time. Even if you cannot go the last few steps to the mine, the hike to the national forest boundary is well worth the effort.
Type of hike:	Out-and-back day hike.
Total distance:	2.6 miles.
Difficulty:	Easy.
Best months:	Mid-June–October.
Elevation gain:	170 feet.
Permits and fees:	None.
Maps:	Kirkwood Creek USGS quad.

Finding the trailhead: From the small town of Lucile, 8.5 miles north of Riggins, Idaho, on U.S. Highway 95, head west crossing the bridge over the Salmon River on County Road 242. Follow CR 242 for 8 miles to Cow Creek Saddle. From the saddle, drive northwest on Forest Road 420 for 1 mile to Kirkwood Corrals. No sign marks the corrals, which are on the left side of the road. This route begins on the south side of the corrals. The GPS coordinates at the corrals are 45 33.517 N 116 25.114 W.

Trailhead facilities: The trailhead has parking for several cars at the corrals but has no other facilities.

Camping and services: Primitive camping is allowed in the national forest around the trailhead. Gas, groceries, and other services can be obtained in Riggins.

For more information: USDA Forest Service at the Hells Canyon National Recreation Area office in Riggins.

Key points:

0.0   Kirkwood Corrals.
0.7   Saddle.
0.9   Cabins.
1.3   Blue Jacket Mine. GPS 45 33.390 N 116 26.498 W.

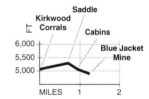

The hike: The trail, which is really a roadbed, first goes through a gate on the south side of the corrals, then heads west climbing gently. The track goes through another gate 0.2 mile from the corrals. Now heading southwest you traverse a gentle slope covered with pines and

Cabin above Blue Jacket Mine.

a few firs. Four-tenths of a mile after leaving the corrals the trace crosses a small ridgeline onto an open slope. Hundreds of Mariposa Lilies bloom on this grassy slope in July along with many other wildflowers. The tread traverses this open slope for 0.3 mile heading west to a saddle. As you cross the open saddle, at 5,220 feet elevation, note the remains of a stone fence to your right. The remains of three cabins are next to the trail 0.2 mile farther along. Two of the cabins are still standing, but the third and largest one is starting to crumble. The route passes the Nez Perce National Forest boundary 0.3 mile after passing the cabins. From this point on to the mine the route is on private land. Permission to pass is always revocable by the landowner, whose rights must be respected. The route continues another 150 yards to a small fenced area at the top of the mineshaft, at 4,910 feet elevation. A rock outcropping a short distance west of the mineshaft offers great views of the canyon below.

Do not try to enter this or any other mineshaft; it could be very dangerous. This mine smells of sulfur, and there is some sulfur lying around on the tailing piles next to it. There are several old roadbeds in the area around the mineshaft, one of them leading around the hill to the lower entrance of the mine.

Options: Make this short hike on the same trip that you hike down to Kirkwood Ranch. See Hike 44 for information about Kirkwood Ranch Trail.

46 Boise Trail North 101

General description:	A hike mostly along an abandoned roadbed from Cold Springs Trailhead to Heavens Gate Trailhead. This trail is the access to Crater and Papoose Lakes and several other trails. The description printed below is from north to south; however, this trail can be easily hiked either way in one day.
Type of hike:	Day hike or backpack shuttle.
Total distance:	10.3 miles.
Difficulty:	Easy.
Best months:	July–September.
Elevation gain:	Approximately 2,300 feet.
Permits and fees:	None.
Maps:	Kessler Creek and Heavens Gate USGS quads. Only a very small section of this trail is on the Heavens Gate quad.

Finding the trailhead: From Riggins, Idaho, drive north on U.S. Highway 95 for 0.5 mile. Turn west on Race Creek Road (Forest Road 241). Follow Race Creek Road for 13.4 miles to the junction with Forest Road 1819 at Buckhorn Spring. Turn left on FR 1819 and go 2 miles to Cold Springs Trailhead. The trailhead is located on a right-hand turn. The GPS coordinates at Cold Springs Trailhead are 45 29.849 N 116 26.905 W.

Boise Trail North 101

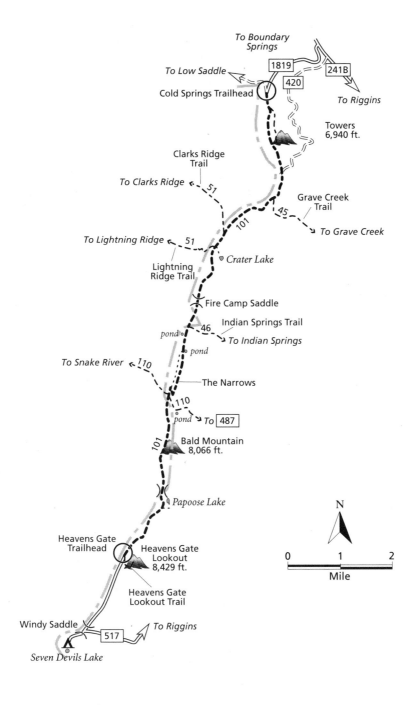

To Boundary
Springs

To Low Saddle
1819
241B
Cold Springs Trailhead
420
To Riggins

Towers
6,940 ft.

Clarks Ridge
Trail
To Clarks Ridge
51

Grave Creek
Trail
45
To Grave Creek
101

To Lightning Ridge
51
Crater Lake

Lightning
Ridge Trail

Fire Camp Saddle

Indian Springs Trail
pond
46
To Indian Springs

pond

To Snake River
110

The Narrows

110
pond
To 487

101
Bald Mountain
8,066 ft.

Papoose Lake

Heavens Gate
Trailhead
Heavens Gate
Lookout
8,429 ft.

Heavens Gate
Lookout Trail

Windy Saddle
To Riggins
517
Seven Devils Lake

N

0   1   2
Mile

To reach Heavens Gate Trailhead, the end of this hike, drive 1 mile south from Riggins on U.S. Highway 95 to the junction with Squaw Creek Road. Turn west on Squaw Creek Road (County Road 517) and follow it for 16.5 miles to Windy Saddle Trailhead. County Road 517 makes a left turn at a junction slightly less than 2 miles after leaving US 95 and becomes Forest Road 517 at the Nez Perce National Forest Boundary approximately 4 miles from US 95. There are road signs pointing to Seven Devils Campground at the junction with US 95 and at other intersections along the way.

Turn right at the junction next to the trailhead and drive 1.7 miles north on FR 517 to Heavens Gate Trailhead. Early in the season, it may be necessary to walk part of the way from Windy Saddle because of snowdrifts, which sometimes block the road. The trailhead is located at the north end of the parking area. The GPS coordinates at Heavens Gate Trailhead are 45 22.229 N 116 29.850 W.

Trailhead facilities: Cold Springs Trailhead has parking for several cars but has no other facilities. Heavens Gate Trailhead has a restroom and parking for several cars.

Camping and services: Primitive camping is allowed in the national forest around Cold Springs Trailhead. Developed campsites are available at Windy Saddle Trailhead, which is 1.7 miles south of Heavens Gate Trailhead, and at Seven Devils Lake, which is 0.5 mile farther to the southwest. Other services, including gas and groceries, can be obtained in Riggins. A cell phone will work most places along this trail.

For more information: USDA Forest Service at the Hells Canyon National Recreation Area office in Riggins.

Key points:
- 0.0 Cold Springs Trailhead.
- 1.5 Junction with FR 420. GPS 45 28.602 N 116 26.532 W.
- 2.1 Junction with Grave Creek Trail 45.
- 3.2 Junction with Clarks Ridge Trail 51.
- 3.5 Junction with path to Crater Lake.
- 3.6 Junction with Lightning Ridge Trail 51
- 4.8 Fire Camp Saddle.
- 5.1 Junction with Indian Springs Trail 46.
- 6.8 Junction withhold Timer Mountain Trail 110 just south of The Narrows. GPS 45 24.920 N 116 28.892 W.
- 8.9 Junction with route to Papoose Lake.
- 10.3 Heavens Gate Trailhead. GPS 45 22.229 N 116 29.850 W.

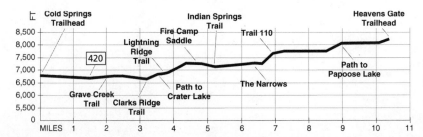

The hike: Boise Trail, which is really a roadbed, heads south from Cold Springs Trailhead. After going 0.3 mile there is a junction with a road that goes to the radio towers on the top of the hill to the left. Bear right (really straight ahead) at the junction and continue to traverse the mostly open slope. The track begins to descend 1.3 miles from the trailhead. After another 0.2 miles is the signed junction with FR 420 (elev. 6,620 ft.). FR 420 heads northeast to Round Knob Trailhead, 0.8 mile away. Continue to head south at the junction, on the old roadbed. From here on, the trail is closed to motor vehicles.

The course (roadbed) generally follows the ridge, going in and out of the timber, as it heads south. The junction with Grave Creek Trail 45, at 6,710 feet elevation, is reached 0.6 mile after passing FR 420. Grave Creek Trail turns off to the left (southeast) and descends to a trailhead on FR 2052. About 1.1 miles after passing the junction with Grave Creek Trail is the signed junction with Clarks Ridge Trail 51. Clarks Ridge trail turns off to the right (northwest) and descends to meet Sheep Creek Trail. The lower parts of Clarks Ridge Trail and Lightning Ridge Trail, which it joins, have not been maintained for some time and are hard to follow.

The path to Crater Lake leaves Boise Trail 0.3 mile past the Clarks Ridge Trail junction. From the unmarked junction the route to Crater Lake heads south, following old blazes. It descends south and very slightly east for 0.3 mile, through thick timber, to Crater Lake. The route can be confusing in places. Watch for cut logs as well as blazes. In the event the route is lost, Boise Trail can be reached by climbing to the west. There are a few small possible campsites around Crater Lake (elev. 6,540 ft).

A short distance after passing the path to Crater Lake is the junction with Lightning Ridge Trail 51. Lightning Ridge Trail turns to the right (west). The junction, at 6,850 feet elevation, is marked with a sign. As is true with Clarks Ridge Trail, Lightning Ridge Trail has not been maintained recently and is difficult to follow lower down on its way to Sheep Creek. Check with the Forest Service before using either of these trails.

Boise Trail crosses a fenceline, through a gate, 0.3 mile after passing the junction with Lightning Ridge Trail. Here the timber thins out and the view gets better. Another three-quarters of a mile brings you to Fire Camp Saddle. The saddle, at 7,210 feet elevation, offers an excellent view of Hells Canyon to the right and the high peaks of the Seven Devils Mountains straight ahead to the south. Soon after passing the saddle the route drops slightly and reenters the timber at the junction with Indian Springs Trail 46. At the signed junction (elev. 7,140 ft), Indian Springs Trail turns off to the left (east) and descends to Indian Springs Trailhead. There are campsites near the junction but no water.

There is a stock pond to the right of the trail, a quarter of a mile past the junction with Indian Springs Trail. After passing the pond the trace climbs moderately, passing another stock pond, this one to the left of the trail. Just past this pond an alternate trail, which crosses The Narrows, leaves the main trail. This alternate path bears to the right and closely follows the ridgeline through The Narrows. The Narrows are a section of the ridgeline that was too narrow to build a road on. The main trail, which is still a roadbed, traverses the semiopen hillside on the left (east) side of the ridge, drops a little, then climbs to a fenceline. The trail crosses the fence through a gate, then winds up through the woods. It soon makes a wide switchback to the right and climbs to the ridgeline at the south end of The Narrows. At the ridgeline the trail switches back to the left (south), and the alternate trail mentioned before rejoins the main trail.

Trail 110, heading east toward Squaw Creek, leaves Boise Trail at this point. A few yards after crossing the ridgeline the trail forks. Bear left at the fork (the right fork joins Old Timer Mountain Trail a short distance down the hill to the southwest) and climb gently for 100 yards to the sign marking the junction with Old Timer Mountain Trail, also number 110. (See Hike 47 for a description of Old Timer Mountain Trail.) There are actually two junctions with Old Timer Mountain Trail. The sign marking the junction is halfway between them. See the map in Hike 47 for clarification.

Past the junctions with Old Timer Mountain Trail, Boise Trail continues to traverse to the south, on the open slope, west of the summit of Bald Mountain. The roadbed ends on this slope. From the end of the roadbed you will climb, on an easy to follow trail, to a saddle on the ridgeline (elev. 7,940 ft) overlooking Papoose Lake. Past the saddle the path follows a ledge and climbs on the east side of the rocky ridge for a short distance. The trail then traverses the east slope of the ridge through thin, partly burned alpine timber.

A quarter of a mile south of the saddle the route traverses above a spur ridge. This spur ridge descends south of Papoose Lake. Following the ridge down is the easiest way to get to the lake. To reach Papoose Lake descend the spur ridge to the east to a small flat area well above and straight south of the lake. From the flat area there is a steep path down a chute to the lake.

Past the route to Papoose Lake Boise Trail traverses south to another saddle. It then contours around the east side of the ridgeline and climbs slightly

Campsite along Boise Trail.

to a meadow near the ridge top. There is a campsite next to the meadow but no water. The course then drops slightly to another saddle on the ridgeline (elev. 7,850 ft). South of the saddle the route climbs for 0.5 mile, making four switchbacks along the way, to Heavens Gate Trailhead at 8,140 feet elevation.

Much of the canyon country to the west of this trail was burned in the 1996 Sheep Creek, Heavens Gate, and Salt Creek Fires. This section of Boise Trail is easy to follow all the way. Wildlife, especially Elk, are abundant at times, and the flowers are great.

Options: Hike to Crater Lake or Papoose Lake as a side trip. The trail to the Heavens Gate Lookout leaves from the east side of the parking area at Heavens Gate Trailhead. The short hike to the lookout is worthwhile. See Hike 48 for details about Heavens Gate Lookout Trail.

47 Old Timer Mountain Trail 110

Highlights:	A hike from Boise Trail down to Sheep Creek Trail, passing through an abandoned mining area along the way, or a steep rugged descent over the top of Old Timer Mountain.
Type of hike:	Internal connecting trail; backpack, with a lollipop loop option.
Total distance:	4.7 miles.
Difficulty:	Moderate to strenuous.
Best months:	Late June–September.
Elevation loss:	3,080 feet.
Permits and fees:	None.
Maps:	Kessler Creek and Old Timer Mountain USGS quads.

Finding the trailhead: To reach Heavens Gate Trailhead, drive 1 mile south from Riggins, Idaho, on U.S. Highway 95 to the junction with Squaw Creek Road. Turn west on Squaw Creek Road (County Road 517) and follow it for 16.5 miles to Windy Saddle Trailhead. County Road 517 makes a left turn at a junction slightly less than 2 miles after leaving US 95 and becomes Forest Road 517 at the Nez Perce National Forest Boundary approximately 4 miles from US 95. There are road signs pointing to Seven Devils Campground at the junction with US 95 and at other intersections along the way.

Turn right at the junction next to the trailhead and drive 1.7 miles north on FR 517 to Heavens Gate Trailhead. Early in the season, it may be necessary to walk part of the way from Windy Saddle because of snowdrifts, which sometimes block the road. The trailhead is located at the north end of the parking area. The GPS coordinates at Heavens Gate Trailhead are 45 22.229 N 116 29.850 W.

From Heavens Gate Trailhead, hike 3.5 miles north on Boise Trail to the junction with Old Timer Mountain Trail. The junction is just south of The Narrows (a knife-edge place on the ridge that Boise Trail detours around).

Old Timer Mountain Trail 110

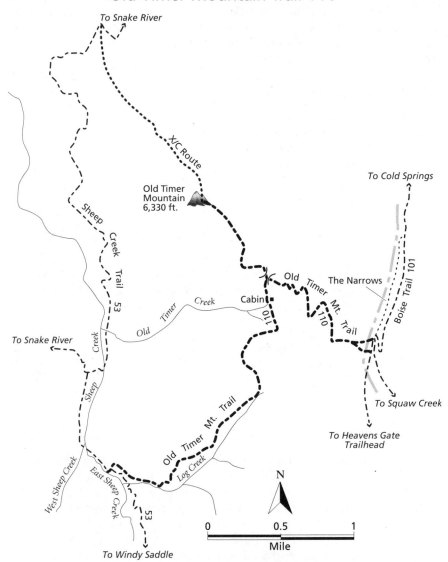

There are actually two junctions where Boise Trail meets Old Timer Mountain Trail. The sign marking the junction is about halfway between them. The trails here form a triangle. This description starts from the northern junction. The GPS coordinates at the northern junction are 45 24.920 N 116 28.892 W. See the accompanying map for clarification.

Trailhead facilities: A couple of dry campsites are located near the junction, but there are no other facilities.

Camping and services: Developed campsites are available at Windy Saddle Trailhead, which is 1.7 miles south of Heavens Gate Trailhead, and at

Seven Devils Lake, which is 0.5 mile farther to the southwest. Other services, including gas and groceries, can be obtained in Riggins. A cell phone will work in most of the open areas near the junction with Boise Trail.

For more information: USDA Forest Service at the Hells Canyon National Recreation Area office in Riggins.

Key points:
    0.0   Junction with Boise Trail 3.5 miles north of Heavens Gate Trailhead.
    0.6   Route to summit of Old Timer Mountain leaves trail in a saddle. GPS 45 25.359 N 116 29.610 W.
    1.8   Remains of old cabin.
    2.9   Trail turns down Log Creek.
    4.7   Junction with Sheep Creek Trail. GPS 45 24.247 N 116 31.312 W.

The hike: Old Timer Mountain Trail heads southwest off Boise Trail on an abandoned roadbed. A couple of hundred yards after leaving Boise Trail, there will be a trail leading to your left. This trail is the other segment of the triangle mentioned in the Finding the trailhead section above. Continue past the junction heading west on the roadbed through a

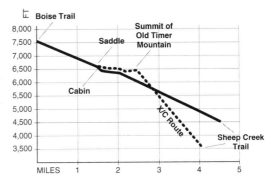

meadow. A couple hundred yards past the junction the track makes a right turn and begins a traverse through the woods, heading north-northwest. The course reaches an open ridgeline 0.5 mile from Boise Trail. Here on the flower-covered ridgetop the route switches back to the left (southwest). Great views of this canyon country can be had at this switchback as well as at the next one. The trace makes five more switchbacks in the next mile as it descends to 6,580 feet elevation in a saddle.

In the saddle the route, which is still a roadbed, makes a switchback to the left. At this switchback a vague path that leads west over the top of Old Timer Mountain and on down to Sheep Creek Trail leaves the roadbed. For a description of this path, see the Options section below.

Turn left at the switchback and follow the roadbed. You will notice evidence of an abandoned mining operation as you cross this open hillside. There is a developed spring on the left side of the route 0.2 mile past the switchback in the saddle. On the right side of the spring, which is surrounded with a log fence, turn left on a steep vague path. Climb steeply up the slope for about 15 yards. Here you will find the remains of an old cabin. About 15 feet past the cabin is a trail. Turn right on the trail and head south-southeast. Follow the trail 0.3 mile to a gully. Cross the gully and climb a few yards to another roadbed. Turn right on the roadbed and hike southwest. Columbines, Fireweed, and Paintbrush bloom along this roadbed in late July. Wild Strawberries carpet the ground in spots as you hike through the burnt timber.

After hiking southwest for 0.2 mile the route rounds a ridgeline into timber that was only partly burned and begins to descend. The course descends south then southeast for 0.6 mile, losing 500 vertical feet before reaching the bottom of brush-choked Log Creek Canyon. The track turns right down the brushy canyon bottom and continues its steep descent. The course remains steep for most of the next 1.8 miles as you hike down through the timber, to the junction with Sheep Creek Trail 53. The junction with Sheep Creek Trail is at 4,460 feet elevation and is 4.7 miles from Boise Trail.(See Hike 43 for a description of Sheep Creek Trail.)

Options: If you are an experienced cross-country hiker and are planning to hike down Sheep Creek Trail to the Snake River, you may want to leave Old Timer Mountain Trail at the saddle 1.6 miles after you left the Boise Trail. This route, which goes over the summit of Old Timer Mountain, is very steep and requires a little scrambling in places. This cross-country route reaches Sheep Creek Trail 4.3 miles closer to the Snake River than does the Old Timer Mountain Trail described above. From the saddle, it is about 2.6 miles, and 3,000 vertical feet, down to Sheep Creek Trail. Do not use this route unless you are sure of your scrambling and routefinding skills. This route is not suitable for stock.

To descend the cross-country route, head northwest from the saddle on a vague path through the forest. The route climbs slightly then contours around a semiopen hillside. The path fades out completely in the open area. Continue to traverse the slope heading north-northwest to a ridgeline, where the track shows up again. The route, that once was a roadbed here, heads northwest along the ridge for 0.3 mile to a small saddle. At this saddle the route

Whitetail deer near Sheep Creek.

230

bears slightly to the right of the ridgeline for a short distance. Then you must climb steeply back to the ridgeline at another small notch in the ridge.

Once you are back on the ridge, follow it to the northwest on a vague path that includes a little scrambling for 0.2 mile to the summit of Old Timer Mountain. The summit, at 6,330 feet elevation, offers wonderful views in all directions. You can even spot a small section of the Snake River over 5,000 feet below the point where you are standing. The GPS coordinates at the summit are 45 25.758 N 116 30.454 W.

To continue down to Sheep Creek Trail, head northwest down a ridgeline. Work your way down the ridge, scrambling through and around the rock outcropping. The route drops about 1,700 feet in the first mile of descent. It then moderates slightly, and you will follow a poor path down the ridge, to the north-northwest. Sheep Creek Trail is hard to spot where this route meets it. There was a small rock cairn marking the spot when I hiked this route in 1999, but it may not be there in the future. The elevation where the route meets the Sheep Creek Trail is 3,560 feet, and the GPS coordinates are 45 26.082 N 116 31.318 W.

To make a loop, turn left on Sheep Creek Trail and follow it south for 4.3 miles to the junction with Old Timer Mountain Trail described above. Then climb back to Boise Trail on Old Timer Mountain Trail.

48 Heavens Gate Lookout Trail

Highlights:	A short hike from Heavens Gate Trailhead to the Heavens Gate Lookout, with its marvelous view of Hells Canyon and the Seven Devils Mountains. The well-maintained trail has heavy foot traffic but little or no horse traffic. The sign at the trailhead says 350 yards, but the actual distance is considerably more.
Type of hike:	Out-and-back day hike.
Total distance:	0.7 mile.
Difficulty:	Easy.
Best months:	Mid-July–September.
Elevation gain:	289 feet.
Permits and fees:	None.
Maps:	Heavens Gate USGS quad covers the area, but a map is not needed to follow this trail.
Starting point:	Heavens Gate Trailhead and parking area.

Finding the trailhead: From Riggins, Idaho, drive 1 mile south on U.S. Highway 95 to the junction with Squaw Creek Road. Turn west on Squaw Creek Road (County Road 517) and follow it for 16.5 miles to Windy Saddle Trailhead. County Road 517 makes a left turn at a junction slightly less than 2 miles after leaving US 95 and becomes Forest Road 517 at the Nez Perce National Forest Boundary approximately 4 miles from US 95. There are road

Heavens Gate Lookout Trail

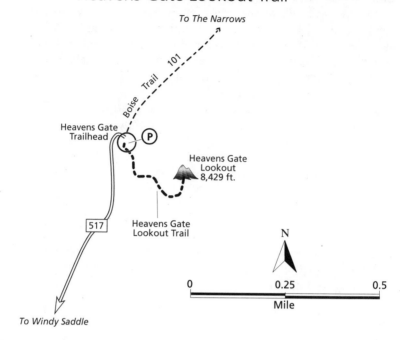

signs pointing to Seven Devils Campground at the junction with US 95 and at other intersections along the way.

Turn right at the junction next to the trailhead and drive 1.7 miles north on FR 517 to Heavens Gate Trailhead. Early in the season, it may be necessary to walk part of the way from Windy Saddle because of snowdrifts, which sometimes block the road. The trailhead is located at the north end of the parking area. The GPS coordinates at Heavens Gate Trailhead are 45 22.229 N 116 29.850 W.

Trailhead facilities: The trailhead has a restroom and parking for several cars.

Camping and services: Campsites are available at Windy Saddle Trailhead and at Seven Devils Lake, 1.7 and 2.2 miles south of Heavens Gate Trailhead respectively. Groceries, gas, and medical services can be obtained in Riggins. Cell phones work well at Heavens Gate Trailhead and at the lookout.

For more information: USDA Forest Service at the Hells Canyon National Recreation Area office in Riggins.

Key points:
  0.0   Heavens Gate Trailhead.
  0.35 Heavens Gate Lookout.

The hike: The trail leaves from the southeast side of the parking area. You will climb gently through

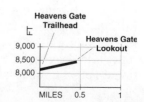

Heavens Gate Lookout.

the thin forest of large Whitebark Pines, making five switchbacks on the way to the lookout. The Heavens Gate Lookout provides a panoramic view of the surrounding area. It is an excellent place to visit before starting a backpack trip into the Seven Devils Mountains, because from the lookout one can get the general lay of the land. The Hat Point Lookout and the Dry Diggins Lookout can be seen from the Heavens Gate Lookout, as can the high peaks of the Seven Devils Mountains. The Wallowa Mountains are in the distance to the southwest, across Hells Canyon in Oregon.

Options: Hike to the Heavens Gate Lookout before you start your backpacking trip into the Seven Devils Mountains.

49 Seven Devils Loop 101, 124

Highlights:	A loop that encircles the highest and most rugged part of the Seven Devils Mountains. While no lakes are actually reached along the loop, it provides the primary access route to side trails that lead to fifteen of the most beautiful lakes in the area. All along the Seven Devils Loop are views of Salmon River Canyon, Hells Canyon, the Seven Devils Mountains, and several other mountain ranges. Many parts of this hike traverse burn areas of varying age, where the regrowth of flowers and young trees is spectacular. Allow as much time as you can to hike the loop in order to explore the peaks and lakes above it and the canyons below.
Type of hike:	Three- to ten-day backpacking loop.
Total distance:	28.2 miles.
Difficulty:	Moderate.
Best months:	Mid-July–September.
Elevation gain:	Approximately 5,000 feet.
Permits and fees:	None.
Maps:	He Devil and Heavens Gate USGS quads. Most of this loop is on the He Devil quad.

Finding the trailhead: From Riggins, Idaho, drive 1 mile south on U.S. Highway 95 to the junction with Squaw Creek Road. Turn west on Squaw Creek Road (County Road 517) and follow it for 16.5 miles to Windy Saddle Trailhead. County Road 517 makes a left turn at a junction slightly less than 2 miles after leaving US 95 and becomes Forest Road 517 at the Nez Perce National Forest Boundary approximately 4 miles from US 95. There are road signs pointing to Seven Devils Campground at the junction with US 95 and at other intersections along the way. Seven Devils Campground is .05 mile past the trailhead. The GPS coordinates at the trailhead are 45 20.818 N 116 30.864 W. Do not try to shorten your hike by parking at the Seven Devils Guard Station; you may be asked to move your car.

Trailhead facilities: The trailhead has restrooms, ample parking, and a few campsites. Horse facilities are located a short distance northeast across the road that leads to Heavens Gate Lookout.

Camping and services: Camping is available at the trailhead and at Seven Devils Lake 0.5 mile to the southwest. Other services and groceries can be obtained in Riggins.

For more information: USDA Forest Service at the Hells Canyon National Recreation Office in Riggins.

Key points:
- 0.0 Windy Saddle Trailhead.
- 0.5 Seven Devils Guard Station.

Seven Devils Loop 101, 124

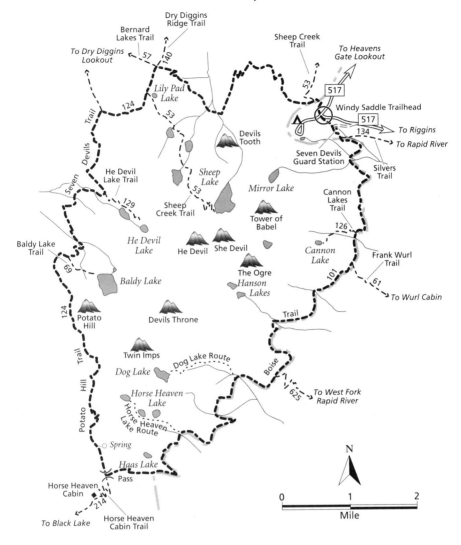

3.4   Junction with Cannon Lakes Trail 126. GPS 45 19.477 N 116 30.060 W.

7.4   Junction with Dog Lake Route.

9.7   Junction with Horse Heaven Lake Route. GPS 45 16.986 N 116 33.158 W.

11.9   Junction with Horse Heaven Trail 214. GPS 45 16.451N 116 34.428 W.

16.7   Junction with Baldy Lake Trail 69. GPS 45 19.108 N 116 35.338 W.

19.8   Junction with He Devil Lake Trail 129. GPS 45 19.993 N 116 34.457 W.

20.9   Junction with Little Granite Creek Trail 112.

21.3   Junction with Dry Diggins Lookout Trail 56.

22.2   Junction with Sheep Lake Trail 123. GPS 45 21.217 N 116 33.728 W.

22.7   Junction with Bernard Lakes Trail 57 and Dry Diggins Ridge Trail 140. GPS 45 21.527 N 116 33.619 W.

27.7   Junction with Sheep Creek Trail 53. GPS 45 21.242 N 116 30.878 W.

28.2   Windy Saddle Trailhead.

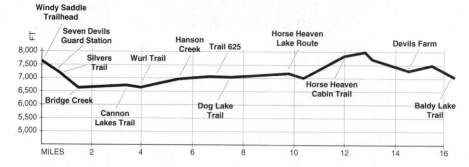

The hike: The first 11.9 miles of this loop hike are along Boise Trail 101. From the parking area at Windy Saddle Trailhead the route crosses the road that leads to Seven Devils Campground. It then descends the grassy and flower-covered slope to the east-southeast. After making a couple of switchbacks you will pass through a gate and enter the timber. In the timber the track makes a couple more switchbacks then passes a small log cabin and some corrals. The course follows a road for a short distance then bears left and crosses another road before reaching Seven Devils Guard Station and Work Center.

The guard station and work center, at 7,270 feet elevation, consists of two cabins and a tent cabin. Hike across the turnaround in front of the guard station, then bear slightly left (east) to a trail sign. The route soon heads southeast again, passing the Hells Canyon Wilderness Boundary sign, as it descends into thicker timber. Three-tenths of a mile after passing the guard station, you will come to the junction with Silvers Trail 134. Silvers Trail turns to the left (east) at the junction. This route descends and forks before reaching Rapid River Trail about 8 miles down, near Rapid River Fish Hatchery. From the junction Boise Trail heads south, passing a wilderness registration box.

The tread crosses an open slope with a great view of the Tower of Babel to the southwest 0.4 mile after passing the junction with Silvers Trail. Soon the track reenters the timber, and crosses a creek. Here you enter the burn area of the 1994 Rapid River Fire. In some places the fire killed nearly all the trees but in many areas the timber was only partly burned. In the burn, flowers cover the ground in many spots.

One mile from the guard station the trail crosses Bridge Creek. For the next couple of miles the course contours along the slope, never gaining or losing much elevation, to the junction with Cannon Lakes Trail 126. Several spots along this section of trail offer views of Rapid River Canyon to the east and the peaks of the Seven Devils Mountains to the west. You will reach the junction with Cannon Lakes Trail at 6,730 feet elevation, 3.4 miles from Windy Saddle Trailhead. At the junction Cannon Lakes Trail turns to the right (west), and climbs to Cannon Lakes. (See Hike 50 for details about hiking to Cannon Lake and Upper Cannon Lake.)

A short distance past the junction the course crosses Cannon Creek. Half a mile after crossing Cannon Creek a poor unmarked path turns off to the left (southeast). This poor path is Frank Wurl Trail 61. Frank Wurl Trail descends about 3 miles into West Fork Rapid River Canyon to meet West Fork

236

Rapid River Trail 113 at the McCrea Cabin. (See Hike 60 for a description of West Fork Rapid River Trail.)

From the junction with Frank Wurl Trail the route continues to contour along the east slope of the Seven Devils Mountains for 1.5 miles to Hanson Creek. There is a fairly good campsite to the right of the trail just before reaching Hanson Creek. About 1.3 miles after crossing Hanson Creek you will reach another unsigned trail junction. The trail that turns off to the left is Trail 625, which descends to the southeast to meet West Fork Rapid River Trail. Half a mile after passing the junction with Trail 625, Boise Trail crosses Dog Creek at 7,030 feet elevation. Twenty feet past the crossing is the unmarked junction with Dog Lake Route. From this junction, 7.4 miles from Windy Saddle Trailhead, Dog Lake is 1.3 miles to the west. (See Hike 51 for a description of Dog Lake Route.)

After passing the junction with the route to Dog Lake, Boise Trail heads on to the south and west, staying relatively level to the junction with the route to Horse Heaven Lake. The route to Horse Heaven Lake is not marked but there is a sign on a tree marking Horse Heaven Creek a few feet past (south of) the junction. Horse Heaven and Slide Rock Lakes are to the right up this poor trail. (See Hike 52 for details about reaching Horse Heaven and Slide Rock Lakes.) The junction with the route to Horse Heaven Lake is at 7,200 feet elevation, 9.7 miles from Windy Saddle Trailhead.

Boise Trail continues south after passing the junction with the route to Horse Heaven Lake. Half a mile from the junction, as the trace enters a rockslide, a cross-country route to Haas Lake leaves the trail. There is no trail to Haas Lake and no fish in the lake, but the lake makes a nice out of the way camping spot. The GPS coordinates where you leave Boise Trail to head for Haas Lake are 45 16.698 N 116 33.370 W. To reach Haas Lake, scramble up over the boulders for a quarter of a mile to the west.

Continuing on Boise Trail, you will cross the boulder field below Haas Lake then climb along a slope through green timber to a ridgeline. At this point the route has left the burn area it has been in nearly all the way from Seven Devils Guard Station. The track turns right as it crosses the ridgeline and heads west, climbing moderately through the meadows and timber along this south-facing slope. The trail enters a talus slope 0.7 mile after crossing the ridgeline. You will make four switchbacks as you climb for 0.7 mile through the talus. The USGS He Devil quad map shows the trail incorrectly in this area.

This slope is a very beautiful place. Take time to sit on a rock and admire the view. As you are sitting watch and listen for the pikas that abound here.

The route reaches a pass and the junction with Horse Heaven Cabin Trail 214 as it leaves the talus slope. This pass, 11.9 miles from Windy Saddle Trailhead, is on the main crest of the Seven Devils Mountains at 7,860 feet elevation. Most maps show this to be a four-way junction, but the trail leading down Two Creek to the west is not visible on the ground and no sign points to it. To the left (south) at the junction Horse Heaven Cabin Trail climbs toward Horse Heaven Cabin, 0.8 mile away. At the junction the trail number changes to 124, and you are no longer on Boise Trail. The section of the Seven Devils Loop from here to the junction with Baldy Lake Trail is sometimes referred to as Potato Hill Trail.

The loop route makes a right turn at the junction and climbs at a moderate grade to the north-northwest. The track soon leaves the open woods of Whitebark Pine and Sub-Alpine Fir for an open grass and flower covered slope. A quarter of a mile from the junction the trail forks. Bear left at the fork to stay on the main trail. There is a spring 75 yards above the trail to the right 0.2 mile after passing the fork. The spring is surrounded with False Hellebore and Monkeyflowers, making it relatively easy to spot from the trail. Past the spring the course traverses open slopes dotted with trees and silvered snags for 0.3 mile to a ridgeline at 8,000 feet elevation. This ridgeline has a very good view of the canyons to the west and several rocks to sit on, making it a great place for a rest break. The USGS He Devil quad map is incorrect in this area. The trail is a couple hundred feet lower than the map shows.

The route makes a right turn crossing the ridgeline, then starts its descent toward The Devils Farm. The trace makes four switchbacks, losing about 300 feet in elevation before turning north to traverse the rocky slope. You will continue to descend at a gentle rate through the boulders and silvered snags, dropping to about 7,350 feet elevation as you cross the boulder-strewn basin called The Devils Farm. From these rough semiopen slopes Hat Point Tower on the Oregon side of Hells Canyon can be seen in the distance to the northwest.

After crossing The Devils Farm the trail climbs slightly to cross a rounded ridge through thin, mostly burnt timber at 7,500 feet elevation. Then you start a gradual descent toward the junction with Baldy Lake Trail 69. Fireweed adds cheer to the burned sections of timber along this part of the hike. The junction with Baldy Lake Trail is reached 4.8 miles from the junction with Horse Heaven Trail and 16.7 miles from Windy Saddle Trailhead. The signed junction at 6,920 feet elevation is in an area of nearly completely burned timber. Baldy Lake Trail turns to the right to climb gently for 0.9 mile to Baldy Lake. (See Hike 53 for a description of Baldy Lake Trail.)

The portion of Seven Devils Loop from the junction with Baldy Lake Trail on to Windy Saddle Trailhead is called Seven Devils Trail. Leaving the junction with Baldy Lake Trail the loop route continues to descend, making several switchbacks before reaching a creek crossing. There is a fair campsite next to the trail just after crossing the creek. The track crosses the outlet stream from Baldy Lake 0.1 mile farther along, at 6,450 feet elevation. The trail follows the creek down for a short distance then begins to climb along a rocky slope. Penstemon and Asters grow from between the rocks and cliffs loom above to the right as you climb. After climbing for 0.4 mile and making a couple of switchbacks the trail makes a hard right turn on a ridgeline and enters green timber. The tread crosses a small stream that runs through a culvert beneath it 0.7 mile after crossing the ridgeline. It then climbs gently for another 0.4 mile to the junction with He Devil Lake Trail 129 at 6,900 feet elevation. (See Hike 54 for a description of He Devil Lake Trail.) At the junction, 19.8 miles from where you started this hike at Windy Saddle Trailhead, Echo, Triangle, Quad, He Devil, and Purgatory Lakes are to the right (southeast).

The loop trail heads north from the signed junction with He Devil Lake Trail. Climbing moderately it soon crosses an open slope with a view of the Wallowa Mountains across Hells Canyon to the west. About 1.1 miles from the junction with He Devil Lake Trail you will reach the junction with Little Granite Creek Trail 112. Little Granite Creek Trail turns to the left (west) and descends about 6 miles to the Snake River, but it has not been maintained in recent years and is difficult to follow in spots. The junction at 7,360 feet is really a trail triangle. Hibbs Cow Camp, which makes an excellent campsite, is about 100 yards off the loop trail on Little Granite Creek Trail.

Seven Devils Trail leads north-northeast from the junction with Little Granite Creek Trail. The track goes in and out of the timber and crosses a couple of streambeds, reaching the junction with Dry Diggins Lookout Trail 56 in 0.4 mile. Dry Diggins Lookout Trail turns to the left to head for Dry Diggins Lookout 2.2 miles to the northwest. (See Hike 55 for details about reaching the lookout from this junction.)

Seven Devils Trail turns right at the junction to head east through ridgetop meadows and stands of silvered snags. The trail appears to fork 0.8 mile past the junction. The right fork is a shortcut to Sheep Lake Trail. Bear left at the fork and hike north for 0.3 mile to the junction with Sheep Lake Trail 123. (See Hike 56 for a description of Sheep Lake Trail.) Sheep Lake as well as Gem, Basin, and Shelf Lakes are to the right at this junction. The junction with Sheep Lake Trail, at 7,390 feet elevation, is 22.2 miles from the starting point at Windy Saddle Trailhead, and you have 6 miles yet to hike to complete the loop.

From the junction with Sheep Lake Trail the loop trail heads northeast through meadows and burnt woods for 0.5 mile to the junction with Bernard Lakes Trail 57 and Dry Diggins Ridge Trail 140. This four-way, signed junction, at 7,310 feet elevation, is on the eastern edge of the plateau you have been hiking across since leaving the junction with Little Granite Creek Trail. (See Hikes 57 and 58 for descriptions of these two trails.) Silver snags surround the junction, and Fireweed covers the ground in spots. Looking to the east the canyons of the Sheep Creek drainage are in view.

The loop route heads east from the junction and quickly begins to descend, making a switchback, through the silvered snags. Leaving the snags you enter a talus slope. The track makes a couple of switchbacks on the talus then gets back into thick green timber. After hiking through the timber for 0.7 mile

The Devils Tooth.

the course crosses the West Fork of Sheep Creek that drains Gem, Shelf, and Basin Lakes. Another 250 yards farther along you will cross another fork at 6,680 feet elevation. This fork drains Sheep Lake. There is a campsite to the left of the trail just past the crossing. Now the route begins to climb making a couple of switchbacks. At the second switchback there is a good campsite a few yards to the right of the trail.

Past the campsite the trace makes another switchback and passes a small pond before entering another talus slope. As you climb through the boulders look behind you (south) for a close-up view of the rock spire called The Devils Tooth. To your right gray cliffs rise above the talus. Penstemon grows out from between the rocks beside the trail as you climb. Leaving the talus slope the track makes eight switchbacks, climbing the steep slope through thin timber to a ridgeline. You then traverse a slope for 0.3 mile to another ridgeline.

On this ridgeline, at 7,950 feet elevation, there is a great viewpoint a few yards to the left of the trail. There is also a campsite here, but no water is available. Once across the ridgeline the trace begins its descent into the East Fork of Sheep Creek Canyon. The route descends through timber making a couple of switchbacks and crossing a grassy slope below gray cliffs for 1.4 miles to the junction with Sheep Creek Trail 53. Watch for Mountain Goats and Mule Deer as you hike this section of trail. At the junction with Sheep Creek Trail you are 27.7 miles from where this hike began and you have only 0.5 mile to go to complete the loop. The elevation at the junction with Sheep Creek Trail is 7,280 feet. Sheep Creek Trail turns to the left (north) to descend 14.2 miles to the Snake River. (See Hike 43 for a description of Sheep Creek Trail.)

Seven Devils Loop climbs northeast from the junction with Sheep Creek Trail. Shortly you will come to another junction. The path to the left goes a short distance to a stock water tank then rejoins the main trail farther along. Bear right at the junction and follow the main trail. The route makes several switchbacks as it climbs the 326 vertical feet to Windy Saddle Trailhead to complete the loop.

Options: Many options for side trips exist along Seven Devils Loop. See the hike descriptions mentioned above for details.

50 Cannon Lakes Trail 126

Highlights:	A hike from Seven Devils Loop to Lower Cannon Lake. If you feel more adventurous, you can continue on a cross-country route to the eye-popping grandeur of Upper Cannon Lake. Considerable routefinding skills are required above Lower Cannon Lake.
Type of hike:	Internal out-and-back day hike or backpack.
Total distance:	3.8 miles.
Difficulty:	Easy to Lower Cannon Lake; strenuous off-trail hike from there to Upper Cannon Lake.
Best months:	July–September.
Elevation gain:	300 feet to Lower Cannon Lake; 1,370 feet to Upper Cannon Lake.
Permits and fees:	None.
Maps:	He Devil USGS quad.

Starting point: Junction with the Seven Devils Loop (Boise Trail 101) 3.4 miles south of Windy Saddle Trailhead.

Finding the trailhead: Follow the driving directions in Hike 49 to Windy Saddle Trailhead. Then hike south as described in Hike 49 for 3.4 miles to the junction with Cannon Lakes Trail. The junction with Seven Devils Loop (Boise Trail) is in a burn area a few yards north of Cannon Creek. There is a sign marking the junction. GPS coordinates at the junction are 45 19.477 N 116 30.060 W. The route from Lower Cannon Lake to Upper Cannon Lake is not suitable for stock.

Trailhead facilities: Windy Saddle Trailhead has ample parking, restrooms, and horse facilities. Seven Devils Guard Station has parking for several cars as well as a horse-loading ramp.

There is a possible campsite next to the junction where Cannon Lakes Trail leaves the loop (Boise Trail).

Camping and services: Developed campsites are available at Windy Saddle Trailhead and at Seven Devils Lake 0.5 mile to the southwest. Other services and groceries can be obtained in Riggins, Idaho.

For more information: USDA Forest Service at the Hells Canyon National Recreation Area office in Riggins.

Key points:
- 0.5 Crossing of Cannon Creek.
- 0.8 Lower Cannon Lake. GPS 45 19.380 N 116 30.592 W.
- 1.6 Crossing of Cannon Creek in a small meadow next to falls.
- 1.9 Upper Cannon Lake. GPS 45 19.295 N 116 31.645 W.

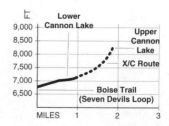

Cannon Lakes Trail 126

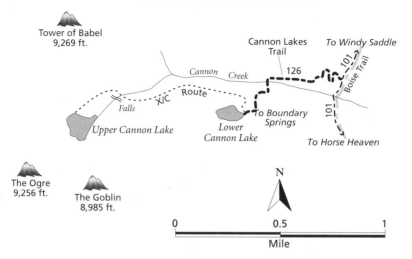

The hike: Cannon Lakes Trail climbs to the west from the junction with Seven Devils Loop. The path soon bears to the right, then makes several switchbacks as it climbs through the burn area. Paintbrush and Fireweed grow up out of the ashes of the burn. The trail flattens out 0.3 mile after leaving the loop trail. It then heads on up the canyon to the west for another 0.2 mile to a crossing of Cannon Creek, at 6,980 feet elevation. Once across the creek the trail winds over a small ridge to the southwest for 0.3 mile to Lower Cannon Lake.

Lower Cannon Lake, at 7,030 feet elevation, is in a mostly burned area. However, the forest is rejuvenating itself, and the flowers can be very pretty. There is some large green timber along the south shore of the lake. A campsite is located at the southwest corner of the lake, near where the trail reaches it.

Lower Cannon Lake is at the end of the maintained trail. From here it is a 1.1-mile cross-country climb to Upper Cannon Lake. The route to the upper lake climbs the small ridge to the north of Lower Cannon Lake. It then follows this ridge to the west approximately 0.3 mile to the place where it steepens. Where the ridge steepens the route bears slightly to the right and traverses the steep side hill on the south side of Cannon Creek. After 0.5 mile of bushwacking along the slope the route enters a small meadow, at 7,780 feet elevation. At the south end of the meadow, the route crosses Cannon Creek, which enters the meadow as a pretty waterfall. After crossing the creek the route climbs steeply to the west and southwest to Upper Cannon Lake.

Upper Cannon Lake, which is out of the burn area at 8,100 feet elevation, is in a far more spectacular setting than is Lower Cannon Lake. High peaks ring the lake, including The Goblin, The Ogre, She Devil, and Tower of Babel. Proximity to these peaks makes Upper Cannon Lake a good

Lower Cannon Lake.

climber's base camp. There are several campsites close to Upper Cannon Lake and trout to be caught.

Options: Hiking to Lower Cannon Lake makes a good, short side trip when you are hiking Seven Devils Loop.

Camp at Upper Cannon Lake and possibly make a climb of one of the peaks near it. See Hikes 72, 73, and 74 for descriptions of the routes to some of these peaks.

51 Dog Lake Route

Highlights:	A steep hike from Seven Devils Loop (Boise Trail 101) to Dog Lake. This route should not be used by stock.
Type of hike:	Internal out-and-back day hike or backpack.
Total distance:	2.6 miles.
Difficulty:	Strenuous. Good routefinding skills are required.
Best months:	Late July–September.
Elevation gain:	890 feet.
Permits and fees:	None.
Maps:	He Devil USGS quad.

Finding the trailhead: Follow the driving directions shown in Hike 49 to Windy Saddle Trailhead. Then hike south as described in Hike 49 for 7.4 miles to the junction with the route to Dog Lake. The unmarked junction is

Dog Lake Route

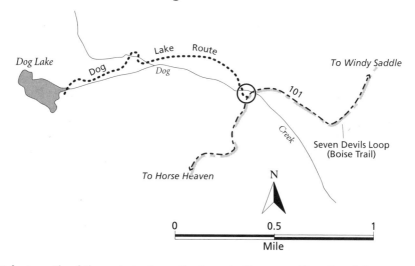

20 feet south of the point where the loop trail crosses Dog Creek in a mostly burned area. The elevation at the junction is 7,020 feet. The GPS coordinates at the junction are 45 17.725 N 116 32.117 W.

Trailhead facilities: None.

Camping and services: Developed campsites are available at Windy Saddle Trailhead and at Seven Devils Lake 0.5 mile to the southwest. Other services, including gas and groceries, can be obtained in Riggins, Idaho.

For more information: USDA Forest Service at the Hells Canyon National Recreation Area office in Riggins.

Key points:
- 0.0 Junction with Seven Devils Loop 7.4 miles south of Windy Saddle Trailhead.
- 1.3 Dog Lake. GPS 45 17.723 N 116 33.225 W.

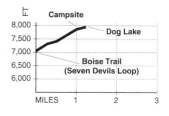

The hike: The route to Dog Lake heads northwest from the junction with the loop trail. A few yards up the course you will cross Dog Creek. There are campsites on both sides of this crossing. The faint path climbs a few yards away from the creek. It then bears left (west) and continues to climb through the burn. There may be many downed logs across the vague path in this area. The route soon bears to the right (northwest) again and climbs steeply. After climbing steeply a bit more, it bears left (west) and enters a boulder-strewn slope, which may be covered with wildflowers. Cairns mark the trace along this slope.

Along the slope the path flattens some as it climbs along the edge of the burnt timber. It soon enters thin timber and crosses a side stream. The faint

Dog Lake.

track may be very difficult to follow in this area. This stream crossing is 0.5 mile from the junction with the loop trail. The route recrosses the stream in a few yards, then crosses it again a short distance farther along. After crossing the side stream for the last time the route follows its south bank for 100 yards or so. Then you climb the ridge dividing the side stream and Dog Creek. From here on up to Dog Lake the path climbs steeply along the left side of the ridge, next to Dog Creek. The course makes a couple of switchbacks and crosses Dog Creek a couple of times, before reaching the lake, at 7,909 feet elevation.

There is a possible campsite in a flat area along Dog Creek a quarter of a mile before reaching the lake. There is also a small campsite next to Dog Lake to the left of the outlet. Some fairly large trout inhabit Dog Lake.

Options: Hike this route as a side trip from Seven Devils Loop.

52 Horse Heaven Lake Route

Highlights:	A hike along a poor path off Seven Devils Loop (Boise Trail 101) to Horse Heaven Lake. Then climb on to the breathtakingly beautiful Slide Rock Lake, nestled close to the spine of the Seven Devils Mountains. Stock should not use this route.
Type of hike:	Internal out-and-back day hike or backpack.
Total distance:	2.8 miles.
Difficulty:	Moderate to strenuous with routefinding skills required.
Best months:	August–September.
Elevation gain:	680 feet.
Permits and fees:	None.
Maps:	He Devil USGS quad.

Finding the trailhead: Follow the driving directions shown in Hike 49 to Windy Saddle Trailhead. Then hike south on the loop trail for 9.7 miles to the junction with the route to Horse Heaven Lake. The route heads northwest off Seven Devils Loop a few feet north of Horse Heaven Creek, at 7,200 feet elevation. There is a sign on a tree marking Horse Heaven Creek, which may be dry. The GPS coordinates at the unmarked junction are 45 16.986 N 116 33.158 W.

Trailhead facilities: None.

Camping and services: Developed campsites are available at Windy Saddle Trailhead and at Seven Devils Lake 0.5 mile to the southwest. Other services, including gas and groceries, can be obtained in Riggins, Idaho.

For more information: USDA Forest Service at the Hells Canyon National Recreation Area office in Riggins.

Horse Heaven Lake Route

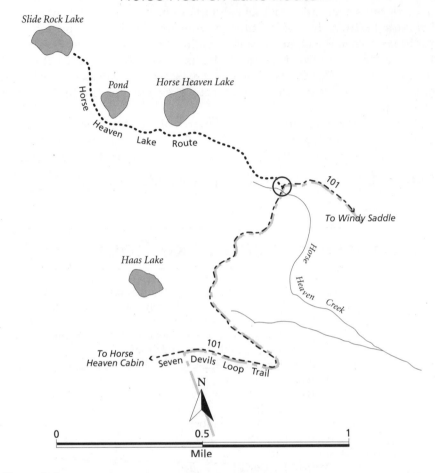

Key points:

    0.0   Junction with Seven Devils Loop (Boise Trail) 9.7 miles south of Windy Saddle Trailhead.

    0.6   Horse Heaven Lake. GPS 45 17.134 N 116 33.522 W.

    1.0   Pond.

    1.4   Slide Rock Lake. GPS 45 17.390 N 116 33.943 W.

The hike: The faint path heads northwest off the loop trail. In a short distance the path fades out completely in a jumble of downed logs. Just before entering the jumbled logs bear to the left and climb a small rise. On the top of the rise the path should show up again. Then follow the vague path northwest. Soon the route climbs along a slope and makes a couple of tiny switch-

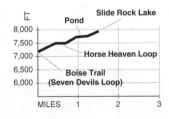

backs. About 0.5 mile from the loop trail the route flattens for a short distance then reaches Horse Heaven Lake at 7,500 feet elevation. The route skirts

Horse Heaven Lake.

the lake on the south side, passing a good campsite. Horse Heaven Lake makes a good out-of-the-way camping spot, quite a few trout await your fly or lure.

As you leave Horse Heaven Lake the path heads up a draw to the west. It then bears slightly right, climbing the sloping side of the draw. Soon you will pass a pond that is to the right (north) of the route. After passing the pond, head northwest and climb toward what looks from here like a small saddle. Work your way up through the boulders and rock outcroppings to Slide Rock Lake, at 7,880 feet elevation.

Slide Rock Lake sits in a spectacular alpine bowl. Rockslides reach the lake along two-thirds of its perimeter. Bluebells grace the lakes outlet, and heather covers the ground between the boulders. There is a marginal campsite just to the right (north) of the outlet. There are trout to be caught in Slide Rock Lake if you brought your fishing gear.

Options: Hike to Horse Heaven Lake and Slide Rock Lake as a side trip while hiking Seven Devils Loop. There are campsites at both lakes.

53 Baldy Lake Trail 69

Highlights:	A hike from Seven Devils Loop to a beautiful mountain lake in a spectacular setting.
Type of hike:	Internal out-and-back day hike or backpack.
Total distance:	1.8 miles.
Difficulty:	Easy.
Best months:	Mid-July–September.
Elevation gain:	300 feet.
Permits and fees:	None.
Maps:	He Devil USGS quad.

Finding the trailhead: Follow the driving directions shown in Hike 49 to Windy Saddle Trailhead. Then hike west and south on Seven Devils Trail for 11.5 miles to the junction with Baldy Lake Trail.

If you are hiking Seven Devils Loop clockwise as described in Hike 49, follow the loop for 16.7 miles to reach the junction where this hike description starts. A sign marks the junction. GPS coordinates at the junction are 45 19.108 N 116 35.338 W.

Trailhead facilities: None.

Camping and services: Camping is available at the trailhead and at Seven Devils Lake 0.5 mile to the southwest. Other services and groceries can be obtained in Riggins, Idaho. Cell phone service can generally be had on the low ridge just west of Baldy Lake.

For more information: USDA Forest Service at the Hells Canyon National Recreation Area office in Riggins.

Key points:

0.0	Junction with Seven Devils Loop (Seven Devils Trail 124).
0.5	Stream crossing.
0.9	Baldy Lake. GPS 45 18.798 N 116 34.573 W.

The hike: Baldy Lake Trail leaves Seven Devils Loop climbing gently to the southeast, through the burnt forest. Young Lodge-

Baldy Lake.

Baldy Lake Trail 69 • He Devil Lake Trail 129

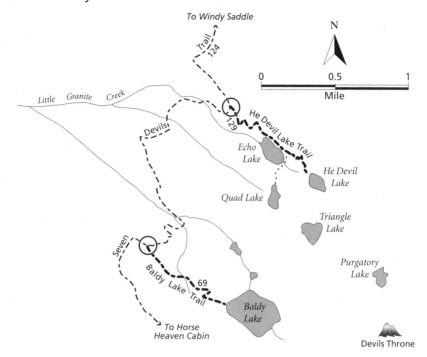

pole Pines grow between the burnt snags, and Fireweed blooms in profusion in August next to the path. After climbing for 100 yards or so the tread bears slightly to the right to begin a traverse of a steep slope. Soon the course leaves the burnt woods and crosses a talus slope. Leaving the talus the trace crosses more moderate terrain through small Lodgepole Pines to a stream crossing at 7,030 feet elevation.

The path winds up a small ridge that is nearly covered with blooming Pearly Everlasting in August. You then make a couple of switchbacks before entering a flat, semiopen rocky area. Hike across the rock-strewn meadow; then descend a few feet to the shore of Baldy Lake.

The lake, at 7,200 feet elevation, has a fair population of Rainbow Trout that are sometimes eager to take a rooster tail. There are campsites along the lakeshore in either direction form the point where the trail reaches the lake.

Options: Use this hike as a side trip when hiking Seven Devils Loop.

54 He Devil Lake Trail 129

Highlights: A hike from Seven Devils Loop (Seven Devils Trail 124) to beautiful He Devil Lake on a well-maintained trail. He Devil Lake is sometimes used as a base camp for climbing He Devil Mountain.

See Map on Page 251

Type of hike: Internal out-and-back day hike or backpack.
Total distance: 2.8 miles.
Difficulty: Easy to moderate.
Best months: Mid-July–September.
Elevation gain: 615 feet.
Permits and fees: None.
Maps: He Devil USGS quad.

Finding the trail: Follow the driving directions shown in Hike 49 to Windy Saddle Trailhead. Then hike west and south on Seven Devils Trail 124 (Seven Devils Loop) for 8.4 miles to the junction with He Devil Lake Trail, or hike 19.8 miles from the opposite direction as described in Hike 49. The GPS coordinates at the junction are GPS 45 19.993 N 116 34.457 W.

Trailhead facilities: None.

Camping and services: Developed campsites are available at Windy Saddle Trailhead and at Seven Devils Lake 0.5 mile to the southwest. Other services, including gas and groceries, can be obtained in Riggins, Idaho.

For more information: USDA Forest Service at the Hells Canyon National Recreation Area office in Riggins, Idaho.

Key points:
- 0.0 Junction with Seven Devils Loop 8.4 miles southwest of Windy Saddle Trailhead.
- 0.7 Upper end of Echo Lake and junction with path to Quad Lake.
- 1.4 He Devil Lake. GPS 45 19.579 N 116 33.771 W.

The hike: He Devil Lake Trail climbs to the southeast from the junction. It soon enters an old partial burn area. The course winds its way up through the partly burned timber for 0.5 mile. It then flattens out and heads along the northeast side of Echo Lake, at 7,245 feet elevation.

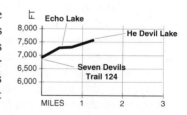

A couple of campsites can be found along Echo Lake, and the lake seems to have a good fish population. At the upper end of the lake is another campsite as well as the junction with the vague path that leads to Quad Lake.

Quad Lake is 0.5 mile from He Devil Lake Trail. To reach it, follow the poor path around the southeast end of Echo Lake, crossing its tiny inlet stream, which

Echo Lake.   GARY FLETCHER PHOTO

may be dry. Then climb very slightly to the south, up a boulder-strewn draw, to Quad Lake. Campsites are very limited at Quad Lake, elevation 7,260 feet.

Leaving Echo Lake, He Devil Lake Trail makes seven switchbacks as it climbs the 0.5 mile to He Devil Lake. He Devil Lake, at 7,505 feet elevation, has a good supply of Rainbow Trout. There are also a couple of good campsites. One of the campsites is next to the point where the trail reaches the lake. The other is near the opposite end of the lake. There is a poor path all the way around the lake. He Devil Lake is at the end of the trail so the return is best made by retracing your steps to the loop trail.

Options: Triangle Lake (elev. 7,523 ft) is a quarter of a mile south of He Devil Lake. It also has lots of trout but campsites are limited. Purgatory Lake is 0.5 mile southeast of Triangle Lake. To reach it follow the streambed up from Triangle Lake. Purgatory Lake, at 7,950 feet elevation, is the highest lake in this drainage. The terrain and vegetation around it are much more alpine than they are around the other lakes.

If your intent is to climb He Devil Mountain, He Devil Lake is a good base camp for starting your climb. Scramble up the slope to the northeast of the lake to a saddle on the ridgeline (elev. 8,550 ft). Then turn right on the ridge and follow the route described in Hike 71 to the summit. This is a mountain climb and should not be attempted by the novice without experienced leadership.

55 Dry Diggins Lookout Trail 56

Highlights:	A hike from Seven Devils Loop (Seven Devils Trail 124) to Dry Diggins Lookout and the best view of Hells Canyon to be had.
Type of hike:	Internal out-and-back day hike, with a loop option.
Total distance:	4.4 miles.
Difficulty:	Easy.
Best months:	Mid-July–September.
Elevation gain:	715 feet.
Permits and fees:	None.
Maps:	He Devil USGS quad.

Finding the trailhead: Follow the driving directions shown in Hike 49 to Windy Saddle Trailhead. Then hike west and south on Seven Devils Trail 124 (Seven Devils Loop) for 6.9 miles to the junction with Dry Diggins Trail 56. The GPS coordinates at the junction are 45 20.962 N 116 34.534 W. The description of Seven Devils Loop (Hike 49) is written in the opposite direction.

Trailhead facilities: None.

Camping and services: Camping is available at Windy Saddle Trailhead and at Seven Devils Lake 0.5 mile to the southwest. Other services, including gas and groceries, can be obtained in Riggins, Idaho. Cell phone service is generally good at Dry Diggins Lookout.

For more information: USDA Forest Service at the Hells Canyon National Recreation Area office in Riggins.

Key points:
- 0.0   Junction with Seven Devils Loop 6.9 miles southwest of Windy Saddle Trailhead.
- 1.7   Junction with Bernard Lakes Trail 57. GPS 45 22.077 N 116 35.042 W.
- 2.2   Dry Diggins Lookout. GPS 45 22.297 N 116 35.314 W.

The hike: The route descends gently from the junction with Seven Devils Loop (Seven Devils Trail 124). You first hike through an open area, then through timber. The tread starts to climb 0.2 mile from the junction, soon passing through an old burn area. It tops a rise (elev. 7,860 ft) 0.4 mile past the burn. At the top of the rise the trail flattens a bit but soon begins to climb gen-

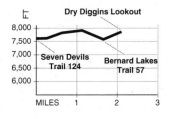

tly again. Three-tenths of a mile after topping the rise the path crosses a ridgeline. This is the highest point on this trail, at 7,950 feet above sea level. After crossing the ridgeline the trail descends through a thick stand of small Sub-Alpine Firs. Watch for the grouse that are common along this slope. The trail soon makes three switchbacks as it works its way down the ridge. After descending along the ridge for 0.5 mile it drops, quite steeply, off the right side.

Dry Diggins Lookout Trail 56 • Bernard Lakes Trail 57

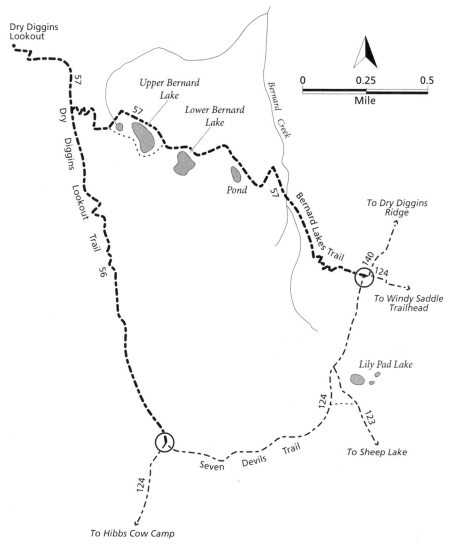

The junction with Bernard Lakes Trail 57 is reached 0.1 mile after dropping off the ridge. At the junction, elevation 7,560 feet, the Dry Diggins Lookout is 0.5 mile to the left (north-northwest).

From here on up to the lookout you will climb to the north-northwest, through semiopen woods of Sub-Alpine Fir and Whitebark Pine. Just before reaching the lookout the trail goes through a gate in the remains of an old fence. Dry Diggins Lookout, at 7,826 feet elevation, is 0.5 mile from the junction with Bernard Lakes Trail and 2.2 miles from the junction with the loop trail.

Dry Diggins Lookout.

Options: Make a loop hike by following Bernard Lakes Trail for 2.5 miles southeast to the junction with Seven Devils Loop. Then turn right on the loop trail and hike southwest for 1.4 miles to the junction with Dry Diggins Lookout Trail, where this hike began. If you are on a backpack around Seven Devils Loop, you may want to use Dry Diggins Lookout Trail and Bernard Lakes Trail as an alternate route. This would add 3.8 miles to your hike, but it would allow you to make the short side trip to the lookout and possibly camp at Bernard Lakes. See Hike 57 for details about Bernard Lakes Trail.

56 Sheep Lake Trail 123

Highlights:	A hike from Seven Devils Loop (Seven Devils Trail 124) to Sheep Lake, at the base of the two highest peaks in the Seven Devils Mountains, passing Lily Pad Lake, Basin Lake, Shelf Lake, and Gem Lake along the way.
Type of hike:	Internal out-and-back day hike or backpack.
Total distance:	6.8 miles.
Difficulty:	Easy.
Best months:	Late July–early September.
Elevation gain:	900 feet.
Permits and fees:	None.
Maps:	He Devil USGS quad.

Sheep Lake Trail 123

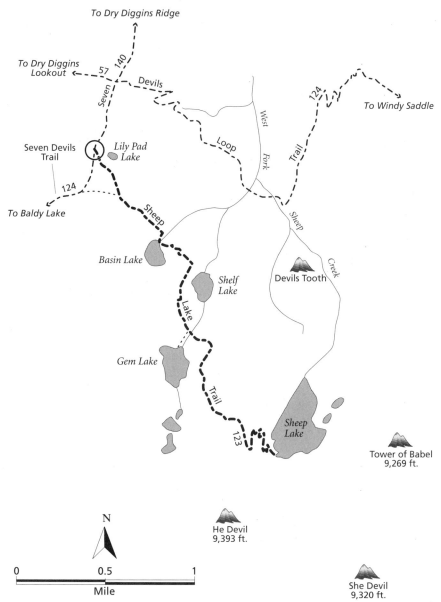

To Dry Diggins Ridge

To Dry Diggins Lookout

57   140

Seven

Devils

West

Fork

124

To Windy Saddle

Loop

Seven Devils Trail

Lily Pad Lake

Trail

124

To Baldy Lake

Sheep

Sheep

Creek

Basin Lake

Devils Tooth

Shelf Lake

Lake

Gem Lake

Sheep Lake

Trail

123

Tower of Babel
9,269 ft.

N

0   0.5   1
Mile

He Devil
9,393 ft.

She Devil
9,320 ft.

Finding the trailhead: Follow the driving directions shown in Hike 49 to Windy Saddle Trailhead. Then hike west and south on Seven Devils Trail 124 (Seven Devils Loop) for 6 miles to the junction with Sheep Lake Trail 123. The description of Seven Devils Loop (Hike 49) is written in the opposite direction. The GPS coordinates at the junction are 45 21.217 N 116 33.728 W.

Trailhead facilities: None at the junction, but a few campsites are available near Lily Pad Lake.

Camping and services: Camping is available at Windy Saddle Trailhead and at Seven Devils Lake 0.5 mile to the southwest. Other services, including gas and groceries, can be obtained in Riggins, Idaho.

For more information: USDA Forest Service at the Hells Canyon National Recreation Area office in Riggins.

Key points:

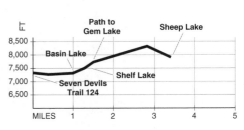

- 0.0 Junction with Seven Devils Loop 6 miles southwest of Windy Saddle Trailhead.
- 0.1 Lily Pad Lake.
- 0.8 Path to Basin Lake.
- 1.2 Shelf Lake below, to the left.
- 1.5 Path to Gem Lake.
- 3.4 Sheep Lake. GPS 45 19.743 N 116 32.463 W.

The hike: Sheep Lake Trail begins at the junction with Seven Devils Loop, in an area of burnt forest. From the junction the route to Sheep Lake heads to the southeast. After hiking a short distance you will pass Lily Pad Lake. The shallow lake is 100 yards to the left of the trail. Soon after passing Lily Pad Lake the tread goes along the left side of a meadow. A side path turns to the right in the meadow and heads west for a quarter of a mile to rejoin the loop trail. Sheep Lake Trail goes on to the southeast along the meadow, crossing a small stream. Leaving the meadow the trail reenters the partly burned timber and soon leaves the burn behind. You will cross the outlet stream of Basin Lake 0.8 mile after leaving the junction with the loop. Just past the crossing a side path, to the right leads 100 yards to Basin Lake.

There is a good campsite where the side path reaches Basin Lake (elev. 7,381 ft). Fishing for Rainbow Trout is very good in the lake. Some of the Bows are quite large, up to 15 inches long, and well fed. They seem to like flies best, but fly fishing is difficult because of all the trees next to the lake.

The course climbs gently to the southeast, after passing the path to Basin Lake. It makes three switchbacks as it climbs to the top a small rise, where it turns south toward Shelf Lake. Shelf Lake is below to the left 0.4 mile after passing the path to Basin Lake. A couple of side paths lead down to a nice campsite at Shelf Lake (elev. 7,460 ft). There are also fish to be caught.

Leaving Shelf Lake you will make a couple switchbacks, then climb gently through thinning subalpine forest and rock outcroppings, for 0.3 mile, to the junction with the path to Gem Lake. The junction is just before crossing the stream that is the outlet of Gem Lake. The path to Gem Lake climbs steeply off Sheep Lake Trail, along the right side of the stream. Gem Lake, at 7,763 feet elevation, is a couple hundred yards off the main trail. There are fish to be had in Gem Lake, but the campsites are very limited.

After passing the path to Gem Lake Sheep Lake Trail climbs moderately, making nine switchbacks. It then traverses above the lake and heads south below towering cliffs. A mile after passing the path to Gem Lake, the route makes another series of six switchbacks as it climbs to a broad saddle on the ridge dividing Gem Lake and Sheep Lake drainages. The route is fairly flat for a few yards crossing the saddle at 8,290 feet elevation.

The track then begins to descend. A short distance down the trail at the first switchback as it descends toward Sheep Lake, a climbing route to the summit of He Devil Mountain leaves the trail. (See Hike 71 for a description of the rough scrambling route to the summit.)

You will make 11 more switchbacks as you descend the 0.6 mile to Sheep Lake. Sheep Lake, at 7,882 feet elevation, is one of the largest lakes in the Seven Devils Mountains. There is a campsite where the trail reaches the lake and several more on the small ridge on its east side.

There are lots of trout in the lake, but they can sometimes be finicky eaters. Small bright spinners will usually catch fish, and flies work on warmer evenings when there is little or no wind. Watch for Mountain Goats on the alpine slopes around the lake. Sometimes the goats will come down to the lake and even enter camps. Be careful about leaving your pack lying around; these goats are notorious for chewing salty pack straps and even getting into tents.

Options: If you are a normal hiker, you will want to return via the same route. But if you are a climber or an experienced cross-country hiker who doesn't mind a rough obscure trail with considerable exposure, you may want to take the route past Mirror Lake and return to Windy Saddle Trailhead via Seven Devils Lake. See Hike 59 for a description of this route. The spectacular setting of Sheep Lake makes it a great base camp for climbing He Devil and She Devil Mountains, as well as Mount Baal and The Tower Of Babel. See Hikes 71 through 74 for a description of these climbing routes.

Sheep Lake Trout.

57 Bernard Lakes Trail 57

See Map on Page 255

Highlights: A hike from Seven Devils Loop (Seven Devils Trail 124), passing Bernard Lakes, to Dry Diggins Lookout and the most spectacular view of Hells Canyon to be had.
Type of hike: Internal out-and-back day hike or backpack, with a loop option.
Total distance: 6 miles.
Difficulty: Easy to moderate.
Best months: Mid-July–September.
Elevation gain: 920 feet.
Permits and fees: None.
Maps: He Devil USGS quad.

Finding the trailhead: Follow the driving directions shown in Hike 49 to Windy Saddle Trailhead. Then hike west on Seven Devils Loop (Seven Devils Trail 124) for 5.4 miles to the junction with Bernard Lakes Trail. The GPS coordinates at the junction are 45 21.527 N 116 33.619 W. The description of the loop trail (Hike 49) is written in the other direction. Dry Diggins Ridge Trail 140 also leaves the loop from this junction. (See Hike 58 for a description of Dry Diggins Ridge Trail.)

Trailhead facilities: The junction with the loop trail has a couple of possible campsites.

Camping and services: Camping is available at Windy Saddle Trailhead and at Seven Devils Lake 0.5 mile to the southwest. Other services, including gas and groceries, can be obtained in Riggins, Idaho. Cell phone service is generally good at Dry Diggins Lookout.

For more information: USDA Forest Service at the Hells Canyon National Recreation Area office in Riggins.

Key points:

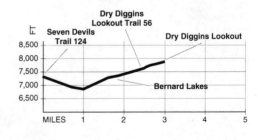

0.0 Junction with Seven Devils Loop 5.4 miles west of Windy Saddle Trailhead.
1.6 Lower Bernard Lake.
1.8 Upper Bernard Lake.
2.5 Junction with Dry Diggins Lookout Trail 56. GPS 45 22.077 N 116 35.042 W.
3.0 Dry Diggins Lookout. GPS 45 22.297 N 116 35.314 W.

The hike: Bernard Lakes Trail heads west through burnt forest from the junction with the loop trail. It soon begins to descend, making several switchbacks, as it works its way down into upper Bernard Creek Canyon. The path crosses two streams in the bottom of the canyon, at 6,910 feet elevation. These streams were dry in September when I hiked this trail but have water in them earlier in the season. You will leave the burn area just before crossing the streams. After crossing the second stream the route climbs, fairly steeply in places, for 0.4 mile to a pond on the left side of the trail. The tread crosses the pond's outlet stream then climbs a bit more. A couple hundred yards past the pond a short side path to the right goes to a viewpoint. The trail crosses a tiny wooden bridge about 300 yards after passing the viewpoint path. This bridge crosses the outlet of Lower Bernard Lake.

Lower Bernard Lake, at 7,260 feet elevation, is a few yards to the left at the bridge. There is a campsite to the right of the trail near the lake. There are fish to be caught in the lake; they seem to be a little finicky during the middle of the day, however. Lower Bernard Lake is 1.6 miles from the junction with the loop trail.

Heading northwest from Lower Bernard Lake the course climbs gently for 0.2 mile to Upper Bernard Lake (elev. 7,300 ft). Campsites are limited at Upper Bernard Lake, but the fishing for Cutthroat Trout is excellent. Lily pads cover the north side of this lake.

The route follows the north shore of the lake for a couple hundred yards then leaves it. It soon passes another lily pad–covered pond. Shortly after passing the pond the trace crosses a tiny stream. Just after crossing the stream the trail splits. Turn right at the split in the trail. The main trail is blazed in this area. There are several campsites to the right of the main trail at the point where the path splits off.

The side path to the left goes back around the pond and around the south side of Upper Bernard Lake. This side path is not suitable for stock and is somewhat difficult to follow. One spot on the side path crosses a rock outcropping on a tiny ledge, requiring the use of handholds.

After passing the split in the trail you will wind and switchback your way up through rock outcroppings to the junction with Dry Diggins Lookout Trail 56. (See Hike 55 for details about Dry Diggins Lookout Trail.) This junction at 7,560 feet elevation is reached 0.3 mile past the split in the trail. The route is a bit rough and rocky at times in this section. At the junction is a trail sign; Hibbs Cow Camp is to the left, and Dry Diggins Lookout is to the right. From here up to the lookout the trail climbs to the north-northwest, through semiopen woods of Sub-Alpine Fir and Whitebark Pine. Just before reaching the lookout the trail goes through a gate in the remains of an old fence. Dry Diggins Lookout, at 7,826 feet elevation, is 0.5 mile from the junction with Dry Diggins Lookout Trail and 3 miles from the junction with the loop trail.

The view from the lookout may well be the best in the Hells Canyon Wilderness. The Snake River, slightly more than 2 miles away to the west, is 6,500 feet below the point where you are standing. To the northwest the Hat Point Lookout Tower can be seen across the canyon. To the southwest the Wallowa Mountains are in the distance. The highest towers and spires of the Seven Devils Mountains are close by to the southeast.

Watch for Mountain Goats on the ridge south of Bernard Lakes and below the lookout.

Upper Bernard Lake.

Options: Make the return trip following the same trail, or make a loop trip by hiking Dry Diggins Lookout Trail back to the loop trail and then following the loop trail for 1.4 miles northwest back to the junction where this hike started.

58 Dry Diggins Ridge Trail 140

Highlights:	A hike that first follows the broad rounded top of Dry Diggins Ridge through timber and flower-covered meadows, then descends steeply to a saddle and the junction with Bernard Creek Trail. Timber obscures the view much of the way, but the solitude of this lightly used route makes it a worthwhile hike.
Type of hike:	Internal connector; backpack, with shuttle and loop options.
Total distance:	4 miles.
Difficulty:	Moderate to strenuous.
Best months:	Mid-July–September.
Elevation loss:	1,330 feet.
Permits and fees:	None.
Maps:	He Devil and Old Timer Mountain USGS quads.

Finding the trailhead: Follow the driving directions shown in Hike 49 to Windy Saddle Trailhead. Then hike west on Seven Devils Loop (Seven Devils Trail 124) for 5.4 miles to the junction with Dry Diggins Ridge Trail. The

Dry Diggins Ridge Trail 140

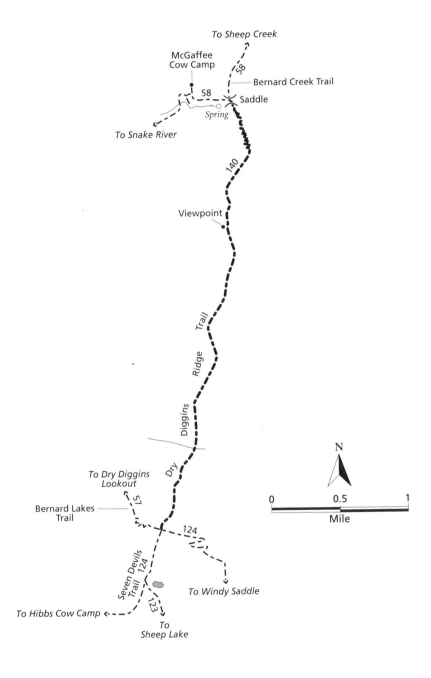

To Sheep Creek

McGaffee
Cow Camp

58

Bernard Creek Trail

58   Saddle

Spring

To Snake River

140

Viewpoint

Trail

Ridge

Diggins

Dry

To Dry Diggins
Lookout

57

Bernard Lakes
Trail

124

Seven Devils
Trail 124

To Hibbs Cow Camp

123

To Windy Saddle

To
Sheep Lake

N

0   0.5   1
Mile

GPS coordinates at the junction are 45 21.527 N 116 33.619 W. The description of the Seven Devils Loop (Hike 49) is written in the opposite direction. Hike 57 (Bernard Lakes Trail) also leaves the loop from this junction.

Trailhead facilities: The junction has a couple of possible campsites.

Camping and services: Camping is available at Windy Saddle Trailhead and at Seven Devils Lake 0.5 mile to the southwest. Other services, including gas and groceries, can be obtained in Riggins, Idaho. For jet boat transportation, contact Hells Canyon Adventures in Oxbow, Oregon. Cell phone service can be had in spots along Dry Diggins Ridge.

For more information: USDA Forest Service at the Hells Canyon National Recreation Area office in Riggins.

Key points:
- 0.0 Junction with Seven Devils Loop 5.4 miles west of Windy Saddle Trailhead.
- 2.5 Viewpoint overlooking the Bernard Creek drainage.
- 3.2 Trail begins to descend switchbacks off end of Dry Diggins Ridge.
- 4.0 Junction with Bernard Creek Trail 58. GPS 45 24.242 N 116 33.014 W.

The hike: From the ridgetop, four-way junction with Seven Devils Loop, Dry Diggins Ridge Trail heads north-northeast. First the route climbs gently through the silver snags of an old burn area. The tread soon leaves the burn behind and contours along the western slope of

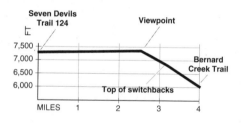

Dry Diggins Ridge. The path traverses patches of dense Lodgepole Pine and fir, and small meadows with flowers. As you get farther along the meadows become larger. In the meadows Dogtooth Violets, Shooting Stars, Flax, Lupine, Paintbrush, and many other wildflowers bloom soon after the snowmelt in early July.

The route crosses a small stream, which may be dry by midsummer, 0.8 mile after leaving the junction with Seven Devils Loop. This may be your only water source along the ridge, but do not depend on its having water during the dryer parts of the year. Past the small stream the route stays in larger meadows much of the time. From a few spots in these meadows Hat Point Lookout can be seen far to the west-northwest across Hells Canyon in Oregon, and the much closer Dry Diggins is in view to the southwest.

About 2.5 miles from the junction with the loop trail the ridge narrows. The trail is slightly to the west of the ridgeline here affording a spectacular view of the canyon below to the west. A tiny section of the Snake River, at the mouth of Bernard Creek, nearly 6,000 feet below the point where you are standing, can be seen. This spot, at 7,360 feet elevation, makes a good place for a rest stop because the more difficult part of this hike is about to begin.

Rest break at the north end of Dry Diggins Ridge.

The path, which is a little vague in places, descends along a ridge to the north, then northeast after passing the viewpoint. The tread is steep in spots so watch your footing. You may notice the remains of a long-abandoned phone line in the trees to your left as you descend. The trail becomes very vague in a small sloping meadow 0.7 mile after passing the viewpoint. Bear slightly left (north-northwest) in the meadow and pick up the trail again at the edge of the timber.

The vague route makes 25 switchbacks in the next 0.8 mile, as you hike steeply downhill through the timber and brush. In spots this section of the trail is braided and in others it is not there at all. Your routefinding skills will be tested as you descend the nearly 800 vertical feet to a saddle and the junction with Bernard Creek Trail. There is a trail sign on a tree at the south end of the saddle marking the junction, but it can be hard to spot. This is the end of Dry Diggins Ridge Trail, at 5,980 feet elevation.

Options: If you wish to continue your hike to the Snake River, where a jet boat pick-up can be arranged to take you downriver to Pittsburg Landing, turn left in the saddle on the vague Bernard Creek Trail. Then descend that trail for 5.9 miles to the river. See Hike 42 for a description of Bernard Creek Trail. A loop can be made by turning right (really straight ahead) on Bernard Creek Trail and following it for 3.4 miles to Sheep Creek Trail. Then ascend Sheep Creek Trail for 5.9 miles to a junction with Seven Devils Loop 0.5 mile west of Windy Saddle Trailhead. See Hike 43 for details about Sheep Creek Trail.

59 Sheep Lake Climbers Route

Highlights:	A steep and sometimes exposed cross-country route from Seven Devils Lake Campground to Sheep Lake. This route is considered easy by climbers' standards, but it is very strenuous when considered as a hike. There is a path most of the way, but it can be difficult to follow and even dangerous to all but experienced, in-shape hikers. Do not even think of taking stock on this route. There is no trail maintenance on this route, but it receives moderate to heavy traffic. This is also an access route to Mirror Lake.
Type of hike:	Out-and-back day hike or backpack, with a loop option.
Total distance:	3.8 miles.
Difficulty:	Very strenuous.
Best months:	Late July–September.
Elevation gain:	890 feet.
Permits and fees:	None.
Maps:	He Devil USGS quad covers the area, but this route is not marked on the map.

Finding the trailhead: From Riggins, Idaho, drive 1 mile south on U.S. Highway 95 to the junction with Squaw Creek Road. Turn west on Squaw Creek Road (County Road 517) and follow it for 16.5 miles to Windy Saddle Trailhead. County Road 517 makes a left turn at a junction slightly less than 2 miles after leaving US 95 and becomes Forest Road 517 at the Nez Perce National Forest Boundary approximately 4 miles from US 95. Road signs point to Seven Devils Lake Campground at the junction with US 95 and at other intersections along the way. Turn left at Windy Saddle Trailhead and drive another 0.5 mile to Seven Devils Lake Campground. The trail leaves from the southwest corner of the campground a short distance past the second restroom. The trailhead has no sign. The GPS coordinates at the trailhead are 45 20.836 N 116 31.076 W.

Trailhead facilities: Seven Devils Lake Campground has campsites and restrooms.

Camping and services: Developed campsites are available at Seven Devils Lake. Other services and groceries can be obtained in Riggins. Cell phone service can be had from Goat Pass.

For more information: USDA Forest Service at the Hells Canyon National Recreation Area office in Riggins.

Key points:
- 0.0   Seven Devils Lake Campground.
- 0.9   First saddle.
- 1.2   Second saddle (Goat Pass). GPS 45 20.297 N 116 31.725 W.
- 1.9   Sheep Lake. GPS 45 19.864 N 116 32.180 W.

Sheep Lake Climbers Route

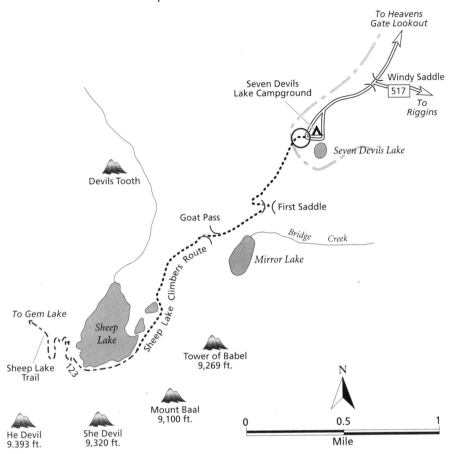

To Heavens Gate Lookout

Seven Devils
Lake Campground

Windy Saddle

517

To Riggins

Seven Devils Lake

Devils Tooth

First Saddle

Goat Pass

Bridge *Creek*

Mirror Lake

To Gem Lake

Sheep Lake

Sheep Lake Climbers Route

Tower of Babel
9,269 ft.

Sheep Lake
Trail

123

N

Mount Baal
9,100 ft.

0   0.5   1

Mile

He Devil
9.393 ft.

She Devil
9,320 ft.

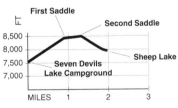

The hike: At the southwest end of Seven Devils Lake Campground the route, which is just a narrow path at this point, heads west. After heading west for 0.1 mile the path forks. Bear left at the fork, and climb for a quarter of a mile to where the path enters an open cirque. The steep route switchbacks up the lower slope of the cirque for another quarter of a mile. It then bears to the right at about 8,100 feet elevation, and climbs steeply for another couple hundred yards. Then the path turns left continuing to climb very steeply, to the south, for 150 more yards. It then flattens out and traverses east the last 200 yards to the first saddle. At the saddle (elev. 8,410 ft), Mirror Lake comes into view to the south and below.

From the first saddle the route traverses to the southwest for 0.3 mile to another saddle on the ridge dividing Mirror Lake and Sheep Lake. This section of the route can be hard to see. It is very important not to climb too high here, because the ridge above the second saddle is difficult to negotiate. The

Hikers on the ledge.

second saddle, sometimes called Goat Pass, is only a few feet higher than the first saddle.

At the second saddle the path shows up again. The route descends steeply to the west for a few feet, then heads southwest, following a ledge. After following the ledge for 0.3 mile it descends a scree slope, then heads south along the eastern shore of a pond before reaching the eastern shore of Sheep Lake.

A poor path goes along the eastern and southern shorelines to meet Sheep Lake Trail at the southeast corner of the lake. There are several good campsites at Sheep Lake, and it has a good population of Rainbow and Cutthroat Trout. It also makes an excellent base camp for climbing He Devil, She Devil, Mount Baal, and The Tower of Babel Mountains.

Options: For a much longer but easier return trip, follow Sheep Lake Trail for 3.4 miles west and north from Sheep Lake to the junction with Seven Devils Loop. Then take the loop for 6 miles east to Windy Saddle Trailhead. See Hikes 56 and 49 for descriptions of these trails.

Several places between the saddles have scrambling routes that can be taken down to Mirror Lake. Hiking to or camping at Mirror Lake makes an excellent side trip. There are fish to be caught in Mirror Lake.

60 Rapid River Trail 113

Highlights:	A hike from Rapid River Fish Hatchery up the rushing Rapid River to the junction with West Fork Rapid River Trail, then continuing up West Fork Rapid River Trail to McCrea Cabin.
Type of hike:	Out-and-back day hike or backpack.
Total distance:	17 miles, to McCrea Cabin.
Difficulty:	Easy to moderate.
Best months:	March–June and September–November.
Elevation gain:	1,785 feet.
Permits and fees:	None.
Maps:	Heavens Gate USGS quad.

Finding the trailhead: From Riggins, Idaho, drive 4.3 miles south on U.S. Highway 95 to Rapid River Road. Turn right (southwest) and go 2.4 more miles to Rapid River Fish Hatchery at the end of the road. The trailhead is on a hard left turn just before entering the hatchery grounds. The GPS coordinates at the trailhead are 45 21.193 N 116 23.835 W.

Trailhead facilities: The trailhead has limited parking but has no other facilities. There is adequate parking from 8 A.M. to 5 P.M. at Rapid River Fish Hatchery a short distance from the trailhead. Restrooms and picnic tables are also available at the fish hatchery.

Rapid River Trail 113

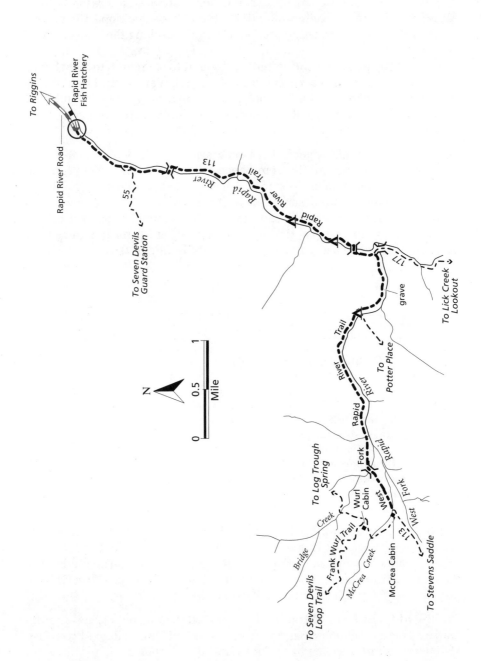

Camping and services: Camping is not allowed at the trailhead. Gas, groceries, and medical services are available in Riggins.

For more information: USDA Forest Service at the Salmon River Ranger District office, 10 miles south of White Bird, Idaho, on US 95.

Key points:
- 0.0   Rapid River Fish Hatchery.
- 0.6   Junction with Trail 55.
- 1.2   First Bridge.
- 4.2   Second Bridge.
- 4.5   Junction with Upper Rapid River Trail. GPS 45 18.427 N 116 25.315 W.
- 5.5   Junction with trail to the Potter Place. GPS 45 18.464 N 116 25.983 W.
- 8.5   McCrea Cabin and junction with Frank Wurl Trail. GPS 45 18.320 N 116 28.680 W.

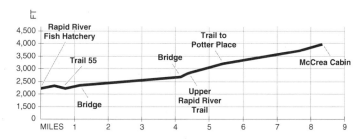

The hike: The trail climbs along abandoned roadbeds heading southwest as it leaves the trailhead. Shortly it passes through a gate and passes a national forest boundary sign, where it enters the Nez Perce National Forest. The canyon narrows 0.3 mile from the trailhead. Here the rushing Rapid River flows through a gorge 100 feet below the trail. In spots the swift waters have undercut the gray, black, and orange cliffs at the river's edge.

Bear left at an unsigned trail junction 0.6 mile from the trailhead. The trail to the right (Trail 55) climbs the ridge of Cannon Ball Mountain and reaches Seven Devils Loop Trail near Seven Devils Guard Station in about 8 miles. Fir and pine trees line the river below the mostly open slopes of the canyon walls as you hike on to the southwest.

The route crosses a wide sturdy wooden bridge, over the pools and riffles of the Rapid River, 0.6 mile past the junction with Trail 55. Once across the bridge the course climbs some distance above river level. Blue Gulch Creek tumbles into the river from the opposite side 0.3 mile after crossing the bridge. Shortly after passing Blue Gulch Creek the tread goes beneath an overhanging cliff for a short distance. Many of the older trees in this area have fire scars.

The course passes a tiny campsite next to the river and soon begins to climb. After climbing a couple hundred feet above river level the trail descends back down to the river and soon passes another campsite. The route then continues upstream, passing yet another campsite to the second bridge over the Rapid River. This bridge, 4.2 miles from the trailhead, is also wide and sturdy. After crossing the bridge the path climbs steeply for 0.3 mile to

Rapid River in March.

ETTORE NEGRI PHOTO

the junction with West Fork Rapid River Trail (also number 113) on a spur ridge. Rapid River Trail becomes Trail 177 at this point and continues up the Rapid River for about 17 more miles to Lick Creek Lookout.

Turn right (west) at the junction and gently climb on West Fork Rapid River Trail, along the open slope above the rushing West Fork of the Rapid River. The route is chipped from the cliffs for a short distance 0.3 mile from the junction. Below the chipped out area the West Fork plunges through a gorge to the left. Before long the route flattens out to pass the grave of J. Jones, who was killed nearby in a mine accident in 1889. The trail enters the timber as it passes the grave.

You will reach the junction with the trail to the Potter Place at 3,170 feet elevation, 1 mile after leaving the junction with Rapid River Trail. The trail to the Potter Place turns to the left (southwest) and passes a great campsite at the edge of a meadow next to the river, then crosses the river to climb steeply toward the Potter Place. The meadow is called Potter's Flat. There is evidence of old mining activity to your right, above the trail, near the junction.

To continue on West Fork Rapid River Trail, hike straight ahead (west-northwest) from the junction. The route leaves the flat area in 0.3 mile, then traverses a slope, climbing gently but continuously for 2 miles to the bridge over Bridge Creek. Along the way it passes beneath some cliffs. The bridge over Bridge Creek, at 3,730 feet elevation, is 7.8 miles from the trailhead. After crossing Bridge Creek the tread traverses a mostly open slope for 0.6 mile to McCrea Creek. There is no bridge at McCrea Creek so ford the stream and continue another 0.1 mile to McCrea Cabin and the junction with Frank Wurl Trail 61. Frank Wurl Trail climbs northwest for about 3 miles to meet Seven Devils Loop. See Hike 49 for a description of Seven Devils Loop (Boise Trail).

McCrea Cabin, at 4,005 feet elevation, is in good condition and is open to the public. Please leave the cabin and everything inside of it in as good or better condition as you found it. Watch out for Rattlesnakes and Poison Ivy along the trail.

From McCrea Cabin, West Fork Rapid River trail climbs for approximately 8 more miles to meet Horse Heaven Cabin Trail 214 at Stevens Saddle. (See Hike 61 for a description of Horse Heaven Cabin Trail.)

Options: Use your map to check out the many other possibilities for continuing along West Fork Rapid River Trail. There are several side trails and mill ruins to explore.

SOUTHERN REGION

Mining once dominated the southern region. Black Lake Road (Forest Road 112), the main access route to the high country, was constructed to serve the mining operation at Black Lake. Kleinschmidt Grade, which climbs from the shore of Hells Canyon Reservoir to the now-abandoned town site of Helena, was also once an oar-hauling road. None of the mines in the region are now in operation, and most have been permanently abandoned.

Hike 70 Red Ledge Mine Trail follows another of these abandoned mine roads from its trailhead next to Hells Canyon Reservoir to the mine. A little farther south along the reservoir are Hikes 67 through 69, whose interconnecting routes wind through and above the precipitous limestone formations of Eckels, Allison, and Kinney Creek Canyons.

If you drive from the reservoir up Kleinschmidt Grade to the tiny hamlet of Cuprum and turn left on Forest Road 111, you will soon reach Lynes Saddle and the trailhead for Hike 66 Horse Mountain Lookout Route. Hike 67 Eckels Creek Trail also reaches Lynes Saddle. Following the remains of Kleinschmidt Grade to its end at Helena and then continuing a little farther north on Forest Road 106 takes you to Hike 65 Sheep Rock National Recreation Trail.

Purgatory Saddle.

Southern Region

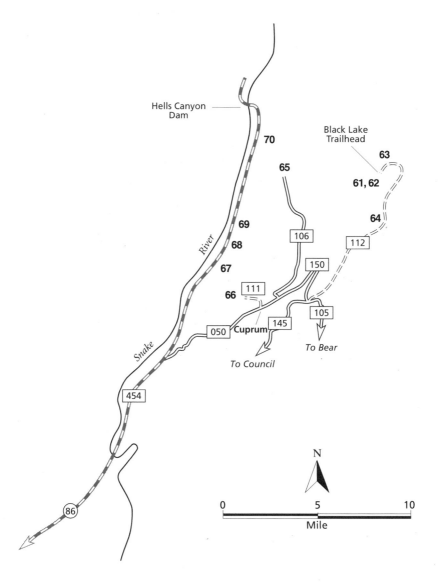

Hells Canyon Dam

70

Black Lake Trailhead

63

61, 62

65

64

69

106

68

112

67

150

66   111

050

Cuprum   145

105

To Bear

To Council

454

N

0   5   10

Mile

Snake

River

86

61 Horse Heaven Cabin Trail 214

Highlights:	A hike from Black Lake Trailhead up through alpine meadows to Purgatory Saddle with a descent past Emerald Lake down Granite Creek Canyon and a climb back to the ridgeline at Stevens Saddle. From Stevens Saddle, the trail follows the ridgeline of the Seven Devils Mountains north to Horse Heaven Cabin, at over 8,200 feet elevation, before descending to meet Seven Devils Loop.
Type of hike:	Out-and-back backpack, with an extended shuttle hike option.
Total distance:	18.2 miles.
Difficulty:	Moderate.
Best months:	August–September.
Elevation gain:	2,800 feet.
Permits and fees:	None.
Maps:	Purgatory Saddle and He Devil USGS quads.

Finding the trailhead: Head east from Interstate 84 at Baker City on Oregon 86. Follow OR 86 for 70.5 miles to the bridge over the Snake River at Copperfield Park. Cross the bridge and turn left on Idaho Power Company Road. Follow Idaho Power Company Road, which becomes Forest Road 454, for 6.1 miles to the junction with Kleinschmidt Grade (Forest Road 050). Turn right and drive northeast, up the steep gravel grade, for 9.4 miles to the tiny town of Cuprum, Idaho. Head straight through Cuprum on what is now Forest Road 105. Follow FR 105 for 7.9 miles to a four-way junction. At the junction, turn left on Black Lake Road (Forest Road 112). There is a sign pointing to Black Lake at the junction. Follow Black Lake Road for 12.3 miles northeast to Black Lake Campground and Trailhead.

If coming from Council, Idaho, drive northwest for 30 miles on the Cuprum–Council Road (Forest Road 002) to the community of Bear. From Bear, head north on FR 105 for 4.5 miles to a fork in the road. Bear left at the fork, staying on FR 105, and drive north for 2 miles to a four-way junction. At the junction, turn right on Black Lake Road (Forest Road 112). There is a sign pointing to Black Lake at the junction. Follow Black Lake Road for 12.3 miles northeast to Black Lake Campground and Trailhead.

Black Lake Road is for high-clearance vehicles only. The GPS coordinates at the trailhead are 45 11.453 N 116 33.656 W.

Trailhead facilities: The trailhead has restrooms and several campsites, but parking is limited.

Camping and services: There are several campsites near the trailhead at Black Lake. Groceries and gas can be obtained in Oxbow, Oregon, and Council, Idaho. Medical services can be obtained in Council. Cell phone service is available at Horse Heaven Cabin and at many spots along the ridge between Stevens Saddle and the cabin.

Horse Heaven Cabin Trail 214

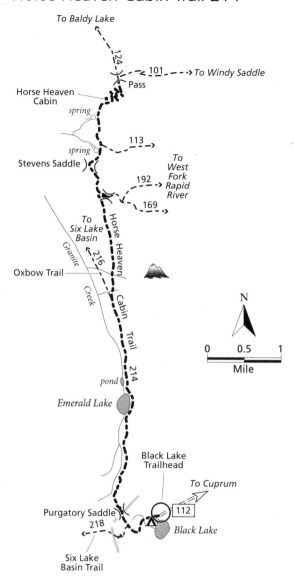

For more information: USDA Forest Service at Council Ranger District in Council or the Hells Canyon National Recreation Area office in Riggins, Idaho.

Key points:

0.0	Black Lake Trailhead.
0.8	Six Lake Basin Trail 218. GPS 45 11.283 N 116 34.081 W.
1.1	Purgatory Saddle.
2.9	Emerald Lake (south end). GPS 45 12.536 N 116 34.255 W.
4.6	Oxbow Trail 216. GPS 45 14.034 N 116 34.587 W.

6.5 Stevens Saddle. GPS 45 14.966 N 116 34.463 W.

7.6 Rapid River Trail 113. GPS 45 15.743 N 116 34.725 W.

8.3 Horse Heaven Cabin. GPS 45 16.165 N 116 34.496 W.

9.1 Seven Devils Loop 101, 124. GPS 45 16.451N 116 34.428 W.

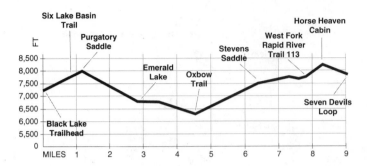

The hike: The wide trail, which was once used as a mine road, heads west as it leaves Black Lake Trailhead. Paintbrush and Lupine line the route as it climbs gently through the open subalpine woods. Shortly after leaving the trailhead the track enters Hells Canyon Wilderness. One of several huge boulders overhangs the trail as you hike through a rockslide area soon after passing the boundary. The course makes a switchback to the right 0.4 mile from the trailhead. A bit farther along the trace crosses a tiny stream. Just past the stream there is a large pine tree with a square hole cut into its hollow core, next to the trail.

The junction with Six Lake Basin Trail 218 is reached 0.8 mile from the trailhead, at 7,730 feet elevation. From the junction an abandoned mine can be seen several hundred yards to the south. Up to this point Six Lake Basin Trail and Horse Heaven Cabin Trail follow the same route. (See Hike 62 for a description of the Six Lake Basin Trail.)

Bear right (really straight ahead to the northwest) at the junction. As you climb above the junction Black Lake comes into view far below to the right. The tread passes a pond then climbs to Purgatory Saddle at 7,950 feet elevation. From the saddle, 1.1 miles from Black Lake Trailhead, the canyon holding Emerald Lake and Granite Creek unfolds below to the north. The course crosses a little north of the saddle's lowest point, then begins its descent on a steep, open, boulder-covered slope. After making seven switchbacks the path reaches the floor of the alpine cirque at the head of the Granite Creek drainage. You then hike down the canyon through forest that becomes larger as you lose altitude. The tread makes a couple of switchbacks in the woods then descends to the south end of Emerald Lake. As you approach the south end of the lake, 2.9 miles from the trailhead, the trail bears slightly to the right.

Emerald Lake, at 6,799 feet elevation, is a good place to turn around if this is to be a day hike. There are several campsites along the shore and plenty of Brook Trout to be caught, making Emerald Lake a worthy destination for a short backpack. Fly fishing is excellent here in the evening and morning.

The route follows the east shore of the lake, crossing a couple of streams, and traversing open and wooded slopes. Paintbrush blooms in abundance on the open slopes, and Lewis Monkeyflowers guard the wet areas. After following the shoreline for 0.4 mile, the trace leaves the lake behind. You will hike past a pond below the lake then continue north. Tan and gray cliffs loom far above to the right as you walk along. The route crosses several small streams, most of which may be dry by late summer, as it descends gently through the thick forest.

About 1.3 miles after leaving the north end of Emerald Lake you will come to the junction with Oxbow Trail 216. Oxbow Trail bears left (northwest) at the junction and heads over Oxbow Saddle to the Six Lake Basin and on down to Hells Canyon Reservoir. Much of this trail gets only limited maintenance and may be difficult to follow.

Bear right (north) at the junction and start to climb, crossing a creek a few yards. Fill up with water here as the other small streams you will cross as you climb may be dry. You will climb across timbered slopes and wide sloping, flower-covered meadows as you gain the 2,250 feet in elevation it takes to reach Stevens Saddle, at 7,520 feet elevation. At the saddle, 6.5 miles from Black Lake Trailhead, is the junction with Trails 189 and 192. Both of these trails lead to the east into the West Fork of the Rapid River drainage.

Turn left at the junction and climb moderately to the northwest. Soon the grade moderates and you cross open slopes with gorgeous views of Emerald Lake up the canyon to the south, and of the canyons to the west. The route crosses a ridgeline, at 7,750 feet elevation, 0.7 mile after leaving the saddle. Once across, the trace descends slightly through the timber to a meadow. In the meadow to the left of the trail is a spring where you can obtain water. Lewis Monkeyflowers raise their pretty heads to give away the location of the spring from a distance. The trail climbs again after passing the spring. In 0.2 mile you will reach the signed junction with Rapid River Trail 113. Rapid River Trail 113 turns right to head east over the ridge and down into the West Fork of the Rapid River drainage.

Climb straight ahead (north) along the ridgeline from the junction. You will reach a developed spring in 0.4 mile. This spring is the water source for Horse Heaven Cabin. The water must be carried from here to the cabin, however. A good campsite is located in the scattered trees to the right (east) of the spring. At the spring the trail forks. Bear right and climb north-northeast across the gentle open slope to Horse Heaven Cabin.

Horse Heaven Cabin sits on the crest of the Seven Devils Mountains at 8,205 feet above sea level. The view from the cabin is awesome in all directions. To the west the country drops away into the depths of Hells Canyon, then rises to include the Wallowa Valley and Mountains. At night the lights of Joseph, Oregon, are visible in the distance. To the north is the rugged heart of the Seven Devils, and to the east is the Rapid River Country. To the south is the southern spine of the Seven Devils Mountains that you hiked through to reach this magnificent place. Several campsites are available around the cabin as well as back down at the spring that you just passed. The cabin is open to the public, but Forest Service personnel have

Horse Heaven Cabin.

priority for its overnight use. Watch for big Mule Deer bucks that frequent the meadows around the cabin.

Leaving Horse Heaven Cabin the trail descends, making five switchbacks as it drops to the junction with Seven Devils Loop 101,124. The route is braided between the cabin and the junction. Try to stay on the main trail, which has a gentler grade than the others do. Staying on the main trail also causes less damage to this alpine environment. The junction with the loop trail is at 7,860 feet elevation, 0.8 mile from Horse Heaven Cabin and 9.1 miles from Black Lake Trailhead.

Options: If you would like to make an extended backpack through the Seven Devils Mountains, use this hike as a starter. Then turn left when you reach Seven Devils Loop. Follow the loop trail for 18.5 miles to Windy Saddle Trailhead. Making this 27.6-mile hike will require a long car shuttle (four-wheel-drive or high-clearance vehicle) to Windy Saddle Trailhead. See Hike 49 for details about the loop trail and driving directions to Windy Saddle Trailhead. For a shorter out-and-back day hike or backpack, just hike the 6 miles to Emerald Lake and back.

62 Six Lake Basin Trail 214, 218

Highlights:	A hike from Black Lake over a high ridge, through beautiful alpine country, to Six Lake Basin.
Type of hike:	Out-and-back day hike or backpack, with a shuttle option.
Total distance:	8 miles.
Difficulty:	Moderate.
Best months:	Late July–September. Black Lake Road may be closed by snow until early August some years.
Elevation gain:	900 feet.
Permits and fees:	None.
Maps:	Purgatory Saddle USGS quad.

Finding the trailhead: Head east from Interstate 84 at Baker City on Oregon 86. Follow OR 86 for 70.5 miles to the bridge over the Snake River at Copperfield Park. Cross the bridge and turn left on Idaho Power Company Road. Follow Idaho Power Company Road, which becomes Forest Road 454, for 6.1 miles to the junction with Kleinschmidt Grade (Forest Road 050). Turn right and drive northeast, up the steep gravel grade, for 9.4 miles to the tiny town of Cuprum, Idaho. Head straight through Cuprum on what is now Forest Road 105. Follow FR 105 for 7.9 miles to a four-way junction. At the junction, turn left on Black Lake Road (Forest Road 112). There is a sign pointing to Black Lake at the junction. Follow Black Lake Road for 12.3 miles northeast to Black Lake Campground and Trailhead.

If coming from Council, Idaho, drive northwest for 30 miles on the Cuprum–Council Road (Forest Road 002) to the community of Bear. From Bear, head north on FR 105 for 4.5 miles to a fork in the road. Bear left at the fork, staying on FR 105, and drive north for 2 miles to a four-way junction. At the junction, turn right on Black Lake Road (Forest Road 112). There is a sign pointing to Black Lake at the junction. Follow Black Lake Road for 12.3 miles northeast to Black Lake Campground and Trailhead.

Black Lake Road is for high-clearance vehicles only. The GPS coordinates at the trailhead are 45 11.453 N 116 33.656 W.

Trailhead facilities: The trailhead has restrooms and several campsites, but parking is limited.

Camping and services: There are several campsites near the trailhead at Black Lake. Groceries and gas can be obtained in Oxbow, Oregon, and Council, Idaho. Medical services can be obtained in Council.

For more information: USDA Forest Service at Council Ranger District in Council or the Hells Canyon National Recreational Area office in Riggins, Idaho.

Six Lake Basin Trail 214, 218
Horse Pasture Basin Trail 173

Key points:

0.0   Black Lake Trailhead.

0.8   Junction with Horse Heaven Cabin Trail 214. GPS 45 11.283 N 116 34.081 W.

1.4   Cross ridgeline.

2.4   Joe's Gap and junction with Horse Pasture Basin Trail. GPS 45 11.283 N 116 35.211 W.

3.0   Six Lake Basin (first lake).

4.0   Junction with Trail 216.

The hike: The wide trail, which was once used as a mine road, heads west as it leaves Black Lake Trailhead. Paintbrush and Lupine line the route as it climbs gently through the open subalpine woods. Shortly after leaving the trailhead the track enters Hells

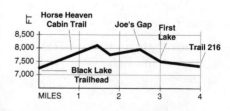

Canyon Wilderness. One of several huge boulders overhangs the trail as you hike through a rockslide area soon after passing the boundary. The course

282

makes a switchback to the right and leaves the roadbed, 0.4 mile from the trailhead. A bit farther along the trace crosses a tiny stream. Just past the stream there is a large pine tree with a square hole cut into its hollow core, next to the trail.

The junction with Horse Heaven Cabin Trail 214 is reached 0.8 mile from the trailhead, at 7,730 feet elevation. From the junction an abandoned mine can be seen several hundred yards to the south. Turn left at the junction and climb to the west and southwest and pass a pond. The path is vague for a short distance in the meadow, near the pond. The route bears to the left and heads directly away from the pond to the south-southwest, and soon becomes obvious again. Soon the track forks. Take the left fork and continue to climb (the right fork is the remains of an older trail). About .04 mile from the junction the course makes a switchback to the right and soon crosses the older trail again. You will make another switchback and reach the ridgeline at 8,150 feet elevation, 0.6 mile from the junction and 1.4 miles from Black Lake Trailhead. Watch for Mountain Goats as you cross this ridge.

The route crosses the ridgeline and bears right at another fork (old trail again). The lake you can see to the south is in Horse Pasture Basin. You will make two switchbacks as you descend about 300 vertical feet before starting a traverse along the slope toward Joe's Gap. Cardinal Flowers, Balsamroot, and many other flowers add color to this rocky slope as you hike along.

Just before you reach Joe's Gap, 2.4 miles from Black Lake Trailhead, you will come to the junction with Horse Pasture Basin Trail 173. Horse Pasture Basin Trail turns to the left and leads southeast to a trailhead on Black Lake Road. (See Hike 64 for a description of Horse Pasture Basin Trail.) A few yards past the junction is the notch called Joe's Gap, at 7,990 feet elevation. At the gap, Six Lake Basin comes into view to the northwest.

The course goes through the gap then makes four descending switchbacks before starting a traverse to the north. This descending traverse crosses a boulder-covered slope; to the left in the distance are the Wallowa Mountains. The traverse ends and the track makes five more switchbacks as it drops to within a few yards of the first lake in the basin. This lake, which is 3 miles from Black Lake Trailhead at 7,530 feet elevation, contains a good supply of wild Rainbow Trout.

The trail crosses the lake's tiny outlet stream and enters burnt timber. In the timber the track makes a couple more switchbacks then crosses a stream. The fire spared the timber along the stream. The path then heads northwest for 0.3 mile to another stream crossing. Another lake with fish in it is located a short distance upstream (northeast) at the crossing. Another .02 mile farther along there is another lake 50 yards to the right of the trail. A path follows the creek to the east-northeast from this lake to the largest lake in the basin. This lake, about 0.4 mile from the trail, has several campsites close to it and contains a good supply of fish.

You will reach the junction with Trail 216 4 miles from the trailhead. Trail 216 descends southwest into Deep Creek Canyon to meet Deep Creek Trail. Past this junction the trail receives limited maintenance and may be hard to follow. Check with the Forest Service if you plan to hike past here.

Pond near junction with Horse Heaven Cabin Trail. Six Lake Basin Trail climbs the ridge on the right.

Options: Return via Horse Pasture Basin Trail to Black Lake Road. This option would require a 5.8-mile shuttle by four-wheel-drive or high-clearance vehicle along Black Lake Road. See Hike 64 for details about Horse Pasture Basin Trail and driving directions.

63 Satan Lake Route

Highlights:	A cross-country hike from Black Lake to the glacial cirque that holds the small jewel called Satan Lake. This is a relativity easy cross-country route to follow, but map and compass skills are still required to do it safely.
Type of hike:	Out-and-back day hike or backpack.
Total distance:	2 miles.
Difficulty:	Moderate, with routefinding skills required.
Best months:	August–mid-October
Elevation gain:	360 feet.
Permits and fees:	None.
Maps:	Purgatory Saddle USGS quad.

Finding the trailhead: Head east from Interstate 84 at Baker City on Oregon 86. Follow OR 86 for 70.5 miles to the bridge over the Snake River at Copperfield Park. Cross the bridge and turn left on Idaho Power Company Road. Follow Idaho Power Company Road, which becomes Forest Road 454,

Satan Lake Route

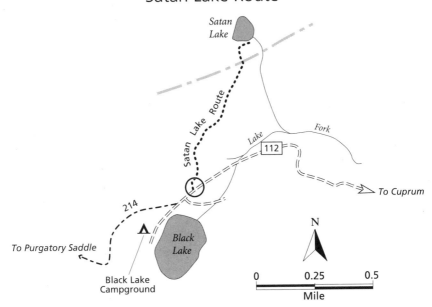

for 6.1 miles to the junction with Kleinschmidt Grade (Forest Road 050). Turn right and drive northeast, up the steep gravel grade, for 9.4 miles to the tiny town of Cuprum, Idaho. Head straight through Cuprum on what is now Forest Road 105. Follow FR 105 for 7.9 miles to a four-way junction. At the junction, turn left on Black Lake Road (Forest Road 112). There is a sign pointing to Black Lake at the junction. Follow Black Lake Road for 12.3 miles northeast to Black Lake Campground and Trailhead. Black Lake Road is for high-clearance vehicles only.

If coming from Council, Idaho, drive northwest for 30 miles on the Cuprum–Council Road (Forest Road 002) to the community of Bear. From Bear, head north on FR 105 for 4.5 miles to a fork in the road. Bear left at the fork, staying on FR 105, and drive north for 2 miles to a four-way junction. At the junction, turn right on Black Lake Road (Forest Road 112). There is a sign pointing to Black Lake at the junction. Follow Black Lake Road for 12.3 miles northeast to Black Lake Campground and Trailhead. Black Lake Road is for high-clearance vehicles only.

From the campground, go back the way you came for 0.2 mile to reach the start of the route to Satan Lake. The route begins 70 yards northeast along Black Lake Road from the road that goes to the unimproved campsites at the north end of Black Lake. The GPS coordinates where the route leaves Black Lake Road are 45 11.476 N 116 33.523W.

Trailhead facilities: None at the spot where this route leaves the Black Lake Road. A restroom, limited parking, and a few campsites are available 0.2 mile to the southwest at Black Lake Campground.

Camping and services: There are several campsites near the trailhead at Black Lake. Groceries and gas can be obtained in Oxbow, Oregon, and Council, Idaho. Medical services can be obtained in Council.

For more information: USDA Forest Service at Council Ranger District in Council or the Hells Canyon National Recreational Area office in Riggins, Idaho.

Key points:
0.0   Black Lake Road.
1.0   Satan Lake. GPS 45 12.018 N 116 33.215 W.

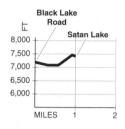

The hike: The route to Satan Lake leaves Black Lake Road following an abandoned roadbed to the north. You will follow this roadbed for 65 yards then the route turns to the right (north-northeast) and descends slightly into the timber. The roadbed continues only a few more yards then ends, so if you miss the path backtrack a short distance to find it. The route heads north-northeast through the timber for a short distance then enters a semiopen slope with a scattering of boulders. Gray cliffs rise above to your left as you descend slightly crossing this slope. Coneflowers, Pearly Everlastings, Asters, and many other flowers line the vague path as you walk along.

You will reenter dense timber, at 7,090 feet elevation, 0.3 mile after leaving Black Lake Road. In this timber the path becomes even harder to see. You will need to bear slightly left and climb to the north-northwest through the timber. The route breaks out of the thick timber in about 0.1 mile, at 7,200 feet elevation. You then traverse across a fairly steep semiopen slope, climbing gradually, just below the gray cliffs for nearly half a mile north-northeast, to what appears to be a flat-topped rock outcropping. Where the path enters this slope and where it exits it are marked with rock cairns, but these cairns may be hard to spot. The route is a very vague braided path across this open area.

The flat-topped rock outcropping, at 7,420 feet elevation, is actually part of the small ridge at the bottom of the cirque that holds Satan Lake. From the ridge, descend a short distance north to the shore of Satan Lake at 7,380 feet elevation.

Satan Lake's shoreline is timbered with Lodgepole Pine, Whitebark Pine, and Sub-Alpine Fir on three sides, but on its west side rockslides reach nearly to the shore. Look for the Gentians that bloom near the tiny outlet stream at the southeast corner of the lake. There is one fairly good campsite a short distance above the lake's south shore. Satan Lake contains a fair population of trout, some of them good sized.

Options: The hike to Satan Lake makes a good day trip while you are camped at Black Lake Campground.

64 Horse Pasture Basin Trail 173

See Map on Page 282

Highlights: A hike from the trailhead on Black Lake Road through the alpine bowl of Horse Pasture Basin to Joe's Gap. From here, descend into Six Lake Basin to spend some time fishing or camping. Horse Pasture Basin Trail is the easiest way to get to Six Lake Basin.

Type of hike: Out-and-back day hike or backpack, with shuttle option.

Total distance: 8 miles.

Difficulty: Easy to moderate.

Best months: Late July–September.

Elevation gain: 980 feet.

Permits and fees: None.

Maps: Purgatory Saddle USGS quad.

Finding the trailhead: Head east from Interstate 84 at Baker City on Oregon 86. Follow OR 86 for 70.5 miles to the bridge over the Snake River at Copperfield Park. Cross the bridge and turn left on Idaho Power Company Road. Follow Idaho Power Company Road, which becomes Forest Road 454, for 6.1 miles to the junction with Kleinschmidt Grade (Forest Road 050). Turn right and drive northeast, up the steep gravel grade, for 9.4 miles to the tiny town of Cuprum, Idaho. Head straight through Cuprum on what is now Forest Road 105. Follow FR 105 for 7.9 miles to a four-way junction. At the junction, turn left on Black Lake Road (Forest Road 112). There is a sign pointing to Black Lake at the junction. Follow FR 112 for 7.3 miles to Deep Creek Trailhead.

If coming from Council, Idaho, drive northwest for 30 miles on the Cuprum–Council Road (Forest Road 002) to the community of Bear. From Bear, head north on FR 105 for 4.5 miles to a fork in the road. Bear left at the fork, staying on FR 105, and drive north for 2 miles to a four-way junction. At the junction, turn right on Black Lake Road (Forest Road 112). There is a sign pointing to Black Lake at the junction. Follow FR 112 for 7.3 miles to Deep Creek Trailhead.

The GPS coordinates at the trailhead are 45 09.256 N 116 33.509 W. Black Lake Road is for high-clearance vehicles only.

Trailhead facilities: The trailhead has parking for three or four cars but has no other facilities.

Camping and services: Several campsites are located at Black Lake Campground 0.2 mile southwest of the beginning of this route. Groceries and gas can be obtained in Oxbow, Oregon, and Council, Idaho. Medical services can be obtained in Council. Cell phone service can be had along much of this route.

For more information: USDA Forest Service at Council Ranger District in Council or the Hells Canyon National Recreation Area office in Riggins, Idaho.

Key points:
- 0.0 Deep Creek Trailhead.
- 0.9 Spring below trail.
- 2.1 First stream crossing; route to lake leaves trail.
- 3.4 Junction with Six Lake Basin Trail at Joe's Gap. GPS 45 11.271 N 116 35.221 W.
- 4.0 Six Lake Basin (first lake).

The hike: Leaving the trailhead at 7,380 feet elevation Horse Pasture Basin Trail first climbs a few feet to the northwest. It then begins a long traverse along the slope on the left side of the ridgeline. The slope the trail crosses is dotted with groves of Sub-

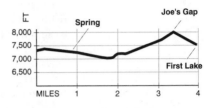

Alpine Fir and Whitebark Pine. Between the groves of trees the slope is covered with wildflowers in early summer (late July). The route, which may be braided from use by sheep, passes a tiny spring 0.9 mile from the trailhead. From the open areas the trail along Deep Creek can be seen far below to the left. The trail rounds a point and begins to head north into Horse Pasture Basin, 1.4 miles from the trailhead. After turning north the path climbs fairly steeply for a short distance.

About a third of a mile after heading north the route crosses a small stream (elev. 7,150 ft) that is the outlet for the lake in Horse Pasture Basin. To reach the lake, cross the stream and climb the small ridge on its north side. Stay parallel to the stream for 0.3 mile to a spring. This spring is 125 yards west of the lake. At times the lake may also overflow into the stream. It's a steep brushy 380-foot climb to the lake. Watch for Lewis Monkeyflowers along the stream.

Horse Pasture Basin Trail climbs after crossing the stream. It crosses another stream 0.4 mile farther along, then soon bears northwest and makes the final climb to Joe's Gap and the junction with Six Lake Basin Trail 218. (See Hike 62 for details about Six Lake Basin Trail.) Some of the lakes in Six Lake Basin can be seen to the northwest from the vantage point of Joe's Gap at 7,980 feet elevation The tread goes through the gap then makes four descending switchbacks before starting a traverse to the north. Look to the left as you cross the boulder-covered slope; you will see the Wallowa Mountains in the distance. The traverse ends and the track makes five more switchbacks as it drops to within a few yards of the first lake in the basin.

Options: A one-way trip can be made by taking Trail 218 back to Black Lake Trailhead. This requires a car shuttle (four-wheel drive) back to Deep Creek Trailhead.

65 Sheep Rock National Recreation Trail

Highlights:	A short loop from Sheep Rock parking area to an observation point and back. This trail offers breathtaking views of Hells Canyon and the Wallowa and southern Seven Devils Mountains. The short hike to Sheep Rock observation point is a good place for persons who are unable or unwilling to make a long hike to get an excellent view of Hells Canyon. While the view from Sheep Rock is inferior to the view from Dry Diggins Lookout, the hike is a much easier 0.5-mile round trip as opposed to a 17-mile trip.
Type of hike:	Short loop day hike.
Total distance:	0.5 mile.
Difficulty:	Easy.
Best months:	July–September.
Elevation gain:	Minimal.
Permits and fees:	None.
Maps:	White Monument USGS quad covers the area, but no map is needed to hike this short trail.

Finding the trailhead: Head east from Interstate 84 at Baker City on Oregon 86. Follow OR 86 for 70.5 miles to the bridge over the Snake River at Copperfield Park. Cross the bridge and turn left on Idaho Power Company Road. Follow Idaho Power Company Road, which becomes Forest Road 454, for 6.1 miles to the junction with Kleinschmidt Grade (Forest Road 050). Turn right and drive northeast up the steep gravel grade for 9.4 miles to the tiny town of Cuprum, Idaho. Head straight through Cuprum on what is now Forest Road 105. Follow FR 105 for 2.1 more miles to the junction with Forest Road 106. Turn left as the sign directs and drive 10 miles to Sheep Rock Trailhead.

If you are coming from Council, Idaho, drive northwest for 38 miles on the Cuprum–Council Road (Forest Road 002) to the junction with Kleinschmidt Grade. Turn right and drive 1.4 miles northeast to the town of Cuprum on FR 105. Follow FR 105 for 2.1 more miles to the junction with FR 106. Turn left as the sign directs and drive 10 miles to Sheep Rock Trailhead.

The GPS coordinates at the trailhead are 45 11.421 N 116 40.032 W.

Kleinschmidt Grade, completed in July 1891, was built by Albert Kleinschmidt to provide access to his copper mines at Cuprum and Helena. The road was built with picks, shovels, dynamite, and horse-drawn scrapers. FR 106 passes several old mining sites and the old Helena town site. Kinney Point Lookout site is a short distance to the left of FR 106 near the Helena town site. A high-clearance vehicle is recommended for driving the road to Sheep Rock. The Hells Canyon National Recreation Area map from the Forest Service will be helpful with finding the trailhead.

Sheep Rock National Recreation Trail

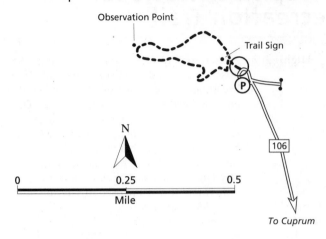

Trailhead facilities: The trailhead has a restroom and parking for several cars.

Camping and services: The closest developed campsites are at the Idaho Power Company at the bottom of Kleinschmidt Grade, 21.5 miles to the southwest via Cuprum. Groceries and gas can be obtained in Oxbow, Oregon, and Council, Idaho. Medical services can be obtained in Council. Cell phone service can be had along much of this route.

For more information: USDA Forest Service at Council Ranger District in Council or the Hells Canyon National Recreation Area office in Riggins, Idaho.

Key points:
- 0.0   Sheep Rock parking area.
- 0.2   Side path to observation point.
- 0.5   Parking area.

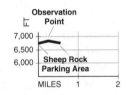

The hike: Starting at the parking area the trail heads to the northwest. It reaches the junction with the return trail and a sign pointing to the observation point a few yards after leaving the parking area. Stay right (straight ahead) at the junction. Just past the junction is a bronze plaque, stating that Sheep Rock is a registered natural landmark. After passing the plaque the trail goes around the north side of the highest outcroppings of Sheep Rock, then it climbs the last few yards to a short side path to the right, which leads to the observation point.

The observation point is marked with an informational sign. From the point the view is spectacular. To the west in the distance is the Wallowa Mountains. Much closer and far below is the southern part of Hells Canyon. Hells Canyon Reservoir is 4,100 feet below where you are standing.

The return trip to the parking area follows a slightly rougher path around the south side of the highest outcroppings. This path parallels the one you

SHEEP ROCK

Sheep Rock was named because of the Bighorn sheep that used to inhabit this area. No doubt this was a favorite hangout for the old rams.

To the North is part of the Red Ledge mine in Deep Creek. It can be located by the reddish color of the rocks. Supplies were first hauled in by wagon to the Peacock Mine-Helena area. Then the supplies were loaded on large wooden sleds and skidded down to the mine and also on down Hailey Ridge to Eagle Bar on the Snake River. A road built down the river in 1927 ended this arduous task.

PAYETTE *National Forest*

came in on for a short distance. It then bears south slightly around the outcropping and makes four switchbacks as it descends to the junction near the parking area.

Options: Various places of interest along the access road to Sheep Rock also contribute to making this a worthwhile trip.

66 Horse Mountain Lookout Route

Highlights:	A cross-country hike along an open ridgeline, with magnificent views of the southern part of Hells Canyon, from Lynes Saddle to Horse Mountain Lookout.
Type of hike:	Out-and-back cross-country day hike, with a shuttle option.
Total distance:	7 miles.
Difficulty:	Strenuous, with routefinding skills required.
Best months:	June–early July for an out-and-back hike; mid-July–September for a shuttle.
Elevation gain:	2,010 feet.
Permits and fees:	None.
Maps:	Cuprum and White Monument USGS quads.

Finding the trailhead: Head east from Interstate 84 at Baker City on Oregon 86. Follow OR 86 for 70.5 miles to the bridge over the Snake River at Copperfield Park. Cross the bridge and turn left on Idaho Power Company

Horse Mountain Lookout Route

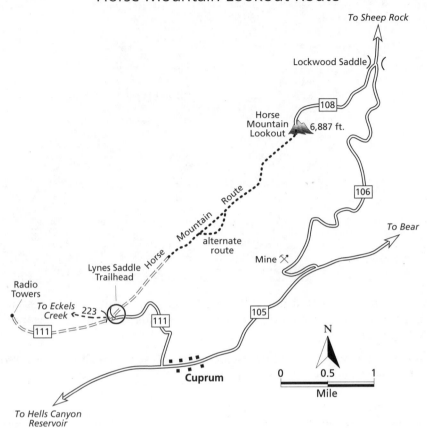

Road. Follow Idaho Power Company Road, which becomes Forest Road 454, for 6.1 miles to the junction with Kleinschmidt Grade (Forest Road 050). Turn right and drive northeast up the steep gravel grade for 9.2 miles to the junction with Forest Road 111 just as you enter the tiny town of Cuprum, Idaho. Turn left (north) and follow FR 111 for 1.6 miles to Lynes Saddle Trailhead at 5,020 feet. Both the Kleinschmidt Grade and FR 111 are rough, steep gravel roads.

If you are coming from Council, Idaho, drive northwest for 38 miles on the Cuprum–Council Road (Forest Road 002) to the junction with Kleinschmidt Grade. Turn right and drive 1.2 miles northeast to the junction with FR 111 just as you enter the tiny town of Cuprum. Turn left (north) and follow FR 111 for 1.6 miles to Lynes Saddle Trailhead.

Lynes Saddle Trailhead is also the upper trailhead for Eckels Creek Trail (Hike 67). The GPS coordinates at Lynes Saddle are 45 05.610 N 116 42.601W.

To reach Horse Mountain Lookout at the end of this hike, go back to Cuprum and then follow FR 105 for 2.1 more miles to the junction with FR 106. Turn left at the sign that directs you to Sheep Rock, and drive 4 miles to Lockwood Saddle and the junction with Forest Road 108. Turn left on FR 108 and drive about 1.5 miles to Horse Mountain Lookout. FR 108 is a four-wheel-drive road.

Trailhead facilities: Lynes Saddle Trailhead has parking for several cars but has no other facilities.

Camping and services: The closest developed campground is the Idaho Power Company Camp at the foot of Kleinschmidt Grade on Hells Canyon Reservoir about 12 miles southwest of the trailhead. Other services can be had in Oxbow, Oregon, and Council, Idaho. Cell phone service is good from Horse Mountain Lookout.

For more information: USDA Forest Service at Council Ranger Station in Council. Further information may be limited.

Key points:

0.0   Lynes Saddle Trailhead.
0.9   End of abandoned roadbed.
1.6   High point on ridge.
3.5   Horse Mountain Lookout. GPS 45 07.343 N 116 40.205 W.

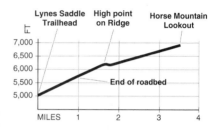

The hike: Climbing northeast from Lynes Saddle the route follows an abandoned roadbed along an open ridgeline. Balsamroot, Desert Parsley, Larkspur, and Lupine add a splash of color along this ridge in June. Another abandoned roadbed bears to the right 0.3 mile from Lynes Saddle. Keep left (straight ahead to the northwest) and follow the ridge continuing to climb. The track steepens 0.7 mile from the saddle. Mountain Mahogany grows from the rock outcroppings next to the trail as you ascend this steep section. Eckels Creek Canyon and Trail can be seen far below to the left, and to the west are the Wallowa Mountains.

After climbing steeply for a little more than 0.1 mile the ridge flattens out for 100 yards. The roadbed you have been following ends here, at 5,680 feet elevation. The path is very vague from here on. Head on up the ridge, bearing right to get around the rock outcroppings, and climb moderately for 0.7 mile to a high point on the ridgeline. In a few spots along this part of the route you may need to use your hands for balance to climb over the rough spots. Be careful where you put your hands, however; there are Rattlesnakes along this ridge. As you gain altitude a few Penstemons grow between the rocks. In spots on the north facing slope to your left Glacier Lilies (Dogtooth Violets) bloom as the snow retreats in June.

Leaving the high point at 6,190 feet elevation, the route continues along the ridge to the northeast, descending slightly through the rock outcroppings. Pass these outcroppings on the right but do not drop more than a few yards below the ridgeline. You will pass a small prospect hole that is just right of the ridgeline 0.4 mile from the high point. The vague path you are following goes just to the right of the hole. About 0.5 mile past the prospect hole the route enters the timber. At the point where you enter the timber you will be about 100 yards to the right of the ridgeline, at 6,280 feet elevation. As you enter the timber you should be on the very vague remains of another abandoned roadbed. The route through the timber climbs gently for 300 yards then turns to the left and climbs steeply for a short distance, nearly regaining the ridgeline. Take careful note of the route as you ascend through this stretch of timber and brush. You will need to follow the same route when you descend. The route turns slightly to the right (northwest) as you near the ridgeline again. Continue to climb staying just right of the ridge along and through the sloping meadows with groves of Aspen to the top of Horse Mountain and Horse Mountain Lookout.

Horse Mountain, at 6,887 feet elevation, offers a panoramic 360-degree view. To the north are Kinney Point and Sheep Rock, in the southern part of the Seven Devils Mountains. To the east the pyramid-shaped peak of Smith Mountain dominates the skyline. To the west the Wallowa Mountains in Oregon rise above the timber and grassland.

There is no water along this route so take what you will need. Even though all of this route is above 5,000 feet elevation, there are Rattlesnakes along this ridge so keep your eyes and ears open, even if there are still snowdrifts on the lee side of the ridge.

Options: On your return trip, you may wish to traverse around to the left of the high point on the ridge 1.6 miles from Lynes Saddle. It is easily possible to do this, but there are some steep, loose side hills to cross. Late in the summer, you can drive to Horse Mountain, making a one-way hike with a high-clearance vehicle shuttle possible.

Old Horse Mountain Lookout.

67 Eckels Creek Trail 223, 222, 514

Highlights: A hike that travels up the rough Eckels Creek Canyon above a rushing stream, then traverses the mid-slopes of Hells Canyon to Allison Creek Canyon, and finally descends this spectacular canyon back down to Hells Canyon Reservoir.

Type of hike: Shuttle day hike.

Total distance: 7.4 miles.

Difficulty: Moderate to strenuous. Good routefinding skills are required to follow parts of this trail.

Best months: April–mid-June and September–October.

Elevation gain: 2,020 feet.

Permits and fees: Register at the trailhead.

Maps: Cuprum and White Monument USGS quads.

Finding the trailhead: Head east from Interstate 84 at Baker City on Oregon 86. Follow OR 86 for 70.5 miles to the bridge over the Snake River at Copperfield Park. Cross the bridge and turn left on Idaho Power Company Road. Follow Idaho Power Company Road, which becomes Forest Road 454, for 12.5 miles to Eckels Creek Trailhead. GPS coordinates at the trailhead are 45 07.154 N 116 44.898 W.

Trailhead facilities: The trailhead has very limited parking and no other facilities.

Camping and services: The closest developed campground to the trailhead is the Idaho Power Company Camp 6.5 miles to the south on Forest Road 454. Gas and groceries can be purchased at Pine Creek 2 miles southwest of Oxbow on OR 86. For medical services, your best bet is to head for Halfway, Oregon, which is another 15 miles to the southwest on OR 86.

For more information: USDA Forest Service at Hells Canyon Dam Visitor Center, Council Ranger District in Council, Idaho, or the Hells Canyon National Recreation Area office in Riggins, Idaho.

Key points:

0.0 Eckels Creek Trailhead.

0.8 Unmarked junction with Trail 224. GPS 45 06.730 N 116 44.263 W.

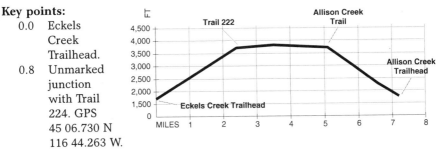

1.5 Cross Eckels Creek for the first time.

2.6 Junction with Trail 222. GPS 45 06.383 N 116 43.153 W.

5.1 Junction with Allison Creek Trail 514. GPS 45 07.587 N 116 43.208 W.

7.4 Allison Creek Trailhead. GPS 45 07.763 N 116 44.199 W.

Eckels Creek Trail 223, 222, 514
Allison Creek Trail 514
Kinney Creek Trail 211, 222, 514

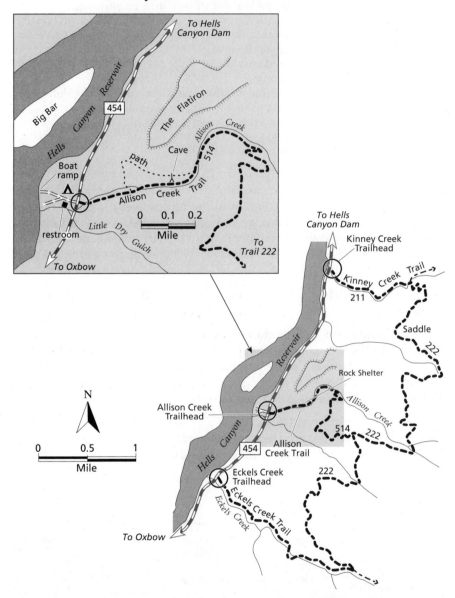

The hike: Eckels Creek Trail heads east from the trailhead, soon passing a trail register box. Register at the box, then follow the tread as it climbs above the brush along the north side of Eckels Creek. Sumac and Balsamroot dot the slope as you climb below the gray and tan cliffs that rise above the south side of Eckels Creek.

The rocky course bears to the left up a side canyon 0.6 mile from the trailhead. You soon work back out of the side canyon and continue to climb well above the frothy waters of Eckels Creek. Below to your right 0.7 mile from the trailhead Eckels Creek splashes over a small falls. Just past the falls, where the route makes a switchback to the left, at 2,420 feet elevation, you may notice a faint path heading off to the right (southeast). This faint path is the remains of Trail 224, which climbs to the south to join Kleinschmidt Grade.

After passing the unmarked junction with Trail 224, Eckels Creek Trail climbs along a rocky slope that blooms with Larkspur, Balsamroot, and Desert Parsley in April. Soon you will make a switchback to the right and cross a spur ridge. The route then passes through several small brushy areas as it traverses the steep slopes. Just before traversing back into the brushy creekbed of Eckels Creek you may notice the remains of a long-abandoned telephone line above the trail. Bleeding Hearts and Dogtooth Violets bloom beneath the brush along the creek.

The trace makes several more switchbacks before crossing Eckels Creek, 1.5 miles from the trailhead. This crossing is generally an easy rock hop, but the rocks may be very slick. The course then makes a couple more switchbacks before recrossing Eckels Creek. One hundred yards past the second crossing the tread makes a switchback to the left and soon leaves the brushy creekbed. You will then climb the open slope for 150 yards to another switchback, on a small spur ridge, next to a large tree. The trail is a little vague at the switchback but soon becomes more obvious. The path then continues to climb to the southeast for another mile, staying above the creekbed, and crossing a couple of side draws to the junction with Trail 222, at 3,630 feet elevation. At the junction, 2.6 miles from the trailhead, there is a plastic signpost with the trail numbers on it but no other information. Both trails have been recently maintained at this point, and the junction is easy to see.

Turn left (northwest) at the junction onto Trail 222, and traverse an open slope. There will probably be Elk and Mule Deer tracks on the trail; both animals are common here in the spring. Hells Canyon Reservoir as well as the benches and rims on the Oregon side of Hells Canyon come into view to the west 0.7 mile past the junction. The trail crosses a draw through some large Ponderosa Pines 1.2 miles after leaving Eckels Creek Trail. Most of the large trees show the scars of a long-ago fire. Just before reaching the draw with the large pines the trail reaches its highest point, at 3,760 feet elevation. The course crosses a rounded ridgeline where it becomes vague 0.2 mile after passing the grove of pines. Bear right on the ridgeline and head east into Little Dry Gulch Canyon along a partially forested north-facing slope. Shooting Stars line the trail in spots, as you traverse toward Little Dry Gulch Creek. The trace crosses Little Dry Gulch Creek, which may indeed be dry, then heads north-northwest. This side of Little Dry Gulch is mostly open but the trail is vague. The route stays nearly level for the 0.7 mile to the junction with Allison Creek Trail 514. Watch for cairns marking the route along this section of trail.

The unmarked junction with Allison Creek Trail is reached 5.1 miles from the trailhead on a grassy ridgeline. At the junction, 3,680 feet above sea level,

Allison Creek Canyon.

the trail is very vague. Turn left at the junction and head southwest to enter a shallow draw. You are now on Allison Creek Trail. The rough rocky route descends this draw for a short distance then bears to the right (west). Shortly it makes a switchback to the left and goes back into the draw. In the bottom of the draw you will switchback to the west (right) again. From this switchback on down, the trail is easier to follow. The route winds down and west to a grassy saddle at 3,000 feet elevation. It then turns right and descends to the northeast into Allison Creek Canyon, making a couple of switchbacks along the way. The route then descends along Allison Creek, crossing it three times before reaching Allison Creek Trailhead. Allison Creek Trailhead, at 1,780 feet elevation, is 2.3 miles from Trail 222 and 7.4 miles from Eckels Creek Trailhead. (For a more complete description of Allison Creek Trail, see Hike 68.)

Rattlesnakes can be found anywhere along this trail and Poison Ivy is abundant in the creekbeds, so watch where you put your hands and feet.

Options: To make a longer (12-mile) shuttle hike, turn right at the junction with Allison Creek Trail and continue on Trail 222 to Kinney Creek Trail. Then take Kinney Creek Trail to Kinney Creek Trailhead. See Hike 69 for a description of Kinney Creek Trail.

If you go straight ahead from the junction with Trail 122, which is 2.6 miles from Eckels Creek Trailhead, you can climb to the southeast for about 2 miles to Lynes Saddle Trailhead on FR 111, above the town of Cuprum. To Reach Lynes Saddle by road, see the finding the trailhead directions in Hike 66.

68 Allison Creek Trail 514

Highlights:	A hike up Allison Creek Canyon through spectacular limestone formations. If you are so inclined, you can also do some very technical rock climbing.
Type of hike:	Out-and-back day hike.
Total distance:	4.6 miles.
Difficulty:	Moderate.
Best months:	April–June and September–October.
Elevation gain:	1,220 feet.
Permits and fees:	Register at the box near the trailhead.
Maps:	White Monument USGS quad.

See Map on Page 296

Finding the trail: Head east from Interstate 84 at Baker City on Oregon 86. Follow OR 86 for 70.5 miles to the bridge over the Snake River at Copperfield Park. Cross the bridge and turn left on Idaho Power Company Road. Follow Idaho Power Company Road, which becomes Forest Road 454, for 13.4 miles north along Hells Canyon Reservoir to Allison Creek Trailhead. The trailhead is on the right side of the road at 1,780 feet elevation. The GPS coordinates at the trailhead are 45 07.763 N 116 44.199 W.

Trailhead facilities: The trailhead has parking for only a couple of cars. Across the road from the trailhead are several campsites, a primitive boat launching area, and restrooms.

Camping and services: Idaho Power Company has a very nice campground 7.4 miles south of the trailhead on FR 454. Groceries and gas are available at Pine Creek, 2 miles southwest of Oxbow, Oregon, on OR 86. Other services are available in Halfway and Baker City, Oregon, and in Cambridge, Idaho.

For more information: USDA Forest Service at the Hells Canyon Visitor Center 1 mile north of Hells Canyon Dam, Council Ranger District in Council, Idaho, or the Hells Canyon National Recreation Area office in Riggins, Idaho.

Key points:
0.0   Allison Creek Trailhead.
0.2   Poor side path to ridge below The Flatiron.
0.3   Path to rock shelter and cave.
1.7   Saddle. GPS 45 07.612 N 116 43.619 W.
2.3   Junction with Trail 222. GPS 45 07.587 N 116 43.208 W.

The hike: Fill out your trail registration card at the registration box. Then begin your hike to the east, up an abandoned roadbed, into Allison Creek Canyon. A short distance from the trailhead the course fords Allison Creek for the first time. Soon the light gray canyon walls of Martin Bridge Limestone begin to close in on the trail. The Flatiron, a huge limestone outcropping, looms high above to the northeast.

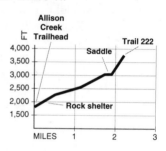

These limestone formations were formed in shallow warm seas about 210 million years ago.

Two-tenths of a mile into the hike you will pass a concrete box. Just past the box, a vague side path turns to the left (north). This path descends steeply for a few feet to cross Allison Creek then climbs very steeply up a shallow draw to the ridgeline below The Flatiron. The side path is used as a return route for rock climbers who have climbed the cliffs to your left. After reaching the ridgeline the path becomes very hard to follow as it traverses to the east along the steep slope to rejoin the main trail 0.2 mile farther up. Use this path only if you are an experienced off-trail hiker, because it is difficult to follow and is exposed in spots.

A few yards after passing the junction with the side path the tread crosses Allison Creek again. Stepping stones ease this crossing, but they are widely spaced and may be slick. The route now follows the north side of Allison Creek for 0.1 mile to another side path to the left. This short path leads to the site of the Allison Creek Rock Shelter at the mouth of a cave. Archeologists excavated this rock shelter in the 1960s.

Inside the cave next to Allison Creek Trail.

The trail crosses Allison Creek for the last time 0.1 mile past the path to the rock shelter, at 2,140 feet elevation. Just before reaching this crossing, the side path mentioned earlier rejoins the main trail. Half a mile past the last creek crossing the course makes a switchback to the right as it ascends the brushy slope. You will soon make another switchback then continue to climb to a rocky spur ridge. On the ridge the view improves as you leave the brush-covered slope. The route heads southeast up the ridge for a short distance, then begins an ascending traverse to the south and southwest along a steep slope that is dotted with Balsamroot and Shooting Stars in the spring. The tread reaches a saddle on the ridge between Allison Creek and Little Dry Gulch 1.7 miles from the trailhead, at 3,000 feet elevation.

This saddle has a great view and is a good place to stop for lunch or to turn around. Above the saddle the trail becomes a little harder to follow; there is usually no trail visible on the ground for a short distance in the grassy saddle. Turn left (east-southeast) in the saddle and climb slightly to the right of the ridgeline. Soon the path will show up as it climbs steeply along the south-facing slope. The route makes several switchbacks before ascending a shallow draw to a grassy rounded ridgeline and the junction with Trail 222. The vague, unmarked junction with Trail 222 is 2.3 miles from the trailhead, at 3,680 feet elevation.

Poison Ivy is abundant along the first mile of this trail and Rattlesnakes can be found anywhere, so watch where you put your hands and feet.

Options: Shorten your hike, without missing much, by turning around at the saddle 1.7 miles from the trailhead, or make a longer return hike via either Kinney Creek Trail or Eckels Creek Trail. You may want to make a short car shuttle to either of these trailheads. See Hikes 67 and 69 for more information.

69 Kinney Creek Trail 211, 222, 514

Highlights: A hike that travels up the | See Map on Page 296

Highlights: A hike that travels up the rugged Kinney Creek Canyon and traverses the wall of Hells Canyon to the spectacular Allison Creek Canyon. Make your return by descending Allison Creek Canyon to Allison Creek Trailhead.

Type of hike: Day hike shuttle, with out-and-back option.

Total distance: 9.2 miles.

Difficulty: Strenuous. Good routefinding skills are required to follow this trail.

Best months: April–mid-June and September–October.

Elevation gain: 2,210 feet.

Permits and fees: Register at the trailhead.

Maps: White Monument and Cuprum USGS quads.

Finding the trail: Head east from Interstate 84 at Baker City on Oregon 86. Follow OR 86 for 70.5 miles to the bridge over the Snake River at Copperfield Park. Cross the bridge and turn left on Idaho Power Company Road. Follow Idaho Power Company Road, which becomes Forest Road 454, for 14.8 miles north along Hells Canyon Reservoir to Kinney Creek Trailhead. The trailhead is a few yards north of the parking area. The GPS coordinates at the trailhead are 45 08.983 N 116 43.499 W.

Trailhead facilities: The trailhead has parking for a couple of cars but has no other facilities.

Camping and services: The closest developed campground to the trailhead is the Idaho Power Company Camp 8.8 miles to the south on FR 454. Gas and groceries can be purchased at Pine Creek 2 miles southwest of Oxbow on OR 86. For medical services, your best bet is to head for Halfway, Oregon, which is another 15 miles to the southwest on OR 86.

For more information: USDA Forest Service at the Hells Canyon Visitor Center 1 mile north of Hells Canyon Dam, Council Ranger District in Council, Idaho, or the Hells Canyon National Recreation Area office in Riggins, Idaho.

Key points:
0.0 Kinney Creek Trailhead.
1.7 Bridge over Kinney Creek.

1.8   Unmarked junction with Trail 222. GPS 45 09.053 N 116 42.496 W.

3.2   First ridge.

6.9   Unmarked junction with Allison Creek Trail 514. GPS 45 07.587 N 116
43.208 W.

9.2   Allison Creek Trailhead. GPS 45 07.763 N 116 44.199 W.

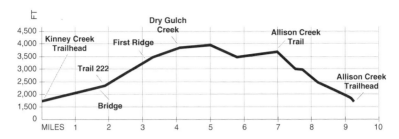

The hike: Kinney Creek Trail leads east from the trailhead, passing the trail registration box, and along the north side of a backwater pond. It then follows the rocky creekbed for a short distance before beginning to climb. Balsamroot, Hackberry, and Desert Parsley line the trail as it climbs the rocky slopes. At 0.5 mile the course makes a switchback to the left offering a view to the west across Hells Canyon Reservoir. Kinney Creek rushes below to the south. The path makes three more switchbacks before continuing up the rugged canyon. After traversing back to the creekbed at 1 mile from the trailhead, the route makes another switchback to the left. Here the tread climbs away from Kinney Creek again. Gray limestone cliffs rise above the south side of the creek as you continue to climb. The trace makes three more switchbacks then descends slightly to a wooden bridge over Kinney Creek. This bridge, at 2,350 feet elevation, is 1.7 miles from the trailhead. Watch for Dippers foraging in the swift waters of the creek below the bridge. For the casual hiker this bridge makes a good turnaround point because the route becomes steeper above here.

Continuing past the bridge the path climbs a few feet, then makes a switchback to the left. A short distance from the bridge is the unmarked junction with Trail 222. Kinney Creek Trail, which is in very poor condition above this point, bears to the left at the junction and recrosses Kinney Creek. Turn hard to the right at the junction onto Trail 222.

Past the junction the route climbs steeply. You will make four switchbacks as you climb the steep mostly open slopes. After making the fourth switchback the path crosses a draw then continues to climb the grass covered slope to a ridgeline. The USGS White Monument quad map shows the trail incorrectly from here to the junction with Allison Creek Trail. The route that is presently in use is somewhat higher and east of the one shown on the map. Dogtooth Violets and Shooting Stars brighten the trailside and Serviceberry bushes dot the slope.

The trail reaches the ridgeline, between the Kinney Creek and Dry Gulch drainages, just east of a saddle at 3,380 feet elevation. This ridge, 3.2 miles from the trailhead, is a good place to stop for lunch, rest a bit and admire the view after the steep climb out of Kinney Creek Canyon.

On the ridge the route becomes vague. Bear left as you cross the ridge, staying nearly level and soon the path will show up again as it continues to climb along the south slope of the ridge. From here to the junction with Allison Creek Trail it is necessary to watch the slopes well ahead in order to see the trail, because there are spots where it is very vague. A few small rock cairns mark the route but it is easy to lose. The vague route works its way in and out of three side draws as it climbs the 1.1 miles to the point where it crosses Dry Gulch Creek. The tread crosses Dry Gulch Creek, which may be dry, at 3,850 feet elevation.

As you cross Dry Gulch Creek the course enters the woods. Aspen, Ponderosa pine, and Alder form a dense forest in the creekbed. Soon the path, which is easier to follow now, traverses the wooded slope. As you climb gently the woods becomes more open. Dogtooth Violets and Buttercups bloom between the trees and brush. After traversing for 0.7 mile you will reach another ridgeline, at 3,930 feet elevation the highest point on this hike. On this ridge as it did on the last one the trail becomes very vague. Round the ridge and descend very slightly; soon the path shows up again on the southwest-facing slope.

From this Bunchgrass-covered slope the view to the right is of Allison Creek Canyon and Hells Canyon Reservoir. Soon The Flatiron, a flat-topped limestone outcropping, comes into view below to the right. Half a mile from the ridgeline, after crossing a rounded subridge, the route reaches a spur ridge. On this spur ridge the vague route descends for 150 feet, making four switchbacks. It then continues to descend now to the east into a draw. Leaving the draw a side path turns to the left and climbs. Ignore this path and hike nearly on the level, to the southeast. In another quarter of a mile the route enters a woods of brush, pine, and fir, as it crosses a tiny stream that may be dry. A short distance after crossing the tiny stream the tread crosses Allison Creek, at 3,490 feet elevation. Just after crossing the creek there is a possible campsite next to the trail.

The route is a little vague in the woods near Allison Creek, but blazes make it easier to follow. Soon after crossing Allison Creek the course begins a gently ascending traverse to the west along the wooded slope. On the traverse the route becomes easy to follow again. As you leave the creekbed the woods open up, allowing a view of the canyon to the west. The unmarked junction with Allison Creek Trail is reached 0.8 mile after crossing Allison Creek, at 3,680 feet elevation. The junction with Allison Creek Trail is on a ridgeline, and true to form this trail disappears on ridgelines. At the junction Trail 222 turns to the left to continue to Eckels Creek Trail. (See Hike 67 for a description of the rest of Trail 222 and Eckels Creek Trail.)

As you cross the grassy ridge, head southwest and enter a shallow draw. The rough rocky route descends this draw for a short distance then bears to the right (west). Soon it makes a switchback to the left and goes back into the draw. In the bottom of the draw you will switchback to the west (right) again. From this switchback on down the trail is easier to follow. The route winds down to the west to a grassy saddle at 3,000 feet elevation. It then turns right and descends to the northeast into Allison Creek Canyon, making a

The Flatiron.

couple of switchbacks along the way. The route then descends along Allison Creek, crossing it three times before reaching Allison Creek Trailhead. Allison Creek Trailhead, at 1,780 feet elevation, is 2.3 miles from Trail 222 and 9.2 miles from Kinney Creek Trailhead. (For a more complete description of the lower part of Allison Creek Trail, see Hike 68.)

Rattlesnakes can be found anywhere this trail, and Poison Ivy is abundant in the creekbeds.

Options: Make an out-and-back hike by returning from the bridge over Kinney Creek or from the first ridge. Or make a longer shuttle hike by continuing on Trail 222 to Eckels Creek and descending Eckels Creek Trail to Eckels Creek Trailhead. See Hike 67 for a description of Eckels Creek Trail.

70 Red Ledge Mine Trail 219

Highlights: A hike from Eagle Bar Trailhead on the east shore of Hells Canyon Reservoir to the abandoned Red Ledge Mine in rugged Deep Creek Canyon.
Type of hike: Out-and-back day hike.
Total distance: 5.3 miles.
Difficulty: Moderate to strenuous.
Best months: Late March–May and September–mid-November.
Elevation gain: 2,360 feet.
Permits and fees: None.
Maps: White Monument USGS quad.

Finding the trailhead: Head east from Interstate 84 at Baker City on Oregon 86. Follow OR 86 for 70.5 miles to the bridge over the Snake River at Copperfield Park. Cross the bridge and turn left on Idaho Power Company Road. Follow Idaho Power Company Road, which becomes Forest Road 454, for 19 miles to the trailhead at Eagle Bar. The trailhead is on the east side of the road. The GPS coordinates at the trailhead are 45 13.143 N 116 42.352 W.

Trailhead facilities: The trailhead has parking for several cars but has no other facilities.

Camping and services: The closest developed campground to the trailhead is the Idaho Power Company Camp 14 miles to the south on FR 454. Gas and groceries can be purchased at Pine Creek, which is 2 miles southwest of Oxbow on Oregon Highway 86. For medical services, your best bet is to head for Halfway, Oregon, which is another 15 miles to the southwest on OR 86.

For more information: USDA Forest Service at Hells Canyon Visitor Center 1 mile north of Hells Canyon Dam, Council Ranger District in Council, Idaho, or the Hells Canyon National Recreation Area office in Riggins, Idaho.

Key points:
0.0   Eagle Bar Trailhead.
2.8   Trail passes through notch.
4.5   First crossing of Deep Creek.
5.3   Red Ledge Mine. GPS 45 13.789 N 116 40.148 W.

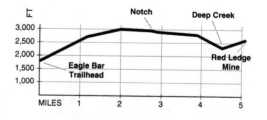

The hike: Although the route to Red Ledge Mine follows an old mine road all the way, it is closed to motor vehicle use to protect wildlife. A locked iron gate blocks vehicle access 50 yards up the trail from the trailhead. Poison Ivy grows beside the tread in spots so watch what plants you touch.

Red Lodge Mine Trail 219

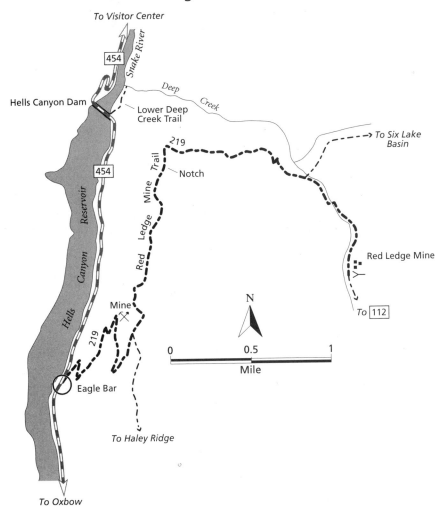

Shortly after passing the gate the course makes the first of six switchbacks as you climb the grass-covered slope. As you hike along the abandoned roadbed you pass a mineshaft, the remains of a long abandoned building, and some rusting mining equipment. Stay out of the shaft; the timbers are rotten and a fall or cave in is always possible. The old buildings are also not to be trusted; besides being dangerous in their own right there is a good chance that a Rattlesnake may be hiding under their old boards.

After climbing the last switchback about 1.3 miles from the trailhead, the route traverses to the north. The traverse starts out on a grassy slope that blooms with Balsamroot in the spring. Before long the terrain begins to get rougher and steeper. The route even follows a ledge for a short distance. Seven-tenths of a mile into the traverse the trace passes through a grove of Dou-glas-fir trees. These trees, at 3,000 feet elevation, are the first shade to be

Abandoned buildings at Red Ledge Mine.

found after leaving the trailhead. P.O. Saddle and Saulsberry Saddle can now be seen to the west, across Hells Canyon Reservoir in Oregon (the power lines go through Saulsberry Saddle).

The course goes through a notch in the rock outcroppings 2.8 miles from Eagle Bar. It then drops a few feet to the west before turning north again. Here Hells Canyon Dam comes into view far below to the left. Soon the route makes a turn to the right (east) and continues its gradual descent into Deep Creek Canyon. The scattered fir trees along this slope show the scars of a fire that burned through here several years ago, but most of them survived. The roadbed crosses a rockslide 0.4 mile into the canyon. Then it climbs for a short distance before resuming its gentle descent toward Deep Creek. Bright red and orange outcroppings come into view far up the canyon as you hike along. These outcroppings are the red ledge the mine is named for.

The route makes a couple of switchbacks as it descends. A little past the switchbacks Oxbow Creek can be seen flowing into Deep Creek from the far side of the canyon. As you near the bottom of the canyon the trail is overgrown with brush in spots. The trail crosses Deep Creek for the first time 4.5 miles from the trailhead, at 2,350 feet elevation. This ford can be dangerous during times of high water. The route heads up the left (northeast) side of the creek staying close to it. About 0.3 mile above the crossing the roadbed is washed out in several places and the brush is thick. This area changes each time the creek floods, so no real trail really exists here. Follow the creek up and the roadbed shows up again just before you reach the abandoned buildings at Red Ledge Mine (elev. 2,700 ft.). If the creek is high it may be very difficult to follow the trail up to the mine, because some crossings may be necessary.

The first claims at the Red Ledge Mine were staked by Tom Heady in 1894. There are 23 patented claims here and much work has been done; however, no ore has yet been produced. Watch for Rattlesnakes all along this trail, especially just below the mine.

Options: The trail continues on another 11 miles, and 4,500 vertical feet, up to Black Lake Road, but it is hard to follow above the mine. Do not try to follow it unless you are skilled in routefinding and cross-country travel. Trail conditions are somewhat better as you approach Black Lake Road. For driving directions to the trailhead on Black Lake Road, see Hike 64.

MOUNTAIN CLIMBS IN THE SEVEN DEVILS MOUNTAINS

The grandeur of some of the most rugged country in the northwestern United States comes into full and unobstructed view from the jagged summits of the Seven Devils Mountains. Below the peaks, the terrain is dotted with alpine lakes nestled in glacier-carved cirques. To the west the colossal gash of Hells Canyon drops away below your feet. In the distance past the canyon, the ridges and peaks of the Wallowa Mountains rise a mile above their surroundings.

To the east, the view is nearly as impressive. Here the canyons of the Salmon River drainage carve their way through the vast expanse of the mountains of central Idaho. In this direction, the mountains seem to go on forever.

All of the mountain climbs described in this section begin at Sheep Lake. Sheep Lake is reached via 9.4 miles of well-maintained trail from Windy Saddle Trailhead or via the rougher but much shorter 1.9-mile Sheep Lake Climbers Route (Hike 59) from Seven Devils Lake Campground. With its many campsites, Sheep Lake is an ideal base camp from which to explore the rugged heart of the Seven Devils Mountains.

Climber ascending beneath "The Roof" on The Tower of Babel.

Mountain Climbs in the Seven Devils Mountains

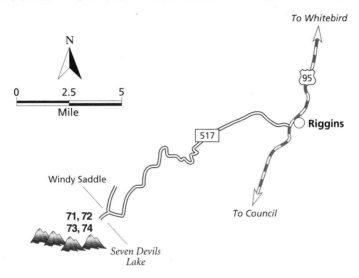

71 He Devil Mountain via Northwest Ridge

Highlights:	A hike and scramble from Sheep Lake to the summit of He Devil Mountain, the highest peak in the Seven Devils. This is probably the easiest way to the summit.
Type of hike:	Out-and-back mountain climb from a base camp.
Total distance:	3.4 miles.
Difficulty:	Easy to moderate by climbing standards; very strenuous by hiking standards.
Best months:	Late July–early September.
Elevation gain:	1,600 feet.
Permits and fees:	None.
Maps:	He Devil USGS quad.

Finding the trailhead: Follow the driving and hiking directions shown in Hike 59 to Sheep Lake. Then hike along the east and south shorelines on a poor path to the southwest corner of the lake, where the path meets Sheep Lake Trail. The GPS coordinates at the junction with Sheep Lake Trail are 45 19.743 N 116 32.463 W.

Sheep Lake may also be reached via Seven Devils Loop (Seven Devils Trail 124) and Sheep Lake Trail. See Hikes 49 and 56 for a description of these trails.

Trailhead facilities: Sheep Lake has many great campsites.

Camping and services: Developed campsites are available at Seven Devils Lake. Other services and groceries can be obtained in Riggins, Idaho. Cell phones work well from the summit of He Devil Mountain.

For more information: USDA Forest Service at the Hells Canyon National Recreation office in Riggins.

Key points:

- 0.0 Southwest corner of Sheep Lake.
- 0.7 Route leaves Sheep Lake Trail.
- 1.7 Summit of He Devil Mountain. GPS 45 19.447 N 116 32.849 W.

The climb: Allow 1.5 to 3 hours to reach the summit and nearly as much time to descend. There may be no water available after leaving Sheep Lake. As is true of most of the peaks in the Seven Devils this route could be very dangerous for novice climbers if it has a covering of snow or ice. There is moderate exposure at a few points along this climb.

From the southwest corner of Sheep Lake hike to the west on Sheep Lake Trail 123, the only maintained trail that reaches Sheep Lake. At the twelfth

He Devil Mountain via Northwest Ridge

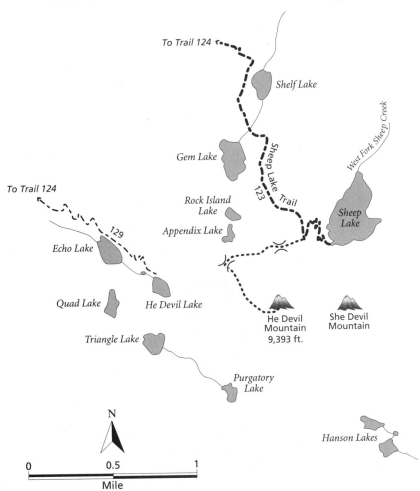

switchback, 0.7 mile from the lake, turn off the trail and head west-south-west. Climb 200 vertical feet to the saddle on the ridge, at 8,380 feet elevation. From the saddle descend slightly to the southwest. Then traverse to the west and southwest to another saddle on the ridge south of Appendix Lake (elev. 8,550 ft). Turn left (southeast) at the saddle and climb the ridge. The route generally climbs just to the right of the ridgeline but is right on top of it in a few spots. Just below the highest outcropping on the ridge (elev. 9,200 ft), bear left crossing the ridgeline. Then traverse a ledge, to the notch below the summit outcropping. From the notch traverse east-northeast for 150 feet. Then scramble up the class 2 and 3 rock to the summit of He Devil Mountain at 9,393 feet above sea level.

Most of the Seven Devils Range is in view from the top of He Devil Mountain, as well as much of Hells Canyon. The Wallowa Mountains across the

He Devil Mountain via the Northwest Ridge. GARY FLETCHER PHOTO

border in Oregon are to the west. Watch for Mountain Goats along this route. The easiest return is via the same route.

Options: Make a base camp at Sheep Lake and climb the other peaks described in this book.

72 She Devil Mountain via Northeast Ridge

Highlights:	A scramble from Sheep Lake to the summit of She Devil Mountain, watching for mountain goats all the way.
Type of hike:	Out-and-back mountain climb from a base camp.
Total distance:	2.2 miles.
Difficulty:	Easy by climbing standards; strenuous by hiking standards.
Best months:	Late July–September.
Elevation gain:	1,400 feet from Sheep Lake.
Permits and fees:	None.
Maps:	He Devil USGS quad.

Finding the trailhead: Follow the driving and hiking directions to Sheep Lake shown in Hike 59. The GPS coordinates where the route reaches the east shore of Sheep Lake are 45 19.864 N 116 32.180 W. Then hike along the east side of the lake to the gully where the climb starts.

Sheep Lake may also be reached using Seven Devils Loop and Sheep Lake Trail. See Hikes 49 and 56 for a description of these trails.

Trailhead facilities: Sheep Lake has lots of good campsites.

Camping and services: Developed campsites are available at Seven Devils Lake. Other services, including gas and groceries, can be obtained in Riggins, Idaho.

For more information: USDA Forest Service at the Hells Canyon National Recreation office in Riggins.

Key points:
- 0.0 Southeast corner of Sheep Lake.
- 0.6 Saddle between She Devil and Mount Baal. GPS 45 19.488 N 116 32.012 W.
- 1.1 Summit. GPS 45 19.434 N 116 32.424 W.

The climb: Allow 1.5 to 3 hours to reach the summit from Sheep Lake and nearly as much time to descend. There may be no water available after leaving Sheep Lake. As is true of most of the peaks in the Seven Devils this route could be very dangerous for novice climbers if it

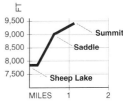

She Devil Mountain via Northeast Ridge
Mount Baal via the South Ridge
The Tower of Babel via the South Ridge

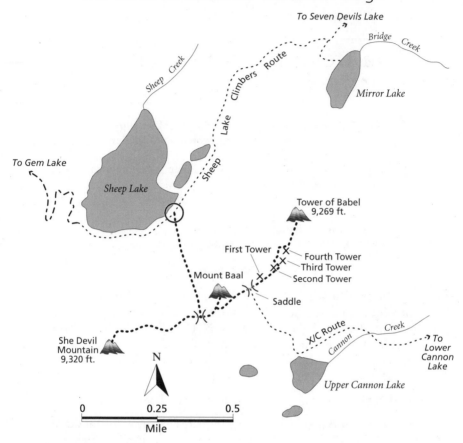

To Seven Devils Lake

Bridge Creek

Sheep Creek

Climbers Route

Mirror Lake

Sheep Lake

To Gem Lake

Sheep Lake

Tower of Babel
9,269 ft.

First Tower

Fourth Tower
Third Tower

Mount Baal

Second Tower

Saddle

She Devil
Mountain
9,320 ft.

N

X/C Route

Cannon Creek

To
Lower
Cannon
Lake

Upper Cannon Lake

0   0.25   0.5
Mile

has a covering of snow or ice. There is moderate exposure at a few points along this climb.

Follow the lakeshore path to a gully at the southeast corner of the lake. Turn left and climb southeast up the gully to the base of the talus slope. Climb south-southeast up the talus gully to the saddle between Mount Baal and She Devil, at 8,980 feet elevation. As you are climbing, the talus turns into scree, making climbing more difficult. For the last 300 vertical feet before reaching the saddle you may want to move right just off the scree and climb alongside of the sloping rock slabs. This saddle can also be reached via Upper Cannon Lake. (For directions to Upper Cannon Lake, see Hike 50.)

Once you are in the saddle the hardest part of the climb (the scree) is finished. Turn right in the saddle and head west on a vague path that is intermittently marked with rock cairns. The route stays to the right of the ridgeline for a time then climbs back to it at about 9,100 feet elevation. After following the ridge for a few yards you will need to bear right of the ridge-

She Devil Mountain from Mount Baal.

line again. Soon the route regains the ridgeline again at 9,200 feet elevation. From here follow the ridge west then slightly southwest to the summit of She Devil Mountain at 9,320 feet elevation. Allow yourself enough time to rest on the summit and admire the 360-degree view.

Probably the most difficult and potentially dangerous part of this climb is descending the talus gully. Take your time and be sure of your footing on the way down. Rolling a two-foot boulder on your leg can easily break it. Coming down this section is grueling for novice climbers.

Options: From the saddle between She Devil and Mount Baal, climb Mount Baal on the same trip.

73 Mount Baal via the South Ridge

<table>
<tr><td align="right">Highlights:</td><td>A rough scramble, but not a technical climb, from Sheep Lake to the summit of Mount Baal.</td><td>See Map on Page 316</td></tr>
<tr><td align="right">Type of hike:</td><td colspan="2">Out-and-back mountain climb from a base camp.</td></tr>
<tr><td align="right">Total distance:</td><td colspan="2">1.6 miles.</td></tr>
<tr><td align="right">Difficulty:</td><td colspan="2">Easy by climbing standards; very strenuous by hiking standards.</td></tr>
<tr><td align="right">Best months:</td><td colspan="2">Late July–September.</td></tr>
<tr><td align="right">Elevation gain:</td><td colspan="2">1,200 feet.</td></tr>
<tr><td align="right">Permits and fees:</td><td colspan="2">None.</td></tr>
<tr><td align="right">Maps:</td><td colspan="2">He Devil USGS quad.</td></tr>
</table>

Finding the trailhead: Follow the driving and hiking directions to Sheep Lake shown in Hike 59. The GPS coordinates where the route reaches the east shore of Sheep Lake are 45 19.864 N 116 32.180 W. Then hike along the east side of the lake to the gully where the climb starts.

Sheep Lake may also be reached using Seven Devils Loop and Sheep Lake Trail. See Hikes 49 and 56 for descriptions of these trails.

Trailhead facilities: Sheep Lake has lots of good campsites.

Camping and services: Developed campsites are available at Seven Devils Lake. Other services and groceries can be obtained in Riggins, Idaho. Cell phone service is good from the summit of Mount Baal.

For more information: USDA Forest Service at the Hells Canyon National Recreation office in Riggins.

Key points:
    0.0   Southeast corner of Sheep Lake.
    0.6   Saddle between She Devil and Mount Baal
          Mountains. GPS 45 19.488 N 116 32.012 W.
    0.8   Summit. GPS 45 19.594 N 116 31.967 W

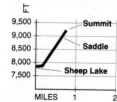

Mount Baal.

The climb: Allow 1.5 to 3 hours to reach the summit and nearly as much time to descend. There may be no water available after leaving Sheep Lake. As is true of most of the peaks in the Seven Devils this route could be very dangerous for novice climbers if it has a covering of snow or ice. There is moderate exposure at a few points along this climb.

Follow the lakeshore path to a gully at the southeast corner of the lake. Turn left and climb southeast up the gully to the base of the talus slope. Climb the talus gully to the saddle between Mount Baal and She Devil Mountains at 8,980 feet elevation. As you are climbing, the talus turns into scree, making climbing more difficult. For the last 300 vertical feet before reaching the saddle you may want to move right just off the scree and climb along the edge of the sloping rock slabs.

Turn left (northeast) in the saddle and climb just to the right of the ridgeline to the 9,100-foot summit of Mount Baal. Watch your step on the summit because the cliffs to the north and northwest drop away for several hundred feet below you. Because you are in the heart of the Seven Devils, the views are magnificent in all directions. A yellow film can in the cairn on the summit contains records of ascents back into the 1960s.

Probably the most difficult and potentially dangerous part of this climb is descending the talus gully. Take your time and be sure of your footing on the way down. Rolling a two-foot boulder on your leg can easily break it. Coming down this section is grueling for novice climbers.

Options: Climb She Devil Mountain on the same trip.

---

74 The Tower of Babel via the South Ridge

Highlights:	A climb from a very picturesque base camp at Sheep Lake to the summit of The Tower of Babel. This route is the most difficult climb described in this book. A novice climber without experienced leadership should not attempt it.
Type of hike:	Out-and-back mountain climb from a base camp.
Total distance:	2.8 miles.
Difficulty:	Class 3 mountain climb, with excellent routefinding skills required.
Best months:	Mid-July–September.
Elevation gain:	1,370 feet from Sheep Lake.
Permits and fees:	None.
Maps:	He Devil USGS quad.

See Map on Page 316

Finding the trailhead: Follow the driving and hiking directions to Sheep Lake shown in Hike 59. The GPS coordinates where the route reaches the east shore of Sheep Lake are 45 19.864 N 116 32.180 W. Then hike along

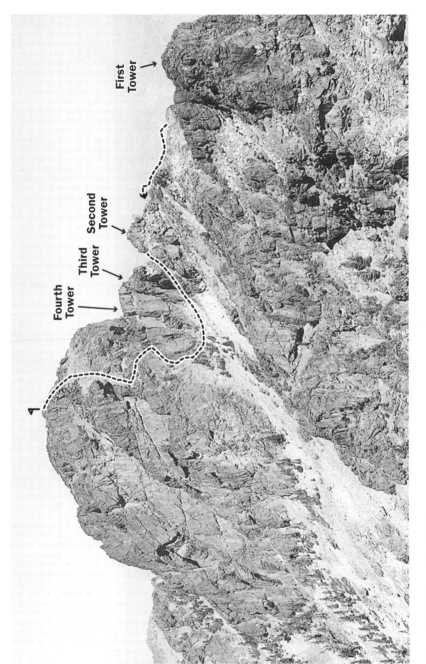

First
Tower

Second
Tower

Third
Tower

Fourth
Tower

1

Tower of Babel from Mount Baal.

the east side of the lake to the gully where the climb starts.

Sheep Lake may also be reached using Seven Devils Loop and Sheep Lake Trail. See Hikes 49 and 56 for descriptions of these trails.

Trailhead facilities: Sheep Lake has plenty of great campsites.

Camping and services: Campsites are available at Windy Saddle Trailhead and at Seven Devils Lake Campground. Gas, groceries, and other services can be obtained in Riggins, Idaho. Cell phones work well from the summit of The Tower of Babel.

For more information: USDA Forest Service at the Hells Canyon National Recreation Area office in Riggins.

Key points:

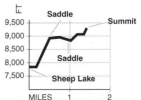

0.0   Southeast corner of Sheep Lake.
0.6   Saddle between She Devil and Mount Baal. GPS 45 19.488 N 116 32.012 W.
0.9   Saddle between Mount Baal and The Tower of Babel. GPS 45 19.604 N 116 31.880 W.
1.4   Summit of The Tower of Babel. GPS 45 19.796 N 116 31.719 W.

The climb: Allow 2.5 to 4 hours to reach the summit and nearly as much time to descend. There is no water available after leaving Sheep Lake. As is true of most of the peaks in the Seven Devils this route could be very dangerous for novice climbers if it has a covering of snow or ice. There is moderate exposure at a few points along this climb.

From the point where Sheep Lake Climbers Route reaches the east shore of Sheep Lake, follow the lakeshore path to a gully at the southeast corner of the lake. Turn left and climb southeast up the gully to the base of the talus slope. Climb the talus gully to the saddle between Mount Baal and She Devil at 8,980 feet elevation. As you are climbing, the talus turns into scree, making climbing more difficult. For the last 300 vertical feet before reaching the saddle you may want to move right just off the scree and climb along the edge of the sloping rock slabs. Turn left in the saddle and traverse northeast, on the scree and through the rock outcroppings, to the saddle between Mount Baal and The Tower of Babel, at 8,940 feet elevation.

There is a gendarme and four towers that you will need to pass around and between, along the ridge from here to the summit. These towers are very prominent when viewed from Sheep Lake but are not as well defined from the southeast side of the ridgeline where you will be climbing. The second tower, which you pass close to its summit, is the least defined of the four.

Climb north-northeast from the saddle, passing a gendarme on the right. Then traverse, still climbing slightly, around the first rock tower. The route nearly regains the ridgeline after passing the first tower. Traverse high around the second tower, then climb a few feet down a chute to gain access to another chute, which is between the second and third towers. Turn left and climb a few feet to the notch between the second and third towers. From the notch descend a short distance down the chute to the west. Then turn right and descend a sloping ledge to the talus slope below the third tower. This ledge is the first class 3 climbing (descending here) you will encounter on this route. Traverse north across the talus passing below the third and fourth towers and a few stunted trees to a gully. This gully may not be obvious as you are crossing the talus. Turn right and climb northeast up the gully to a large chockstone. Pass the chockstone on the left on some small ledges, and climb a few more feet up the gully to another notch, just past the fourth tower. In this notch turn left, climbing over a boulder, then proceed up more small ledges and over the boulders until you are beneath an overhanging roof. Once past the roof, scramble up and to the north over easier terrain to the summit of The Tower of Babel.

The fantastic view sprawls out in all directions from the 9,269-foot summit. Take the time to boulder hop north from the very summit to the top of the cliffs above Mirror Lake, but be very careful; the boulders may not be as stable as they look. Falling off this ridge could very likely be fatal.

Options: It is possible to hike and scramble up or down from the saddle between Mount Baal and The Tower of Babel to Upper Cannon Lake. For a description of the route to Upper Cannon Lake from Windy Saddle Trailhead, see Hike 49 and Hike 50.

Appendix A: Additional Information

USDA FOREST SERVICE

Hells Canyon National Recreation Area
Wallowa Mountains Visitor Center
88401 Highway 82
Enterprise, OR 97828
541-426-4978

Hells Canyon National Recreation Area
2535 Riverside Drive, P.O. Box 699
Clarkston, WA 99403
509-758-0616

Hells Canyon National Recreation Area
P.O. Box 832
Riggins, ID 83549
208-628-3916

Wallowa Whitman National Forest Headquarters
1550 Dewey Avenue
P.O. Box 907
Baker City, OR 97814
541-523-6391

Wallowa Whitman National Forest
Pine Ranger District
General Delivery
Halfway, OR 97834
541-742-7511

Payette National Forest
Council Ranger District
500 E. Whitley
P.O. Box 567
Council, ID 83612
208-253-0100

Nez Perce National Forest Headquarters
Route 2 Box 475
Grangeville, ID 83530
208-983-1950

Idaho County Search & Rescue
Idaho County Courthouse
Grangeville, ID 83530
208-983-1100

Wallowa County Search & Rescue
Wallowa County Sheriff's Office
Wallowa County Courthouse
Enterprise, OR 97828
541-426-3131 or 911

Spence Air Service
P.O. Box 217
Enterprise, OR 97828
541-426-3288

Hells Canyon Adventures Inc.
4200 Hells Canyon Dam Road
P.O. Box 159
Oxbow, OR 97840
541-785-3352
Fax 541-785-3353
E-mail: jetboat@pdx.oneworld.com
1-800-HCA-Flot (422-3568)
www.hellscanyonadventures.com

Beamer's Hells Canyon Tours and Excursions
1451 Bridge Street
Clarkston, WA
or
P.O. Box 1243
Lewiston, ID 83501
509-758-4800 or 1-800-522-6966
www.hellscanyontours.com

Snake River Adventures
227 Snake River Avenue
Lewiston, ID 83501
1-800-262-8874
Email: snkrvadv@valint.net
www.snakeriveradventures.com

Appendix B: Glossary

Bat door—A broad mesh diron door used to allow bats to enter a cave or mineshaft but keep people out.

Benchmark—A disk, usually made of brass, secured to solid rock or placed on top of a pipe that has been driven into the ground to mark an exact spot. Benchmarks are usually placed by the U.S. Geological Survey.

Blaze—A mark on a tree formed by cutting away a small section of bark with a hatchet or axe. A blaze may consist of one or two marks. Blazes can usually be seen some distance ahead while hiking.

Braided trail—A section of trail formed by two or more interconnecting paths.

Cairn—A stack or pile of rocks that marks the trail or route.

Cirque—A bowl-shaped area where a glacier has eaten its way into a mountain slope and then melted. A cirque is formed at the head of a glacier.

Complete burn—An area where all of the trees were killed in a forest fire.

Connecting trail, Connecting route—A trail that connects two or more other trails and does not reach any trailhead.

Cornice—A wind-caused snowdrift that overhangs a cliff of steep slope.

Chockstone—A rock that is stuck in a crack between bedrock walls or other rocks.

Fault—A fracture in bedrock where a displacement has occurred.

Fault zone—The area along a fault.

Gendarme—A rock pinnacle on a ridgeline.

Internal trail—A trail that begins and or ends at a junction with another trail or at a jet boat or aircraft drop-off point.

Notch—A naturally carved out section of a ridge. A notch is smaller than a saddle and has rock outcroppings on both sides.

Outcropping—Bedrock protruding through the surface of the ground.

Partial burn—An area burned in a forest fire in which only part of the trees were killed.

Pika—A small mammal that lives in steep rocky areas or talus slopes. Pikas are related to rabbits and do not hibernate.

Pit house—A Native American dwelling. Usually only a depression in the ground remains today.

Prospect hole—A test hole dug in a vein of mineralized strata to check the strata's mineral content for a possible mining operation.

Red digger—A species of ground squirrel.

Scree—Loose rock on a slope. The size of the rocks are smaller than they are in talus. Scree may be very tiring to climb.

Second-growth forest—Forest that was logged many years ago and has regrown to medium-sized timber.

Side draw—A smaller draw or gully on the side of a larger draw or canyon.

Spur ridge—A smaller ridge on the side of a main ridge. Spur ridges may be very steep.

Spur trail—A short side trail.

Subdraw—Same as a side draw.

Su ridge—Same as a spur ridge.

Talus slope—A slope covered with large rocks or boulders.

Thorn brush—The local name for native or black hawthorn.

Traverse—The crossing of a slope, climbing or descending but usually in nearly a straight line. The term is also used to describe a route that follows a fairly flat ridgeline.

USDA—United States Department of Agriculture.

USGS—United States Geological Survey.

Wash—A creekbed that is dry most of the time. A wash usually has steep unstable banks.

Waterspout—A local word for a flash flood in a steep creekbed.

Winter range—The area where migrating animals spend the winter.

Appendix C: Hiker's Checklist

Use the following lists to help you prepare for your Hells Canyon and Seven Devils Mountains hikes. Your equipment need not be new or expensive, but it should be well tested.

Equipment
- ☐ Daypack or fanny pack
- ☐ Plenty of water bottles
- ☐ First-aid kit
- ☐ Survival kit
- ☐ Compass
- ☐ Maps
- ☐ Toilet paper
- ☐ Sunscreen
- ☐ Flashlight or headlamp with extra batteries
- ☐ Pocket knife
- ☐ Sunglasses
- ☐ Anti-fog solution (if you wear glasses)
- ☐ Snakebite kit

Optional
- ☐ Tick removal kit
- ☐ Snakeproof gaters or chaps
- ☐ Binoculars
- ☐ Camera and extra film

Added Equipment for Overnight Trips
- ☐ Tent and waterproof fly
- ☐ Sleeping bag and stuff sack
- ☐ Sleeping pad
- ☐ Water filter or purification tablets
- ☐ Additional water bottles
- ☐ Cooking pots and holder
- ☐ Cup, bowl, and eating utensils
- ☐ Light stove and plenty of fuel
- ☐ Resealable plastic bags
- ☐ Nylon cord (50 feet)
- ☐ Small towel
- ☐ Personal toilet kit

Optional
- ☐ Paper towels
- ☐ Stuff sacks

- ☐ Notebook and pencil

Clothing
- ☐ Large-brimmed hat or cap
- ☐ Sturdy hiking boots (well broken in)
- ☐ Hiking shorts or long pants
- ☐ Long-sleeved shirt
- ☐ Light windproof parka
- ☐ Rain gear
- ☐ Mittens or gloves

Additional Clothing for Overnight Trips
- ☐ Warm hat (stocking cap)
- ☐ Long underwear (during fall, winter, and spring)
- ☐ Sweater or insulated vest
- ☐ Waterproof wilderness parka
- ☐ Long pants
- ☐ One pair of socks for each day plus one extra pair
- ☐ Extra underwear
- ☐ Extra shirts
- ☐ Sandals (for wading streams)

Food
- ☐ For day hiking, take high-energy snacks for munching along the way. For overnight trips, bring enough food, but do not overburden yourself with too much. Include plenty of snacks. Plan meals carefully, bringing just enough food plus some emergency rations. Packaged freeze-dried foods are the lightest to carry, but they are expensive and are not really necessary. Bring plenty of cold and hot drinks.

Appendix D: Further Reading

Islands and Rapids: A Geologic Story of Hells Canyon. Tracy Vallier. Lewiston, Id.: Confluence Press, Lewis-Clark State College, 1998.

Snake River of Hells Canyon. Johnny Carrey, Cort Conley, and Ace Barton. Backeddy Books, 1979.

Hells Canyon: A River Trip. Captain Elmer Earl. Lewiston, Id.: Lewiston Printing, 1990.

Home Below Hells Canyon. Grace Jordan. Lincoln: University of Nebraska Press, 1954.

Hells Canyon: The Deepest Gorge on Earth. William Ashworth. Hawthorn Books, 1977.

Index

About the Author

Growing up in Oregon's Willamette Valley, Fred Barstad developed an interest in Oregon's mountains at an early age. With his parents, he hiked and fished extensively in the Cascade Range.

By the time he was a teenager in the 1960s, this interest had become an addiction to the high and remote country. Fred has climbed most of the Cascades volcanoes in Washington and Oregon, some of them many times. He has also climbed Mount McKinley in Alaska, Aconcagua in Argentina, and Popocatepetl, Citlaltepetl, and Iztaccihuatl in Mexico. Since his first visit to Hells Canyon in 1962, Fred has been intrigued by this vast and rugged wilderness.

Fred now lives in Enterprise, Oregon, near Hells Canyon. This is his fifth FalconGuide, and he intends to write several more. He devotes his time to hiking, climbing, skiing, and snowshoeing when he is not working on a book.